Bicycling Bliss

Riding to Improve Your Wellness

Portia H. Masterson

Self-Propulsion Publishing
Golden, Colorado

Disclaimer

Information in this book is for educational and instructional purposes based on the research and experience of the author. It is intended to complement medical care and not replace it. **Bicycling Bliss** does offer many suggestions to improve your wellness. But remember it is your responsibility to tune in to your body's response and determine if the exercises and practices benefit you. Pain is your body's signal that something is wrong. Don't ignore it. The publisher and author are not responsible for any adverse effects or consequences resulting from the use of any of the suggestions or procedures discussed in this book.

First edition: 2004, second printing

Masterson, Portia H., 1941-
    Bicycling Bliss: Riding to Improve Your Wellness
    Includes bibliographical references and indexes
    ISBN: 0-9753868-1-6 (pbk.)   13-digit ISBN 978-0-9753868-1-1 (pbk.)
    1. Cycling - Training. 2. Physical Fitness. 3. Health. 4. Human mechanics.
    5. Mind-body relations. 6. Breathing exercises. 7. Sports clothing. 8. Recipes.
    9. Nutrition. I. Author. II. Title

    GV1041 .M36 2004   LCCN: 2004302564
    613.71 or 796.6

To purchase additional copies, e-mail **portia@bicyclingbliss.com** or visit our website at **www.bicyclingbliss.com**

Self-Propulsion Publishing
P.O. Box 16334
Golden, CO 80402-6006 USA

Editor: Elizabeth Gold, ElizGold@aol.com
Interior design: Char Campbell, Desktop Publisher
Cover design: E. Magine & Assoc., Mona Simon
Cover photo: Jim Yost Photography, Angela Roz models at Red Rocks Park, Morrison, CO
Drawings: Pat Conrad, Susan Hart, Ted Rains, and by permission of H. David Coulter
Photographs: Jim Yost; Bernhard, Kirk, & Portia Masterson; and Brett Butler
Printed in the U.S.A. by United Graphics, Inc.

With love and admiration to
my sons, Bernhard and Kirk,
my fellow adventurers

Acknowledgments

I am greatly indebted to friends who have given so generously of their time and expertise to enable me to develop *Bicycling Bliss* as you see it here. Self-Propulsion customers and staff have posed questions, provided feedback, and shared their experiences as my teachers and my motivation to write. Special thanks to Andrea Felton McAdoo, P.T.; Carrie Bentley, M.S., P.T.A.; Becky Brinkman, D.C.; and Sue Boatwright, certified Rolfer, who were my first instructors in human anatomy and healthful body use. My sons, Bernhard and Kirk, and my counselor, Betsy Vollmer, have advised and supported me these many years. My Taiji instructors, Michael and Sara Stenson and Larry Welsh, M.Ac., nourished my cultivation of qi. My Yoga teacher, Michael Bonamer, and friend Pat Kraker introduced me to the wellsprings of Yogic and Buddhist teachings and practices.

As *Bicycling Bliss* took form, friends read and critiqued my drafts, which resulted in new content and more fluid expression. Fred Clements posed thoughtful questions that led to substantial changes in style and content. Merle Baranczyk and Tina Obrecht edited text to clarify syntax and meaning. Bernhard and Kirk critiqued various parts of the text along the way and were my dependable computer consultants and website designers. Alexandra and Marjorie Eddy read every word of an early draft with such thoroughness that they enabled me to lift my writing style to a new level. Tom Beckwith counseled me in the rudiments of book production. Mary Lou Parsons and Pete Siemsen eliminated mistakes in the galley proofs.

Creating the illustrations has been one of the most fun aspects of learning. Susan Hart drew the first illustrations of torso position in 1997. Ted Rains, retired engineer turned amateur artist, drew the bicycle equipment. Pat Conrad began with the line drawings of Yoga postures and strengthening exercises and progressed to many splendid anatomic drawings giving form to my design requests. Edd Hamilton enhanced my amateur photos in the darkroom. Jim Yost brought his years of professional photography experience to the project to illuminate technical points.

Volunteer models enthusiastically posed to document equipment and body use. Angela Roz brought personality to the cover; Peter Heppner modeled Yoga poses for Pat Conrad; and Ken Brown, Rex Bryan, Shelley Ervin, Mary Lou Parsons, and Ted Rains modeled for the photo session.

H. David Coulter of Body and Breath provided the anatomic illustration from *Anatomy of Hatha Yoga* based on the drawings from the 1800s of Philibert C. Sappey and J. G. Heck. I also thank Simon & Schuster for permission to reproduce Walter C. Willett's Healthy Eating Pyramid.

My professional book production team has not only created a high quality publication but their expertise and commitment raised my expectations and energized me in the final stages of book preparation. Mona Simon designed the cover. Char Campbell designed the interior pages, and Elizabeth Gold, editor, guided me in restructuring the text and improving the syntax. Ann Marie Gordon of United Graphics, Inc., orchestrated printing.

And finally, thank you to all the manufacturers of the bicycle industry for your products, support services, and permission to discuss your contributions to cycling.

Portia H. Masterson
Golden, Colorado
April 2004

Table of Contents

Expand Your Expectations of Cycling

Integrate cycling into your life through nine recommendations, from how to evaluate and fix problems caused by incorrect postures and movements to how to develop a personal riding style that keeps cycling fun, healthy, and enticing. Bliss comes from practicing simplicity, moderation, self-nurture, reflection, relaxation, and being fully present.

Cycling Builds Fitness, Develops Life Skills, and Improves Attitudes

Explore the benefits of riding, from physical agility to psychological and spiritual balance. Cycling develops problem-solving skills, nurtures self-sufficiency, and increases confidence.

Balanced Muscle Alignment and Reduced Tension Enhance Riding Comfort and Control

Discover the origins of discomfort, from bicycle setup to incorrect riding technique. Improving your bike handling skills depends on comfort and relaxation.

Tools for Integrated Wellness

Increase ways of optimizing fitness, from cardiovascular exercises to cultivation of vital energy. Integrated wellness begins with correct breathing and is enhanced by inner and outer disciplines.

Riding Style Modifications Optimize Comfort, Efficiency, and Wellness

Improve your riding through exercises, from foot alignment to shoulder and neck relaxation. This core chapter outlines the function of each body part and provides exercises to correct problems as well as methods to optimize technique.

Customized Bicycle Setup Supports Riding Style

Fit your bike to your body by focusing on details, from how to match body-to-bike measurements to understanding how cog and chainring choice affect pedaling. Find answers to common questions about bicycle modifications.

Sustained Riding Performance Depends on Balanced Resources

Understand the elements that contribute to stamina, from the value of oxygen, fluids, food, and sleep to the value of building confidence. Conscientious care for your body improves your endurance.

Proper Clothing Extends Riding Seasons

Ride in all types of weather with tips, from understanding clothing technology to riding in wind and rain and hot and cold weather. Clothing and textile designs are available to make riding comfortable in varied weather conditions.

Riding With Contentment in Urban Areas Requires Special Attention

Increase your joy when riding in traffic by focusing on the essentials, from precautions that reduce chances of collision and injury to games that help when you're sharing the road with distracted motorists.

Introduction

- How to Use **Bicycling Bliss**
- Cultivating Effective Practice
- Letting Go of Cherished Assumptions about Cycling
- **Bicycling Bliss** Emerged Out of My Search for Solutions to Riding Challenges

As an avid bicyclist for more than 50 years and as a bicycle store owner for half that time, I've heard or experienced many cycling stories of frustration, injury, and fear. Fortunately I've been able to balance these disturbing tales with reassuring stories of cycling triumphs and years of blissful cycling moments.

Summing up all my years of pedaling through life is the reality that **bicycling is fun!** When it's not fun, it is because of inadequate information. To bridge this information gap, I have spent the last few years collecting information that will be useful to everyone who wants to enjoy bicycling as a holistic approach to living well. With customers and friends, I have questioned, listened, observed, experimented, and researched writing this book as my contribution to helping more cyclists experience fun, fitness, and freedom.

Bicycling Bliss is written for people who want to improve their health and fitness through cycling. It will guide you in developing a healthful riding technique, in improving your riding performance and pleasure, and in establishing a rewarding program of integrated wellness based on cycling. This book acknowledges that riders and potential riders are at all levels of fitness and are as diverse as a cross-section of the general population. Whether you are large or small, lean or obese, strong or frail, recovering from sickness or injury, old or young, or differently-abled, you can develop a personal riding style that meets your individual needs.

Some of you are experienced riders who have never received instruction, some of you are beginners, and some of you probably fall somewhere in-between those categories. There are no prerequisites for this book — **Bicycling Bliss** is designed to provide insights to cyclists of all levels. My own experience is that no matter how satisfactory my current cycling performance is, I can always refine my technique and discover new ways to increase my riding pleasure. I'm certain you will find that the same is true for you.

This book is organized for easy and frequent reference. I hope you will refer to the text often as you practice new riding techniques and conditioning exercises. Illustrations of human anatomy, bicycle components, and a glossary of terms will make new vocabulary understandable. Food pyramids, recipes, and recommended readings encourage you to explore new eating habits and further your knowledge from specialists in subjects introduced in **Bicycling Bliss**.

How to Use *Bicycling Bliss*

The chapters are arranged to progressively build a solid understanding of how to optimize your cycling performance through proper use of your body and by nurturing yourself as an athlete. I hope you will read from cover to cover. However, I know many of us open a book and go directly to the part that interests us most or search for a solution to a specific problem. If this is your approach, make use of the cross references to gain a complete picture on each issue. If you are a novice, select the most helpful suggestions and work them through step by step. Avoid becoming overwhelmed by trying to improve several aspects of cycling at once.

The biomechanics of your body and the mechanical variables of your bicycle are interrelated. During optimum performance, you and your bicycle function as one unit. For simplicity, I discuss each part of your body and your bike separately. But remember that all body parts are interrelated in complex ways, and that each aspect of your bike setup influences other performance factors.

Modifying your riding style and modifying your bike are interdependent. When you are experimenting with a new riding technique, your bike may hinder you from experiencing the full benefits. Similarly, it is possible to modify your bike setup but benefit only partially because you cling to your old riding style. A sore neck and upper back may lead you to install a new stem on your bike to bring the handlebars closer to your shoulders. But after making this modification, you will probably continue to ride with stiff elbows, dropped head, and scrunched shoulders. Until you change your riding technique by flexing your elbows downward and relaxing your arms, shoulders, and neck, and lifting through the top of your head, you will continue to experience discomfort. Look in Chapter 5 under "Your Neck and Shoulders" to learn how to retrain your body use and what stretching and strengthening exercises to practice to eliminate your discomfort.

Bicycling Bliss is based on the following concepts:

1. Discomfort on your bike is an indication that something is wrong and needs to be changed.

2. If you hurt during or after a ride, you will seek to understand the underlying causes

of discomfort and make corrections rather than continuing to damage yourself.

3. Four factors contribute to riding comfort:

    a. **Your bicycle setup:** This requires that you have a bike frame that fits your body proportions and then modify the bike so your riding position enables you to relax and tune in to your body. The most common modification is to reposition your handlebars closer to your shoulders.

    b. **Biomechanically sound use of your body:** This requires that you understand how to use your body, heighten your awareness so you are conscious of habitual movements, and invest the time and energy to reshape your riding technique.

    c. **Balanced and symmetric muscle development:** Even with optimum riding technique, you will need to establish a daily strengthening and stretching routine to strengthen weak areas and to elongate chronically contracted muscles.

    d. **A modified life style that will support health and fitness excellence.**

Cultivating Effective Practice

It takes courage to let go of the familiar. Rather than engaging yourself in an intellectual debate about change, just begin to experiment. Try something new and then observe what effect it has for you. Trust your experience. If you like the results, incorporate them into your style.

Avoid laboring over the pros and cons of a new technique. Just give it a whirl. Your mind and body will feel liberated by new thoughts and new movement patterns, and you will feel rejuvenated. Although experimentation is the characteristic learning pattern of children, you can enjoy it at any age.

Active children possess the natural gift of responding to their bodies' messages that tell them which muscles affect a particular skill. This is how they actively learn physical skills every day. On the other hand, as we move into adult life, daily pressures often cause us to ignore signs of fatigue and strain and we tend to push ourselves to exhaustion. Eventually this causes a limited ability to receive critical feedback about body needs as well as diminished body awareness and kinesthetic sense. In fact, it is common for adults learning a new physical skill to tense up or to exert all their muscles. As the exercise becomes more familiar, they respond to body feedback (or coaching) and release the muscles that are not helping with the new skill. With practice, everyone can learn to use only the muscles that contribute to improved performance.

Practice regularly and in a sustained manner. Riding several times a week will facilitate change more quickly than taking long rides on the weekend. Short frequent rides enable you to give full attention to your new form. You are more likely to be successful when you are fresh and relaxed. When you devote time and attention to your practice, you will experience the benefits more quickly, and the results will motivate you to continue. On the other hand, focusing on the anticipated end results will probably cause the benefits to elude you. If you put your energy into the process of each technique, you will enjoy results sooner.

The quality of your practice is critical. No practice is better than wrong practice. Surely you have had the experience of needing to relearn a skill after learning it incorrectly. It is tedious and requires patience and perseverance to overcome established habits. It will be worth your time to ensure that you are practicing the correct form. You might watch yourself in the large windows of buildings you ride past. If you have a video camera, ask someone to record your form so you can critique yourself.

Now let's imagine that you are practicing a different use of your elbows while riding. You have always ridden with them rigid and hyperextended. You've just learned that you could gain better control of your bike and reduce hand and shoulder discomfort by flexing your elbows down toward your hips. With your hands on flat handlebars, you bend your elbows. It feels like you are following the instructions but instead of dropping your elbows downward, you have bent them out to the side. Instead of being more comfortable, your deltoids are fatiguing while you ride, and you remain sore the next day. Getting accurate feedback from a video, mirror, or friend will help you avoid setbacks by ensuring that you are working toward the right goal from the start.

Letting Go of Cherished Assumptions about Cycling

I ask you to sensitively search your assumptions about cycling for ideas that diminish your riding pleasure and the benefits you derive as you read **Bicycling Bliss**. You may be able to identify these assumptions in beliefs you hold about your skills, in your cycling goals, or in your understanding of riding technique and equipment choices.

Listen to how you characterize your riding skills in casual comments to friends. You might say, "I have lousy balance." "I can't get used to toe clips." "I have poor stamina." The more often you repeat these limiting statements, the more ingrained they become in your subconscious, and the more difficult they are to overcome. Try rephrasing these statements as working challenges. For example, "I am improving my balance." "I'm setting myself up for success in learning to use toe clips." "I'm building my stamina."

Too frequently, we criticize ourselves when we fall short of our own expectations. Be sure your expectations are appropriate. When recently learning to use a new computer program, I became frustrated every time I got stuck and was unable to make it do what I wanted. I concluded that I was computer challenged. A friend who had experience using this program offered to work with me. To my surprise and relief, she had to try several times to create the desired effects and was frequently annoyed. It turned out this program is not easy to use, and I needed hands-on instruction and patience. When you find yourself in a similar position, talk to other cyclists and look up your concern in the index of **Bicycling Bliss** to determine if your expectations are appropriate for your experience level. Then learn to go beyond your frustration.

There are always other riders who are more accomplished than you, regardless of your skill level. Be sure your riding goals are appropriate for your experience and stamina levels. Avoid aspiring to goals shared by friends or promoted in the media that are destined to end in personal disappointment and even disenchantment with cycling altogether. Four months after Marilyn bought a new bike, she said cycling wasn't for her because she could not easily ride the hills between home and town. I assured her that the one block-long 12 percent grade and steady climb on the way home were demanding, and that she should choose another route while she developed her riding technique and built up her cycling muscles and aerobic stamina. When I reminded her that she should have her gear indicators on "1" on both shifters when the going got tough, she revealed that she tried to stay in her middle chainring all the time. Her misconception of gear use destined her to a miserable riding experience. Rather than informing herself about riding technique, she assumed misery was a part of cycling and wanted to quit.

Clinging too tenaciously to riding styles or equipment can also sabotage your pleasure in cycling and your desire to continue. Claudia owns an expensive Italian bike with Campagnolo® components. It has drop handlebars and two chainrings. She suffers continually from neck pain but rides 30 miles a day anyway. She knows that a more upright riding position and easier gearing would relieve her discomfort but she is too attached to the classic appearance of her bike to make appropriate modifications. A willingness to change would help her avoid permanent damage and provide a pain-free riding style.

I encourage you to honestly and willingly examine your riding satisfaction. What types of rides cause you discomfort or dissatisfaction? If you already are aware of some inadequacies, start seeking solutions there. Or are there skills you are already working on that you would like help refining?

In the pages that follow, I hope you will find encouragement and guidance in improving your riding technique and your equipment choices to help you experience bicycling bliss.

Bicycling Bliss Emerged Out of My Search for Solutions to Riding Challenges

My early riding experiences were probably typical of most kids. I began riding to be part of the neighborhood fun. I knocked around in my street with my buddies, jumped dirt hills in the vacant lots, and rode to friends' homes to play. My bike was fun and gave me independence and the sense that I was capable of creating my own adventures. In junior high, my bike became my main transportation. Although my friends were not riding in the fifties and sixties, I continued to get around by bike and loved the intimacy with nature and the sense of discovery it provided. When I married and became a mother, my sons rode in my Gerry carrier and child seat until they became able riders themselves. We lived in Tucson, Arizona, where the flat terrain and dry, warm desert climate was an ideal environment for developing family riding skills.

In 1977, we moved to Golden, Colorado, where my first friends were employees at the local bike store. When the store closed in 1980, one of the mechanics started searching for another job in Golden. Seven friends pooled their resources to open a new bike store and provide work for Karl. As part owner of Self-Propulsion, Inc., I also became the business manager. Business partnerships can be very trying, so after eighteen months I became the sole owner, the chief mechanic-in-training, and a single mom. This rapid transformation taught me to embrace challenges and to realize that the intense learning required by dramatic changes can be exhilarating.

What an eye-opener! I had ridden for thirty years on the same old 3-speed, carried my stuff haphazardly on my handlebars, and worn whatever was appropriate for my destination. Suddenly my eyes were opened wide to the advantages of quality bikes, appropriate accessories, and cycling specific clothing. With the support of employees, friends, and my neighboring bicycle retailers, I developed my skills as a mechanic. I soon recognized the great need for better riding conditions and became active in bicycle and pedestrian advocacy. I was a founding member of the Colorado Bicycling Advisory Board and co-authored the first Colorado state bicycling manual. In the mid-eighties when mountain biking began, I helped build acceptance of mountain bikes on Jefferson County Open Space trails. Work in the community was rewarding but the most satisfaction came from day-to-day interaction with cyclists in the store and seeking solutions for their needs. Although my personal riding style had focused on transportation, at Self-Propulsion I learned to appreciate the wide variety of rider styles and needs, everything from racers to the "every-third-Sunday" riders.

Striving to meet the equipment and health challenges presented by Self-Propulsion's customers led to my disenchantment with the state of the bicycle industry and its preoccupation with high-end equipment and extreme riding styles. In hopes that I might understand these forces, which still limit the satisfaction of most riders, I became active in the industry. In an effort to promote change, I became a board member and eventual president of the National Bicycle Dealers Association. The years of my tenure, from 1988 to 1995, provided great personal opportunities. I worked with leaders in the industry and made presentations at regional bicycle conferences in New Jersey, Pennsylvania, Minnesota, Ontario, and Indiana. Each of these events enabled me to attend seminars and meet experts in cycling, urban planning, and advocacy. They strengthened my abilities as a spokesperson for healthy communities and rider and pedestrian interests. However, my broadening perspective of cycling only intensified my dissatisfaction with the cycling establishment. I therefore withdrew from my work in the bicycle industry to devote my full attention to the needs of my customers and my community. For more details of my family cycling adventures and in-store testing, refer to Appendix A.

In 1996, I began writing a guide for Self-Propulsion customers to help them improve their riding technique. In my efforts to address riders' needs, I learned a lot about common discomforts that limit and discourage cyclists. For each problem riders presented, I suggested changes in their bike setups and riding techniques. As an experienced bicycle mechanic, I was able to guide customers in their equipment choices. Our customers were well-educated and committed cyclists who were willing to trust my advice, experiment with my suggestions, and report their experiences back to me. With each success and failure, my knowledge increased and gradually my confidence grew. Soon customers began to ask for more details. Was this information published so they could continue to improve their comfort and efficiency? When I told them that I didn't know of a reliable resource to refer them to, they encouraged me to write one. Since I love to write, I began the project, starting out with earnest research. I searched the literature on cycling, anatomy, biomechanics, and general wellness to broaden my understanding. Fortunately, many of our customers are healthcare professionals and they were generous with their time and knowledge to answer my many questions. My employees shared their observations and insights, and we all tested new ideas on our own rides.

I was also able to draw on my undergraduate studies at Oregon State University (OSU) in clothing and textiles. I did two years of graduate study in textile chemistry at North Carolina State University. During the ensuing years, I have designed and sewn clothing and equipment for family and friends. My studies at OSU included foods and nutrition, and I have continually updated these early studies. I love to cook and have enjoyed many leisure hours developing recipes to match the best nutritional information with my tastes. You'll find my current favorites in Appendix E.

Over the last eight years, the simple origins of my writing have evolved into a full-fledged, thoroughly researched book. The concepts and exercises have been tested repeatedly. Traditional cycling solutions have been critically analyzed to sort out the wisdom from the myths. Whether you are a cyclist with years of experience or a novice, search the pages for concepts, exercises, and equipment suggestions to make your riding more enjoyable and to support a lifetime commitment to your health and fitness.

And above all, always remember: **bicycling is fun**.

chapter 1

Expand Your Expectations of Cycling

- Integrate Cycling into Your Life
- Honestly Evaluate the Detrimental Aspects of Cycling
- Focus on the Process of Riding
- Use Comfort as an Indicator of Efficient and Healthful Form
- Develop a Personal Riding Style
- Make Riding Fun
- Strengthen and Bring into Balance All Elements of Human Nature
- Cultivate a Conscious Awareness
- Let Go of Your Old Ways

What role does cycling play in your life now? These nine steps will expand your expectations and your satisfaction from cycling.

1. Integrate cycling into your life. By incorporating cycling into your daily routine, you will reap benefits that will improve your life skills and attitudes.

2. Honestly evaluate the detrimental aspects of cycling and develop a cycling-specific conditioning routine to counter them.

3. Focus on the process of riding and direct your attention inward.

4. Use comfort as an indicator of efficient and healthful form while riding and conditioning.

5. Develop a personal riding style that serves your current life needs.

6. Make riding fun so you can maintain a passion for a healthful fitness routine the rest of your life.

7. Strengthen and bring into balance all elements of human nature: physical, mental, emotional, social, and spiritual.

8. Cultivate a conscious awareness to enable you to assess your needs, learn new skills, and fully appreciate your experiences.

9. Let go of your old ways so you are free to experiment and to define a new direction.

These are essential steps for learning and improving your skills and attitudes. I hope the technical understanding of how to use your body to optimize your riding experience will foster a zeal for knowledge, a culture of self-nurture, and the desire to initiate change — and that it will result in a new sense of ***bliss***.

What do I mean by "bliss?" I draw on Eastern traditions to understand bliss. **Bliss is an enduring form of contentment derived from being fully present and practicing simplicity, moderation, self-nurture, reflection, and conscious breathing**. Bliss can be sustained by avoiding complexity; excesses; self-abuse; high-pressure scheduling; a scattered, driven mind; and striving to surpass friends in demonstrations of wealth, image, physical prowess, and risk taking.

1. Integrate cycling into your life.

My son Kirk wisely observed that a passionate involvement in some physical activity is essential to maintaining a healthy body weight as well as abundant wellness and balance in your daily activity schedule. So remove cycling from the "Physical Fitness Department" and establish a daily, moderate-intensity riding routine. Your attitude will mellow, and your life perspective will broaden. I am confident that **you can develop a riding style that will transform your life style**. Knowing that the quality of your performance at work and at home will improve with your dedication to improving your cycling technique will make it easier to commit appropriate time to riding and conditioning.

Riding shorter distances four to seven days a week will acquaint you with the full benefits of cycling. Avoid the popular practice of strenuous, high-mileage weekend rides. These extended rides may provide you with relief from your work routines, increase your physical fitness, contribute to weight control, and provide renewal in the outdoors but they do have detrimental impacts. Hurting muscles indicate muscle damage rather than increased muscle strength; riding to exhaustion is abusive; and these excesses tend to keep you in overdrive and support a high-pressure life style.

Imagine yourself getting out for a 30-minute ride four times a week. Use your creative problem solving skills to design a variety of schedule changes that will enable you to experiment and adapt. You could keep a bike at work and ride at lunch. Maybe take turns with your partner in looking after the kids. Perhaps riding all or part way to work is attractive to you. If you think a brief ride won't fit into your schedule, you probably need to ask yourself who has control of your life.

Those of us who exercise regularly know that **effort creates energy!** It is your choice to overcome fatigue with moderate exercise or succumb to lethargy. When you exert yourself, all systems speed up, and you actually increase your energy level. Moderate exercise increases your sense of well-being and helps you work more efficiently. With increased vitality and focus, your greater efficiency will create time for exercise. Eventually you will observe that you are less effective on days without exercise. You might be motivated by the extensive documentation that exercise five days a week reduces the risk of cardiovascular disease, diabetes, and hypertension. This schedule also mitigates the effects of arthritis, diabetes, MS, and other debilitating diseases. For a detailed list of benefits refer to

"Establishing a Moderate-intensity Aerobic Exercise Routine," pp. 86-92 in Chapter 4.

Here are some ideas to get you started. Identify a circuit at home or at work that you can ride every day for about 30 minutes. Designate a certain time and stick to the schedule faithfully. Ride at a moderate pace so you don't have to change clothes or clean up. Yes, it is possible to ride in business suits and dresses in many climates. You may find it easier to establish a leisure riding style by riding a bike that puts you in a more upright position. If you are embarrassed to ride in business clothes in an upright position, try imagining that you are an aristocrat surveying your estate. Have fun, use a little humor! You might find that a bit of levity on your noon ride will make it easier to be amused by the next challenge at work.

A 30-minute ride both renews and builds fitness. If you are accustomed to high energy workouts, use this time to improve your riding form or breathing technique. Even the most accomplished riders can always refine their technique. You may want to focus on the psychological benefits of riding. Lift your eyes to the sky and lighten your perspective. Just relax and let go of trying to achieve anything. By enjoying a renewing interlude in the workday you will reduce your yearning for unwholesome snacks and beverages later in the day. Adapt your 30-minute "perspective break" to your daily needs. There will be days when a walk would be more therapeutic or a few stretching exercises in the park would be more refreshing. Taking these few moments every day for self-nurture can liberate you from an otherwise confining work routine.

2. Honestly evaluate the detrimental aspects of cycling and develop a cycling-specific conditioning routine to counter them.

The human body requires stretching to maintain healthful alignment, muscular flexibility, and joint mobility. It is admirable if you routinely ride your bike and receive regular body work (such as massage, Rolfing, Shiatsu, or chiropractic manipulation), **but everyone will benefit from daily stretching for maintenance**. If you are riding more than 20 miles per week, you will cause harmful muscular imbalances unless you complement your cycling with stretching! Muscles work by contracting. The more any muscle is used, the shorter and tighter it becomes. No massage or manipulation, relaxation technique, or magic will lengthen that muscle to its healthy configuration except stretching. Tight muscles cannot contract over their full range and limit the opposing muscles from contracting fully.

They cause many different problems including:

1. Discomfort from misaligned posture

2. Reduced mobility due to inflexibility in the joints

3. Discomfort from muscular imbalance that increases risk of strains and other injuries

4. Pain or numbness from pinched nerves

5. Malfunction of glands and organs compressed by tight muscles or impaired by internal tension

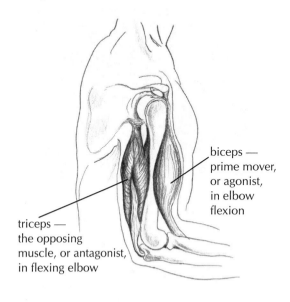

biceps — prime mover, or agonist, in elbow flexion

triceps — the opposing muscle, or antagonist, in flexing elbow

The biceps of the arm is the prime mover (agonist) of the upper arm when lifting your hand toward your chest. As the biceps contracts, the triceps is the antagonist (opposing) and must release completely to allow full contraction of the biceps. Full contraction results in full range of movement and full power. If the triceps is chronically tight it impairs movement of the biceps. In this illustration, the supporting muscles (synergists) are not shown for simplicity. Contrast the action of these muscles when you flex and extend your elbow while pumping up your tires with a floor pump. As your arms straighten out, the triceps become the prime mover, and the biceps become the opposing muscles.

The musculoskeletal problems characteristic of cyclists form an impressive list:

- Tight, shortened hamstrings

- Tight, over-developed quadriceps

- Tight pelvic structure, including hip joint inflexibility, tight buttocks muscles, and pinched sciatic nerve

- Weak abdominal muscles

- Collapsed chest and shortened pectoral muscles

- Tight upper trapezius muscles and hunched shoulders

- Compressed cervical spine (vertebrae of the neck)

- Tight triceps, forearms, and hands

- Numb hands and feet

This is not a pretty picture. It is also completely avoidable. Ten to thirty minutes of stretching each day will minimize these problems. Take a Yoga or stretching class to familiarize yourself with the areas of your body where you have limited flexibility. Refer to "Understanding Yoga Postures and Stretching" in Chapter 4, pp. 96-101.

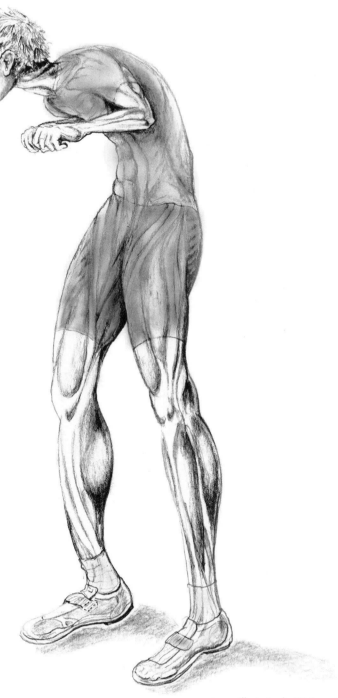

The unfortunate Timothy McTight is a high-mileage cyclist who has not committed himself to a daily stretching practice or to developing good riding form. Imbalanced and tight muscles limit his health and riding performance.

Illustration by Pat Conrad

You will enjoy an enduring enthusiasm for cycling when you have the courage to honestly search your perspective of cycling for limiting misunderstandings or fears. I hope that by addressing these concerns, you will be able to deal with the fears that diminish your passion for cycling. Let's explore the common fears — for personal safety, of losing control, of falling, or of looking foolish.

Fear for Personal Safety

If you live in a densely populated urban area, you are familiar with safety issues caused by disturbed individuals, reckless drivers, and inadequate space on the roads. You can overcome these concerns by creatively finding suitable places to ride. I also recommend carrying a canister of pepper spray attached to your handlebars with Velcro® for quick access. Yes, I have heard all the arguments for and against this practice but I am not going to carry a gun and some means of personal protection is advisable in many riding locations. Another way to feel secure is to ride in groups. By all means, don't take risks. Always be a responsible, alert user of public roads and trails. I often ask fearful riders if they have given up driving a car based on increased safety concerns on the road. I believe that with creativity, you can overcome personal safety issues.

Fear of Losing Control of Your Bike

Riding more frequently and learning to relax on your bike will develop your bike handling skills. Chapters 4 and 5 will instruct you in techniques for gaining full control of your bike. Meanwhile, you can increase your confidence by selecting appropriate places to ride, riding speeds, and riding styles. When I first learned to ride a unicycle, I became impatient with my faltering style. I hoped that riding more miles would help me gain strength and skill. For four consecutive days, I commuted the five-mile round-trip to work on my unicycle. Yes, some nights I was pretty tired climbing the last hill home after a full day's work but I was rewarded by a dramatic improvement in skill and a visible change in the shape of my thighs. When we yearn for results, we are more likely to make the necessary commitment.

Fear of Falling

During my first 40 years of riding, it was a high priority for me not to crash. As a child, I had been denied timely medical attention for a broken finger and concluded that I should avoid injuring myself. (This may have been a blessing in disguise since I still have a pain-free body and everything still works well.) A few years ago I caught a pedal and piled up while riding single track and recognized this latent fear. I also realized that when I ride relaxed at conservative speeds, crashes produce only minor scrapes. Now I enjoy freedom from this fear and can laugh at my goofy tumbles. You might find that wearing protective clothing and taking a few intentional, low-speed tumbles on a grassy surface would help you overcome your fear of falling.

Fear from a Bicycle Crash that Resulted in Serious Injury, Pain, and a Prolonged Recovery Time

The trauma of a serious childhood crash keeps many riders off bikes for years or even decades. Increasing your knowledge of cycling while developing your skills and confidence gradually with patience will enable you to overcome these fears. Acknowledge that you have changed in the ensuing years and can select different equipment and places to ride until you have proven to yourself that these fears are no longer appropriate. Most important is to stop the broken record in your head that instills the idea that you are afraid of riding. Replace it with the affirmation that "I enjoy riding a bike with skill and confidence."

Fear of Looking Foolish

Cycling is a highly revealing sport. Your physical stamina is conspicuous in a group, especially if you can't keep up. Most cycle clothing indiscriminately reveals every desirable curve and every unwanted bulge. It takes fairly confident riders to expose themselves to peer scrutiny. This became apparent to me when Self-Propulsion sponsored a women-centered riding group. Participants were eager to organize rides and events but when the event day came, turnouts were usually small. I know there are many reasons why people don't come to events but I feel certain that some novice riders hesitated to come because they were afraid they would appear inadequate.

Golden is nestled in a narrow valley in the foothills of the Rocky Mountains. To go home, everyone has to go up steep hills. This can be daunting on a bike. It is so challenging that many citizens do not ride the short distance into town to do errands. It seems simple enough to me to just push your bike up the steepest sections on the way home. However, most people don't want to be seen pushing their bikes because it makes them feel inadequate. I don't think the motorists who speed by them are in a good position to be critical. Perhaps you can overcome the phobia of pushing your bike by realizing how enabling it is. My sons and I often tour high in the mountains where the going is steep and rough, and the oxygen is scarce. In order to overcome the immediate obstacle and continue toward our destination, we get off our heavily-loaded bikes and push. We call this "bike-assisted hiking." Bernhard frequently encourages reluctant bike-pushers by telling them that "Pushing is good exercise, too." Try it. You'll like the freedom and the opportunity to use different muscles. It feels so good to stretch out your neck and hamstrings and give your butt a break by letting blood and lymph fluids flow and nerves regain sensation.

Whatever your fears, you may gain some courage by recognizing that you can only do the best you are able to do *now*. It doesn't matter who you used to be or who you hope to be. You must start where you are today. Perhaps Ganbold's story will inspire you. In 1999, I was delighted to meet Ganbold. He had been the Mongolian national bicycle racing champion throughout the eighties and coached the national cycling team through much of the nineties. He had moved to the U.S. with his wife and three daughters in 1996. He and his wife were working several jobs to support their family and striving to adapt to a new language and a new life style.

In spite of his heavy work schedule, Ganbold decided to try racing in Colorado. He trained as much as possible, purchased a racing license, and got ready for an early season road race. His family and friends and I gathered on that cold spring morning to cheer him on at a Boulder stage race. I really admired him for what he was able to do. He had to register as a novice, Category 4 racer. I asked if he had explained his experience to the licensing board, and he told me there was no space for that on the license application. Here was a man who had raced for years in Europe and Asia and had placed well on many occasions. He enjoyed the respect and admiration of his entire nation. Yet he was able to remember all of that glory in his heart and pursue his love of racing with amateurs no matter how it appeared to others.

Ganbold lines up at the starting line of a Boulder stage race on a cold spring day. During this return to bicycle racing after years away from training, his passion for the sport enabled him to finish strong when most of the others in his category dropped out under tough conditions.

Much of the road race was on dirt roads. Ganbold had never raced his road bike on dirt. The course was so challenging that of the 120 starters, only 23 finished – and he was among those few strong finishers! He did the best he was able to do under the challenging circumstances and made a splendid showing. He later conceded that bicycle racing was not reasonable for him anymore – now that he was a family man with many responsibilities. But he had given it his best and received the love and admiration of friends and family.

3. Focus on the process of riding and on optimizing the physiological and biomechanical functions that contribute to performance.

Make each ride an opportunity to improve your form and to learn something new about how you use your body. Continually build your fitness and health by remaining flexible about target goals of distance, speed, or total elapse time. Bicycle computers are useful tools to help you measure your performance but avoid letting them push you to unrealistic target goals. Be critical of advice on riding technique given by friends and popular magazines and determine whether it is based on good health and improved fitness.

Use the illustrations in **Bicycling Bliss** to learn more about your anatomy and body function. Riding techniques are grounded in human physiology and biomechanics. You will be able to appreciate why it is more important to understand how to breathe to optimize oxygenation than to digress into discussions of the discomforts of lactic acid buildup during high-intensity exertion. When you ride at moderate intensity, you minimize the likelihood of experiencing lactic acid burn.

Knowledge of how your body works will increase your sensitivity to subtle changes in performance and to minor discomforts. When you are able to interpret their meaning, you can begin preventative care before the warning signs develop into pain and injury. Most musculoskeletal problems do not require prolonged medical attention if you intercept them in the beginning stages. Better still, use your daily stretching and strengthening exercises to tune in to your condition. When you detect muscle imbalances and weaknesses, you can select appropriate exercises to counteract them and restore balance and strength. If you detect tenderness, reduce your training level and take preventative measures. With care, you will not need to stay off your bike to recuperate from injury.

Using your wellness as your guide, give attention to adequate fluids, food, sleep, and clothing every time you ride. This will make you feel good and increase your stamina. Equip your bike with a seat bag or rack and tour packs or use a hydration system to carry your essential fluids, energy-rich food, and protective clothing. Inform yourself about how each of these things improves your performance and pleasure. Chapters 7 and 8 will help you learn to optimize your resources and choose appropriate clothing. It is also wise to learn the basics of bicycle maintenance. Refer to Leonard Zinn's books (see recommended readings), which provide current and thorough explanations of bicycle maintenance. Enjoy peace of mind by being ready for the unexpected. Learn from other people's mistakes. It is more fun than making them yourself. Besides, you have to learn from others' mistakes because you won't live long enough to make them all yourself!

4. Use comfort as an indicator of efficient and healthful form while riding and conditioning.

Few cyclists make comfort a high priority. Unfortunately, many riders assume that discomfort is a part of bike riding. Let me correct that misconception.

- Riding in a comfortable way is more efficient. When you work against discomfort, you become tense and waste energy that could propel your bike.

- By making choices that ensure both physical and psychological comfort, you are building fitness, renewing your psyche, and reducing the likelihood of mishaps.

- Sensitivity to discomfort is the alarm system that warns you that you're doing harm to yourself.

- Riding in comfort makes you eager to get back on your bike and thus helps you maintain your enthusiasm and your fitness.

- Appreciating comfort is *not* a sign of weakness but a tool for evaluating wellness.

When riders persevere in spite of discomfort, they increase the likelihood of overuse injuries and mishaps that result from poor judgement. Tuning in to your comfort level is a vital tool in optimizing your form.

If you live on a high-pressure schedule, you probably push yourself past your comfortable stamina level for work and home responsibilities. You may have learned to shut off your body's need for rest, quiet, food, and water. After disregarding your basic needs for extended periods, you may have lost your ability to notice what you really lack. Have you noticed yourself getting a snack when you probably need sleep instead? Or you may indulge in some entertaining distraction when you actually need a nourishing meal.

You will increase your appreciation of genuine comfort by using **self-nurturing interludes**. What is an interlude of self-nurture? (If this sounds hokey, be patient, you may like it.) It is a healthful activity that replenishes your psychological reservoir. When you feel out-of-sorts, you can put one of these activities on your schedule and look forward to comforting yourself. Choose activities that provide you with lasting pleasure. You guessed it, one such activity is riding your bike in a nurturing way. Other activities I would suggest are:

- Practicing Yoga, Qigong, Taiji, or acupressure

- Creating a piece of equipment, garment, or gadget that you haven't been able to make time for. Working with your hands is grounding and gives the immediate satisfaction of creating a product.

- Creating artwork

- Making music

- Leisurely preparing a favorite, nourishing meal

- Reading a book just for fun

- Writing in your journal

- Meditating

- Performing some personal care like taking a soothing bath or filing your nails

- Going for a stroll

- Washing your bike and fussing to make it sparkle

Whether you include eating a snack on your list of interludes depends on your current weight. If your weight-to-height ratio is healthy, and you feel energetic most of the time, eat a wholesome snack from time to time for self-nurture. If you are overweight, substitute another self-nurturing activity when you want to snack. With some retraining, you will be surprised to discover that substituting some favorite stretches for snacking will be satisfying and you will feel better afterwards, both physically and mentally.

If you are going to use snacking as an interlude, here are some guidelines:

1. Select foods that are low on the glycemic index and are otherwise nutritious and healthful. (Refer to Chapter 7, pp. 297-301.) Consider non-fat yogurt with fresh fruit; roasted walnuts, fresh fruit or vegetables that are specially cut and served; stone-ground whole wheat, low sugar-content muffins you can make and have on hand. Try the recipes in Appendix E.

2. Place the measured amount you are going to eat in a dish. It's easy to overindulge when you eat an unknown quantity directly from the storage or serving container.

3. Sit down to eat and give your full attention to appreciating the flavor and texture as well as to chewing and thoroughly assimilating the food.

4. Satisfy your craving for food with beverages. Select those without sugar or stimulants because they will help you stay fully hydrated.

5. Carry wholesome food with you when you are away from home. This will help you resist the temptation to buy unwholesome snacks.

It will take time and thought to implement these new snacking habits, but they will make a substantial contribution to your long-term health. Contentment is a matter of changing your life style to care for all your needs. If you don't take care of yourself, who will?

We can increase the benefits of self-nurturing interludes by bestowing them with special status. These guidelines will help you increase their value:

1. Consider the interludes as special treats that you deserve. Avoid letting them become commonplace experiences.

2. Design the activity creatively so you will anticipate it with pleasure. That does not mean that every time you ride your bike it must become a special ritual. Create a special style of ride or location for your interludes.

3. Tailor the activity to meet your immediate needs. If you usually go for a brisk walk but feel tired one day, slow down the pace and search your body for hidden tension.

4. Choose a setting that enables you to give full attention to yourself and your experience. Full participation in the activity will heighten your pleasure.

5. Give attention to the esthetics of the activity. Make a ritual based on enjoyment of all your senses: sight, hearing, taste, touch, smell, and movement. Be sensitive to your mental, emotional, and spiritual needs.

6. Observe your breathing and balance your exhalations with your inhalations.

Practicing self-nurturing interludes will help you learn to identify false cravings and counter-productive behaviors. The more often you feel good, the more you'll be able to identify and avoid abusive behaviors. Hopefully you will begin to avoid overeating, involvement in poor relationships, remaining in poor jobs, and subjecting yourself to frenetic schedules.

5. Develop a personal riding style that serves your current life needs.

The first step in cultivating your own riding style is to identify your riding pleasures and priorities. You'll find a list of questions you can ask yourself to help you identify these in Chapter 7, "Selecting Compatible Riding Companions," pp. 321-322. Your priority list might include getting a fitness workout, developing your riding technique, burning some calories, enjoying nature, seeking renewal, exploring and seeking adventure, or enjoying social interaction. Have more fun by varying your priorities from ride to ride or by choosing different companions.

It is challenging to create your own riding style. Most cycling images are limited to a few styles. Group and event rides frequently have an underlying competitive element.

I would support Dr. Andrew Weil's admonition that if you can't leave your competitive drive behind, it is better to ride alone. For examples of more diverse riding styles you might look to Holland, Denmark, or China where cycling is a respected part of the culture.

As you seek to discover a personally satisfying riding style, try freeing yourself from the pressure to look and perform like other riders. Consider the futility of trying to create an image to please others. When cyclists ride through stop signals without hesitating, the riders' perceptions are quite different from the motorists who are looking on. The law-breaking riders are probably feeling quite smug, imagining that speed is more important than good judgement. In contrast, the motorists are increasing their intolerance of cyclists. In a society that places a high priority on appearances, I like this quote, "We can never know the true impression we have on other people."

If you were to adopt a generic riding style, you would build generic fitness. Your body responds specifically to your training technique. After you have identified your riding goals and priorities, you will want to choose riding styles that result in the desired fitness goals. For example, if you want to improve your technique, you will benefit most from riding alone at a pace that enables you to focus on your breathing and your form. If you want to build muscle strength, you should ride with a load, climb hills, or pedal at a cadence between 50 and 70 rpm. If you want to develop speed, a fluid form, or rehabilitate an injury, ride light at a cadence above 80 rpm. If you seek mental, emotional, and spiritual renewal, focus on breathing, staying in the moment, and riding within your stamina level. The conscious choice of a purposeful riding style can make each ride more fulfilling and produce the desired health and fitness results.

Our varied styles are strongly influenced by our different perceptions and our responses to those perceptions. Racers are more likely to tolerate the sensation of "burning" muscles, while most recreational riders dislike that feeling. You may enjoy the exhilaration of being buffeted by the wind while others dislike the hard work and uncertainty of wind strength and direction. Mountain bikers find the demands of riding single track centering while others consider it fatiguing. When you are puzzled by the divergent riding styles of your friends, think about how their perception differs from yours and avoid assuming they are simply crazy.

Be confident in your own choices. The herd instinct is strong among humans as well as ruminants. Often while advocating the option of a flat handlebar road bike, customers asked me, "If drop bars are of questionable value, why is everyone riding with them?" I could only assume that most people want to do what everyone else is doing and avoid the hassle of critically evaluating each situation themselves or of being different. Think for yourself and make no apologies for your individuality.

Experimentation will help you discover a style that serves you well and facilitates an evolving riding style. Cycling is superbly adaptable. The gears help compensate for varied stamina levels. Different tires or different tire pressure can increase your comfort and stability. Replacing your drop bars with flat bars and a more upright position can eliminate neck and shoulder strain. Riding rolling terrain or less demanding trails can make your ride more appropriate when you are tired or scattered. You may find that you want to give up some of your favorite ride routes and establish new ones as your life circumstances change.

Portia's Proposal For Peaceful Pedaling

(Warning: not for adrenaline junkies)

I would like to paint you a picture that I hope will inspire you to create a vision to fulfill your riding aspiration. I ask you to consider a style of riding that brings joy and satisfaction during the ride, pleasant memories, and lasting health benefits. The goal of this style is to maintain balance and fun. It has also helped me develop skills to address life's challenges.

Keep a mellow, sustainable pace that allows conscious breathing, relaxed body, and mindfulness. That means being fully alert and engaged in your present activity, surroundings, and circumstances, responding with grace and humor.

Go prepared for changes in your condition or aspirations, in terrain, in weather, or in

Kirk and I quietly explore the shores of Lake Hofskol in Mongolia.

food needs. Carry plenty of weight so that your exertion level does not depend solely on riding speed or terrain. The weight could be ballast (gallon jugs filled with water can be emptied along the way if you get tired of the weight), but for peaceful pedaling you will need rain wear, extra wind and insulative protection, extra food, and maps so you will be ready to adapt to changing conditions. You can then be free of worries about capricious weather, running low on energy, or not finding an alternative return route. You can actually use all the energy you have saved by not worrying, to move your bike forward.

What will you do now without the excitement of risk? **Just ride along in peace!** You can be content, stay in the moment, and experience the many facets of your surroundings. You can be mindful, adjust your pace, clothing, energy output, or food intake so that the ride is enjoyable all the time. Oh, there will be times when you take refuge under a tree and sit and eat your lunch in your rainwear soggy with perspiration and rain. No, this is not comfortable, but even so, you can still be content. Feel those warm, fit muscles underneath all the mess and look around at the scenery. How nice it is to be prepared to be in harmony with nature! Or if you prefer more comfort, how nice to feel the freedom to take refuge indoors.

Bernhard enjoys lunch while his wet rainwear and clothing dry out. We learned it is usually better to take refuge during brief, intense rain storms than to continue riding and make a mess of ourselves and our bikes. Now we carry a poncho or tarp to cover us until the storm passes.

All this is possible when you maintain a frame of mind that allows you to embrace change. How delightful it is, to be able to move into alternative strategies as conditions change or do not meet your expectations. Conscious breathing brings contentment and relaxation within your reach, whatever the circumstances. You can enjoy freedom from the fear that things won't go as you planned or desired. Your increased adaptability allows you to adjust to different courses of action without stressing out. While these principles apply most obviously to self-contained, long-distance touring, you can also enjoy them on day rides or on your bicycle commute.

How often do you make yourself miserable wishing you were somewhere else, doing something else, being someone else, or possessing something else? Because all these yearnings are of your own making, you are free to change your attitude and let the frustration slide away. Michael Bonamer, my Yoga teacher, says, "Troubles disappear when you cease to compare." This may mean comparing your reality with your hopes; comparing what you've accomplished with what you might have done; or comparing what that other person did that violates your priorities. I just remember, **we each do the best we are able to do at the time**. Under the circumstances, with the understanding I have, my current fatigue level or my resources, I do the best I can (just as others do). I have learned to be gentle with myself and with others. What do I know of other people's burdens?

"So," say the proponents of extreme sports, "This stuff is for wimps and old women!" (I guess so. Here I am.) Certainly this is only one approach and not for everyone, but I find it healing and think that you might not have explored such experiences. However, because extreme sports are so popular these days, I have given them some thought. Some proponents say they seek extreme experiences to learn about themselves and to gain strength while others enjoy them for notoriety or to set records. I find that when the goals are extreme, and the activities involve high risks, the lessons to be learned emphasize the skills and behaviors needed for high-stress situations. When we seek out extreme activities, we develop and reinforce the skills needed for these extremes. How, then, might you develop skills and enhance your sensitivity to subtler needs and feelings? Could you calm your fears and strengthen your commitment to peace and contentment by maintaining an attitude of flexibility, openness, and nurture? There surely are many different ways to increase your understanding of life.

6. Make riding fun so you can maintain a passion for a healthful fitness routine the rest of your life.

Children love to ride bikes because they bring fun, fitness, and freedom! Is that still true for you today? If you have lost these thrills, can you bring them back to your current riding style? Riders often tell me they don't want to ride mountain trails because they can't enjoy the scenery and intimate contact with nature while concentrating on the technical aspects of trail riding. I understand that. I just don't let these two priorities conflict. When the technical demands of the trail distract me from savoring my natural surroundings, I just get off and push my bike. I follow my fitness pursuits in a fun and spontaneous way!

I am indebted to Charles Roy Schroeder, Ph.D., author of *Taking the Work Out of*

Ali, Jenny and I enjoy serenity and companionship riding the Colorado Trail.

Working Out for his thoughtful study of our attitudes toward exercise. Since we commonly bring the seriousness and intensity of our work to our exercise, let me share with you his insights on how to make exercise more fun.

Schroeder's analysis of our attitudes and reasons for exercising are both realistic and creative. He suggests that we exercise as **medicine, play, sensory experience, and art**. Exercise as medicine needs little explanation in our sedentary society. Inactivity breeds lethargy, and lethargy causes us to resist physical activity as if it were work. When we select activities that are fun, we are less likely to think of them as medicine. The very nature of imposed pressure causes us to shut out our sensations, focus on the end goal, and lose the immediate pleasure of being fully present and fully sensual. We displace the opportunity to feel fully alive and capable with a grudging attitude that we have to exercise or we will suffer undesirable consequences. Not only that, we dread that we will have to exercise for **the rest of our lives!** That perspective could stop us right now unless we can make exercise so attractive that we **anticipate and delight in this prospect**.

A playful attitude toward exercise fosters anticipation. Our energy begins to build even before we start riding. Contrast this response to the drained, low energy feeling you experience when you consider a task as drudgery. Think about the elements of play that will make us eager to exercise: distraction from worry, spontaneity, the resulting sense of release and renewal, and improved health and fitness.

A spontaneous dash into Buffalo Creek provided hilarity, cool refreshment, and great memories.

Probably the most neglected element of exercise is sensory experience. The conscious attention to our sensation of coordinated movement is known as kinesthesia. Schroeder gives us a splendid analogy to illustrate the rewards of tuning in to our body sensations during exercise. He compares the typical workout routine to orchestral musicians tuning up their instruments. The activity is certainly part of the practice but it does not create music. When we bicyclists exercise while being tuned in to the freedom and expression of movement, to the sensations of muscles, tendons, and joints working together in healthy coordination, we create the harmony and pleasure of orchestral music! Schroeder calls this "body music." Full body awareness will enable us to continue a regular, life-long exercise program as pleasure and self-nurture rather than obligation and discomfort.

The theory of exercise as art may stretch your imagination. In practice, you can probably appreciate moving in esthetically pleasing patterns. Since you can control your movement patterns, why not gain pleasure from making them esthetically pleasing? I hope you have observed bike riders who were music in action. All their movements were fluid, balanced, and efficient. Though the movements that propel your bike are quite repetitive, cycling also lends itself to making body music. Schroeder describes the kinesthetic pleasures of riding:

...While bicycle riding, you typically feel a generalized joy of movement. If you concentrate on your leg muscles, you'll realize some of the sensation comes from the rhythmic changes of muscle tension. By shifting your attention to the knees and ankles as they alternately extend and flex, you will become aware of the different but still enjoyable feeling. In other words, both muscle and joint sensations contribute to the total body music you will be experiencing.

Next, divert your attention to the pressure of your feet against the pedals, or to the gentle vibrations in your body as the tires roll over the finely pebbled surface of the road. The cool wind flowing over your skin and tousling your hair adds a further satisfying touch as does the texture of clothes as they caress your skin. By pedaling fast enough, acidic wastes in the leg muscles increase and produce an exquisite burning sensation that adds a dash of spice to the body music. (Schroeder, p. 23)

While riding you can also experiment with various rhythms, cadences, exertion levels, and torso positions. One of the reasons I do not ride a bike with suspension is because I love to "dance" on my bike and feel the contact with the earth beneath. Perhaps you can imagine "dancing" on single track. I like to experience my balance, agility, flexibility, alignment, and grace. But it is also fun on the road to use exaggerated movements, turning

Bernhard and Kirk demonstrate the ease of riding no-handed to encourage me to learn.

to watch traffic approaching from behind, stretching to see a passing bird. On your next ride, use your imagination and explore some self-expression.

Experiment with bringing closure to your riding experience. Rather than bounding off your bike and moving directly on to the next pressing task, incorporate some stretches into your ride ritual. What differences do you feel compared to your pre-ride warm-up? Maybe your wind-down could include cleaning your bike. Make a gradual transition while you process and appreciate the pleasures of your ride.

Enjoyment of any exercise requires that you:

- Overcome personal limitations

- Develop control

- Become good at the activity (Schroeder, p. 150)

In the following chapters, I will guide you through how to achieve each of these steps to make riding fun and healthful.

Yoga lends itself well to enhancing your kinesthetic pleasure. During each posture while some muscles are being stretched, others contract. You move different joints and combinations of joints. You can vary the speed of movement and the energy level. You will find that each modulation brings pleasant new sensations. The classically slow movements of Yoga lend themselves to exploring the nuances of movement. You can vary the sequence of several postures. You can contrast the way this repetition or side of your body feels with your memory of previous repetitions. Each of these variations allows you to attach different meaning to your perceptions. Take care to close each posture with special attention to how the completion feels and your appreciation of the benefits. Placing emphasis on kinesthesia integrates your mind and body during physical activities.

7. Strengthen and bring into balance all elements of human nature: physical, mental, emotional, social, and spiritual.

Top performance in sports depends on optimizing all your inward and outward capabilities. Coaches and competitors have long utilized sports psychology to improve athletic performance. Now the array of essential tools for improving athletic performance is greatly expanded:

1. Practicing routine exercise to develop and maintain strong bodies

2. Understanding biomechanics and biofeedback for efficient use of your body

3. Cultivating conscious breathing to optimize oxygenation and adjust your attitude

4. Stretching to keep your body flexible and in balanced alignment

5. Identifying your goals and expectations to guide and motivate disciplined performance

6. Planning to ensure the best quantity and quality of nutrients, sleep, and contemplation

7. Practicing techniques to cultivate and ensure the even flow and distribution of your vital energies (qi)

8. Learning to visualize the desired performance and manifest it through affirmations and intention

9. Quieting your mind and clearing your emotions so your effort will be focused

10. Disciplining yourself to perform at your best even when you think mediocre is good enough

Avoid the common error of committing most of your effort to developing physical strength while neglecting your other resources. Integrated cycling incorporates all your capabilities in order to sustain optimum fitness, health, and contentment.

8. Cultivate a conscious awareness to enable you to assess your needs, learn new skills, and fully appreciate your experiences.

Conscious awareness is essential to implementing change. Begin by making an accurate evaluation of your current condition and your riding technique. Your accuracy will depend on awareness of your sensations and movements. While you are implementing change, you will need to give your attention to biofeedback and kinesthesia. Finally, your ability to perceive your improvement and appreciation of the benefits will be enhanced by conscious awareness.

What is the price of being half-present? For cyclists it means more mishaps. Most of Self-Propulsion's customers ride the same roads and trails. Many of them ride on the same high-quality Continental® tires and tubes that we sell. Why then are a few riders plagued by bad luck and have lots of flats? I believe inattentiveness is a key factor! Perhaps they are riding too fast to respond to debris in their path or maybe their minds are wandering away from their riding. Surely their problems would be diminished if they were fully present and attentive to their surroundings.

To experience the difference that increased focus can make, experiment with these practices:

1. Avoid hurrying. Distinguish riding under pressure from riding at high-exertion levels. You will need to know your priorities and direct your full energy to doing what is of greatest importance.

2. Be realistic in scheduling. Eliminate activities and commitments that will drag you down. Just say no. It seems that any task requires three times more effort and time than you expect. Adjust your schedule as each day unfolds so you can arrive at each commitment focused and ready to engage in the task.

3. Avoid multitasking. Certainly retailing and many other careers require juggling several jobs at once. But only give your attention to more than one thing at a time when it is unavoidable. Don't *plan* to multitask. Sometimes people applying for jobs at Self-Propulsion indicated that they were skilled at multitasking. I shuddered to think of the poor quality work they would do while giving only part of their attention to each job. The nature of our society scatters our minds and dissipates our energies. We need to invest time into concentrating our resources.

4. Accept yourself as lovable, capable, and worthy, just as you naturally are. Avoid wishing that your circumstance were different from your current situation. You are unlikely to be able to enjoy what you are doing now if you don't bring all of your attention to your current activity.

5. When you find your mind wandering, gently bring it back to the present and think about what you are doing. Are you bored or do you feel like time is dragging? Your perception will change when you bring all your attention to your immediate task. It may also help to think about the importance of the job you are doing, how fortunate you are to be capable of doing this job, and how you may benefit from doing it.

6. Practice conscious breathing to bring yourself into the present moment. Tune in to your breathing several times a day, particularly when you need an attitude adjustment.

7. Visually study your surroundings. When you are riding, study the riding surface, look at the details of the flora around you, study the clouds. If you are sitting still, select an object and concentrate on tracing its outline and contours. Pretend you are an artist and are going to draw this object. Or if you are inclined, take up paper and pencil and actually draw it. Creating something with your hands is excellent therapy for focusing the mind *and* opening new thought channels.

8. Limit your audio stimuli. Make time each day to relax or work in a silent environment. Just turn off the CD player or TV and experience the silence. Our environment is so noisy that I always carry earplugs. How satisfying it is to discretely slip them in my ears when people near me are jabbering loudly on their cell phones.

Quieting the racing mind is essential to being present. You give your body a rest, but your mind just keeps working 24 hours a day. Our minds tend to get so wound up that it is difficult to stop them. Look away from this page for a moment and consciously stop thinking. How many seconds was it before thoughts started streaming through your head again? You will find it easier to practice quieting your mind in a silent, secure place away from distraction. By practicing these skills under ideal conditions, you will be able to concentrate better in more distracting circumstances.

Both journaling and contemplation will help quiet your mind. You will find sections on both these practices in Chapter 4, pp. 131-135. Let me emphasize that taking time to process your many concerns, experiences, and feelings will contribute to a quiet mind. Putting them on the back burner just lets them boil over. By taking time to reflect, you will find that many problems are resolved when you give them your full attention. Writing them in a journal will crystallize your thoughts and putting them on paper often releases them from your mind.

Regularly practicing quieting your mind and living consciously will facilitate learning, help you implement change, improve your bike handling skills, help you avoid crashes, and result in fewer flats and mechanical mishaps.

9. Let go of your old ways so you are free to experiment and to define a new direction.

Trying to adapt to a new technique while hanging on to the old way usually intensifies the problem. It surely litters the mind and confuses the body. Just as releasing muscle tension enables the muscle to work through its full contraction, releasing old habits frees you to test new ideas and redirect your energies.

Riders who are willing to experiment with new ways demonstrate just how satisfying change can be. Mary Ann came to Self-Propulsion distressed that she would have to give up riding if she could not find a new bike that relieved her hand pain. She had always ridden a mountain bike and hoped that a drop handlebar road bike would relieve her pain. We discussed the causes of hand pain and the importance of relaxing her grip on the bars. I suggested further that she visualize opening her shoulder joints in order to minimize nerve impingement. Then we talked about the potential hand strain from using drop bars with dual control levers. First she test rode a bike with a short top tube and drop handlebars to determine if that would be comfortable. She did not like it at all and was immediately discouraged. Her mountain bike with high rise bars caused so much pain that she was skeptical about a road bike with flat handlebars providing relief. I was delighted that she was willing to give the flat handlebars a try but she was only marginally impressed.

Returning later that week for another test ride, she was amazed to find she could ride pain-free on flat handlebars. Indeed, Mary Ann did buy the Bianchi® Strada, a performance road bike with flat handlebars and bar ends. We made a few adjustments at her request and hand pain became a forgotten issue. Later as we reflected together on her shopping experience, Mary Ann told me she was so sure that drop bars were what she needed that it was difficult to accept my suggestions. Since she was too stubborn to give up cycling, she was willing to let go of her preconceived notion that drop bars would solve her problem. Surely during the days between test rides, she processed the new information and returned more willing to experiment. Mary Ann is an impressive example of how the willingness to experiment can result in great satisfaction.

Many riders come to Self-Propulsion seeking relief from discomfort on their bikes. They bring their bikes and explain their problems. I ask for clarification and study them on their bikes. Some problems are so common that solutions are clear-cut. Even so, I choose my words thoughtfully, ask if they have tried this or that solution, and make suggestions gently. Nevertheless, many riders resist making changes.

I have been so impressed by people's defensive responses that I made a pact with myself. You might like to try this technique too. Whenever anyone offers suggestions or criticism to me, I ask them one question to try to better understand the suggestion or to learn how to implement it. This demonstrates to the speaker that I respect their comments and helps me avoid responding defensively. This requires that I open up to this person's ideas, making it easier to discover the wisdom or truth in it that is useful for me. At a recent seminar by Gay and Kathlyn Hendricks on conscious relationships, they had the large audience practice saying aloud, "You know, I might be wrong." I was so delighted by the simple effectiveness of this exercise that I have shared it with many friends. Just telling the story repeatedly has lightened my attitude and lowered my defenses. Try saying that a few times over the next few weeks. You too may be a little more accepting of your human fallibility.

Now in my sixth decade, I have finally figured out that my current ideas are just that. They are not some ultimate wisdom, but rather only my current understanding. I have discovered a delightful freedom in knowing that my ideas, understandings, and practices are continually evolving. In fact, I expect them to evolve so there is no need to defend them but simply offer them to others for whatever value they might provide in their current circumstances. *Bicycling Bliss* offers my current understanding of cycling for wellness. During the eight years of writing and researching, I have broadened and refined my understanding and I know that will continue.

Another reason people resist change is that they actually love their problems. Problems give them something to talk about, and they receive special attention for them. They love the familiarity of these old problems and don't want to trade them in for new ones. They are choosing to stay where they are — enduring discomfort rather than discovering a healthful new way. For example, riders resist raising their seats because they want to be able to put their feet squarely on the ground when they stop. It doesn't occur to them that they are choosing to sacrifice the health of their knees and the pleasure of increased stamina in order to achieve this single goal. When you find yourself resisting change, try to identify your own self-imposed limitations. Once you recognize them you may be able to let them go.

I know that adjustment to change can be stressful but the resulting growth and learning will support your effort. Yes, the transition to the new way can create uncertainty but the other choice is imprisonment by our own self-imposed beliefs. Ask yourself if you would like to be the same now as you were five or fifteen years ago. That realization can motivate you to purposely choose what you want to become and to consciously put your energies and imagination into getting there. Think of life as an opportunity to create a fine piece of art. It is your job to discover your rough places (your inadequacies) and polish them to a new, pleasing form.

In writing *Bicycling Bliss* I have assumed that your desire to be healthy and contented is strong enough to give you courage to change ingrained habits. The information on optimum riding technique will provide you with a basis for change. I also describe the processes to guide change and improve your riding skills, life skills, and attitudes. In this high-tech world, change is even more certain than death and taxes. Accepting change can be remarkably liberating. So strive to develop an attitude that embraces change, the confidence that you can affect change, and the skills to implement it.

Conclusion

Cycling is so exhilarating! Each year of riding exposes you to new discoveries and benefits. It is the true mark of cycling's enduring value that each decade adds new dimensions and appreciation of your experience.

I hope *Bicycling Bliss* will support you in your discovery process. I ask you to expand your expectations of cycling and anticipate gaining more than physical fitness from riding.

chapter 2

Cycling Builds Fitness, Develops Life Skills, and Improves Attitudes

- Physical Fitness is the Foremost Benefit of Cycling
- Cycling is Accessible to Most People
- The Psychological Benefits of Cycling
- Bicycle Riding Teaches Us Many of Life's Lessons
- Cyclists Help Build Healthy Communities

Physical Fitness is the Foremost Benefit of Cycling

Whatever your riding style, physical condition, age, or infirmity, you will improve your health by riding a bike. Whether you enjoy a leisurely style or ride long distance at high energy, you will feel fit, free, and capable.

Riding builds **strong aerobic capacity** when you ride regularly at moderate exertion levels for 30 minutes or more. It is **non-weight bearing** so you can build strength and increase the range of movement of your hips and knees with limited risk to your back and joints. The **wide gear range** makes it easy to begin cycling at any strength or stamina level. That is why physical therapists frequently recommended cycling to build strength and mobility during recovery from illness, injury, or surgery. Cycling provides a psychological bonus for anyone with restricted mobility. It helps them build their sense of self-sufficiency, independence, and capability.

Over the years, I have enjoyed the success stories of many riders. Some customers have demonstrated courage and discipline to overcome remarkable challenges. I first met Debbie while she was walking along Golden Road in her characteristic halting gait. As the months went by, we greeted each other with increasing enthusiasm. One day she came into the store to buy a tire for one of her kid's bikes. Even though cerebral palsy challenged her physically, she said she had always wanted to ride a bike. Her unhesitating determination to ride led us to explore the possibilities with her. She had demonstrated she could walk a mile or two but her balance was limited as was use of her right side. After considerable discussion, we agreed to install 20-inch stabilizing wheels (adult training wheels) on an old ten-speed she had. As I test rode the rig, I was apprehensive because the three back wheels made the bike list badly on sloping pavement making me feel precarious. After several

With courage and patience, Debbie learned to ride a bike to do errands in spite of limited strength and control of her right side.

experiments with equipment, we ended up with a 21-speed mountain bike with step-through frame and both gear and brake controls on the left side. When Debbie came to get her custom bike, her courage and determination shone through. She persevered until she succeeded in stepping through the frame from the height of the curb. She needed our help to place her right foot on the pedal, and we strapped it on with a toe strap to prevent it from involuntarily flying off as she rode. To our amazement and admiration, she did succeed in riding home: two-miles of up-hill in busy traffic. After weeks of practice in her apartment parking lot and many crashes, she became quite confident riding to the grocery store. Debbie is a shining example and inspiration to all because she did not let cerebral palsy, finances, or even risk of injury prevent her from riding a bike. Her zeal was so radiant, we invited her to work part-time at Self-Propulsion for several summers.

We have had several customers who can ride bikes better than they can walk. For several years, Self-Propulsion sponsored a group of senior riders. They organized their own rides and encouraged each other back to health after illness or surgery. Many were strong, high-mileage riders, and when adversity struck, they pooled their courage to support each other's return to strength. Ed is an engineer who worked in construction all his life. His back was causing discomfort and difficulty in walking. After a couple surgeries, he needed to walk with two hiking staffs, and his daily rides became shorter. Even so, he tenaciously continued daily rides around his neighborhood. Ed encouraged his friend Farrel to start riding when Farrel was in his early seventies. Farrel was skeptical but eventually bought a fine mountain bike. His wife had a progressively degenerative illness, and bike riding gave Farrel some freedom and sustained his enthusiasm for life. He worked up to riding over 3,000 miles annually, learned to use toe clips, and was an inspiration for many younger riders. As Ed's riding range decreased, Farrel and Ed regularly rode the "Tour de Pleasant View," a small community about a mile from their neighborhood. Along about that time, Farrel was diagnosed with cancer. After surgery and some recovery time, Ed got him out on his bike daily to ride in the high school parking lot across the street from Farrel's house. This outing they fondly referred to as the

"Tour de Parking Lot." I give these examples to help you overcome any obstacles that prevent you from riding a bike and enable you to enjoy the benefits these courageous riders sought.

Balance and agility are essential to optimum health and fitness. The relaxation and quick response skills required to ride a bike will enhance your balance and agility. As you cultivate your sensitivity to movement and kinesthetic sense, your movement will become more fluid, and awkwardness will become an embarrassment of the past.

Cycling also **enhances your sensory perceptions**. As you pass through neighborhoods or wooded meadows, you enjoy their colors, aromas, and sounds. You can hear your heart beat, feel your lungs expand and contract, and enjoy the sensations of a finely tuned body. Your increasing awareness of yourself and your surroundings helps prevent illness and enables you to take better care of yourself. When you ride regularly, you'll probably be able to buy new rainwear with the money you'll save from not going so often to the family medical clinic.

Cycling is Accessible to Most People

Bike riding is economical and adaptable, making the benefits available to almost everyone.

The basic equipment for bike riding is **economical**. Of course there are lots of expensive accessories you could buy but they are not needed to derive the best physical and psychological benefits of cycling. A safe, basic bike (bought from a specialty retailer), sealant in the inner tubes, and a helmet will get you started. You should budget $400-$500 for these. As your mileage increases, you will need to add a rear view mirror, bottle holders, toe clips and straps, frame pump, and seat bag to carry an emergency repair kit. These probably represent another $75. When you amortize these expenses over several years, bike riding is remarkably affordable. As Jeff recently reported in praise of his ten-year-old bike, the initial investment has cost him ten cents a day. Inform yourself about basic maintenance, and those expenses can be kept to a minimum.

Other elements of economy are worth noting. You can ride a bike without paying for a lift ticket, a greens fee, or athletic club membership. You can leave your car in the garage and just roll out of your driveway to enjoy a free cruise in your neighborhood, county, or state. This convenience also lends simplicity to bike riding. As more trails are built, riding opportunities increase.

Using your bike for **basic transportation will save you money!** Economical bikes are suitable for errands and commuting to work or school. Just compare the expense of rainwear, cargo racks, and packs with the cost of driving. The savings are substantial. Or consider how little medical care you could buy with the cost of bike locks and lighting systems. What other physical fitness activity can be incorporated into your daily routine to save money *and* improve your health? (I haven't seen any sailboats in the grocery store parking lot lately.)

Bicycle riding adapts to your current physical and psychological conditions. Once you invest in a bicycle, you can ride whenever you make the time for it. If you slack off and get out of shape, you can always start riding again. If work takes you away from home often, your bike is waiting for you when you return. When the children grow old enough to cruise around the neighborhood, you can ride with them and teach some important safety lessons along the way. You can easily adjust time and riding style to squeeze a ride into any schedule because bicycle riding is so versatile (more on that later). Compared with many other forms of recreation, bike riding is cheap and predictable. It can improve your health and your perspective.

The Psychological Benefits of Cycling

The bicycle is a **human-scale vehicle!** It is an intimate machine that comes close to being an extension of our bodies. Surely this contributes to our bonding with our bikes. Cycling is several times more energy efficient than walking since propulsive energy moves our bikes and bodies forward without our legs having to bear our weight. (Van der Plas, p. 13) It is my experience that bike riding speed is about as fast as the human psyche comfortably moves. Jet lag is only partly physical – the rest of the drag is our psyches trying to catch up with us. Automobile travel not only thrusts us into new situations before we are ready but can also fill us with frustration and little time to process those feelings. But when we travel by bike, even on short trips, we arrive at our destination better grounded and ready for the encounters before us. Perhaps that is why everything is more fun when we get there by bike!

When I ride I feel **so alive, so aware, so in touch** with all sensory things around me. My perspective clears, concerns for the minutia of life fall away, and in focusing on my basic needs, I discover an uncluttered world. This is especially true on all-day or multiple-day tours. No matter how disturbing the world scene is, I can always find joy, peace of mind, and harmony while riding my bike.

Another element of cycling contentment is **your identity as a bike rider**. That has been a part of my self-image since I bought my first bike. No matter what transitions and transformation I have experienced, cycling and my relationship with my trusted bikes have provided a rudder.

Many riders find that their regular riding schedule **provides a rhythm** to their lives that is difficult to orchestrate in an otherwise wacky world. Have you had the pleasant experience of feeling overwhelmed and then gained perspective and a sense of control from an hour's ride? On our bikes we have full control of our speed, direction, and destination.

That can be just enough sense of control to give us courage to address the challenges waiting for us at work and at home. Runners often acknowledge the uplifting effects of endorphin production while running but any aerobic activity, including cycling, changes your chemistry to make you feel good.

Surely the **love of nature** draws many riders to cycling. The bicycle provides an appropriate scale and speed to explore new places, study the flora and wildlife, and observe weather patterns. This intimate contact with the many facets of nature is grounding and makes us feel more human, more aware of our place in the larger scheme of nature.

Riding a bike is not only an outdoor adventure but also an indoor adventure, **exercising our psyches, emotions, and spirits**. Each ride provides time to reflect on our lives. Some rides challenge us through adverse conditions, fatigue, hunger, or not knowing where we are at the moment. With practice, we can learn to accept the emotional highs and lows we experience on tours. On my first two solo tours, I was surprised at my psychological ruminations and my wide swings of mood. When the weather was beautiful, my stomach full, and the going not too strenuous, I would feel euphoric. Late in the day when I was hungry, searching for a place to camp, and pushing slowly up a steep canyon, I would wonder why on earth I was subjecting myself to this punishment. After three days of touring, my psyche was squeaky clean. I had exercised my emotions, processed my worries, cast them aside, and was free!

A friend organized a ride from Idaho Springs to Central City when my sons were eight and twelve years old. The route began at 8,000 feet and climbed to over 9,000 feet, wandering on back roads through a historic mining district. Bernhard, Kirk, and I had always ridden together, so I had packed all the food on my bike, and Bernhard carried all the tools and pump on his bike with only diluted apple juice for sustenance. (This pre-dated energy beverages.) Kirk rode slowly on his heavy 20-inch-wheeled Schwinn, which I had converted to a 10-speed. Kirk and I amused ourselves by stopping at every mine shaft to throw rocks in and listening for how far they fell. Before we knew it, Bernhard, and in fact the other 15 riders, had left us far behind. Now I was concerned. What would I do if I had a flat? (No sealant in those days either.) What would Bernhard do if he got hungry? It was a steep ride of about ten miles, and I was concerned that he would run out of energy. I hoped some of the men would share food and encouragement with him.

Early afternoon, Kirk and I made it to Central City. The ride ended at a historic bar, and I was happy to see Bernhard being included by the older riders. When I asked him how he had gotten along, he replied that he had gotten hungry, low on energy, and been left behind by the other riders. As he sat by the side of the road feeling hungry and alone, he remembered my warnings that bicycle touring created some unusual lows as well as highs. With that as comfort, he got back on his bike and rode on into Central City. What a demonstration that even a boy can be empowered by accepting his true emotions, whether they are difficult or enjoyable. From these beginnings, it is no wonder he became a capable outdoor-adventure leader during his college and post-college years.

After many years of three- and five-day, self-contained tours, I have been able to identify three distinct psychological stages of adventure. I have been able to transfer these insights from touring to any other venture. I might describe these phases as follows:

1. **The Uncertain or Anxious Phase** - After extensive planning, I am on location (the adventure begins). I formalize the details of the ride route (develop the detail of my plans) and become familiar with the local customs and climate (observe the early fulfillment of my accomplishments).

2. **Contentment in the Adventure** - Now I am settled into a routine, the route is unfolding, the suitability of the plan is confirmed or modified, and the weather patterns are evident. (I'm building confidence in the suitability of my plan.)

3. **Euphoria** - The adventure is drawing to a close. I am filled with new experiences, processing new memories, cleansed by journaling and living a simple life. (The fruition of my plans are manifest, and I feel empowered.)

Bicycle Riding Teaches Us Many of Life's Lessons

Riding a bike lets us control our movements and at the same time transports us to unexpected and unusual situations. From this position of confidence in our riding skills and physical strength, we seem to learn the lessons from adventures more willingly than in work and home environments. Bicycle riding **compresses many of life's lessons** into an acceptable framework for learning.

Probably the exhilaration of riding as a child is based on the newfound sense of freedom and **independence** our first bicycles provided. Our bikes were our enablers and our companions when we ventured out into new territory in our neighborhoods. It seems that adults who resume riding after years away from bikes experience a similar excitement and vulnerability while exploring new territory on their bikes. Cycling encourages us to develop greater independence.

In a society dependent on automobiles, discovering **freedom from a motor vehicle** is truly liberating. What an irony that our obsession with motor vehicles, which purportedly increases our freedom, actually results in bondage. Few U.S. citizens can figure out how to get a few blocks from their homes without the aid of a car. Those of us who ride our bikes most of the time are free and confident that we are capable of transporting ourselves and our necessities by our own strength and skills. We may be overly conscious of being outside the social mainstream but in fact, we are leaders, showing the way to a sustainable mode of mobility.

True independence flows out of **self-sufficiency**. Cycling is quite simple. It is easy to identify what our needs will be on a particular ride and prepare adequately for the unexpected. Sealant in the inner tubes, a few basic tools, some mechanical knowledge, food, extra clothing, and maps, and I am on my way. It is simple and on a more human scale than traveling by car. One of the reasons the bike maintenance classes I teach are so popular is that riders want to feel self-sufficient. In the year after my own divorce, four of my women-rider friends also became single. They didn't want to give up their riding freedom just because they had lost their family mechanics. So we formed a post-divorce maintenance group where I taught them some mechanical skills. It was a jolly support group formed around bicycle maintenance.

Becoming proficient at riding and maintaining a bike gives riders a **sense of accomplishment**. When riders set goals for a ride, event, or season, and achieve those goals, their satisfactions are high. Others find satisfaction in learning to take care of themselves and improving their health habits through cycling. In later discussions of optimizing your resources, choosing appropriate clothing, and thoughtful ride preparation, you'll learn techniques to improve your performance and feel even greater achievement.

As your stamina builds and your confidence as a rider increases, you may find completing a challenging ride is **empowering**. After all, if you can reach your cycling goal, isn't it likely that you can meet other challenges? Not only will your mood be lifted after a long ride but you will willingly undertake challenges that may have intimidated you before the ride.

Dealing with the unexpected during a ride and doing maintenance work **improves our problem solving skills**. By focusing on each step of the problem-solving process, we can learn to avoid getting worked up when complications occur. During my early on-the-job training as a bicycle mechanic, I learned this priceless lesson. Let's take repairing a flat tire as an example. You are out riding on a gorgeous day and hear the disturbing sound of air hissing out of your tube. You stop to confirm that your ride is temporarily interrupted while you replace the tube. (This example comes from the era before sealant.) But you are genuinely distressed by this disruption. You keep thinking about your time schedule and getting back to your riding pleasure. First you have trouble getting the tire off the rim. Then you have trouble inflating the new tube with your frame pump. With each setback you become more irritated. Why aren't you long since back on your bike?! As your patience evaporates, you become more clumsy. Now you've pinched your replacement tube with your tire lever and are ready to scream. There is another way to approach unexpected challenges.

Focusing on each individual step in the repair process (or any problem solving process) can enable you to do your best work and enjoy each step along the way. Complications surely will arise and when they do, you are ready to take on the challenge of this additional problem without cursing the setback. Before becoming a bicycle mechanic,

I would not have described myself as a patient person. Now with years of experience, I accept the need to solve the problem presented, put my shoulder to the task, and don't waste any emotional energy on wishing things had gone differently.

Cycling offers an economical way to **learn how to care for equipment**. These lessons are especially valuable for children. They can learn how to keep their bikes running smoothly, how to avoid mishaps, and how to save money. It is much cheaper for kids to learn on their bikes than it is to learn later on the family car. Parental guidance and mutually agreed upon written contracts outlining who is responsible for maintenance and the repair needs of the bike can save money and avoid nagging and arguments. A wise elementary school principal told me that the earlier children learn a lesson, the less it costs in money and emotions.

When we don't prepare for long rides and then suffer from exposure or mechanical breakdowns, we have no one to thank but ourselves. **Learning to take responsibility** for poor choices is truly liberating. Accepting responsibility allows us to move on to problem solving and putting the incident behind us. Rather than fretting and grumbling, we can simply identify what needs to be done and figure out how to proceed. Perhaps you have already learned to ask yourself what you can learn from each challenge that comes along. Just think, it is probably a lesson we need to learn. If it were not, we would not consider it a challenge. We would simply deal with the circumstances and move on.

In any case, we can **enjoy laughing at our self-imposed dilemmas**. When we blame someone else for the messes we get into, there is nothing to laugh about. When we accept our contribution to an undesirable situation, we can indulge in a hearty laugh or at least in a bemused smile at our own predicament.

Bike riding provides many opportunities to cultivate **self-discipline**. I believe that self-discipline will provide more satisfaction than any other life skill. Even though you may just want to rush off on a ride, you can learn to look ahead and see that you could be stranded by a breakdown if you don't discipline yourself to check the mechanical condition of your bike before setting out. If you chose to participate in a strenuous cycling event, you will be well rewarded by disciplining yourself to train. We have delighted in watching riders significantly improve their fitness through self-discipline. Refer to "Establishing a Moderate-intensity Aerobic Exercise Routine," in Chapter 4, pp. 86-92. Jim and Phil of *The Wharton's Stretch Book* advise you to set goals and commit to a fitness routine *once*. When it comes time to implement the goals and fitness routine, don't renegotiate, don't discuss, just begin without wavering. When you've promised yourself something good, follow through. You'll probably find that the rewards of your routine will far outweigh the inconvenience of integrating training into your schedule.

How I Developed Psychologically and Spiritually through Bicycle Touring

More than twenty years of adventure bicycle touring have transformed me from an uncertain explorer to a contented, even fearless, life traveler. The first years were characterized by a mother's natural defensiveness. We took our first tour when Bernhard and Kirk were twelve- and eight-years old. As a single parent with only two brief tours for training, I assumed an instinctive maternal response: I am not afraid, I have children to protect. I still remember Kirk's nightly ritual of asking for reassurance that there were no mountain lions, bears, or lightning storms coming in the night. I would tell him frankly that these threats could be in the area but I had done my best to select a safe campsite.

As the kids grew older, and our collective experience and confidence increased, I was able to get in touch with my true feelings. This meant that I too spent some anxious nights high in the mountains. There was a ride we took on the Rainbow Trail near Salida, Colorado, where Kirk and I had commented all afternoon on the abundance of bear scat and claw marks on the trees. Stormy weather at noon had interrupted our lunch so we were low on energy. At dusk, a heavy fog engulfed us, and it began to rain steadily. We set up our tents and hung our tarp over both of them for added protection from the elements. All night long big raindrops from the trees drummed on the tarp. When I woke to that noise, I wondered how I could defend us if one of the local bears decided to make a tasty treat of me or Kirk packaged neatly in our tents. Our pepper sprays were useless inside our tents. At breakfast we talked about our anxieties during the night. By mid-morning the sun burned off the fog, and our concerns were soon forgotten in the beauty of the morning. (Since that experience, Bernhard and Kirk have used pea-less marine whistles to turn away a bear visiting in the night.)

Bernhard and Kirk perform the nightly task of protecting food and trash from bears. Poor aim and the quest for the right poles and rock transform a mundane chore into an entertaining evening ritual.

Our first night above timberline was another uneasy one. There was no place to secure our food while camping on the barren slopes above Leadville on Mosquito Pass. We were still shaken from our encounter that afternoon with about 30 large, fearsome-looking dogs. We had been chatting while pushing our bikes through the undergrowth on an abandoned railroad grade. Absorbed in the moment, we had disregarded all the barking in the distance. Finally the barking became so loud that we looked in shock to see all these dogs just below us! Our adrenaline surged until we saw that all the dogs were chained. That night, in addition to rain, boulders could be heard rolling off nearby cliffs. This time when we discussed our night fears, I insisted that we would have to find a way to be at peace at night in the mountains. I worked on the problem during the next day's ride. I reminded myself that worrying does not solve problems, and that darkness alone is not a threat. The following nights I found contentment under a brilliant display of stars as well as during turbulent thunderstorms by remembering my realization on the futility of worrying about what I feared could happen.

In the years after both Bernhard and Kirk went off to college in Oregon, I continued my adventures alone. About this time I began studying Yoga. During each class we practiced breathing techniques and meditation. One morning during my regular Taiji practice, I had a transforming experience. I was feeling puny and vulnerable. At one point in the form, I felt strong and confident and my sense of weakness suddenly vanished. Here was a miraculous transformation brought on by meditation! Now I had a resource I could always tap into to regain my strength and contentment.

My study of Yoga and daily meditation practice also transformed my response to the elements of nature. Any residual fear was replaced by harmony and unity with nature. All the creatures, plants, and natural elements were now my friends. Instead of just talking to the birds because they were my only companions, I would project my love and positive energy toward my fellow creatures. I don't feel vulnerable among friends. On one of my first solo tours in the evening light above Crested Butte, I began the ritual of seated meditation each evening and morning in addition to my Taiji and journaling. That moved me permanently from timidity to contentment.

From this contentment, I am able to tap into more subtle feelings of place and nature. Sleeping on the ground and sitting on the ground to meditate, I feel the Earth's energy perhaps in the tradition of Native Americans. I also experience emotional and spiritual bonds with the people who have invested their lives on our prairies and mountain passes. Especially on our national grasslands, I feel a closeness to the Native Americans, explorers, homesteaders, and ranchers. I sense a melancholy mood spreading across these remote plains from the hopes and sufferings that our early people experienced here. At the close of each summer's excitement, I retreat to some part of the grasslands for a quiet soul-searching. In the quiet of solo touring, I uncover my essential self, uncluttered by drives and distractions. I find that exploring these vast open spaces on my bike facilitates probing of my own depths for hidden sadness as well as growing strengths. I continue to explore new terrain on my bike in search of new revelations and experiences.

Cyclists Help Build Healthy Communities

Cycling is an unusual sport in that it depends on public roads and trails. It is in your best interest to **work on trail maintenance and advocate for bike-pedestrian path and bike-friendly road planning**. The federal government requires public input during transportation planning. Contact your local authorities to get involved in local and statewide planning. This is an important responsibility and one of the privileges of living in a democracy. You will need to study policies and exercise patience and persistence but bicycle and pedestrian advocacy is an excellent way to serve your community.

Many communities have special programs for **at-risk kids learning bike maintenance skills** while refurbishing recycled bicycles. Some of these programs are well established: teaching business skills, supporting responsible performance in school, and helping the kids recondition and own bikes. Their well-earned bikes give them independence in transportation and experience in sustainable, healthful transportation. These programs are another example of how bicycles help build a healthy social fabric.

Riding a bike for recreation or transportation **helps draw together the social strata of the community**. Fearing people we don't know who are different from us causes much of the polarization in our society. Riding a bike enables us to reach out to people we would be unlikely to meet elsewhere. The bicycle is a humble vehicle, and we are easily approached by people along the way. I have found this especially true when I do not wear Lycra® cycle clothing. When I wear plain clothes to protect myself from the sun or cold, pedestrians and motorists alike interact with me graciously and with respect. This is a valuable asset when touring in other countries. The world opens a friendly heart to the humble and approachable.

Every time **you ride your bike instead of driving your car, you contribute to the health of your community**. You keep the air cleaner, and everyone breathes easier. If this sounds far fetched, look at these numbers:

- Forty percent of daily auto trips are within two miles of the driver's home.

- It is estimated that an eight-mile trip by bike reduces air pollution by nearly fifteen pounds of contaminants.

- American workers could eliminate U.S. dependence on oil imports by biking to work just two days a week. (Earl Blumenauer, Oregon congressional representative, June 2001)

I replace my brake pads under the watchful eyes of Mongolian neighbors. The day before, we had ridden the length of their valley in heavy rains. At times they rode their horses alongside us. That evening they came and taught Bernhard and Kirk the traditional knots for securing horses. This morning they returned. They tested our knot skills, experimented with riding my bike, and watched all our morning activities. While there, I imagined that I fit into the Mongolian scene. When I saw this photo upon our return to the U.S., I was startled by the contrast of our appearances.

Each time you ride for practical transportation, you become stronger, you arrive at your destination with an improved perspective, and you reduce traffic congestion as well as wear and tear on the infrastructure. You can set an example for your children and your neighbors' children. You can help families and children understand the importance of their transportational choices to their own health and the health of the community.

Many riders are disciplined and creative about recreational riding in ways that can be applied to transportational riding. The advantages of making some trips by bike are so great that I encourage you to find solutions to your obstacles.

Bicycle commuting is an ideal way to incorporate exercise into your daily schedule. If your commute is too long to be realistic for you to ride the entire distance, ride as much as is feasible and drive the remaining distance. Or, drive to work with your bike and leave the car there and ride home. The next day ride to work and drive home. If your commute seems too short, you can add a few miles by taking a longer route. More people explore the advantages of bicycle commuting as our cities become increasingly congested. We all enjoy breezing past cars jammed in traffic while we are free on our bikes. Here are a few suggestions I hope will help you get started bicycle commuting.

1. Begin your transportational riding during pleasant weather.

2. Start with short trips that are easily within your stamina range.

3. Seek out low-traffic volume, direct routes to places you frequently ride. On each trip, explore a different route to find the one that works best for you. I try to avoid main thoroughfares and look for neighborhood through-streets. These have less traffic and fewer stop signs. Check your local bike map for bicycle-friendly streets. Your local bike store can also be a good source of route information.

4. Time yourself by bike and by car so you can budget the appropriate time needed. Sometimes it is faster riding than driving especially when you don't have to find a parking place or don't get stuck in gridlock. You will need to plan time for dressing for the ride, locking up your bike, and dealing with the unexpected.

5. Ask the businesses, libraries, or community centers where you go if bike security is an issue and if you can bring your bicycle inside for safety. I take my bicycle into all our local stores and have rarely had anyone object. (I do clean up the floor after my bike if it makes a puddle since it is not fully housebroken.)

6. Install a cargo rack on your bike so you can safely transport your riding supplies and other cargo. If you think a cargo rack looks funky, balance this concern with the benefits of improved fitness and reduced air pollution. If you have a problem fitting a rack on your bike, check out Old Man Mountain® racks that are sturdy and designed for full-suspension bikes and those without eyelets. You might also find a seat-post mounted rack to your liking.

7. Get an inexpensive or used bike for transportational riding and outfit it with a rack, fenders, and lights. This will make it more practical and give you peace of mind about leaving your bike in public places. I certainly wouldn't leave my nicest bike behind the gum ball machines at the grocery store either.

8. If you are worried about personal grooming, you will need to get over the appearance of your hair and the odor of perspiration! Would you rather get out of shape, waste a lot of gasoline, and pollute the air for the sake of stylish hair? Liberate yourself and restyle your hair to something plain that withstands being

compressed by your helmet. Now what about perspiration? Adjust your clothing and riding energy so you don't get sweaty when riding to business meetings or social occasions.

Try the advice of Jerry, who was a successful architect and an active, respected member of the Denver business and cycling community. He rode everywhere by bike in his business suit. He advocates pacing yourself, adjusting your clothing to avoid sweating, and taking the "three-minute shower" upon arrival. Before you are overtaken by the flush of warmth at the end of a ride, go directly to the rest room and run cold water over your wrists for three minutes. A high volume of blood flows through your wrists close to the surface, and the cold water will lower your body temperature quickly. Odors can be reduced by drinking lots of water, avoiding spicy foods, and shaving your armpits. Wiping your armpits with rubbing alcohol will quickly eliminate odors. These practices are all in your control so if you want to ride to a place that has no showers, make a plan to arrive smelling sweet.

Becka used another system to enable her to ride to work ten miles from home. Her job required that she wear a dress and hosiery. She would rise in the morning, eat breakfast, slip into her riding clothes, and ride to work before personal grooming. Upon arriving she disappeared into the women's restroom. She would emerge 45 minutes later tastefully groomed and professionally attired. She carried a pack with her work clothing, hair drier, and toiletries. For her trip home, she slipped back into her riding clothes. When you give time and attention to the challenges of transportational riding, you will find solutions. Yes, these strategies require planning and commitment, but I never heard Jerry or Becka complaining that they couldn't find time to ride, had trouble with weight control, or that they were bothered by the small things in life.

Based on 22 years of regular bicycle commuting, I have identified three stages of development. Stage I is characterized by, "Shall I ride or drive?" Each morning this question must be answered again based on the day's needs, weather conditions, your stamina, and your confidence level. Stage II is characterized by disregard for the motor vehicle. No consideration is given to driving, you just get on the bike and go. You have the clothing and other necessary equipment to make each ride enjoyable. Stage III is characterized by good judgement. Bike commuting is solidly established, and you have nothing to prove to yourself or your colleagues. You are free to drive when that is better for your health, your family, or you just feel like it. During this stage you extend your riding distances making many more trips by bike. It is a blissful condition.

As I wrote this section on the benefits of cycling, I felt uncertain how persuasive it would be to casual riders. I asked a cycling friend if I would be better off elaborating on the *pleasures* of cycling in contrast to the *benefits*. Were they actually different or was I just expressing them differently? Perhaps it would be better understood to replace "riding a bike enhances your sensory perception" with "you will take fresh notice of the clouds scudding across the sky; smell the savory cooking in Hispanic neighborhoods; hear the call of the meadowlark; and on a stunningly cold night ride, watch the fog rolling down a hillside off a lake." Or would you identify with "the exhilaration of successfully maneuvering your bike through a labyrinth of large rocks along the trail"? Personally, I love the feeling of warm capable muscles moving my bike and me methodically up a long climb. My friend Shelley just laughed at my academic debate and replied, **"The primary benefit of cycling is the pleasure of riding a bike!"** So there you have it.

Considering all these pleasures, it is astonishing that an estimated 11 percent of adult U.S. citizens never learned to ride a bike (NBC affiliate 9News, Denver, Colorado). Some people are embarrassed to talk about this, feeling a sense of inadequacy. Now everyone can enjoy quick success in learning to ride or in teaching someone else to ride. *Pedal Magic*® is a brilliant technique developed by Reginald Joules, a management scientist, who used the method to teach his wife and teenage nieces to ride. The process is patented so you will need to buy the 20-minute CD ROM by the same name. Both the learner and the teacher need to watch the video together. The joy of the system is that it eliminates the fear of falling and the humiliation of blundering. The first practice stage requires just enough space for a bicycle and two people, making this step possible to accomplish indoors. When these conditioning exercises are second nature, the learner usually rides off with control and delight! If you are a parent of young children, avoid using training wheels. They actually teach the child to use the wrong maneuvers when trying to balance and deprive children of the joy of learning a new skill quickly. If your child has already used training wheels, *Pedal Magic*® offers corrective exercises to help your child overcome the wrong habits that are already established. *Pedal Magic*® enables anyone to learn to ride the same day they get a new bike. Go to http://www.pedalmagic.com for more information and to purchase the CD ROM.

Conclusion

Cycling is a universal and powerful tool for building health and fitness and self-discovery. Most people can ride with satisfaction by choosing wisely from the wide variety of bike designs and by making full use of available components. Dependable equipment is available at a wide range of prices enabling anyone to gradually purchase the basics for safe cycling. Although we tend to accept the personal motor vehicle as the norm in transportation, the bicycle is more efficient. Its human scale transports our psyches to our destination at the same time as our bodies with the added bonus of our feeling refreshed, renewed, and able. Recreational riding stimulates our senses and brings us in closer contact with our surroundings. Riding often helps us better understand ourselves and our society while cultivating a higher level of self-sufficiency.

chapter 3

Balanced Muscle Alignment and Reduced Tension Enhance Riding Comfort and Control

- Paying Attention to What Feels Good and What Doesn't Will Keep You Riding with Enthusiasm
- The Influence of Riding Position on Your Cycling Experience
- Comfort, Relaxation, and Bike Handling Skills Are Interrelated
- Origins of Cycling Discomfort
- Creating and Maintaining Cycling Comfort

Paying Attention to What Feels Good and What Doesn't Will Keep You Riding with Enthusiasm

Many riders measure their riding satisfaction in terms of distance or speed or by comparing their stamina to the performance of their riding companions. These criteria have several drawbacks. For one, focusing on end goals tends to diminish sensitivity to your ever-changing physical, mental, and psychological conditions, making it more difficult to adapt to your true needs. Rather than improving your fitness level, you are more likely to over-train or lapse into sloppy and often harmful riding forms. By shifting your focus to the process of riding, you will feel renewed by the satisfying movements of your body, by revitalizing diaphragmatic breathing, and by tuning in to your natural surroundings.

Widespread acceptance of abusive riding styles damages the health of riders and the image of cycling. Many riders persevere toward their goal until they hurt. Their discomfort may be caused by not fueling themselves for sustained endurance or by not wearing appropriate clothing to protect them from the weather. Some people accept crashing and injuries as an unavoidable part of riding. What motivates these riders to willingly compromise their health? I have posed this question to customers in an effort to understand the causes of self-abuse in recreation. Some of their explanations may help you identify old, unhealthy habits of your own. Look through this list of responses that offers some of the reasons why cyclists abuse themselves:

- They pursue exercise and recreation with the same compulsion they pursue their careers: with immoderate drive and with unsupportive companions.

- Some people fail to distinguish their personal riding priorities from the all-out performance of professional athletes. Racers are inclined to justify damaging their health for the compelling goals of winning and professional advancement.

- The influence of our Puritan ancestors contributes to our feeling guilty about pleasure.

- Childhood abuse makes it difficult to recognize abusive behavior as adults.

- They believe the jingle: no pain, no gain.

- Some people have a serious disconnect between head and body. Their life styles require a lot of mental activity and create so much tension that sensitivity to bodily needs is easily lost.

- Residual emotional pain as well as chronic muscle tension set up the tendency to ride beyond a comfortable level in an effort to experience feeling in an otherwise numb body or existence.

- They feel guilty if they don't meet some idealized physical image.

- Some fear that others will interpret self-nurture as weakness.

- Perpetual sleep deprivation, which is prevalent in today's society, impairs judgment.

- Advertising says it is cool to smoke, to participate in extreme, high-risk sports, and to eat junk food. This causes people to feel inadequate the way they are. The message is hammered home that being part of sensational activities and consuming harmful products is what counts.

It is my hope that by learning to tune in to your riding form and your total condition that you will be able to identify abusive riding styles and purposely choose healthful and nurturing alternatives.

The media and the Internet are full of misinformation about cycling. Riders would be more likely to improve their fitness in wholesome ways if cycling experts provided accessible health-based cycling information. On one extreme you will find advice for competitors about how to win, and on the other is superficial advice for beginners that sounds like "Cycling for Dummies." Neither body of information credits the reader with critical intelligence or makes it fun and easy to learn new techniques. All of this information needs to be adapted to the needs of recreational riders who want to improve their general well-being by riding.

The bicycle industry and media target a narrow market of high risk, trend-obsessed riders. Their preoccupation with equipment, competition, speed, and extreme riding styles obscures the pleasures of cycling from many people. If you are a bicycle commuter, a self-contained tourist, a woman, a differently-abled rider, or a strong older rider, you may have difficulty finding appropriate products and receiving respectful service. Elitist and exclusive attitudes in specialty bicycle stores are a further deterrent. Certainly more riders would evolve into cycling enthusiasts if they were greeted with acceptance and respect in their search for products and information. It is my genuine hope that **Bicycling Bliss** will support riders in developing satisfying, personal riding styles independent of these challenges.

Another reason enthusiasm for cycling is not reaching its potential is the lack of comfortable equipment. Bike and component manufacturers focus a disproportionate amount of time and resources on developing products for competitors rather than for non-competitive, pleasure riders. This means the selection of mid-range bikes ($600-$800) for health and fitness riders is sadly neglected.

The Influence of Riding Position on Your Cycling Experience

In recent years, the shape and physical condition of U.S. citizens have changed dramatically. Waistlines have expanded, and tension, discomfort, and injury in the neck, shoulders, and back have become commonplace. At the same time, the top tubes of bicycle frames have become longer, and stems have pushed handlebars lower and farther forward requiring riders to bend forward about 45 degrees with fully extended arms. This position intensifies the chronic muscle tensions riders bring to their bikes from high-pressure life styles. Leaning and reaching so far forward also impairs breathing by confining the chest and diaphragm. As one of our customers with ample girth and large breasts exclaimed, "Designers just don't understand that breathing is not optional when you ride a bike!" These health and design trends have made cycling increasingly uncomfortable and discourage many riders from riding regularly.

These bike designs challenge fun-loving, health-seeking riders. Saddle discomfort increases as the perineum is pressed firmly against the saddle. Weight and pressure on the hands increases, and the upper trapezius (muscle at the top of your shoulders) must contract continually to extend the arms forward. Contracted shoulder muscles combined with hyper-extended necks is a sure formula for upper back and neck pain.

Riding with more than a 45-degree forward lean can make bike handling more challenging. On descents, it places too much weight over the front wheel, increasing the risk of going over the handlebars. It also makes it difficult for riders to shift their weight by moving their buttocks off the back of the saddle because their arms are already fully extended. Generally speaking, the mobility of riders on their bikes is reduced by this stretched out position, making weight shifts and control more difficult.

These problems would be diminished by changing the bike setup. Bringing handlebars closer to the rider's shoulders eliminates neck, shoulder, and wrist discomfort aggravated by the bike. There are three dimensions to consider when adjusting the handlebar grip position: height, distance from the saddle, and width of the bars. Even though bikes are designed with height adjustment in the seat posts, few bikes allow the stems to adjust the handlebar position for individual comfort needs.

You may wonder if this design requiring a forward lean of more than 45 degrees dramatically increases riding performance since manufacturers create so many bikes that require it. For the same degree of forward lean, bike handling is actually improved by bringing the handlebars close enough to the rider's shoulders to allow the elbows to flex. The closer the flexed elbows come beneath the shoulders, the more relaxed the upper trapezius can be during dynamic riding. Flexed elbows increase the rider's agility on the bike and facilitate control by weight shifts. This change in arm position has little effect on your weight distribution over the wheels since the forearms are a small percentage of total body weight.

Then you may question further, if flexed elbows actually improve bike handling and control, could it be that this change in arm position diminishes your ability to generate power? Biomechanically, the large buttocks muscles work more effectively with the pelvis tilted forward at 30 to 45 degrees. The closer the pelvis comes to a vertical position the less active these large muscles are. For riders who want maximum power output, the 45-degree pelvic tilt is a wise choice. For recreational riders who place a higher value on comfort and renewal, a more upright position is more comfortable.

The distance between the saddle and the handlebars influences mobility and comfort but does not dictate the rider's position. All riders can use their elbows to raise and lower their torsos to adjust their position to riding conditions. They can sit more upright to see and be seen better or to enjoy a change in position. They can lower their torsos and tilt their pelvises forward to increase power output, to assume an aerodynamic position, and to move their weight along the length of their bikes to increase traction during steep ascents.

Now you can see that **the forward tilt of the pelvis influences your potential power output and the forward lean of the torso influences bike handling. However your hand and arm positions are a matter of personal preference. This means that when you select a bike or modify your current bike, the frame should fit your body proportions whereas handlebar position should be customized to your personal desire. Your frame size and riding position are separate but interrelated issues.**

The three illustrations that follow represent a continuum of riding positions from upright to a forward lean of more than 45 degrees. These positions represent the full spectrum of riders' positions as well as the possible evolution of an individual rider's form. Where does your current style fit in the continuum? Weigh your priorities against the benefits and detriments when you evaluate your bike setup and your riding position.

Benefits of the Dynamic Position

- Dynamic bike handling
- Distribution of weight over both wheels
- Complete body workout
- Greater ability to generate power
- Lower center of gravity/ more stability
- Aerodynamic efficiency
- Enhanced control of your bicycle by shifting your weight
- Faster response when necessary to change direction or speed
- Enables full use of torso to control bike and for propulsion

Detriments of the Dynamic Position

- More pressure on the perineum and hands
- Increased neck strain from hyperextension
- Increased tension in shoulders
- Discomfort in upper back from neck and shoulder tension
- Increased lower back strain at high power output
- Decreased ability to see and be seen by traffic
- Impaired circulation through the groin

Vertical	**30 to 45 degrees forward**	**More than 45 degrees**

Illustrations by Susan J. Hart

Static Style

Energy style: casual

Suitable for road & bike path
Percentage of weight on rear/front tires: 70/30

Versatile Style

Energy style: moderate power output

Suitable for road, paved & dirt trails
65/35

Dynamic Style

Energy style: high energy output

Suitable for road & all trails

60/40

For a detailed discussion of the physical factors that influence your choice of position, refer to Chapter 5, "Optimum Use of Your Back," p. 219. However, there are some equally important subtle factors you will want to consider in choosing your riding position.

Comfort, Relaxation, and Bike Handling Skills Are Interrelated

If you try to adapt your position to the demands of a particular bicycle, you risk diminishing your riding performance and your development as a rider. Your bike should be modified to meet your current preference rather than you adapting to the current bike setup. It is important to understand the subtleties of choosing a riding position so you will not be dissuaded from your best choice by well-meaning friends, sales staff, or your reluctance to spend the money to modify your bike. Neglecting to modify your bike setup and to optimize your position will unwittingly sabotage your development as a cyclist or diminish the healthful benefits of riding.

While I was learning to ride a unicycle, I discovered that relaxation is the key to controlled movement. You steer a unicycle primarily with the hips. In the beginning it was quite obvious that fatigue and stress made my spine and hips tense and rigid so I had difficulty getting on and turning. To counteract this rigidity, I learned to take a moment before starting to ride to breathe diaphragmatically and swing my hips side-to-side to limber up my spine and hip joints. By reducing tension and increasing my flexibility, my unicycle riding skills developed quickly.

Transferring my unicycle experience to bike riding, I realized that **tense riders have limited control because instead of moving freely and letting their bodies respond intuitively to their bikes, they are rigid and must think through each movement to guide their bikes. They end up steering primarily with their handlebars rather than by the fluid movement of their hips and shoulders.**

Tension can result from either mental or physical causes. My unicycle experience was caused by my stressful life style: managing a small business, precarious financial condition, and the demands of single parenting. But tension can also result from enduring discomfort. The relationship of discomfort, tension, and control can be a troubling circle.

Modifying the bike setup, understanding good riding technique, and reducing life style stresses will help break this vicious cycle. But just modifying your bike setup can make a substantial contribution to your bike handling skills and to building your confidence. **Comfort, relaxation, and bike handling control are interdependent and form the foundation of cycling pleasure.**

Contrast the discomfort-tension cycle below with the pleasure cycle of riding a bike that is set up for your personal comfort.

The Discomfort-tension-poor-control-anxiety Cycle

A person rides a bike that causes discomfort.

Effort to achieve a comfortable position on the bike causes tension to build.

Tension prevents the rider from sensing the movements necessary to control the bike.

Limited control makes the rider anxious.

Anxiety increases physical tension.

Increased tension intensifies discomfort and further limits the rider's control of the bike.

The Comfort-relaxation-control-pleasure Cycle

A rider sits comfortably on the bike.

Comfort enables the rider to relax and develop a can-do attitude.

Relaxation enables the rider to tune in to the body and respond to the bike and terrain, resulting in skillful bike control.

The rider gains a sense of control that brings focus to riding skills and builds confidence.

Increased confidence enables the rider to develop greater power and bike handling skills.

Joy in riding increases mental and physical comfort.

Since comfort is the key to relaxation, bike handling skills, and pleasure in cycling, what are the causes of discomfort and how can we eliminate them?

Origins of Cycling Discomfort

Why do riders who have ridden a bike with comfort and satisfaction lose that satisfaction after years of pleasure riding? Why do some riders have their bikes set up just the way they like them but still continue to be uncomfortable? The answer is because nothing is as simple as it first appears. The underlying causes of rider discomfort require a commitment to health and fitness excellence – the basic elements needed to create bicycling bliss. Key causes of discomfort are:

1. Most stock bikes must be modified to accommodate individual body proportions, desired riding position, and sensitivities due to overuse or injury.

2. Most riders are untutored and ride with poor technique.

3. Too frequently cyclists ride beyond their conditioned stamina level and fail to respond to fatigue.

4. All people move in habitual patterns that create musculoskeletal imbalances and tensions.

5. It is normal in our society to live with excessive stress, intensifying subconscious anxiety, and unresolved emotional burdens that result in chronic body tension.

Let's consider each of these factors in detail.

1. Most stock bikes must be modified to accommodate individual body proportions, desired riding position, and sensitivities due to overuse or injury.

If you have long arms, you may like your handlebars farther from the saddle. If you have a short torso, moving your handlebars closer will make you more comfortable. Use the guidelines for bike fitting in Chapter 6 to help you identify appropriate modifications to your bike to accommodate your body proportions.

Physical injuries also contribute to cycling discomfort. Although car crashes are frequently the cause of these injuries, many others are from high-risk sports activities. If you are past 50 years old, it may be comforting to know that physical impairments are not necessarily age related. Shoulder problems are as likely to originate from snowboard crashes as from misuse injuries that become apparent in later years. Set up your bike to protect these sensitivities while you work on resolving them.

2. Most riders are untutored and ride with poor technique.

The old adage that you never forget how to ride a bike refers only to balancing.

The bike Richard selected for commuting has an unusually short head tube. Installing a tall stem brought him up where he could see and been seen better in traffic.

Carolyn rides for fitness several times a week, year-round. She enjoys the comfort of an upright position but wants plenty of clearance over the top tube. A small frame with extra long seat post and stem achieved these goals. She likes the hand position on wrap around classic touring bars.

Caitlin had a severe neck injury while Alpine skiing as a girl and had several cervical vertebrae fused. She came to us after a fruitless search for a performance road bike that let her sit upright. We selected a small frame with short top tube and installed a tall stem and riser bars to accommodate her needs. This is how she looked as she bought her bike. During the next few weeks, riding upright strengthened her neck and increased her confidence so she began to lower the handlebars, improving her ability to handle the bike skillfully.

The truth is that most adults remain untutored about riding technique. In Chapter 5, "Riding Style Modifications Optimize Comfort, Efficiency, and Wellness," you will learn which muscles and movements propel you forward and how to balance muscle use. But let's look at two common causes of discomfort, one due to muscle imbalance in the lower back and the other due to nerve impingement in the upper back and neck.

Lower back discomfort is aggravated by an imbalance in power output on the downward and upward strokes of the pedals. The gluteus maximus muscles of the buttocks originate at the top of the pelvis and lumbar spine of the lower back. They are the primary extensors of the hip and are used to push the pedals down. The powerful iliopsoas muscles (iliacus and psoas major) are active on the upward pull on the pedals. They are deep in the pelvic bowl and also attach to the pelvis on the inner surface of the ilium and the lumbar spine, respectively. Their contraction pulls forward to where they attach to the upper femur. Premature fatigue and discomfort in the lower back are often the result when the upward pull on the pedals, which pulls the top of the pelvis and lumbar spine forward, is not balanced by the downward stroke, which pulls them back. Refer to the illustrations in Chapter 5, pp. 188-189.

A common cause of neck and upper back discomfort is drawing the shoulders up in a shrug and dropping the head and neck forward. This creates an extreme neck curvature while the surrounding muscles are contracted. The resulting tensions compress the nerves that innervate the hands as they pass from the neck through the shoulders and into the arms and hands causing tingling, numbness, and pain in the wrists and hands. In cycling, knowledge is power.

3. Too frequently, cyclists ride beyond their conditioned stamina level and fail to respond to fatigue.

Even when you have learned to ride with maximum efficiency and control, you are likely to lapse into poor form when fatigue or distractions overtake you. You can maintain optimum form and avoid injury by adjusting your ride plans to your current condition. If you persevere to reach your goal without responding to your body's messages of fatigue, you are certain to become uncomfortable.

4. All people move in habitual patterns that create musculoskeletal imbalances and tensions.

We all move in habitual patterns. Perhaps the most common is extending the head forward so the cervical spine no longer maintains its natural curvature. Certainly this results from working at desks and carrying the heavy burden of responsibilities. Eventually this abnormal head carriage leads to tight muscles in the back of the neck and weak muscles at the front. When you get on your bike with these conditions, you further exaggerate this distortion. The chronically tight muscles are weakened since they no longer have full range of contraction. When you start riding your bike, and your usual head carriage is abnormally far forward, the muscles at the back of your neck strain to hold your head up. Soon discomfort or pain results. In contrast, if you regularly release your head and neck upward, maintaining your natural cervical curve, you will rarely have neck discomfort on or off your bike. Chronically tight muscles in one part of your body are not an isolated phenomenon but predictably result in compensating tension somewhere else.

Even after acknowledging these sources of discomfort, you may still be reluctant to accept the idea that cycling is not the primary cause of discomfort on your bike. Yes, you probably first notice these discomforts on your bike but that is because your upper body remains fairly static on your bike and because pedaling is highly repetitive, using the same muscles without much variation. Consequently, any tensions or sensitivities caused by daily pressures or misuse are aggravated by riding and manifest as discomfort or even pain while you ride. At this point you can no longer disregard the problem and assume the pain is caused by cycling since you first noticed it on your bike. Instead, you need to search for the underlying causes of chronic muscle tension in your daily movement patterns and in the sources of stress and anxiety in your life.

5. It is normal in our society to live with excessive stress, intensifying subconscious anxiety, and unresolved emotional burdens that result in chronic body tension.

Personal experience convinced me that daily tension causes discomfort on my bike. I first became bothered by neck discomfort on long rides about the time I began writing **Bicycling Bliss** and spending long hours at the word processor. During this time my neck and shoulders were stiff with limited range of movement. I concluded it was caused by the self-imposed discipline of spending every spare moment on my writing and by holding myself in the same immobile position at the computer for hours at a time. I suspected that the tension I created at the word processor transferred to my bike, intensifying neck discomfort and pain. I found some relief from Rolfing and massage.

One morning as I was riding home from Rolfing and enjoying my freedom from discomfort, that sharp discomfort suddenly hit me in the neck. This really disturbed me since I knew I was relaxed and properly aligned. The discomfort struck just as I set my writing goals for the day. That was a physical response to self-imposed pressure I had experienced many times before. So I gave myself a brief lecture that I could only write as much as focus and inspiration permitted and that pressuring myself would only fog my mind and give me a pain in the neck. To my delight, the sharp discomfort in my neck left as abruptly as it had come!

If taking full responsibility for your physical discomfort makes you unhappy, the good news is that if you caused the problem, you can also eliminate it. Remember, accepting responsibility does not mean blaming yourself, it only means acknowledging your part in creating the problem. All people who live with the pressures of high-tech urban living will have to deal with tension related discomforts eventually. If you live in a human body, I strongly recommend that you purchase and study Dr. John Sarno's book, *The Mindbody Prescription: Healing the Body, Healing the Pain* (1998). Dr. Sarno is a specialist in rehabilitative medicine. Early in his practice (1965), he observed that medically accepted treatments for back pain did not result in predictable outcomes. Many years of research resulted in his identifying Tension Miositis Syndrome (TMS) and developing a treatment. *Miositis* refers to the changed state of the muscle tissue. (Sarno, *Mind Over Back Pain*, 1982, p. 15) Chronic muscle tension constricts blood and lymph vessels that nourish and cleanse the involved muscles. This results in an inadequate supply of nutrients, especially oxygen, and the accumulation of chemical waste products. Muscle spasms, nerve pain, and trunk deformities follow.

The most common areas affected by TMS are the upper, outer buttocks, the top of the shoulders, and sides of the neck. These common tensions affect nerves of the lumbosacral plexus in the lower extremities and the brachial plexus in the upper extremities. (Sarno 1982, p. 64.) Refer to the illustrations on p. 167, p. 244. Continued damage results in burning, numbness, tingling, and weakness. Surely you are familiar with these problems. You may recognize another characteristic of TMS where the patterns of pain move to various parts of the body and recur with increased frequency over the years, progressively interfering with life style and physical activities. (Sarno 1982, p. 15)

Though we tend to assume that these pains are caused by some physical incident, the root causes of TMS are psycho-physiological rather than musculoskeletal. (Sarno 1982, p. 50) The pain is our mindbody's distraction technique to obscure emotions our subconscious deems totally unacceptable. The underlying emotions are usually associated with our needs to be responsible, achieving, or strong in order to win love, approval, or admiration. Some personality types are prone to anxiety based on being overly conscientious, responsible, hardworking, and often compulsive. (Sarno 1982, p. 50) This is not to say these people are making these problems up but rather that their self-imposed drives create anxiety and manifest as physical tension. If these people are inclined to suppress their emotions or "put things out of their minds," the emotions relocate to the subconscious where they create anxiety and ultimately some physical disorder. (Sarno 1982, p. 53)

Placing the sources of anxiety and anger before us helps us realize their impact on our inner mind. Making a list of all the pressures in our lives and anger left over from childhood can help us identify and deal with these sources of pain. Consciously working through these emotions will reduce their negative effect in the subconscious. (Sarno 1998,

p. 146) By experiencing the emotions at the root of the pain, the mind no longer benefits from the distraction technique of creating pain, and the pain goes away. This is where a properly trained psychotherapist is needed.

Knowledge therapy is the primary treatment for TMS. Understanding the mechanism, identifying the causes of emotional distress, being confident of the harmless nature of the physical condition, and becoming a participant in healing are most important in overcoming TMS. (Sarno 1982, p. 93-94) **Non-compulsive exercise is a valuable secondary treatment as it increases circulation while stretching lengthens contracted muscles. Fortunately all living beings have elaborate healing mechanisms built in. The best therapy is to recognize and unleash our great capacity of self-healing.** (Sarno 1982, p. 82)

Of course when you experience pain it is necessary to eliminate the possibility of physiological disorders. But contrast the impact of the diagnosis of TMS with that of most pain sufferers. The diagnosis of TMS is knowledge-based and supportive. The sufferer is reassured of the harmless nature of the physical pain. With understanding, you can replace fear and anxiety with confident participation in the healing and self-restoration process. However, in the typical scenario of a person's first visit to most doctors, anxiety is intensified by a diagnosis that calls chronic muscle tension a chronic degenerative musculoskeletal problem and the ultimate threat of surgery. Just imagining the pain, expense, and prolonged disability anticipated with this diagnosis causes TMS to worsen. When TMS is diagnosed early, recovery occurs in four to eight weeks. (Sarno 1982 p. 98-99) Treatment depends on thwarting your brain's distraction strategy, which can be accomplished by:

- Repudiation of any structural diagnosis that there is a physical reason for the pain and knowing that TMS is a different physical process

- Acknowledgment of the psychological basis for the pain

- Acceptance of the psychological explanation and all its ramifications as normal for healthy people in our society (Sarno 1998, p. 141-142)

The resolution of your pain does not require that you remove the pressures and emotions that cause them but that you accept how the mind communicates with and affects the rest of the body. The conscious mind communicates with the unconscious. The more forceful that communication, the greater the effect. Contemporary research demonstrates how the mind communicates with the body and affects healing. (Sarno 1998, p. 145) Whenever TMS pain occurs, you might say "Okay, I don't like the situation I'm in but I'm not going to let it go to my pain area." Or "My (fill in your pain area) is acting up. What's going on in my life or in my mind to make it hurt?" The goal is to change the unconscious mind's reaction to emotional states.

John Sarno's work is important for cyclists because it confirms and expands in detail the premise that chronic cycling discomfort among recreational riders is caused by life style choices that increase anxiety and emotional distress. You can choose whether to establish your priorities and base your life style choices on them or to allow your choices of how you think, use your body, eat, sleep, and exercise set your priorities.

When you understand that chronically tight muscles reduce power output, you may find it easier to make appropriate life style changes.

1. Tight muscles are mechanically weakened. Throughout the pedal stroke muscles work by contracting. When a muscle is chronically tight it is shortened and can only generate power through a limited contraction. Both regular stretching and conscious release of tension can restore muscles to their full elongation and power.

2. TMS reduces circulation to the tight muscles, limiting the flow of oxygen and nutrients and depriving them of adequate fuel.

3. The energy used to tension these muscles can not be used to propel your bike.

4. This tension and resulting postural misalignments cause harmful compensations in other parts of your body. The resulting decrease in stamina and comfort may discourage you from riding often and consequently reduce the fitness benefits you could have gained. If you decide to ride through the discomfort, eventual injury will keep you off your bike for an extended period.

Here is another instance where a preoccupation with building muscle strength can obscure the fact that we can increase our fitness more effectively by releasing tension and increasing pleasure.

Creating and Maintaining Cycling Comfort

Fortunately, resolving the causes of cycling discomfort leads to life style changes that transform the quality of your health and fitness. The first steps are specific to cycling but for optimum results you will need to learn how your body, mind, and spirit work together and to increase your sensitivity to their interactions. Refer to "Vital Energy" in Chapter 4, p. 142.

The essential steps to cycling comfort are:

1. **Set up your bicycle so you can maintain a relaxed riding position.** This is the easiest step to implement and ensures that you are not aggravating tension on your bike. Refer to the details in Chapter 6, "Customized Bike Setup Supports Riding Style."

2. **Retrain your body for optimum riding technique.** This one may involve years of increasing awareness and rewarding self-discovery. Refer to Chapter 5, "Riding Style Modifications Optimize Comfort, Efficiency, and Wellness."

3. **Institute a daily stretching, strengthening, and conscious breathing practice.** This will enable you to bring a relaxed, balanced body to your riding. Refer to Chapter 4, "Tools for Integrated Wellness."

The following steps would be a basic beginning for improving your cycling comfort:

1. Simplify your life to provide time and energy to make the above changes. Consciously remove clutter from your life to enable you to see the realities more accurately.
2. Select life goals as the basis for your life style choices that will ensure health and fitness excellence.
3. Seek out instruction on retraining your body for balanced use from Chapter 4, "Tools for Integrated Wellness" and the recommended readings.
4. Quit your job and escape with your loved ones to a pastoral setting and commit your lives to sustainable living and bicycle riding. Oops! That's probably not too realistic.

Conclusion

Your search to improve your cycling comfort is an opportunity to increase your awareness. Most chronic discomforts that you experience on your bike can be resolved by addressing your underlying anxieties and by corrective exercises that will develop your awareness of healthful equilibrium. With practice, your increasing awareness and sensitivity to discomfort will enable you to identify sources of tension, causes of overuse, injury, and the onset of inflammation in their initial stages. **Comfort is the body's system for telling you everything is all right. Discomfort is the alert system warning that something is wrong.** Taking preventative measures in a timely manner will help you avoid injury before severe damage is done.

Chapter 4, "Tools for Integrated Wellness," introduces you to methods for understanding your life as a fascinating, complex entity. The effort you invest in increasing your knowledge of your patterns of response to life's situations will be a source of revelation and amusement. Lighten up, hang loose, and have more fun!

Tools for Integrated Wellness

- Expanding Your Understanding of Wellness
- Effective Breathing Integrates the Mindbody and Optimizes Performance
- Establishing a Moderate-intensity Aerobic Exercise Routine
- Alexander Technique
- Understanding Yoga Postures and Stretching
- Strength Training for Building Balanced Bodies

- Empowering Yourself with Affirmations and Visualizations
- Journaling for Reflection and Quieting Your Mind
- Beginning a Meditation Practice
- Responding to Seasonal Change
- Some Basics on Massage
- Pressure Point Therapy
- Vital Energy
- Practicing Tools for Integrated Wellness Will Improve Your Cycling Performance

People who cannot find time for recreation are obliged sooner or later to find time for illness.
~John Wanamaker

If you have been a cyclist for many years, you probably need to broaden your fitness practices. Cycling develops excellent cardiovascular and leg strength but will create harmful musculoskeletal imbalances if you do not compensate with regular stretching and strengthening exercises. **Fitness experts agree that optimum physical fitness and athletic performance depend on physiological balance created by a program that integrates these four fitness categories:**

> **cardiovascular**
> **stretching**
> **strengthening**
> **balance/agility**

The exercises and body use techniques presented in Chapters 4 and 5 of **Bicycling Bliss** provide you with practices in these four categories. These are needed to achieve balanced physical, psychological, and spiritual fitness. Here is a summary of these categories and their functions:

1. Vigorous, sustained exercise develops the heart, respiratory, and circulatory systems by elevating your pulse rate. On a more subtle level, cardiovascular fitness requires body alignment and freedom from tension to allow you to inhale and exhale to full lung capacity. Understanding the mechanics of breathing and how to breath effectively are just as important to health as developing cardiovascular strength.

2. Stretching exercises elongate your muscles and release tension that interferes with effortless movement and the full contraction of opposing (antagonistic) muscle groups.

3. Strengthening exercises develop your muscle contracting capacity and balance the strength of opposing and supporting (synergistic) muscles and muscle groups.

4. Balance and quick, appropriate recovery response depend on the coordination of mental and physical alertness, freedom from tension, flexibility, and equalized flow of energy throughout your body. Mind and body must be fully integrated. Joints must be surrounded by muscles balanced both in strength and freedom from tension enabling full range of motion. Vital energies must flow equally to all parts of the body.

This chapter provides basic understanding of practices and programs to help you attain integrated fitness and health. Chapter 5 instructs you in specific exercises to benefit each part of your body. As you begin practicing various exercises, refer to this chapter to refine your technique.

Cycling is remarkably effective in developing and maintaining your cardiovascular system, balance, and agility skills. But if you are not already systematically performing stretching and strengthening exercises, now is the time to start. The wisdom of "use it or lose it" is so profound it is generally ignored. But if you have already lost *it*, the exercises and supporting knowledge in **Bicycling Bliss** will enable you to regain *it*. In fact, the more time you invest in cultivating integrated wellness, the more you enrich your life. Notice that time is the primary investment. Satisfaction and health benefits can be derived with a minimal investment in equipment.

As you establish a disciplined exercise program, you will need to improve your diet and balance your intellectual, social, and spiritual practices. Disregard for these key factors will limit your fitness potential. Just as your riding skills depend on parallel development of confidence, strength, and technique, your total wellness depends on simultaneous development of yourself physically, emotionally, intellectually, socially, and spiritually.

Expanding Your Understanding of Wellness

For many of us, wellness is the absence of sickness or pain. We attribute our departure from wellness to infection or injury. This limits wellness to the periods between health problems and usually results in a passive approach to caring for ourselves. We tend to ignore our well-being until we feel lousy with infection or musculoskeletal discomfort. Often we greet our afflictions with disbelief or irritation. How could we be subjected to this displeasure or inconvenience? We may even review our recent activities or social contacts to try to identify who did this to us. As with other challenges, accepting responsibility for our condition frees us to find solutions to our problems. We can shift quickly to a proactive mode. Long-term recovery requires that we look within ourselves. We must examine our attitudes and behavior patterns to determine what we did to weaken our natural defenses and our powerful healing mechanisms.

The root of the word "health" is wholeness. Health depends on a dynamic and complex equilibrium of all the elements within our beings and our surroundings. That equilibrium is temporary as we shift back and forth from periods of relative illness to periods of relative wellness. The shifting is similar to the dynamic balance we keep when riding our bikes through obstacles — at times we lean right and at times we lean left. Sometimes we get too far out of balance and crash. So it is with health. Variations from illness to wellness are natural and to be expected. It is okay to be sick. If we are attentive and respond quickly to subtle changes on our bikes, we can maintain our equilibrium. This is also true of our health; the sooner we notice a problem, the less work it will be to correct our imbalances and return to wholeness. Unless we learn to notice and be bothered by the early subtle stages of illness or injury, we will lose the chance to manage our bodies through their changing cycles by simple means. The loss will make us more and more dependent on outside practitioners and costly intervention. (Weil, 1983, p. 58)

We can learn to minimize illness and injury. Preventative maintenance works just as effectively on ourselves as it does on our bicycles. Fortunately, the tools for maintaining ourselves are more varied, give us more pleasure, and are usually free! These tools include getting adequate sleep, reducing self-imposed pressures, eating a well-balanced diet, exercising regularly, and turning inside to nurture our subtle energies. We should start with a realistic appraisal of our health assets and deficiencies. Everybody is different, just as our facial features and body types are different. By identifying our weak points, we can work toward changing our behaviors to strengthen these areas and can recognize when they are out of balance and take early action. Learning to value our assets and appreciate them daily will maintain them and lift our moods.

The fundamental key to long-term wellness is internal adjustments to maintain balanced wholeness. We are the only ones who can tune in to these subtleties and make needed changes. No one and no product or equipment can do that for us. This requires that we personally implement preventative maintenance practices as well as take responsibility for the poor choices we have made in the past that have damaged our health.

The current disarray of the health care industry should be adequate motivation for you to care for yourself. Although we are fortunate to have some brilliant and dedicated health care professionals, the majority are too eager to prescribe drugs or surgery. Both physicians and patients are preoccupied with relieving symptoms rather than determining the underlying causes and reestablishing wholeness by healing those imbalances. Because most people have relinquished responsibility for their well-being, ineffective and harmful medical practices continue to flourish.

Furthermore, Western or allopathic medicine is only just beginning to recognize subtle and integrated wellness and curative practices. Methods from other cultures that have been respected for thousands of years are still viewed with skepticism in the West. Dr. Andrew Weil's 1983 book *Health and Healing* offers critical and caring discussions of diverse healing traditions. Ken Cohen's *The Way of Qigong* criticizes the inconsistencies in measuring the effectiveness of Eastern and Western medical practices. Many accepted medical procedures used in the U.S. today are not supported by documentation that shows that they cure the problems they are applied to. In Sue Crossen's *Back Pain Breakthrough* you will find a compelling story of her search for relief from back pain and the inadequacies of the current approach to musculoskeletal pain. Many of the authors who have strongly influenced my understanding of health and fitness have broken from the status quo in Western medicine. Doctors John Sarno, John A. McDougall, and Andrew Weil developed revolutionary, effective health and healing concepts and programs after they completed their medical training in the U.S. During their residencies and early practices, they became critical of the inconsistent results from accepted medical curative methods and struck out to discover healing techniques that successfully and consistently heal the root causes of illness.

Gradually, health practices from other cultures are gaining popularity in the U.S. Unfortunately, as the postures of Yoga and the martial applications of Indian, Chinese, and Japanese healing arts become popularized in the U.S., they suffer from the same preoccupation with external aspects that limit many of our Western values. Limiting these practices to exercise alone dramatically diminishes their value. I encourage you to delve into the philosophical and spiritual teachings of these arts. They will enrich your life in meaningful ways.

Whatever our health and healing practices, there are times when it is necessary to seek professional help. Emergency and traumatic injury and illness as well as long-standing conditions require professional care. This is also true of psychological problems. Tuning in to the subtleties of mindbody health necessitates that we clear out excess emotional baggage. I have transformed the quality of my life through long-term counseling, so I am frustrated when friends are reluctant to seek professional help. I ask, "If you broke a leg would you go home and sit in the middle of the living-room floor convinced that you could heal the leg yourself?" And yet our psyches are so much more important than our legs in the search to find satisfaction and productivity in life. Why wouldn't you give your psyche equal opportunity to heal fully? Remedial care and preventive maintenance for your body, mind, and spirit can make good health the norm in your life and enable you to intervene before any infirmity becomes incapacitating.

Perhaps it is convenience that leads us to compartmentalize our lives and treat our bodies as if they were separate vehicles. Human life is certainly one of the miracles of creation. The interactions of our bodies, minds, psyches, and spirits are fascinating *and* powerful. Our attitudes and behaviors are just as important to our health as the condition of our bodies, emotions, social support systems, dedication to learning, and spiritual resources.

Dr. Andrew Weil at the University of Arizona's Integrative Medicine Clinic has thoughtfully identified the diverse components that contribute to well-being. Regularly assessing wellness can help prevent the painful loss of healthful equilibrium. **Begin by asking yourself what good health means to you. Then evaluate your physical state and identify any health problems. Critically assess your diet, activity level, life relationships, stress coping skills, family health risks, meaning in life, and contentment level.** Taking the time to write your answers down can provide you with insights to improving your health and changing your life style. They will also provide a good basis for evaluating your riding style. Combining this information with a general physical check-up will give you a foundation for improving your total wellness.

As you identify what you need to improve, the next challenge is finding the will to change. Since the health of U.S. citizens has reached an alarmingly low point, you will find abundant information to persuade you of the importance of change and to sustain your motivation along the way. Structured programs are available to guide you to better nutrition and physical fitness. these make it easier for busy people to establish new habits without working through each detail. However, before you accept one of these programs critically evaluate it. Is it balanced or does it simplistically promote one group of foods while eliminating other essential nutrients? Even some of the popular programs are harmful. Andrew Weil (2000, pp. 31-33) and Walter Willett (pp. 45-48) both give credible and brief evaluations of several popular diet plans.

Lasting change will require patience, satisfaction with small increments of change, and appreciation of the subtle inner workings of change. Resist the urge to forcefully implement rapid change. **I have identified three fundamental steps in the re-education process:**

1. **Understand what you need to achieve to improve your wellness.**
2. **Let go of your old habits and ideas.**
3. **Intentionally direct your energy toward the new ways.**

Taking time and effort to work through each of these steps will make you more comfortable with your new ways. These apply to redirecting your life goals as well as to retraining your attitudes, relationships, eating habits, and athletic performance.

Effective Breathing Integrates the Mindbody and Optimizes Performance

Conscious breathing is an essential part of healing and spiritual practices in many cultures. By observing your breathing patterns, controlling your breathing, and learning to apply various breathing techniques, you can optimize your physical performance, focus your mind, alter your emotions, mitigate pain, and transform your spiritual experiences. You can increase your understanding of yourself and greatly enhance your satisfaction in life by retraining yourself to master your breathing skills.

Breathing is the bridge between our voluntary and involuntary functions. Dr. Andrew Weil clearly describes this relationship in *Natural Health, Natural Medicine*:

"The breathing function is unique in the human body. It is the only involuntary function which can also be controlled voluntarily. It is controlled by two separate sets of nerves, one belonging to the voluntary nervous system and the other to the involuntary (autonomic) system. Breathing is the bridge between these two systems. Much illness comes from imbalance in the functioning of the autonomic nervous system. Our conscious minds have no direct access to this system. There is reason to believe that by working with breathing, you can change your autonomic tone and affect many of the 'involuntary' functions. Regulating your breath can influence your blood pressure, calm a racing heart or help your digestive system. Practicing simple breathing techniques can give you influence over certain 'involuntary' functions. Increased awareness of breathing can expand your consciousness, further communication between mind and body and so improve your health."

My Personal Journey Developing Conscious Breathing Skills

As a cyclist, I had given casual attention to my breathing while riding above 10,000 ft. elevation but still found it necessary to stop often to catch my breath. I first discovered how deficient my breathing was when I was unable to follow the recommended breathing patterns in Taiji and Yoga classes. Even though I taught breathing techniques in childbirth education classes for many years, I hadn't transferred what I knew about pain mitigation by breathing to day-to-day use. I guess I thought that I knew how to breathe. Only when I began to ask questions, read, and practice breathing techniques, did I realize how dysfunctional my breathing was. Now, after seven years of steady practice, I know that conscious breathing transforms both the quality of my life *and* my athletic performance.

As I began to assess my breathing style, I discovered that there were times when my breath was shallow or erratic. Worse yet, I sometimes simply held my breath. I breathed mostly in my chest and made limited use of my diaphragm. In my effort to improve, I discovered that I was afraid of controlling my breathing. I guess I thought that I might asphyxiate myself. As soon as I identified that fear and accepted it as part of me, I was able to leave it behind and move on to learning control. The next discovery came as I tried to use my diaphragm while riding. I did not coordinate the expansion of my abdominal muscles with inhaling. As I tried to train myself to support the movement of my diaphragm with my abdominal muscles, I often became confused. During an exhalation, I'd find myself expanding my abdominal muscles instead of contracting them. This problem is so common that it has been named: "paradoxical or reverse breathing." I could see clearly that I had a challenge to pursue! Normally, breathing is reflexive. Without training, it is usually inefficient and inadequate for optimum athletic performance. As I became aware of my faulty breathing patterns and learned to correct them at will, I discovered other benefits of diaphragmatic breathing: improved focus, increased energy, more uniform level of exertion, the feeling of contentment, and a sense of ability to deal with present and future challenges.

Will You Benefit from Developing Your Breathing Technique?

Stress is an inevitable part of modern life. Fortunately, breath control counteracts our emotional response to stress and serves as a tool to meet life's challenges with equanimity. The pressures of meeting so many daily challenges distract us, and we become tired, tense, and often obsessive. These reactions dampen our sensitivity and make our body functions erratic and inefficient. Different states of mind are actually accompanied by characteristic breathing patterns. That means we can change undesirable states of mind by altering our breathing patterns. Yes, we can consciously reduce anxiety and calm ourselves in demanding and stressful situations by conscious breathing!

Daily stress and the resulting tension and imbalance cause turmoil in our body functions. These imbalances contribute to most illnesses and many aches and pains. In times of extreme anxiety, we all have experienced digestive and elimination problems but *underlying stress* causes more subtle changes in body functions. Eventually these changes create problems, and illness finally gets our attention. In addition, tension in the respiratory system results in inadequate oxygen supply to all parts of the body — further diminishing their function even at the cellular level. Breath training is a wise place to begin improving our health since it influences every aspect of our lives.

As a cyclist, you will appreciate that conscious breathing will improve your athletic performance, facilitate relaxation, and heighten your awareness of your surroundings. You can increase your stamina, lower your breathing and pulse rates, and benefit from rejuvenation. More specifically, effective breathing moderates your riding experience so uphill climbs will not be so draining. The pleasure of gliding down hills will increase because your heightened awareness will enhance your ability to take in the details of the descent. Improved circulation helps keep your extremities warm during cold weather rides.

You can influence the quality of your sleep. You will simply enjoy riding more!

Resist the urge to skip over this instruction because you believe your breathing skills have been adequate all these years, and you have other things to think about. Breathing problems affect most of us. Breathing therapy specialists believe that at least 60 percent of U.S. citizens are dysfunctional breathers. Gay Hendricks' observations of children revealed that most children have lost their natural, diaphragmatic breathing style by the time they reach kindergarten! I have also made some disquieting observations. I often discussed breathing techniques with customers at Self-Propulsion. When they assured me that their breathing was well developed, I thoughtfully observed their breathing habits while we continued to visit. Many times I discovered they did not support their speech with adequate breath or they held their breath and then took quick, catch-up breaths to compensate. So do stay tuned, you are bound to learn something.

In Gay Hendricks' definitive book *Conscious Breathing, Breathwork for Health, Stress Release, and Personal Mastery* he lists these benefits:

Conscious breathing:
- Releases stress and tension
- Builds energy and endurance
- Contributes to emotional mastery
- Prevents and heals physical problems
- Contributes to graceful aging
- Manages pain
- Enhances mental concentration and physical performance
- Facilitates psychospiritual transformation

How Your Breathing Works

If you were asked how you breathe, you might explain that air comes in your nose, goes down your windpipe, and fills up your lungs. Your lungs oxygenate your blood, and the spent air is expelled back up the windpipe and out the nose. But what parts of your body make this miraculous oxygenation process happen? The lungs and bronchial tubes are where this process occurs but the air is moved by the work of surrounding muscles. The engine of breathing is the **diaphragm**. This dome-shaped muscle and tendon span the entire torso and separate the chest cavity from the abdominal contents. Its muscle fibers radiate horizontally from the central tendon across the top surface of the dome. The diaphragm attaches to the lower ribs and in the rear to the lumbar spine. Although it arches upward to the base of the lungs, much of its vertical height is pressed against the lower ribs. The lungs never move down that far. As it contracts, it draws downward, expanding the lower part of the lungs to fill the void. To facilitate the diaphragm's movement, the abdomen wall needs to round out and let the abdominal contents move out of the way. As the diaphragm relaxes and returns to full height, the lungs are pushed up and contract. To expel the maximum amount of oxygen-depleted air from the lungs, the abdominal muscles must contract, pushing the abdominal organs, diaphragm, and lower lungs upward, pressing out more air. This final step is especially important during exercise.

Of course you notice that your chest also moves when you breathe. Both your rib cage and clavicle expand your lungs by their flexibility and the work of the intercostal muscles that support and control your rib cage. The lungs move up into the clavicular area by the contraction of your neck (scalenes) and shoulder (sternocleidomastoids) muscles during strenuous exertion or conscious breathing exercises.

The neurological benefits from using your diaphragm are also dramatic. During active breathing, the nerves of the chest trigger the sympathetic nervous system that elicits the fight-or-flight response. In contrast, diaphragmatic breathing triggers the parasympathetic nervous system that lowers your heart rate and has a calming effect. Using conscious, diaphragmatic breathing enables you to enjoy high energy cycling and contentment *while* you ride and rejuvenation *afterwards*!

Regaining Your Natural Breathing Skills

You can better appreciate your own need to retrain your breathing technique by evaluating your day-to-day breathing habits. Observe the rate and depth of your breathing at work, at home, and while doing errands. Do you notice that in some situations you breathe faster, for example, before or while you are giving a presentation? If you often feel breathless, are you holding your breath? Do you yawn or sigh often? When you take a deep breath, does your chest expand? During high exertion, do you gasp for breath? Do you generally have tight muscles and are you prone to sore muscles? Do you sleep poorly? All of these behaviors are symptoms of inadequate breathing technique. We are pretty casual about a body function that is essential to life itself.

First let us identify our breathing components. (I wonder if Shimano® could develop a SIBS, Shimano Integrated Breathing System, operated by pinky controls?) It will be easier to identify your breathing components while you lie on your back on the floor. Beginning at the top, run your hands along your collarbones (clavicle) from your shoulders to your breast bone (sternum). Now move down to your ribs and feel the solid structure of your rib cage and its remarkable flexibility as you take several deep breaths. Next, follow down the sternum and notice how large your rib cage is. Your lungs and heart fill this space. Notice that your rib cage increases in circumference toward the bottom, just as your lungs are larger at the bottom.

continued on page 78

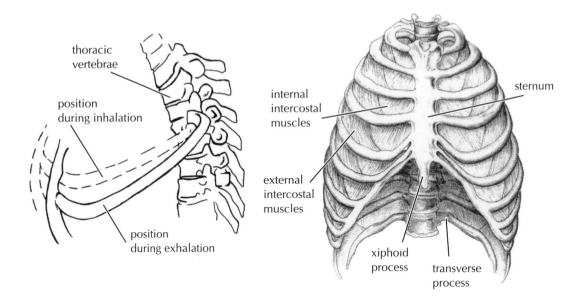

During inhalation the external intercostal muscles lift the ribs, which pivot at the transverse process of each thoracic vertebra, increasing the volume of the chest. Notice how changing the angle of the rib increases the circumference of the chest.

Observe the direction of the external intercostal muscles that are external to the ribs and draw the ribs up during inhalation. The internal intercostal muscles are in between the ribs, inside the external intercostals. They tie perpendicular to the external intercostals and draw the ribs down during exhalation. In the front near the sternum they are not overlain by the external intercostal muscles. Not shown are the innermost intercostal muscles that have the same slant as the internal intercostals and are inside the ribcage.

Learn to use the muscles that affect breathing and release the others. During inhalation the muscles of the chest, back, and abdomen affect vertical lengthening. During exhalation the emphasis is on horizontal contraction. While you are sitting erect, observe this distinction. You can increase lung capacity by releasing tension in your neck, shoulders and chest and by countering gravity's downward pull with upward release. This will free your upper ribs to float upward.

References:

Coulter, H. David, pp. 74-82

Iyengar, B.K.S, pp. 17-31

Netter, M.D., Frank H., *Atlas of Human Anatomy*, Icon Learning Systems, NJ, 2003. ISBN 192900711-6, Plate 191

Poltin, Kevin T., and Gary A. Tribodeau, *Mosby's Handbook of Anatomy and Physiology*, Harcourt Health, 2000, p. 428. ISBN 0323-01096-2

The Mechanics of Active Breathing

Exhalation

Inhalation

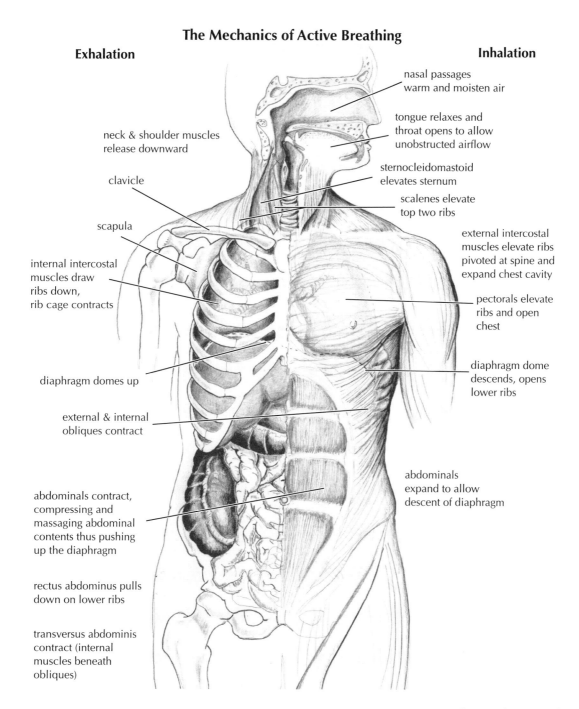

nasal passages warm and moisten air

tongue relaxes and throat opens to allow unobstructed airflow

neck & shoulder muscles release downward

sternocleidomastoid elevates sternum

clavicle

scalenes elevate top two ribs

scapula

external intercostal muscles elevate ribs pivoted at spine and expand chest cavity

internal intercostal muscles draw ribs down, rib cage contracts

pectorals elevate ribs and open chest

diaphragm domes up

diaphragm dome descends, opens lower ribs

external & internal obliques contract

abdominals contract, compressing and massaging abdominal contents thus pushing up the diaphragm

abdominals expand to allow descent of diaphragm

rectus abdominus pulls down on lower ribs

transversus abdominis contract (internal muscles beneath obliques)

Illustrations by Pat Conrad

Now you can locate your diaphragm, the primary motor of breathing. At the bottom of the sternum is a short cartilage extension (the xiphoid process) where the diaphragm attaches. You can distinguish the xiphoid process because it is more sensitive than your sternum. On your sides you can feel the two lower ribs that are not attached to your breastbone, therefore allowing for more expansion during diaphragmatic breathing. The diaphragm is attached to the six lower ribs and to the lumbar spine. (Iyengar, p. 30)

Perhaps you have not thought of your abdominal muscles as part of your respiratory system. They need to coordinate with and support the movement of your diaphragm. You can locate the muscles you need to use in natural breathing by placing one hand on your abdomen, one on the xiphoid process, and pretending to blow out a candle. Notice how your abdominal muscles draw in and then relax. Contrast this movement with tense abdominal muscles characteristic during anxiety or stress by lifting your head off the floor. Feel the tightness from your pubic bone into your chest. Now that you have distinguished the movement of your diaphragm and the contrasting behaviors of your abdominal muscles, you can understand the use of the abdominal muscles in natural breathing. When your diaphragm contracts downward with each inhalation, let your abdominal muscles relax and your abdomen protrude. With each exhalation, your diaphragm relaxes and returns to its dome shape, expelling the air from your lungs. You must expel the maximum amount of spent air from your lungs for maximum efficiency. When the diaphragm is relaxed, it has reached its maximum height. Only by contracting your abdominal muscles and pressing your abdominal organs up against your diaphragm can you push the diaphragm higher. This compresses the lower lungs and expels more air. Let your abdominal muscles contract and pull inward, supporting the diaphragm for a complete exhalation. The natural movement of your diaphragm depends on relaxed expansion and firm contraction of your abdominal muscles. When your diaphragm and abdomen muscles work together, there are several benefits:

1. You move more air in and out of the lower lobes of your lungs, resulting in more efficient oxygenation.

2. Your abdominal organs and heart are massaged by the movement of your diaphragm and your abdominal muscles. This movement increases circulation and improves function.

3. Your abdomen muscles are strengthened by constant use.

4. You will experience a calming effect.

With knowledge of the placement of your breathing components, observe how you use them. Place one hand on your waist, one on your chest, and breathe deeply. Does your chest rise and fall or is most of the movement at your waist? Natural breathing is driven by the diaphragm and causes movement at your waist. If you feel most of the movement in your chest, you are a chest breather and will benefit greatly by retraining yourself to breathe naturally. Shift the movement of breathing to your diaphragm by pushing up at your waist against your hands.

Once you have distinguished the movement of your diaphragm, support its movement with your abdominal muscles. When your diaphragm contracts downward with each inhalation, let your abdominal muscles protrude. With each exhalation, let your abdominal muscles contract and pull inward, supporting the diaphragm for a complete exhalation.

At times you may find unusual difficulty in moving your diaphragm. This happens when your abdominal muscles and organs are tense. As your diaphragm contracts downward, it is restricted by your rigid abdominal organs. This condition is usually caused by psychological tension and the "flat-tummy, body-beautiful" syndrome but also may result from abdominal surgery, injury, or other trauma to the pelvis. You can relax these organs by doing stretches for the diaphragm and abdomen, getting a professional massage, or practicing Yoga, Qigong, and acupressure. Visualization is also a useful tool as you release tension and promote healing. Be creative and imagine your abdominal organs as calm, contented, appreciated, and relaxed.

When the diaphragm is restricted in movement by prolonged periods of stress, breathing shifts up into the chest. Not only is a smaller volume of air moved but limited oxygenation takes place in the upper lungs. The lower lobes are larger in volume and richer in capillaries. Gravity pulls on your body and increases the volume of blood flow to the lower lobes. This is why approximately 80 percent of your blood accessible for oxygen exchange is in the lower lobes. If you are a chest breather, you rarely access the 80 percent of the blood supply in the lower lobes. Most of your air movement is in the upper lobes, which do oxygenate the blood but remove carbon dioxide less efficiently than the capillary-rich lower lobes. Diaphragmatic breathing will dramatically increase the amount of air moved and reduce breaths per minute from 14 or 15 to 8 or 12. (Hendricks, p. 45)

The movement of your rib cage may also be restricted by tight muscles and poor posture. If your shoulders are stooped, and your head is carried forward, your rib cage is permanently compressed. Cyclists must be especially watchful to keep their chests open. Be sure your handlebars are close enough to your seat to enable you to ride with your elbows bent back toward your hips. Rather than rounding your shoulders, broaden your upper back and shoulders energetically without straining while keeping your chest open.

The specific muscles you use to breathe not only influence your oxygenation efficiency but connect intimately to your psychological state. Because our fight-or-flight nervous system is associated with chest breathing, shallow breathing in the upper lungs and chest originates from and results in stress and anxiety. Next time you give a presentation or demonstrate a skill, notice if your breathing has moved up high into your chest. Is this condition fun? No! Generally, life is more fun without anxiety, and now you have a tool to change your attitude and improve your performance! Consciously move your breathing down to your diaphragm, and engage your parasympathetic or calming, nervous system. Just as Andrew Weil stated, now we can influence some of our autonomic systems through the breathing "bridge." Later we will explore John Douillard's work, which demonstrates how controlled breathing influences pulse rate during athletic performance.

There are three different breathing styles that we are discussing: diaphragmatic, conscious, and three-part breathing. *Diaphragmatic breathing* is natural and uses the respiratory system the way it was designed to function. The diaphragm, abdominal, and intercostal muscles are used to move air in and out of the lungs in contrast to chest breathing, which is more restrictive and high in the lungs. *Conscious breathing* can also be called controlled breathing. It includes any breathing style or technique that we consciously control. During retraining from chest breathing to diaphragmatic breathing, you will need to be conscious of your breathing. There are a great many types of psychospiritual, therapeutic breathing techniques that are conscious. *Three-part breathing* is one of these techniques that will help you identify and control the action of all your lung capacity.

Using Three-part Breathing to Develop Your Conscious Breathing Skills

Three-part breathing uses the muscles of the abdomen, diaphragm, chest, and clavicle to expand and contract the lungs. Three-part breathing will help you develop the full volume of your lungs. With one slow and conscious breath, begin to expand your lungs with your diaphragm while releasing your abdominal muscles. Move upward into the chest and finally lift your collarbones. It may help you expand your lungs up under your clavicle by knowing that you will contract muscles in your neck to lift your sternum and clavicle (sternocleidomastoids) and to lift your top two ribs (scalenes). The expansion of your rib cage can also be facilitated by visualizing broadening across your upper (thoracic) back. Reverse this process by deflation, starting at the collarbones and letting your lungs empty all the way down to your diaphragm. Finally, contract your abdominal muscles. It takes a bit of coordination, doesn't it? Practice it for a while until the results are fairly predictable. You will get some indication of how effectively you have been using your lungs by observing how much you are expanding your chest. If you have to concentrate to systematically fill the lungs from one end to the other and then empty them in reverse, you will need more practice to derive maximum benefit from controlled breathing.

If you have respiratory problems, this exercise can be particularly challenging and all the more valuable for you to practice. Respiratory problems are aggravated by poor posture, misshapen chest, obesity, emotional disorders, lung troubles, smoking, and uneven use of your respiratory muscles. (Iyengar, p. 31) Notice that many cyclists have poor posture from extended hours of riding. This poor posture can result in rounded shoulders, collapsed chest, and compressed diaphragm. Failure to correct these problems causes many subtle changes in your body and mind as well as gross ones like fatigue, bad attitude, poor stamina, and heart disease.

During conscious breathing practice, the length and depth of each breath should be relaxed and effortless. Give conscious attention to the manner and sequence in which muscles are used. Practice gently and slowly. You will know you are trying too hard if you experience dizziness, tension, or discomfort. If these occur, pause and rest before resuming practice. If you have health problems where difficult breathing is a secondary symptom, use Gay Hendrick's program *Conscious Breathing* and consult with your physician.

With these cautionary comments in mind, try the *breath of joy* to use all parts of your lungs and observe the dramatic effect conscious breathing can have on your energy level and mood. Stand with your feet at shoulder width. Raise outstretched arms in front of you to shoulder level and partially inflate your lungs with your diaphragm. From this position, sweep your arms in an upward arc that ends at your sides at shoulder level and inflate your lungs further with your chest. Finally, arch your arms up over your head and complete the inflation of your lungs into the clavicular region. Now release all this air with an audible, complete exhalation as you drop your arms down past your hips, ending the movement near the floor as you drop down into a crouch, completely releasing your shoulders and arms. Repeat this several times taking care not to hyperventilate. Use this technique when you are feeling tired, tense, or melancholy. You too, will find joy.

Establishing a Rhythm

When you can depend on the coordination of your respiratory muscles, begin work on a consistent rhythm, which we will call SELF breathing: Slow, Even, Long, and Full. Your current breathing style may be to exhale, hold, inhale, and hold. Now try keeping your diaphragm moving all the time. Slowly, inhale and without a pause slowly exhale. Strive to match the inhalation and exhalation in duration and quality. It may help to visualize each inhalation-exhalation cycle as a loop in a spiral rather than an out and back pattern.

As you gain confidence, lie down and practice SELF breathing while stretching or holding Yoga postures. If you are a Taiji practitioner, let your SELF breathing flow easily with your form. When you use SELF breathing while bike riding, you will probably need to slow your pace to an exertion level that allows you to breathe rhythmically without panting.

When you lapse back into panting during exertion, try this experiment: pant a few breaths and observe how effectively your respiration returns to normal. Then engage your new skills and return to SELF breathing, exhaling completely. If your new skills are sufficiently developed, you will observe a quick and dramatic return to normal breathing. This surely demonstrates the greater efficiency of trained breathing.

Exhaling is the Work Phase of Breathing

Have you ever noticed when you pant your inhalation is stronger than your exhalation? While a powerful inhalation is automatic, you need to train yourself to balance each inhalation with a strong and complete exhalation. The function of the inhalation is to bring fresh, oxygen-rich air into the lungs to oxygenate blood to feed every cell. The function of the exhalation is to push out the spent, oxygen-depleted air to make space for fresh air. Have you ever felt as though you were going to burst while gasping for breath during extreme exertion? That means your exhalation needs work. While you are sitting, try expelling all the air from your lungs by a firm contraction of the diaphragm, abdominal muscles, and intercostal muscles of your chest. You can feel really empty. Whenever you find yourself gasping, focus on complete exhalations that go beyond your untrained habits and expel the last spent air from your lungs. Then inhale through your nose.

An effective technique for developing your exhalation is 1:2 breathing where you consciously exhale for twice as many counts as you inhale. Follow these steps to get started:

1. Begin conscious breathing using SELF breathing.

2. Establish a count for each inhalation. You can probably count to three or six on each inhalation but don't strain, just breathe in a sustainable pattern.

3. Now multiply the inhalation count by two. If you had three counts while inhaling, you will exhale to the count of six.

4. Ensure that your counting beats are uniform. Count one, two, three as you inhale and four, five, six, seven, eight, nine as you exhale. This will cause you to use conscious effort at the end of the exhalation.

If you practice while sitting and expanding your chest fully, you might count three on the inhalation and six on the exhalation. When you're riding or walking, a 2:4 count is more likely to be sustainable. Individual lung capacities vary as well as personal breathing patterns, so find the count that you can maintain for prolonged periods. As you become proficient at this technique, your stamina will increase. Take care to inhale only as long as the count and not until your lungs are ready to burst. Counter-intuitively, the diminished emphasis on inhaling actually increases your capacity to bring in fresh, oxygen-rich air. That is because the complete exhalation has removed more of the spent air and made space for fresh air to rush in more efficiently. When you first begin breathing practice while riding, you may find 1:2 breathing easier than SELF breathing. Use the same diaphragmatic technique emphasizing the exhalation with the 1:2 rhythm in contrast to the evenly balanced inhalation and exhalation of the SELF breathing. You will find that focusing on your breathing while riding will bring you into the present moment and clear your mind of chatter.

John Douillard is a pioneer and leader who trains athletes in breathing technique. He uses Ayurvedic techniques to improve athletic performance. Remarkably, he has discovered that controlled, diaphragmatic breathing allows pulse and breath rates to remain low during high exertion! As with SELF breathing, Ayurvedic breathing opens up the lower lobes of your lungs. Douillard's studies confirm that it is worth the effort to learn to use your full lung capacity because the performance of all your body systems depends on delivery of oxygen and removal of carbon dioxide.

Ayurvedic breathing uses the nose instead of the mouth, with several benefits. Breathing through the nose will condition the air to body temperature and moisture *before* it reaches the lungs. The nose, designed as the breathing instrument, has turbines and turbinates (spiral, spongy bones in the nasal passages) to drive air into the lower lobes of your lungs. To practice nasal, controlled breathing, make a raspy sound at the back of your throat with the muscles and vocal chords used in clearing your throat. This closes off airflow through the mouth and opens the throat connection to the nasal passages. Another technique for opening the nasal and throat passages is to create a yawning sensation in the back of the mouth. If you must breathe through your mouth, place your tongue behind your upper, front teeth to slow the passage of air though your mouth and condition the air to some degree. Mouth breathing is often necessary at cooler temperatures due to nasal congestion. You can also protect yourself from breathing cold air by covering your mouth with a neck gaiter or face mask made of two layers of polyester fleece. This provides an external temperature gradient and protects your lungs from the harsh effects of cold, dry air.

For further discussion of diaphragmatic breathing for high levels of athletic performance, read John Douillard's *Body, Mind and Sport* or listen to his audio tapes *Invincible Athletics*. Ayurvedic breathing benefits extend beyond increased efficiency and lower heart and breath rates. They also produce a tranquil, rejuvenating state, making physical workouts renewing rather than exhausting.

Points to Remember While Practicing Breathing

1. Breathe with your diaphragm.

2. Release your abdominal muscles and let them move out with each inhalation. A flat tummy may look good in a swimsuit but it precludes healthy breathing technique.

3. Empty your lungs completely, expelling all the old air so new oxygen-rich air can flood into your lungs. Exhalation is the active phase of breathing. Draw your diaphragm up and compress your abdominal and chest muscles to complete each exhalation.

4. Use all three regions of your lungs: the lower lobes at the diaphragm, the chest, and high at the clavicle. Relax, expand, contract.

5. Relax and open the back of your nose and throat by simulating yawning and allow air to flow unobstructed.

6. Be patient and allow years to retrain your breathing. Stress will make your breathing rise up in the chest. You will consciously need to shift your breathing back down to your diaphragm.

Overcoming Challenges You May Encounter While Practicing Your Breathing Technique

I hope you clearly understand the concepts and benefits of controlled diaphragmatic breathing. You will need to make retraining a priority and to incorporate it into your daily living as well as your athletic activities. Brief practice in using your diaphragm and abdominal muscles will not translate automatically into increased stamina in cycling. Let's look in more detail at some of the challenges and benefits you might experience along the way.

Some people discover a fear of asphyxiation when first trying to control their breath. Simply acknowledging the fear and practicing in comfortable and secure surroundings will probably overcome this anxiety. Seek out Yoga classes where breathing is taught with each posture. When you are first working to coordinate new breathing skills, it is encouraging to work in a class of like-minded people and to receive effective coaching from a knowledgeable teacher. If you are accustomed to controlling your breathing while swimming, you may find breath training quite natural.

Anxieties and other emotions may well up while you are practicing breathing. Rather than ignoring them, participate in those feelings and breathe into them and the part of your body where you sense them. Breathing through them may enable you to handle them and eventually release them. Consciously breathing into and relaxing both physical and psychological pain will diminish it and facilitate healing. I recommend Gay Hendricks' *Conscious Breathing: Breathwork for Health, Stress Release, and Personal Mastery* as an excellent resource for using breathing for general health and healing.

During intense exertion or stress, you may hold your breath and tighten your abdominal muscles. Use conscious breathing to overcome these counterproductive practices and be especially alert when you are doing aerobics, isometrics, and Yoga postures. Holding your breath increases tension and reduces your ability to improve muscle tone. If you find yourself holding your breath, back off the activity and focus on your breathing.

Restrictive clothing around your waist will interfere with your progress in breathing technique. Avoid confining clothing that interferes with the full use of your diaphragm and abdominal muscles. Instead, you might try suspenders, loose-fitting waistbands, or bib shorts and tights. Riding with a forward lean of more than 45 degrees compresses your diaphragm and interferes with breathing performance unless you are able to maintain your lumbar curve. Most people find this uncomfortable since it presses the pubic bone into the saddle.

Breath training while cycling requires full concentration. I recommend you ride alone while you are coordinating your breathing skills. Trying to superimpose breath training on group rides may discourage you from slowing your pace to optimize your breathing performance.

The great swimming and cross-country skiing coach, Sven Wiik, often challenged his athletes to focus on their technique. He would ask his swimmers to concentrate exclusively on their form for just one lap of the pool. He reported that their success rate was poor, and their minds usually wandered off to other matters to the detriment of their swimming skills. How often have you gone out for a ride to relax and renew and found your mind churning? Conscious breathing can keep you in the moment so you can be alert and engaged in your surroundings, your physical sensations, and your companionship of friends while cycling. It can also *improve your technique*.

Relaxation, Renewal, and Recovery Depend on Diaphragmatic Breathing

Conscious breathing heightens your awareness and physiologically transforms your mind and body functions. Diaphragmatic breathing enables you to relax, rejuvenate, and pace yourself so you can recover quickly.

Relaxation is a fine art and must be well developed before you can relax at will. This does not mean being limp but effortless and light using only those muscles that support your action and releasing all others. It is the key to efficiency. Keep in mind that you need to learn how to relax at will in a quiet place before you can incorporate the practice into your bike riding and other demanding situations. Hendricks assures us that it is not possible to remain anxious while breathing diaphragmatically (Hendricks, p. 160) so practice conscious breathing regularly. You can practice discretely anytime or anyplace. Remember to coordinate your breathing with your stretching and strengthening exercises.

Each ride can be rejuvenating when you use diaphragmatic breathing. Begin slowly and gradually build up your energy level to prepare your mind and body for increased exertion. Shift into diaphragmatic breathing immediately and use it to pace yourself. Any time you begin panting or breathing too hard to maintain control of your breathing rate, slow down and reduce your exertion level to a sustainable breathing level. Eventually your breathing skills will enable you to ride at high exertion while maintaining a lower breathing and pulse rate. The surprising result is improved endurance while completing your ride feeling refreshed and renewed.

Avoid becoming obsessed by challenges encountered during a ride and with distance goals that distract you from accurately accessing your stamina level. This could be a compulsion to ride all of a steep, technical climb without walking or to complete a pre-determined mileage even though you are exhausted. I have learned to stop every hour, get off my saddle, and stand astride my bike. From this perspective, I can accurately evaluate my comfort and stamina levels. I check my shoulders and neck for tension, my perineum for numbness or chafing, and my fuel level to see if I need to eat something. After a thoughtful assessment, I often need to adjustment my clothing, my pace, or my route plan.

I discovered this technique when riding at night in blizzards. Several times I rode to evening meetings or home from work during challenging conditions, pushed myself too hard, and arrived at my destination drenched in sweat and feeling weary and scattered. I resolved to avoid this foolishness in the future and sort out the causes of this behavior. I realized that I had not honestly accessed my psychological comfort about riding in blizzards. Since I needed to travel and traveled by bike, I just launched myself into the storm. This made me feel at risk so I shifted into overdrive and rode compulsively. I realized that psychological comfort is as important as physical comfort. How could I enjoy riding in these circumstances and still deal with poor visibility and sketchy traction? First, I would take time to enjoy the beauty of the blowing snow and white landscape. Then I would stop every half hour and tune in to my comfort level. I was delighted to discover these techniques enabled me to pace myself, have fun, and arrive home refreshed. I was satisfied that my bike was reliable transportation and I had once again found contentment in nature.

Just as I discovered, you too can use conscious breathing to appreciate your immediate circumstances and to gauge a sustainable energy level and an adequate fuel level. Riding harder than you can adequately fuel yourself with oxygen and calories results in the production of byproducts in your system that prolong recovery time. Use your breathing to pace yourself, maintain good judgment, and ensure quick recovery.

Establishing a Moderate-intensity Aerobic Exercise Routine

I've heard it said that U.S. citizens are quick to take action but short on planning. The behaviors of many recreational cyclists confirm this adage. They are eager to get out and ride but unlikely to develop a plan for consistent fitness or to plan adequately for their ride needs. The first task is to develop a ride schedule. The second task is to equip yourself properly so each ride will be fun and safe. Thirdly, care for the mechanical needs of your bike as an extension of caring for yourself.

Regular, moderate-intensity exercise makes it easier to develop and maintain your fitness base and to increase your riding confidence. I recommend a minimum of 30 minutes of daily exercise. Forego the 50 milers on the weekends until you have built a fitness base adequate for longer distances. It is truly remarkable how, over time, short daily rides can build substantial muscular and aerobic fitness. This exercise pattern makes riding more fun because you will feel energized and refreshed at the end of each session and eager to get back on your bike the next day. It also facilitates learning new techniques because you increase your familiarity with your bike and are alert and focused throughout each ride. Brisk exercise at least five days each week is the regimen that most effectively reduces risks of serious illness. Daily moderate exercise takes more months to develop high-performance fitness and does not produce an adrenaline rush but it will help you develop the healthy attitude of a self-nurturing person. Now that is something to feel good about.

A daily exercise routine of moderate intensity produces healthful and lasting results. You can be sure you are building fitness when you experience the following benefits:

1. Increased energy
2. Lower heart rate
3. Improved quality of sleep
4. Balanced appetite, that is, the absence of cravings and immoderate eating
5. A desire to continue exercise for the pleasure of it
6. A general sense of well-being
7. Increased focus and contentment
8. Improved biomechanical form and increased appreciation for your fit body

With such a desirable list of benefits, why do so many fitness buffs seek out extreme exercise? Perhaps it is impatience to achieve fitness results quickly that causes riders to overdo on weekends in an attempt to compensate for inactivity during the week. But let's look at the pitfalls of over-training through high-intensity, prolonged exercise.

1. Whenever you ride hard enough to experience soreness the next day, you create microscopic tears in your muscle fiber membranes and protein filaments. (Burke, p. 38) Rather than building up your body, you are actually tearing it down.

2. This damage causes increased blood flow and swelling within the muscles requiring a return to light exercise and potentially leads to lost training time for recovery.

3. The burning sensation in your muscles indicates lactic acid build-up and intensifies soreness and fatigue.

4. Riding while fatigued causes your riding form to deteriorate, making retraining difficult and discouraging.

5. Over-using your muscles and regressing to poor form increase your risk of injury either on the bike or in the days following.

6. Collectively, over-training and its physiological and psychological changes result in a general deterioration in athletic performance.

7. Central fatigue impairs your judgment and increases the likelihood of mishaps.

I hope this reality check encourages you to begin a daily, moderate-intensity exercise routine.

The term **moderate-intensity exercise is so commonly used that it requires special definition for *Bicycling Bliss*. For our purposes, moderate-intensity exercise means the**

maximum pace you can sustain for three hours. To establish what pace this is for you, you will need to frequently access your heart rate, breathing, muscle fatigue, mental focus, and psychological comfort. If you are pushing too hard in one of these aspects, reduce your output until you get to a sustainable exertion level. ***Bicycling Bliss*** emphasizes moderation and awareness. Riders who are beginning a fitness program or who have endured an exhausting work schedule in recent days will ride more slowly than cyclists who have already built a strong fitness base or who are well rested. Consequently, a moderate-intensity pace will vary widely under different circumstances for any one individual. Within any group, moderate-intensity exertion for some riders would be low-intensity for others. It is essential to make your exercise routine enjoyable and know that you are truly building fitness. If it takes five years to build the fitness base that has tangible health benefits for you, that is just fine because you are active and enjoying it. Only then will your program be *sustainable* and keep you fit and fun-loving past mid-life.

Notice the difference between this definition and the definition of moderate-intensity used by athletic trainers. These pulse-rate based systems require that you establish your personal maximum aerobic output and then work at a percentage of your maximum, based on age and condition. They tend to be inflexible and do not adapt as well to your immediate needs. They may distract you from tuning in to your condition. Pace is critical to your short-term and long-term goals, to your exercise routine, and to your daily work routine. It requires constant awareness of your breathing and of the details of the exercise process. When you do this, you will know when you are breathing harder, perspiring, and maintaining a steady, moderate-aerobic workout.

Pacing and a moderate exercise program translate into increased balance and moderation in your life. Since rest and recovery are essential to building muscle strength, a daily exercise program naturally incorporates the pattern of exercise and recovery necessary to incorporate it into a busy schedule. For example, exercising five days each week allows for two days off to accommodate variations in your business and family schedules.

Develop your program gradually with sensitivity to your individual physical and mental conditions. Any changes in distance or pace should be made wisely and gently with a watchful eye on the quality of your exercise session. Keeping an exercise journal will help you monitor your progress and help you discover patterns in your wellness. Bear in mind that all the tools discussed in this chapter and the resources discussed in Chapter 7 are part of your wellness program. Avoid neglecting sleep or proper nutrition to pack your exercise into an over-scheduled day. The goal is to increase well-being, not to sacrifice your health to build "body beautiful."

Here are some suggestions for establishing a daily exercise program that you can maintain.

Scheduling, Location, and Distance:

- Select a route around your neighborhood to make your daily riding routine manageable.

- Take time to leisurely and creatively evaluate local streets and trails for suitability.

- Change this route occasionally for variety and as your abilities change.

- Now design an alternative plan for poor weather so it will be easy to change plans and not use it as an excuse to skip exercise. This could be a different ride route, stretching, swimming, or creative dance. Make it something fun you can do for at least 30 minutes of conscious breathing.

- Target a realistic number of days each week, say four or five. Then identify the time of day that is most appealing to you. That could be morning or evening but some people find time and a good route at work and ride during lunch break. If you ride immediately upon waking, no grooming or bathing is necessary before you ride. If you ride last thing in the evening you can make your cleanup your nightly bathing routine.

- Now make a *realistic* weekly and monthly schedule.

- Start with an appropriate distance for your current fitness level. Be sure to warm up gradually and cool down purposefully. If 30 minutes of riding seems inadequate for your current fitness level, make those 30 minutes more demanding. You might ride a mountain bike, reduce your tire pressure, or carry a load to increase your exertion level. You'll develop your own tricks.

- Bicycle commuting is an ideal way to get your daily ride into the schedule with very little additional time required. Refer to "Cyclists Help Build Healthy Communities" in Chapter 2, pp. 45-46.

- Avoid jamming your exercise into an already packed schedule. More self-imposed pressure will not contribute to your wellness. Review your current schedule and select something to eliminate so your exercise can take that time slot.

- As you establish your routine, your energy and focus will increase, making you more effective and efficient during each day so you may even make time for reflection.

Maintaining a Moderate-intensity Exertion Level:

- Use conscious breathing, both in the planning phase and during exercise.

- Avoid using stimulants. By their very nature, they push you out of balance and encourage obsessive behavior.

- Seek out compatible companions to share your exercise routines.

- Break away from the riding styles projected by the media; many of them are excessive.

- Allow time to develop the fitness level you desire. Avoid committing to events or vacation touring rides that are well beyond your current stamina level.

- Respond to your physical and psychological needs and customize your exercise to your condition. When your legs are leaden, take a short spinning ride to loosen up or declare a rest day. Over-training is the most common cause of injury and burnout.

If you doubt that you can build and maintain the fitness you desire with these constraints, refer to John Douillard's *Body, Mind and Sport*. His research has been with competitive athletes, and he explains in detail how conscious, diaphragmatic breathing makes it possible to build fitness while simultaneously allowing you to experience relaxation, rejuvenation, and quick recovery.

Getting Started:

- Start during warm weather with longer daylight hours. As your fitness and confidence increase, you will experience the benefits of regular exercise. As the days become shorter and cooler, you can gradually adapt to more challenging conditions. With proper planning and equipment, you will be able to maintain your routine most of the year. Refer to Chapter 8, pp. 327-357, to enable you to make informed clothing choices and Chapter 9, pp. 368-370, on selecting appropriate illumination.

- The first weeks of your new routine will be more difficult than after your routine is established. The more often you do any task, the easier it becomes. Not only do you do a better quality job but you do it with less effort.

- Phil and Jim Wharton (*Active, Isolated Stretching*) advise that once you have committed to a fitness program, do not renegotiate your commitment each day. Just go out and do it without questioning your commitment.

Variety is the Key to Maintaining Your Enthusiasm and Motivation:

- Change your routine on whim or for the weather. Identify several ride routes and select the one that interests you today. You may enjoy the social aspects of going to a gym to exercise. But if time is at a premium, create something fun to do at home.

- Fun is important to your success. If you are watching the clock (or odometer) you are not having fun. Be creative and playful so you are not conscious of the passing of time.

- Establish some form of support system so you have someone with whom to share your experiences. If a friend or family member is not available, keep a training journal and use it for reinforcement.

- Toss aside some of your cherished laborsaving devices. Bypass the elevator and take the stairs. Park a few blocks away from work or the store and walk a few minutes. Retire the power mower and human power a reel-type mower. Maintain a brisk pace at each of these tasks and you will feel results.

Riders Who Have Used Cycling to Dramatically Improve Their Fitness Have These Tips to Share:

- Ride every day.

- Make every ride a pleasure ride so you will look forward to your fitness routine.

- Establish some parameters that allow you to observe your progress.

- Find a companion of similar abilities to help you keep your commitment and add to the fun.

- Set realistic goals so you will be encouraged by success.

- Establish a routine but provide some variety for interest.

- Make this a time of sharing with someone you want to spend more time with.

- Be willing to invest in needed equipment. This is an investment in your wellness.

- Be sure to eat and drink adequately so your exertion level is comfortable. If you ride before breakfast in the morning, use an energy beverage or snack to avoid running on empty.

- Ride during the workday and carry a cell phone to stay in contact with business associates.

- "Break loose from the excuse circuit. Whatever niggling thing is keeping you from riding, get rid of it. Lost gloves? Buy another pair. It's raining? Go get a raincoat. Just contrast these expenses with the cost of filling up with gas for a month," says Rex Brian, who shed more than 30 pounds following his own advice while running his own consulting business and parenting four teenagers with his physician wife.

Most people who maintain daily exercise routines find that they have more energy, are better able to handle the challenges of life, and sleep more soundly. Over a year's time, 30 minutes of activity a day adds up to a lot of calories burned, so you can surely take more pleasure in food. Active people also have higher metabolic rates — a perk that increases their nutritional choices.

Beginning a regular exercise program gradually does not exclude moderate-intensity endurance rides of four hours or more. After your commitment to cycling is well established, you may want to explore the benefits of longer rides. They can transform your performance and your sensitivity to your needs. It takes about eight to ten weeks of endurance training to build a good endurance base. Endurance rides result in the following beneficial physiological changes:

- An increase in the number of capillaries surrounding muscle cells
- An increase in the number of red blood cells
- An increase in enzymes that speed the chemical reactions in your body
- An increase in the transport of oxygen to your cells

All of these things mean your performance and endurance are optimized, and your body responds more quickly to fuel and exertion requirements. You will also become more aware of your exact fuel and rest needs. Endurance training should also be designed with the same attention to your general well-being and avoidance of excesses as a beginning exercise program.

Alexander Technique

In searching for a better understanding of kinesthesia on the Internet, I "discovered" the Alexander Technique. What a classic example of not "finding" something until you are ready for it. After becoming an appreciative student of Alexander Technique, I found an article about it in a newsletter at home. However, I had passed it by because it was not meaningful to me at that time. First I read Robert Rickover's *Fitness without Stress*. The title intrigued me since it seemed to be an excellent fit for **Bicycling Bliss**. Indeed, it provided an outstanding introduction to Alexander Technique.

The technique was developed by F. M. Alexander (1869-1955). He was a successful Australian dramatist during the late 1880s. His career suffered when his voice began failing him in the middle of a performance. Doctors were unable to help him overcome this problem so he decided to study his voice weakness and cure himself. It took him 10 years but he solved his problem! His transformation was so dramatic that some of his colleagues asked him to instruct them in his technique. Gradually his success as a teacher led him to England and eventually to the United States. Alexander discovered and demonstrated the unique role of the body in the development of conscious learning. His technique is a tool for heightening self-knowledge and changing old habits.

Alexander identified tension and compression in his neck as the cause of his voice failure. Most of us can share his concern about neck tension. However, *he* was able to develop techniques for retraining himself that were effective and led to a wider understanding of how we use and misuse our bodies.

Alexander Technique is based on the idea that from a young age, we unconsciously develop habitual movement patterns. Some of these habits help us work efficiently but others are limiting and even harmful. We don't notice the harmful habits until they cause us pain or injury. Then we usually blame the pain on stress, the work environment, poorly designed furniture, or a poor bicycle setup. We rarely search our own habits for the cause and take responsibility for our own predicament. How many times have you heard, "I wasn't doing anything and suddenly my back went out." Well, it was not so "suddenly." Rather, it was the result of years of harmful movement patterns that are so ingrained in our habits that we don't recognize them until they finally create pain or discomfort.

I was excited to find confirmation of my premise that discomforts while cycling are caused by movement habits we develop through life's routines. They show up while cycling because the motions we use in cycling are repetitive and because many riders push themselves past their comfortable stamina levels.

Just as Alexander did, we can choose to retrain ourselves in healthful, properly aligned movement patterns when we commit adequate time and dedication and seek out proper instruction. The desired result is graceful, poised, effortless movement and a well-aligned spine.

Successful retraining depends on the following key elements:

1. Heightening your sensory awareness of the difference between beneficial and damaging uses of your body

2. Consciously controlling otherwise automatic and faulty response patterns to any given stimulus

3. Aligning the head, neck, and back to improve the quality of body use

4. Learning that letting go of harmful habits is more important than acquiring the "right knowledge"

5. Focusing on observation, the process of change, and abandonment of the egocentric concern with results

Working through Alexander Technique analysis and retraining empowers students to learn how to change old habits. It gives them a sense of control over their own lives. They discover that the quality of their lives is improved by using their bodies to optimize healthful alignment. They are able to take responsibility for their own well-being and give up the victim mentality that "Life/stress just makes me this way." They feel "connected." Indeed, many movement patterns reflect mental attitudes. Alexander students often find that physical retraining can also be freeing intellectually and spiritually. It can even lead to increased awareness of reality.

There are several noteworthy applications of these principles and benefits to athletes.

1. Currently, the characteristics that we associate with "the fit body" are based on habitual tension, which results in inflexibility. It is more important to use the appropriate effort to perform a task and to relax tension that is not useful. This is the definition of efficiency in athletic performance.

2. Preoccupation with winning usually means that other important aspects of life and health are sacrificed. Athletes are frequently encouraged to continue training at high performance levels even when it is destructive to their bodies and general well-being.

3. Athletes will benefit from avoiding the common preoccupation with the *quantity of exertion* and instead emphasize the *quality of movement*: balance, coordination, and the ease of breathing.

4. Many exercise programs do little to improve the way we use our bodies. In fact, they often exaggerate our worst habits. Watch a group of joggers or cyclists and observe how awkwardly some of them move.

5. Lack of body awareness is a major contributor to exercise-related injuries.

Books on Alexander Technique are by nature somewhat nebulous. Human movement and posture patterns are too complex to be understood in a short time. We need to give attention to the integrity of the entire body. Instruction by a certified teacher is essential in diagnosing the needed changes and in guiding retraining. During bike fittings I observe that *telling* people how to change is not adequate. It is more effective to gently guide their bodies and physical responses while they listen to verbal instructions.

To gain first hand experience with the technique, I took classes from a local, certified instructor. I learned that there are two basic approaches instructors use to support changing movement patterns: energetic and practical. The energetic style guides the student's body energy, intention, and visualization and is true to F. M. Alexander's teachings. The practical style is more familiar and uses muscular exercises to correct old patterns. It can be helpful during the retraining process. Whenever I observed myself moving in the old patterns, I redirected my energy, using different muscles and quality of movement, until this became the new instinctive pattern.

The energetic style required that I change my thought process and vocabulary to eliminate the usual concepts of "striving" and "trying." Integrated and balanced body use manifests as effortless movement. That means that retraining focuses on letting go of the old ways and manifesting the new movement patterns by intention, visualization, and energy direction. The energetic approach requires us to make basic changes. Using our muscles is only one element of movement. Guiding the student with the hands while giving verbal instruction facilitates learning new movement patterns. This two-pronged teaching method allows our "body's intelligence" to respond to the physical guidance and helps us mentally conceptualize the intended movement. I found I needed to identify the energy location and direction to implement the new movement pattern. I needed to create new visions of movement focusing on lengthening and broadening my muscles to enable my body to work as an integrated whole.

Rather than further damaging the body by imposing a new muscular pattern on top of an old one, it is better to adopt the new movement patterns immediately. This is in contrast to the common practice of over-compensating for an inadequacy or harmful habit hoping to achieve balanced use sometime in the future. For years I tried to balance the strength of my legs by working my weaker left leg harder in hopes that it would someday equal the strength of my dominant right leg. I did not see that this created two imbalances instead of one. What a revelation to discover that I could reduce the power output of my right leg, visualize energetic balance while pedaling, and achieve balance immediately! Yes, this meant riding at a slightly lower energy level for a brief time but it enabled me to enjoy the pleasure and health benefits of balanced, integrated body use immediately! By putting my energy and focus into balance, I could achieve the desired effect without causing strain or damage to my hips or back. I have extended this retraining beyond cycling. Whenever I observe myself lazily using the superior strength of my right leg to get up off the ground or take a large step up to a higher lever, I consciously lead with my left leg as often as my right.

Alexander Technique places great importance on how we carry our heads. My retraining process has made me a believer in the interrelationship between head carriage and alignment of the entire length of the spine. Like many who spend a lot of time at desks and on bikes, I had carried my head so far forward that it created undue tension throughout my spine. Years of Taiji practice have diminished the degree of forward carriage but not eliminated it. My Alexander Technique instructor identified that I carried my hips too far forward. My pelvic rotation was fine but I needed to shift my hips back and my chest forward (actually raise my awareness of the front of my thoracic spine). To my amazement and delight, when I made this adjustment in spine alignment, *my head floated effortlessly on top of my neck.* It seems magical to me that a small correction in carriage of my hips opened my chest and effortlessly realigned my head position. Although I could feel the benefits of this adjustment immediately, retraining my body took more time. After a month of shifting my alignment many times a day, I miraculously *felt* the energetic change one morning during Taiji practice. To make this realignment lasting, the release of the hips and firming of the abdominal muscles was a small part. The primary dynamic was visualizing a lifting and elongation of the entire spine. It was a shift of my energy rather than a well-defined muscular action.

I was fascinated that the vital change needed to be effected right at my diaphragm. Could it be that this spinal misalignment is related to years of dysfunctional breathing or even weak abdominal muscles? I am delighted that the effective use of my diaphragm accompanied by relaxation of the adjacent organs facilitated the energetic and perceptual transformation of my spinal alignment. Through Yoga and Rolfing I have become aware of the front of my thoracic spine and I have opened my chest. My perception of my body has become three-dimensional. The better I understand the human body, the more I appreciate its miraculous design. With this one change in alignment, my entire body feels light and free. All movements are effortless, energizing me to meet daily challenges with enthusiasm! Such subtle fine-tuning of body alignment certainly requires analysis and instruction by a certified Alexander Technique instructor. You will find a list of instructors in your area at http://www.alexandertech.com/teachers.

Surely this new buoyancy I have found is convincing evidence that Alexander's initial premise is true: habitual movement patterns cause destructive tension and compression in the spine. Conversations with many customers convince me that this was not just a problem for Alexander's contemporaries but also an increasingly common problem among cyclists today. In fact, it appears that neck problems occur among all ages, social groups, and professions. Time to lighten up!

Understanding Yoga Postures and Stretching

Daily routines usually involve a limited range of movement. Regular stretching will improve your range of motion, body alignment, circulation, breathing, and centering.

Because cycling is a highly repetitive activity with a limited range of movement, the muscles that stabilize your body and power the bike forward can suffer from tightness and overuse. Since muscles work by contracting, they become shorter with constant use. If you do not stretch, they remain tight and create imbalances in your body alignment. Listen to any group of riders and you will soon learn where tension develops in a cyclist's body. Remember Timothy McTight? Refer to p. 13. Stretching or Yoga postures are essential for elongating shortened muscles.

Yoga postures guide you into new movements and help free you of habitual movement patterns. Mindful stretching will help you discover the idiosyncrasies of your body and help you select and practice the exercises where your movements are most limited.

Yoga improves circulation in several ways. Improved breathing increases the flow of oxygen to all parts of the body. Twisting postures compress body parts, squeezing or pressing the old blood and lymph fluids out of those tissues just like wringing out a dishrag. With the release of each posture, fresh blood returns, cleansing, healing, and energizing the tissue. Postures that move your head below your heart or your legs above your hips assist blood flow in the veins and counteract gravity's constant pull on your body.

As you develop your breathing skills, Yoga becomes a remarkable tool for quieting your mind, developing your focus, and increasing your awareness. Maintaining your focus while you ride will improve your riding technique and your bike handling skills as well as prevent mishaps.

Combine all these benefits and you can see that a daily stretching practice and stretching before you ride can make a noticeable difference in your riding performance. You can improve your coordination through freer, easier movement and greater receptivity to your body feedback. I hope you will find that the centering effects of Yoga together with increased flexibility and sensitivity to your whole body will improve your riding technique and bike handling skills. Your body can relax and flow and respond spontaneously without your mind's interference. Your stamina can improve through more efficient breathing and body use. Stretching will benefit both casual and high-performance riders. Lance Armstrong reported that one hour of stretching daily contributed substantially to his training for winning the 2001 Tour de France.

Maintaining a Yoga or stretching practice requires self-discipline. The first step is to design a practical and realistic schedule. You will do well to establish your practice during the off-season of cycling or when you have a less hectic schedule. Then when you feel stressed-out you can turn to your Yoga to reduce tension and regain a balanced perspective. Just as you carefully schedule training rides in advance of a major cycling event, you need to schedule and develop your stretching routine well in advance of the most demanding workload and riding season.

When you begin a regular practice, the vast selection of Yoga postures can be overwhelming. I recommend that you select one or two postures that you like or that are challenging for you to perform and practice those for an entire week. It takes only a few minutes of quality time morning and evening to notice your improvement. The second week, add one more posture. As you become proficient at five or six postures, drop one and add another. In this manner you will learn a repertoire of postures. Then when your shoulders need attention, you can select several postures beneficial for your shoulders. Use the lists and instructions in **Bicycling Bliss** to remind you of postures that benefit any specific part of your body.

Experiencing immediate benefits will keep you motivated to follow your practice schedule. Bob Anderson (*The Stretching Book*) says it takes a year of practice before you mentally connect with stretching and fully enjoy the ease and commitment to your practice. The quality of your practice is more important than its duration. So use these guidelines to increase the benefits of stretching and Yoga.

1. Warm up gradually. Cold, tense muscles resist elongation. Trying to stretch without preparation can result in injury or can even increase tension. Begin slowly and gently, preparing your mind and body for exercise. The moving elephant posture is a fun and effective warm-up (refer to the following description). Before practice, take a moment to relax. Sit quietly and observe your breathing. If you are breathing in your chest or your breath pattern is erratic, begin slow, controlled breathing using your diaphragm. Try to balance the duration of your exhalations and inhalations. Make the transition between exhalation and inhalations smooth and fluid.

2. Breathe continuously throughout each stretch. The benefits of elongation and strengthening will be limited if you hold your breath during any part of a stretch. Give attention to your breathing throughout each sequence. If you are unable to breathe evenly, ease up on the stretch. Mentally direct your breath into the muscles you are elongating. In some postures your movement is coordinated with your breath. The general rule is to exhale when you fold over the diaphragm and inhale as you straighten up. If the breath pattern is not clear to you, experiment until you discover what feels natural and enhances your stretch.

3. Move without force. Instead, cultivate these two types of movement:

   a. Release into each posture using relaxation, exhalation, and gravity to increase the stretch. Sink downward with each exhalation. Let go of tension and exertion.

   b. When moving against gravity or improving the alignment of your posture, use gentle muscle strength, intention, and an inhalation. Use the inhalation to open, expand, and extend.

Breathe regularly throughout each posture and focus on isolating the muscles you need to contract and those you need to elongate. Through these two different aspects of practice, you will open your joints, increase your range of movement, build your strength, and avoid the risks of bouncing movement.

4. Be clear about your intention in each stretch. When practicing Yoga and stretching, draw your attention inward. Close your eyes and scan your body with curious interest in what you are feeling. When you are stretching during a ride or in a group, let go of any competitive urges or preoccupation with your appearance. Observe your flexibility, relax tense areas, become aware of your body alignment, the quality of your stretch, and the nature of your breathing. You might ask, "Where are the tight spots?" "How does my body respond to the structure of the pose?" "Does the pose elicit any emotions?"

Are you doing what you intended to do? This is especially important as you are learning each posture. If you are practicing without an instructor, look at yourself in a mirror or large window to confirm that you are moving in the direction you intend.

Be aware of your movement esthetics. Practicing postures should lift your spirits and give you pleasure. Avoid angular, jerky, or bouncing movements. They can make you uncomfortable and scatter your mind. Using fluid movements will help you maintain a quiet attitude. Complete each posture purposefully, returning to the beginning position. Enjoy this moment by bringing your attention to the areas you have worked. What are you feeling? Listen to your entire being. For all standing postures return to the mountain pose, p. 101.

5. Choose the duration and intensity of each stretch based on your present condition. Initially, you might hold each stretch 10 to 30 seconds to limber up. As you become more flexible, experiment with holding stretches longer than 30 seconds. Each time you practice, hold postures only as long as you are able to maintain a quiet mind, a steady body, and conscious breathing. If you are exerting yourself or beginning to shake, you have gone too far. Back off or come out of the posture. These parameters will help you avoid pain, which is a clear indication that something is wrong. When you discover extremely tight muscles, you may experience some discomfort. Bring your attention into the area of discomfort and imagine breathing into it. Or imagine the discomfort draining out of the limb or torso. This will relieve your discomfort and reduce the likelihood of muscle soreness the next day. If you have impairments or injuries, facilitate healing by only doing 75 percent of what you normally would.

6. Select postures that meet your immediate needs.

    a.   Forward bends are quieting, cooling, and relaxing.

    b.   Backward bends increase mental clarity and awareness and are energizing and warming.

    c.   There are postures that are performed standing, sitting, and lying down. Lying postures are especially enjoyable at the end of the day or after exercise.

    d.   Stretch opposing muscles in pairs. For example follow, the downward-facing dog with the upward-facing dog.

7. Repeat each stretch twice on each side of your body. This process increases your pleasure by letting you observe immediate improvements. During the first repetition, your mind and body become familiar with the posture. The second time, they acknowledge that familiarity, and you will notice greater ease and improved form. Thoughtfully observe the differences between the two sides of your body. Accept these differences but use the information to help you develop balanced alignment and strength.

8. Keep these principles of body use in mind.

    a.   Point your feet straightforward or at the recommended angle, bringing relaxed awareness to the soles of your feet. Distribute your weight evenly across the bottom of each foot and both feet evenly. Relax and spread your toes.

    b.   Align your knees so they are directly over the respective feet. Do this when your legs are bent or straight. In straight leg poses, contract the thigh muscles and draw your kneecaps up while engaging the hamstrings. Use balanced isometric tension and avoid locking or hyper-extending your joints past 180 degrees by strong contraction of the quadriceps femoris without a balanced contraction of the hamstrings.

c.   During forward bends, pivot at the hips rather than rounding your spine forward.

d.   Give attention to all of your body: front, sides, and back. Observe your joints as well as your muscles. While observing your breathing, also observe the flow of energy.

e.   When making adjustments to your position, begin at the base and work up. For standing poses, begin at your feet. For seated poses, begin at your seat bones and at the alignment of your pelvis. Since the pelvis is the base of the spine, its placement determines the curvature of the length of the spine. A neutral position balances the engagement of the muscles of the buttocks and the abdomen.

9.   *Acknowledge and accept your unique body type.* If you have tight joints, you especially will benefit from stretching. Stretching is not about flexibility but about getting at tight places and releasing them. If you are quite limber, complement your stretching with strengthening exercises to support loose joints.

10. *Use proper equipment.* Many postures will be more fun and relaxing if you use a "sticky mat." These are available through Yoga centers and catalogs. They prevent you from slipping on the floor so you will be able to relax appropriate muscles fully. Wear loose-fitting clothing or knits that allow you to move freely. Remove your shoes and socks. Be sure to regulate your body temperature by adjusting your clothing. Being too cool or too hot will diminish the benefits of centering.

For more details on stretching and stretches for specific parts of the body, refer to Bob Anderson's *Stretching* or to your favorite Yoga manual. Classes will help you get started and maintain your practice. Try several teachers until you find one you can appreciate.

I have used Yoga and stretching interchangeably to encourage those of you who already have a regular stretching practice. However, there are several distinctions between Yoga and conventional stretching. The postures are esthetically pleasing and cultivate a grace that provides another dimension of interest. The essential goal of Yoga is to cultivate physical, mental, and spiritual balance. It is slow and steady, giving the practitioner greater control, safety, and efficiency. The mind must be receptive to the messages the body is sending and make appropriate adjustments. There is a constant interplay between mind and body. You will need to perceive sensations, accept them, and make needed adjustments and refinements. When your mind wanders, draw it back into your body.

Yoga is a philosophy developed in India over many thousands of years. It is much more than just postures (*asana*). Its primary purpose is to quiet the mind and senses in order to develop a steady, balanced awareness. Yoga teachings promote discipline to practice the postures, meditation, and simplification of life style. Because of the rich and ancient traditions of Yoga, it touches people in many different ways. Depending on your personal goals, you may experience increased contentment, increased wellness, and improved balance of body, mind, and spirit. The essence of Yoga is to reduce your suffering by reaching into your inner being and developing a fearless, joyful heart and increased spiritual awareness.

The Mountain Pose is the Basic Resting Position for Standing Postures.

It helps cultivate a sense of balanced alignment in your carriage. Stand upright with your feet together and pointing forward. If your pelvis is wide or you are improving your balance, you may feel more stable with your feet six inches apart. Distribute your weight evenly across the soles of your feet, front-to-back and side-to-side. Let your arms hang along your sides, turning the creases of your elbows and thumbs forward and gently extending your fingers toward the ground. Align your pelvis and knees by engaging both your quadriceps and hamstrings. Do this by drawing your kneecaps up and your seat bones and tailbone down and forward. Open your chest, lifting your thoracic spine forward. Broaden across your shoulders and upper back and lift through the top of your head. Relax your jaw, mouth, and face. Now close your eyes, breathe diaphragmatically, and give attention to how this feels. Engaging your quadriceps and hamstrings lifts your kneecaps and perfectly fits all parts of the knee joint together. If you have sensitive knees, this practice with strengthen them gradually so over time they can withstand intense contraction of the surrounding muscles. (Coulter, p. 311)

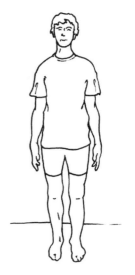

Mountain pose

Yoga Sequences for Warming Up

Warming up before moderate physical activity reduces the risk of soreness or injury and improves physical performance.

How does that work? Your warm-up activity increases blood flow to the muscles and joints to be used during exercise. Either breathing harder or gradually working the muscles and joints you want to warm up can accomplish this. Moving directly into vigorous activity without preparation reduces flexibility in your joints and elasticity in your connective tissue. It makes movements awkward, reduces efficiency, and increases the risk of injury and mishaps.

You can either begin your ride slowly and gradually increase your exertion level or start your exercise session with one of the following Yoga sequences. Indoor warms-ups are especially beneficial when you are going outside to exercise on a cold day.

The Elephant

Preparation for the elephant

Preparation for the elephant — Stand with your feet parallel and at shoulder width. Fold your arms across your chest, clasping each arm just above your elbows. Now bend forward pivoting at the hips and keeping your weight forward on your toes. Stop when your torso is horizontal. Let your arms hang relaxed toward the floor. Lift upward with your tailbone. Looking toward the floor, extend through the top of your head, maintaining the natural alignment of your neck and spine. When you have experienced a healthy stretch through your hamstrings and a realignment in your hips, let your torso, neck, and arms relax downward. Breathing should be conscious but will be somewhat shallow with the compression of your diaphragm. Return to a standing position letting your legs do the work by pressing down on your toes and pivoting at the hips. You can work your back and abdominals more by returning to upright by stacking each vertebra gently on top of the previous one. Another option is to finish with a back bend by moving past vertical to arch your back, release your head back, and fully extended your arms upward. Back bends are energizing and will balance your forward bend. Notice in the illustration that the weight is centered over the feet rather than forward on the toes.

The elephant — Repeat the warm-up. At the lowest point in the posture, let your arms unfold so your hands reach the floor.

Be sure your head hangs relaxed so you gaze back between your legs. Keep your arms and legs as straight as possible and imagine you are an elephant. Now walk forward about 20 feet and then back up to your starting place. Breathe continuously throughout your walk. Release your neck and head. When you are finished, return to a standing position and focus on the changed condition of your body and breathing. With your heart and lungs lowered, your breathing and circulation are quickly deepened. Your hamstrings are stretched and wrist and ankles strengthened.

The elephant

The Downward-facing Dog, Upward-facing Dog, and Child's Pose Sequence

This sequence strengthens your shoulders, arms, wrists, and hands while stretching and relaxing your lower back and your hamstrings. It alternately inverts your internal organs, stretches them, and finally compresses them. This exercise benefits digestion, and breathing. It requires good traction on the floor and is easier to perform on a sticky mat. If you do not have a sticky mat, you can use gloves and bare feet that don't slip on your exercise surface. This sequence is an excellent energizer used immediately upon rising in the morning. It balances energy throughout your body and restores flexibility to your spine and the joints of your limbs.

Downward-facing dog — Starting on your hands and knees, point your index fingers forward and spread your fingers and thumb widely apart. Press the base of your index and middle fingers firmly onto the floor to engage your wrists and forearms. Be sure that your knees are directly beneath your hips and your hands directly beneath your shoulders. Now straighten your legs to form a triangle with the floor, your buttocks forming the apex, and your hands and feet forming the third side with the floor. Pivot at the hip joints. Keeping your arms and back straight and extending your arms fully at the shoulders, let your head hang relaxed toward the floor. Rather than arching your back, keep it flat by rotating your pelvis so that your tailbone is lifted up, and your navel is pressed down. Draw your abdominal muscles toward your spine. So how are your hamstrings doing?

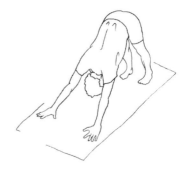

Downward-facing dog

There are several alternatives. If you are able, bring your heels to the floor, feet pointing toward your hands. If your heels don't contact the floor, spread your feet apart to slightly *wider* than hip width. Now alternately flex first one knee and then the other while pressing the opposite heel toward the floor and stretching your hamstrings. Breathe regularly and diaphragmatically for as long as this posture is comfortable. If you find it too strenuous, practice it daily, limbering and strengthening your shoulders, arms, and hands. Gradually your hamstrings will lengthen, and your shoulders will come closer to the floor, resulting in two nice straight sides to your triangle. This is a moderate inversion that should be safe for people with high blood pressure or heart problems. It massages your internal organs, brings blood to your lungs and brain, and rejuvenates you when you are tired (or trying to wake up).

Upward-facing dog — Relieves the back, shoulders, and hamstrings with a backward arch that opens the front of the spine. Continuing from the down dog, reposition your feet so they are resting on the tops with your toes pointed away from you. This can be accomplished one at a time as you gradually lower your hips so that your torso is supported by your arms. You can also make this transition by rolling over your toes onto the tops of your feet. Only your hands and feet will touch the floor. Contract your gluteus maximus and hamstrings so your knees do not contact the floor. Lift from the top of your head and direct your conscious breathing into the parts of your body that are feeling sensitive. Shifting your shoulders slightly forward of your hands makes it easier to open your shoulders and chest.

Child's pose — Relieves the small of your back, opens your upper back, and provides total relaxation. Continue from the upward-facing dog, bringing your knees on to the floor and sitting back on your feet. Bring your chest down onto your thighs and place your forehead on the floor, completely releasing your neck and tailbone. Place your knees far enough apart to allow space for your abdomen and chest but close enough to let your shoulders fully release toward the floor.

Upward-facing dog

Bring your arms down along your sides so your hands are by your feet with palms up. Breathing will be more shallow while your diaphragm is confined. Relax fully and enjoy the sensation of wellness. To come out of the pose, lift your head and shoulder on an inhalation. Here is a nice variation for your neck. While your forehead is on the floor, gently sway your shoulders from side to side over your knees. Let your forehead roll gently back and forth, pivoting your neck while it is fully relaxed.

Child's pose

The Sun Salutation

The sun salutation is an ancient tribute to the sun as the source of life. Practicing it with a sense of reverence and gratitude can increase its benefits. You may enjoy performing this sequence outdoors facing the rising sun. It will help you develop conscious breathing since breathing coordinates with each movement. It is adequate by itself because it works all parts of your body. Its benefits include increasing back flexibility, opening the chest, firming abdominal muscles, stimulating digestion, and relieving constipation. Best of all, it raises your energy level and lifts your spirits.

Practice gently, with grace and fluidity. This will help balance your energy. The pace you choose will correspond to your breathing rate. While moving rapidly may scatter your mind, moving too slowly may cause you to strain. Be conscious of each movement and each breath, giving attention to how each side of your body feels, to signs of progress with each repetition, and to your general wellness.

1. Stand erect, feet parallel, toes spread, with your weight evenly distributed across the entire sole of each foot. Place your hands in the prayer position, palms together over your heart. Give attention to the balance of energy in your entire being. Bring your breathing to a conscious, diaphragmatic, restful rhythm.

2. Inhaling slowly, lift your hands up over your head, following them with your head and eyes. Let your hands come to rest when your arms are fully extended. Let your

continued on page 107

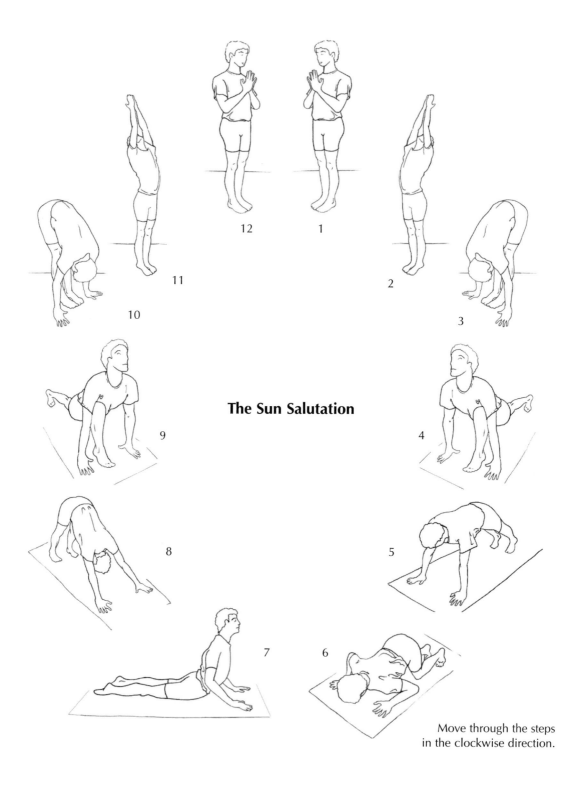

The Sun Salutation

Move through the steps
in the clockwise direction.

head relax backward as far as is comfortable with your thumbs above your eyes. If you have any impairment to your neck, do not drop your head back. (Here you may enjoy the variation of arching backwards on the exhalation by firming your buttocks and moving your hips forward and inhaling as you return to an erect posture.)

3. Exhaling slowly, bend forward, placing your hands (or finger tips) on the floor. Pivot at the hips, keeping your back flat until your torso is horizontal. Round your back as you bring your forehead toward your knees, keeping your legs as straight as is comfortable.

4. On the inhalation, step back into a lunge with your left foot as far behind you as possible with your toes on the floor. Raise your head up to look forward. Keep your left leg as straight as possible and let your perineum (floor of the pelvis) sink toward the floor.

5. While suspending your breathing, place your right foot back beside your left foot. In this plank position, keep your torso horizontal so it is parallel to the floor.

6. Exhaling, lower your knees to the floor, then your chest, and finally your chin or forehead.

7. Inhaling slowly, lower your hips to the floor, let the tops of your feet rest on the floor and lift your shoulders off the floor using your back muscles. (You may recognize this as *cobra pose*.) When you have raised your shoulders as far as possible with your back muscles, support your raised shoulders with your arms, drop your shoulder blades, keep your elbows close to your torso and bent back toward your hips. Let your head relax back and look upward. Reduce any possible strain on your arched back by pressing your pubic bone against the floor.

8. Exhaling, bring your toes back onto the floor and then bring your hips up to form the *downward-facing dog*. Pivot at the hips, keeping your legs as straight as possible, and let your head hang down between your arms. Try to form an inverted "V" with straight and elongated arms, shoulders and back. Bring your heels as close to the floor as possible.

9. Inhaling, lunge forward with your left leg. Bring your knee to your chest and your toes as close to forward alignment with your fingertips as possible. Look forward. Again, let your perineum sink toward the floor.

10. Exhaling, bring your right leg forward, placing your right foot parallel to your left foot. Keep your legs straight and bring your forehead toward your knees.

11. Inhaling, stand up while keeping your arms alongside your ears until they are over your head, reversing the opening motion. (If your back is sensitive, move your arms in arcs to your sides to reduce back strain.)

12. Exhale while bringing your hands down to your chest in the prayer position. Bring your

attention to the refreshing sensation of your entire being and let your breath return to normal before repeating the sequence with your right leg.

Always practice this sequence in pairs to benefit both sides of the body. Repeat as many pairs as you like but always return to balance between each set.

The sun salutation is taught in many different forms. If you are used to a different sequence, practice the one you prefer. There are also variations: you might like to add a back rotation after step 4, shifting your weight onto your left hand and foot and bringing your right hand and arm up directly above your left hand so your shoulders are vertical. Keep your hips as close to horizontal as possible to optimize the rotation of your spine. You can hold this position for several breaths or for only one complete inhalation and exhalation before returning to the position in step 4 and proceeding to step 5.

Strength Training for Building Balanced Bodies

If you enjoy working out on weight machines, you can appreciate the value of exercising indoors in a controlled environment. I've never gotten closer to this equipment than the doorway of the weight room. Strength training conjures up images of people sweating and grimacing, entangled in bulky metal contraptions. The equipment reminds me of medieval torture devices. If you too have been put off by the complexity of weight training equipment and the risks associated with heavy weights, let me introduce you to resistance training exercises that can be done at home using little or no equipment. The purpose of these exercises is to make strength building more accessible to everyone and to help you develop a strong and balanced musculature.

This program is to help recreational athletes build and maintain health and fitness. The old adage, "use it or lose it," is strong motivation to develop your own resistance training routine. I hope this essential guidance will get you started building strength, confidence, and an increased sense of well-being.

I have chosen these exercises with two goals in mind:

- **to build strength in muscles that are not worked during cycling and**

- **to strengthen the muscles that support (synergists) and those that oppose (antagonists) the heavily used cycling muscles.**

These exercises use your body weight, dumbbells, and ankle weights. All of these fit in the category of free weights since you can carry them around, and gravity provides the resistance. I will not include barbell exercises. Free weights allow more creativity in use than weight machines and are excellent for developing your synergistic muscles (those that play a secondary role in producing a desired movement). They also allow greater variety of muscle involvement and require greater coordination and attention to balance. These characteristics develop increased joint stability. In contrast, weight machines are highly specific in the muscles they work. Regardless of the resistance training you choose, however, the equipment is not as important as your attention to maintaining good technique. (A noteworthy similarity to cycling!) As you gain experience, you will enjoy the transition from lifting in prescribed movements to concentrating on the specific muscle groups you are working.

Another approach is to use tubing for resistance. Although bicycle inner tubes are sometimes used, surgical tubing is more predictable and more elastic. I mention tubing because tubing is light and compact for resistance training while traveling. To prepare the equipment, purchase 12 feet of tubing and create handles at the ends by tying off a section threaded through PVC pipe. A webbing strap with "D" rings will enable you to secure the tubing around immovable furniture for some exercises. For safety, check the tubing regularly for nicks or cuts so you won't risk having it snap back and hurt you. Resistance can be increased by shortening the tubing, stepping away for the anchor point, or doubling the tubing over. Obviously, it is not as easy to quantify the resistance with tubing. Some of the exercises described here work with tubing such as upright rowing, bent over rowing, and the diagonal hip swing. Refer to Cook and Stewart's *Strength Basics* for a variety of exercises using tubing.

As I reviewed strength-training manuals for just the right exercises, I was surprised and pleased to discover several exercises I do in Yoga. I have been aware of the strength needed to perform Yoga postures and have appreciated that in doing them, I was gradually strengthening weak muscles. However, I had no idea that I would find some Yoga postures popular among body builders! While reflecting on this discovery, I chuckled to think of the wisdom of ancient Yogis to include strengthening with stretching in a regimen to balance one's being. Of course, balanced musculature would be essential to balanced living! For this reason I have included reference to Yoga postures and indicated the muscles they strengthen.

Cross-training is another way to strengthen muscles underused in cycling. Sports that work the upper torso are a wise choice for cyclists: flat-water kayaking, canoeing, rowing, cross-country skiing, and swimming can be enjoyed depending on the convenience of water and the climate where you live.

You can also build strength with yard work and household chores. I love to maintain a vegetable garden and enjoy digging as therapy as well as good exercise. With our severe drought in recent years, I have expended many calories hauling five-gallon buckets of "gray water" to water my yard. To increase my bone density, I made a weight vest with sixteen pounds of weight on my shoulders to wear for 30 minutes a day. An unexpected bonus of wearing this vest is the passive stretch to my upper trapezius and my improved posture. What regular lifting do you enjoy? All this utilitarian lifting contributes to our overall strength but is not specific in developing our weaker muscles and those that will balance our strong cycling muscles. Weight training tailored to these needs will better prepare us for more demanding activities and reduce the risk of injury from misuse and overuse.

How Resistance Training Builds Strength and Increases Coordination and Control

When muscle cells are not used, they atrophy. (Remember: *use it or lose it.*) With consistent daily use, muscles maintain their strength. When you work your muscles beyond the demands of your normal activity, you stimulate them to adapt to the increased workload thereby increasing strength and stamina. When a rest period follows each workout, the muscles rebuild to meet the greater demand. **Progressive resistance exercise** means you increase the level of exertion by *small* increments from week to week to stimulate muscles to adapt to an ever-increasing load. The same rest-rebuild principle applies to both strength training and aerobic exercise: overuse without adequate rest prevents the body from rebuilding and diminishes the fitness benefits.

Notice the difference between progressive resistance training with weights and over-extending yourself while riding either by excessive exertion levels or riding substantially greater distance than you are conditioned for. Measuring weights or counting reps enables you to accurately quantify the resistance increments. You can progressively increase the intensity of your work load in small amounts, continually building strength. Bike riding has too many variables to accurately assess your work load. Riding until exhaustion or soreness sets in means that you are breaking down muscle fiber to such a degree that you may require time to heal the muscle damage rather than progressively building up strength.

Let's look at the structure of muscle tissue and coordinated performance of groups of muscles in any body part. Muscle is made up of tiny threadlike tissue called *myofibrils*. These are bundled together to form *muscle fibers*. Groups of the fibers are clustered into *motor units*, all under the control of a single nerve. In any exercise movement, the muscles directly responsible for the action are called the *prime movers*. These are assisted by dozens of helper muscles called *synergists*. *Stabilizers* secure the limb or joint while the prime mover and synergist muscles carry out the motion. *Antagonists* are the opposing muscles that can reverse the movement on command.

We will concentrate on exercises:

- To strengthen the synergists used in cycling

- To strengthen the stabilizers especially in the back and the abdomen

- To strengthen the muscles that are typically weak among cyclists — especially the feet and ankles, abdominals, spinal erectors, triceps, wrists and hands, and neck

Let me emphasize the importance of developing the antagonists of the legs used during the down stroke in pedaling. You need to do this while riding by developing your power on the full rotation of the crank! Don't leave this essential aspect of developing muscle symmetry in your legs to a resistance training program. Well-balanced opposing muscles work in concert and enable you to ride with greater efficiency and reduced risk of injury.

What does strength training do for you?

- Increases your strength

- Builds balanced relationships between muscles

- Prolongs the duration you can enjoy any activity before you get tired

- Protects your joints against strain and pain by strengthening the muscles around the joints and reducing stress on the joints themselves — Take note of this benefit if you have arthritis or other joint inflammation. Improved disposition is an important side benefit.

- Builds denser bones — Muscles and tendons pulling on the bones promotes bone cell activity. Bones benefit from this stress during workouts and during normal activity due to stronger muscles. Listen up all you women over 55 years!

- Helps with weight control — Muscle tissue is active and consumes more calories than fat tissue. As with any regular exercise, strength training boosts your metabolic rate.

- Energizes — With greater strength, it is easier to move.

- Improves your appearance — Your physique will change as stronger muscles reshape your body.

- Increases coordination — Stronger synergistic and antagonistic muscles results in more controlled movement. Imagine several people trying to lift a large, heavily loaded banquet table. If even one person fails to lift at the right moment, the table will not rise or will lurch and spill the food. However, when each person lifts equally at the right moment, the table lifts off the floor smoothly in a controlled manner.

- Reduces frailty even past seventy, making strength training the true fountain of youth

Let's clear up a few myths.

- Spot reduction is not possible. You cannot perform certain exercises and lose weight in specific parts of your body. Consuming fewer calories than you burn will reduce overall body fat but not in designated areas. However, resistance training can increase muscle tone in specific areas, changing your contours.

- You do not have to consume large quantities of protein and vitamin supplements to gain strength. It is less expensive and easier to eat a well-balanced diet. You may need to increase your caloric intake when you increase your activity level.

- If you taper off or stop resistance training, your muscles will not turn to fat. Muscle and fat tissue are distinctively different. If muscles are less active, they get smaller. Just think about what happens when a leg is confined to a cast. It atrophies. It does not turn to mush.

So with a clear understanding of all the benefits of resistance training, let's get started!!

The Basics You Should Know for Healthful Strength Training

Terms that are used for strength training are *lifts*, *reps*, and *sets*. *Lift* refers to each exercise. *Rep* stands for repetitions and is one complete movement of each exercise. A *set* is any fixed number of repetitions.

1. Always take a rest day between strength training sessions. Schedule a 48 to 72 hour break. The *adaptation response* requires this rest in order to build strength. The one exception to this rule is working the abdominals. You can exercise them daily because they are small muscles, and it is difficult to overload them using your body weight. You might enjoy working your upper body on Mondays and Thursdays and lower body on Tuesdays and Fridays. To maintain fitness and health, you will only need two or three sessions a week of 30 to 45 minutes each.

2. Warm up and cool down as a part of each session. If you are doing a 30-minute workout, warm up for 5 minutes, train for 20 minutes, and cool down for 5 minutes. Try the warm-ups described in stretching on pp. 102-108. Or you might walk up and down stairs, and jog in place and then move your arms in all directions slowly without straining: over head, across your chest, and towards your back. It is wise to design your cool-down to include stretches that release the muscles you have worked against resistance. For example, the inner thigh lifts contract the muscles of the inner thigh and groin. Stretch those out gently by sitting on the floor (pelvis vertical), placing the soles of your feet together, and using your leg muscles to gently press your knees toward the floor. (See inner-thigh stretch, p. 186.) Continue each exercise session without interruption to avoid cooling down.

3. Before you begin each session, visualize the exercise you will perform. This will increase the neuromuscular excitation of muscle fibers for greater involvement and improved outcome. (Cooper, p. 200)

4. Perform each exercise with slow, smooth movements. This reduces the chance of strain and optimizes strength-building results. Slow fluid movements recruit more

motor units and involve more muscle fibers in each direction of the movement. Each rep should last about nine seconds, four in each direction with a pause in between. You may find it helpful to count the seconds aloud. This ensures continuous breathing, prevents hyperventilation, and will help you pace yourself throughout your practice.

5. Continuous breathing will keep you tuned in and relaxed. Watch this carefully because you may tend to hold your breath during overload exertion. Generally the breathing pattern for each lift will be to exhale during increased resistance and inhale while lowering resistance. Remember: "Exhale on effort." Let your breath return to normal between sets.

6. Stabilize your body in the starting position. Maintain proper posture by relaxing, elongating through the top of your head, and maintaining the natural curvature of your spine. This means the back of your neck releases and allows your chin to drop. Keep your neck in line with your spine, your shoulders down and back, your tailbone slightly tucked, and your knees not locked or bent. If you have difficulty maintaining this stability, you need to develop more vital strength by working your spinal erectors, abdominals, and shoulders.

7. Keep your joints slightly flexed at the full extension of each exercise. Avoid locking them and causing undue stress.

8. Plan your workouts between meals when possible. If you train too soon after a meal your blood will be in your digestive tract and diminish your effectiveness. On the other hand, if you are hungry you could get light headed. Remember: adequate hydration is important during any exercise.

9. Over time, gradually increase the intensity of your workouts so joints, tendons, ligaments, and muscles develop together. Train consistently and intelligently.

10. Listen to your body to determine the appropriate intensity of each workout and when to increase the progressive exertion level as the weeks go by. Maintain a comfortable exertion level. Discomfort means something is wrong.

11. When you use weights, begin your program with weights that seem too easy while you learn to do the exercises and develop your form. By the fourth session you should be using enough weight so the sixth or eighth rep is challenging. When you progress to 12 to 15 reps, add more weight.

12. You may enjoy setting goals and recording your progress. Keeping track of frequency of sessions, number of reps and sets, rate of movement, number of holds, and amount of weight will ensure that your work increments are small and progressive.

One of the rewarding aspects of strength training is the noticeable increase in strength and coordination. Rapid improvement occurs during the first few weeks but you will improve indefinitely as long as you continue to progressively increase resistance.

Like any specialty, strength training uses some jargon. The names of some muscles and muscle groups have common short forms. You will see the following:

Abdominals or abs - obliques and rectus abdominus — Details to follow.

Hamstrings — the muscles at the back of the thigh that attach at the back of the knee by tendons that look like cords or strings. The one toward the inside of the leg is the semitendinosus. One half of its length is tendon and is not as resilient as muscle. The upper end attaches to the seat bone affecting the lower back. That is why the hamstrings require consistent, patient work by athletes. (Couch, p. 79) Refer to the illustrations in "Your Knees" in Chapter 5, starting on p. 175.

Paraspinals — the muscles on either side of the spine that stabilize and extend the back into an arch. Also referred to as spinal erectors.

Quads — the quadriceps group

Refer to the Glossary, p. 377 and illustrations of anatomy in Appendix D, p. 405-411 for further understanding of these terms.

Strength Training Exercises for Cyclists

It is simple to increase the intensity of your workout when using weights by just adding more weight. For exercises without weights, you can increase the intensity by the following variations:
- Increase the height of the lift.
- Move extra slowly.
- Prolong the holds where you are resisting gravity.
- Add holds at about 30 and 60 percent of the full movement.
- Add a rotation to straight lifts such as the abdominal roll-ups by moving your shoulder toward the opposite knee.

Abdominal Muscles

We'll start with the abdominal muscles since weakness there is a primary cause of lower back problems. Strong abdominal muscles, which balance strong lower-back erectors, maintain the healthy lumbosacral angle of the pelvis. They also support the abdominal organs, improving their function, and control the contours of your tummy. They are also the muscles used to support abdominal breathing. Do these exercises three to four times a week, performing 5 to 25 reps. It is important to work both prime movers and antagonists in one session. Notice that the reverse trunk rotation also engages your back muscles. To maintain optimum function and appearance of your abdomen, tone the muscles through regular exercise and then let them release while inhaling and contract while exhaling to support the diaphragm.

Key muscles of the abdomen are the vertical *rectus abdominis* (from the breast bone to the pubic bone) and three layers that encircle the abdomen. The outermost are the *external obliques* running from the lower eight ribs and sides of the waist downward toward the pubic bone in the same direction as the external intercostal muscles of the rib cage. The middle layer is the *internal obliques* running in the opposite direction from the sides of the waist up to the four lower ribs in the same direction as the internal intercostal muscles. The innermost layer is the *transversalis* surrounding the deep abdominal area and running horizontally from front to back. The *pyramidalis* are small muscles just above the pubic bone. Refer to Appendix D for anatomic illustrations of the superficial, intermediate and deep muscles of the body, pp. 405-413.

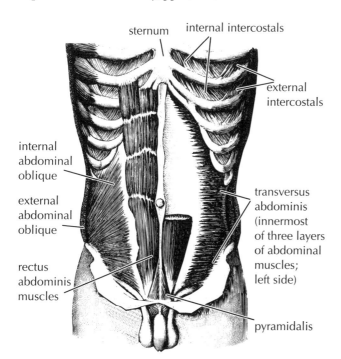

sternum

internal intercostals

external intercostals

internal abdominal oblique

external abdominal oblique

rectus abdominis muscles

transversus abdominis (innermost of three layers of abdominal muscles; left side)

pyramidalis

The key muscles of the abdomen form three layers with the outermost rectus abdominis and innermost transversalis sandwiching the external (cut away in this illustration) and internal abdominal obliques. (*Anatomy of Hatha Yoga*)

Transpyramid exercise — The transversalis and pyramidalis muscles are not involved in bending the spine so they are not strengthened by most exercise. They are important in breathing and maintaining a firm lower abdomen. Sit or stand, exhale slowly and when you get to where you would normally stop exhaling, forcefully breathe out more, lifting with your abdominal muscles. If you like, you can assist with your hands on the lower abdomen. Relax, take several normal breaths, and be careful not to hyperventilate. For the best results, repeat this 2 to 5 times several times a day. Do not get overzealous and do more than five at a time.

Abdominal roll-downs

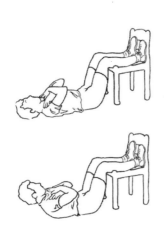

Abdominal roll-ups

Abdominal roll-downs — Strengthens the upper abdominal area. The stabilizers are the hip flexors. Roll-downs are less intense than roll-ups and do not require a chair. *Starting position* - Sit on the floor, feet flat, with knees bent, held together, and near the chest. Extend your arms straight out in front of you at shoulder height. *Movement* - Slowly lower your torso only as far as you can and still maintain control. At this point, come back up to your starting position. Lower on the inhalation to a four-second count, hold and come up on the exhalation to a four-second count.

Abdominal roll-ups — Strengthens the upper abdominal area. The stabilizers are again the hip flexors. Contrary to common instructions, do not hold your feet down for roll-ups. This causes the powerful hip flexors to take over much of the work *and* stresses your lower back. *Starting position* - Lie on your back with knees bent and lower legs resting on a bench or chair. Depending on your strength, place your arms along your sides, cross them on your chest, or place your hands over your ears with your elbows toward your back, when you are ready to increase your load. Placing your hands over your ears will prevent you from straining your neck by pulling on your head. *Movement* - Leaving your middle and lower back flat on the floor, slowly raise your head and shoulders off the ground 20 to 30 degrees. Pause and slowly lower. Use about a four-second count in each direction to get started. Throughout the movement, look at the ceiling and not at your knees to maintain a neutral neck position. *Variations* - To increase the intensity, you can eliminate the lower leg support, holding your lower legs horizontal in the air. Lift your shoulder at a variety of angles: in addition to lifting straight forward you can also lift toward each knee.

Reverse trunk rotations — Primarily works the internal and external obliques located in the midsection and used for rotation. Refer to the illustrations on pp. 76-77. At the same time, you will balance the abdominal work by engaging several key back muscles. *Starting position* - Lie on your back on the floor, bring your feet close to your buttocks, and rest them flat on the floor. Hold your knees together throughout the exercise.

Extend your arms at shoulder height with your palms on the floor. While performing this rotation, strive to keep both shoulders on the floor. *Movement* - Slowly and smoothly rotate your hips to bring your knees to your left side and touch the floor, exhale. Turn your head to look in the opposite direction of your leg movement. During the inhalation, bring your knees back to center so your thighs are vertical. Repeat to the right. Notice that the breathing coordinates with the action of the diaphragm during the rotation. *Variations* - This exercise is so versatile you can easily adapt it to your immediate needs and never get bored with it. These exercises are listed in order of increasing intensity.

Reverse trunk rotations

   a. Draw your knees close to your chest and raise your feet off the floor. Rotate to the left and bring your knees toward your left elbow, hold, raise to the center, and repeat to the right.

   b. Raise your feet off the floor, maintaining your thighs at right angles to your spine. Lower your left knee to the floor, again keeping your knees together. Hold, raise to the center, and repeat on the right side.

   c. Over time, gradually straighten your legs and lower your extended legs as far toward the floor as possible while maintaining control and being able to raise them back to vertical.

Always repeat an equal number of reps on each side, maintain good form, and stay in touch with all your body sensations. Have fun with these rotations and make them part of your life-long fitness routine!

Yoga postures for the abdominals:

   a. The cat, p. 227, stretches and strengthens key abdominal and back muscles.

   b. Leg lifts, p. 228, strengthen key abdominal muscles and engage back stabilizers.

During your cool-down, use the camel on page 186 to stretch out the abdominal muscles you have worked.

Full Length of the Back

The full length of the back stabilizes your cycling posture, your control, and the propulsion of your bike, yet full back strength building exercises are disguised as upper or lower back work. The following three Yoga postures will strengthen your back for more power, control, and pleasure.

Spinal twist

a. Variations on the cat, p. 227, strengthen the stabilizing back muscles that run diagonally across the length of your torso. The prime movers are the gluts, hamstrings, paraspinals, upper trapezius, and latissimus dorsi.

b. The cobra, pp. 218-219 strengthens erectors and stretches abdominals. Let me encourage you to continue practicing the cobra and experience the delight of rapid improvement. When I first began, I could barely lift my shoulders off the floor. Although I still cannot straighten my arms at the height of the posture, I can lift my shoulder up quite well before assisting with my arms. Give attention to the nuances of this posture to protect your lumbar spine.

c. The spinal twist, p. 217, strengthens rotators, posterior spinal surface muscles, and the quadratus lumborum, an important lower back muscle.

Upper Body

The upper body work is divided into pushes and pulls. If you ride with a forward lean of more than 15 degrees, strong triceps will increase your comfort. If you sprint and climb steep hills often, strong biceps will help power you. Many high-energy riders pull on their handlebars. I caution you that this puts unusual stress on your stem and handlebars, making it advisable to replace them regularly. When you value endurance over speed, this upper body energy would be better used propelling your bike with your legs.

Neck

Neck muscle fatigue and pain plague many cyclists. Poor riding posture aggravates neck discomfort but the underlying causes are weakness and tight muscles in both the front and back of neck! Refer to the exercises in Chapter 5, pp. 239-240. Have fun with this sequence. You lie down for this one.

Upper Body Pushes

Warm up your shoulders and arms with a variety of movements in all directions as described under strength training basics number two, p. 112. It's hard to surpass the effectiveness of pushups. But before you groan too loudly, try these many variations to provide some variety and to work your way gradually into full-body push-ups.

Push-ups — Especially for deltoids, pectorals, and triceps but they also engage as stabilizers the abdominals, paraspinals, gluteals, and hip flexors. Perform any of these variations as slow, smooth, controlled let-downs. This will help you get started at any strength level. The same principles apply to all variations. Stabilize your position, place your hands shoulder width apart in such a position that in the lowered position your hands are just under the shoulders. Bending at the elbows, slowly lower yourself until your nose or forehead lightly contacts the push-up surface, hold, and slowly push yourself up to the starting position. Place your feet or knees at about shoulder width. Do not lock your elbows and resist resting in a full down position. Either of these practices will make initiating the push-up more difficult.

Wall push-ups with arms extended

   a.   **Wall push-ups** — Stand at arm's length from the wall. Feet shoulder width apart and knees slightly bent. Place your hands palm down against the wall at about mid-chest height. Be sure your spinal alignment includes keeping your head and neck in line with a straight back. Lower yourself to the wall and follow the general instructions for push-ups.

   b.   **Counter push-ups** — These are similar to wall push-ups except your hands are on the edge of the counter, and your feet are backed away far enough so your upper chest will come to the edge of the counter.

   c.   **Knee push-ups** — Get down on your hands and knees. Protect your knees from the floor with some padding.

Place your hands only as far forward as allows you to lower yourself slowly with control and then back up again. This could be from kneeling on all fours to full extension with your torso, hips, and knees all in a straight line.

d. **Standard push-ups** — Begin on all fours, extend the legs straight back, supported on the balls of your feet. Keep your torso and legs in a straight line. Move as described above.

I remember with amusement two young men who were touring by bicycle across the U.S. They camped for the night in our backyard, and the next morning we saw both of them on the patio doing push-ups at a lively pace. I thought perhaps the Marines had invaded during the night. When we inquired about the extreme number and speed of their exercise, they explained that they were so concerned about losing their upper body strength during their weeks on bikes that they decided to do 100 push-ups every morning! That's one way to go at it.

Dips — Strengthen your chest, shoulders, triceps, and back. You'll need two chairs with the seats at the same height. Place the chairs about 24 inches apart, seats facing each other. Place your palms on the seats of the chairs and slowly lower yourself bending until you feel a gentle stretch on the chest muscles. Slowly extend your arms to push yourself back up to the starting position. Keep your shoulders down in the lowered position and do not lock your elbows in the raised position. Letting your elbows bend out to the side, as illustrated, strengthens your deltoid muscles for general shoulder strength. You may choose to let your elbows bend toward your back, strengthening your triceps, which are important in maintaining flexed elbows while riding with a forward lean of more than 15 degrees.

a. **Modified dips** — Follow the above movement description. Place your feet directly under your buttocks and bend your knees. In this manner you can use your legs to assist your shoulders, chest, and arms while raising and lowering.

Modified dips

b. **Standard dips** — Follow the movement pattern for the
modified dips. Place your extended legs in front of you,
slightly bend your knees, and rest your heels on the
floor.

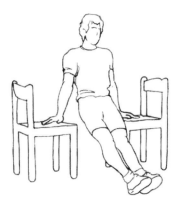

Standard dips

Yoga postures — These postures worked together strengthen
wrists, arms, and shoulders. Refer to pp. 103-105, downward-
facing dog, upward-facing dog, and child's pose sequence.
For best results, hold each position one minute or longer.
Give special attention to flattening your back and arms in
downward-facing dog and keeping your knees off the floor in
upward-facing dog.

Wrist rolls with weights — These strengthen your wrists and
increase their range of motion as well as counteract the
negative effects of repetitive motion stress. Find a solid metal
rod, dumbbell, or other heavy object that weighs about three
pounds and is about the diameter of your handlebar grip.
Sitting in a chair, grasp the weight with your fist, palm upward,
supporting your forearm against your thigh. To a slow four-
count, let your wrist roll back as far as comfortable and then
pivot it back up toward your forearm as far as is comfortable.
Repeat this slowly several times. Repeat with your other hand
and wrist.

Wrist forward and back bends with weights — Standing with
your arms hanging at your sides, grasp your dumbbells or other
weights in each hand. Alternately bend your wrists up toward
the front (thumbs on top) and then up toward the back (little
fingers on top). Keep your arms straight and breathe evenly.
Move slowly to a slow four-count in each direction as far as is
comfortable.

Manual bike tire inflation — (or if you're ambitious, try your
car tires) This is an excellent resistance exercise for your
shoulders and triceps so don't shy away from it. Grab the
chance to develop your upper body.

Upper Body Pulls

You will need some weights for these lifts. Dumbbells work
well because they are balanced, and the small-diameter middle

Bent-over rowing

Dumbbell flyes

reduces the chance of hand strain. How much weight you work with will depend on your strength when you begin your program. This could be anywhere from three to twelve pounds.

Bent-over rowing — Strengthens the biceps and upper back, especially the latissimus dorsi. The primary stabilizers are the trapezius, deltoids, and pectorals. This requires one dumbbell and a chair. *Starting position* - Stand to the left of a stable chair with a dumbbell in your left hand. Move your left foot back about 12 inches and support your weight on both feet while keeping your knees flexed. Bend over at the hips and place your right hand on the chair to support your torso while keeping your right elbow slightly bent. *Movement* - Slowly pull the dumbbell up until it lightly touches your ribcage and rotate your left shoulder slightly upward at the top of the movement. Slowly lower the dumbbell to its starting position. Perform the desired number of reps and then reverse your position and repeat with the dumbbell in the right hand.

Dumbbell flyes — Strengthen the chest and shoulders, especially the pectorals. You'll need two dumbbells and a bench although these could be done on the floor as a second best choice. *Starting position* - Grasp two light dumbbells and lie on your back on a horizontal bench with your feet on the floor, arms extended straight up with hand above your shoulder and palms facing each other. Open your chest, keep your back on the bench, and keep your neck aligned with your spine. If this puts strain on your lower back, you can put some support under your feet to raise them higher and relieve the back strain. *Movement* - Keeping your elbows flexed, slowly move the dumbbells out to the sides in a semicircular arc until you feel a slight stretching sensation in the chest muscles. Do not lower them below shoulder height. Reverse this movement bringing the dumbbells back to the starting position. Perform the desired number of reps.

Upright rowing — Strengthens the shoulders, arms, and back. Two dumbbells are used. *Starting position* - Grasp two light dumbbells. Stand with your feet at shoulder width and elbows slightly bent with dumbbells resting just in front of your upper thighs. Bending at the hips, lean your torso forward slightly to avoid arching your back. *Movement* - With your knuckles facing away from you, slowly pull the dumbbells straight up in a vertical line to mid-chest height. Concentrate on lifting the weight with your elbows rather than your hands. At the top of the movement, your elbows will be slightly higher than your hands and at about shoulder height. Shoulders rotate slightly to the rear. Slowly lower the dumbbells back to the starting position. Perform the desired number of reps.

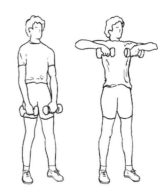

Upright rowing

Lower Body

Because your lower body works constantly while riding, these exercises give attention to muscles that are synergists during pedaling. Evaluate your riding style to determine whether you would benefit from resistance training for your quadriceps, gluteals, and iliopsoas. When you use your gears effectively and maintain a minimum cadence of 80 rpm, resistance training on your bike is limited. You can increase the resistance training on your bike by climbing hills or riding with a load of 30 pounds or more. If you ride rolling and flat terrain most of the time, you will increase your stamina by incorporating exercises that build up the strength in your pedaling muscles. With free weights these could include lunges, single leg squats, and step-ups.

You may want to use ankle weights for these lower body exercises. Avoid walking while wearing weights because they slow the response time of your feet and could cause you to fall. Try these exercises first without ankle weights and add weights when your technique is good and when you need the progressive resistance.

Outer-thigh lifts — Strengthen your outer thighs (tensor fascia latae), buttocks (gluts), and lower back. The stabilizers are the abdominals and paraspinals. *Starting position* - Lie on a padded floor surface on your right side while keeping your body in a straight line. Comfortably support your upper torso on your right elbow and use your left hand to help balance your body. Keep your feet aligned forward. *Movement* - Extending the heel of your left leg, raise your left leg smoothly and slowly upward

Outer-thigh lifts

Inner-thigh lifts

about 12 to 16 inches. (If you are not using weights you may be comfortable raising your leg higher.) Do not twist your body out of your original linear position. Slowly lower your leg to the starting position. Perform the desired number of reps and then switch onto the left side to repeat the exercise.

Variations to help you find a position you like.

a. Keep your right shoulder on the floor and rest your head on your right arm.

b. Support your head on your right hand with elbow bent.

Inner-thigh lifts — Strengthen the inner thigh and groin. The stabilizers are the paraspinals, abdominals, and hip flexors. The muscles of the inner thigh are usually weak. Keeping them well-toned will support healthful knee alignment. If your pelvis is wide, this exercise is especially beneficial for your knees. *Starting position* - Start in the same position as for the outer-thigh lifts. Bend your left knee and hip and place the sole of your left foot on the floor in front of your right knee, allowing enough space to lift your right leg. Keep one hip above the other. *Movement* - Slowly, keeping your right foot flexed and aligned forward and your right leg straight, lift your right leg as high as comfortable without leaning your hips forward or back. Slowly lower your leg and repeat the desired number of reps. Roll onto your left side and repeat lifting the left leg.

Toe raises — Strengthen the calves (gastrocnemius and soleus muscles) and feet. Synergist is the peroneus on the outside of the ankle. *Starting position* - Place your toes and the balls of your feet on a two-by-four, shoulder width apart and with your feet aligned forward. For support, position yourself between two chair backs or beside a door frame. To develop your balance, only use support as you begin to lose your balance. *Movement* - Slowly let your heels relax down to a comfortable point below your toes. Slowly rise up as high as you can on the balls of your feet and then return to the starting position. Experiment with holding for a while on the highest and lowest range of movement.

Variations to increase the resistance over time:

a. Use only one leg at a time, keeping your hips level.

Toe raises

b. Hold a dumbbell in the hand of the leg being exercised.

c. To work the synergists, rise up and place more weight on the inside of the ball of the foot and then with more weight on the outside ball.

Ankle rocker — Strengthens and stretches the tibialis anterior, gastrocnemius, soleus, and peroneus. This is a standing variation on the foot circles described on p. 171. *Starting position* - Stand with your feet three to six inches apart and aligned forward. *Movement* - Rock slowly around on the outside edges of your feet starting at your heels, roll to one side, to your toes, and to the other side. Your knees should make small, circular motions in the same direction your feet are rocking. Repeat in the opposite direction.

Ankle rocker

Diagonal hip swings — Strengthen the quadriceps, hip abductors, adductors, and extensors. You will probably want to use ankle weights as soon as you feel coordinated performing this exercise. *Starting position* - While supporting yourself with your left hand on a chair or door frame, bear your weight on your left leg and swing your right leg back and out to the side at a 45-degree angle. Keep the toes relaxed and your right foot flexed without pointing it. On the next four count, swing your leg back through the starting position and across to the left at a 45-degree angle. Perform the desired number of reps, face the other way, and repeat swinging the left leg. Maintain your vertical alignment and avoid leaning with the swing.

Yoga postures:

a. Warrior strengthens the quads, pp. 211-212.

b. Bridge strengthens the gluts, quads, and inner thighs. It also opens the diaphragm and stimulates the thyroid glands. Refer to p. 213.

Diagonal hip swings

When you have built the strength you desire, your emphasis will shift to maintenance. This is the time to be creative. Your understanding of the principles of resistance training will enable you to develop variations on individual exercises and to design your own routine. These variations will help you maintain your interest and enjoyment. Here are some guidelines for this new phase:

1. Retain your favorite exercises.

2. Vary others to maintain your interest and challenge.

3. Substitute appropriate new exercises, train with a partner or with background music, change the time and location of your practice.

You may come to a point in your training routine when you don't recognize any visible progress. This is known as the sticking point. Continue to work through this with confidence that progress is being made under the surface. It is just like planting a seed in the ground. You can't know that anything is happening until it sprouts.

Empowering Yourself with Affirmations and Visualizations

Your mind is a powerful tool that you can engage to improve your health and your performance as well as to achieve your goals. This may sound strange if you believe your mind is the essence of your being. Instead, consider your mind as one tool in your box of resources along with your body, psyche, spirit, vital energy, social relations, and nature's renewing energy. Too often we waste our mind's power by letting it race uncontrolled, chasing after scheduling demands and daily worries. When we understand how our minds work and how to quiet and direct them, the results will be nothing short of amazing.

The decisions we make, the attitudes we hold, and the limitations we impose on ourselves are created by our minds. However, it is the subconscious that directs, regulates, and implements our actions. Yes, 90 percent of our power resides in our subconscious, leaving 10 percent of our power in our conscious control. How convenient it would be if we could just lift the lids on our subconsciouses and set the dials. Lacking such direct controls, how can we influence them? We must program them with persuasive directives so they become part of our operating systems.

Human internal structure functions much like our state governments. The governor (our conscious minds) offers ideas and direction but most actions depend on the legislature for implementation. However, legislators (our subconsciouses) are influenced by special interest groups, campaign contributions, and lobbyists – all pulling emotions this way and that. Programs may result that benefit the citizens of the state but all too often, intentions become blurred, emotions run high, factions develop, and the final actions rarely bear much resemblance to the ideas of the governors. Only if governors are focused and demonstrate outstanding leadership abilities are legislatures likely to implement their wishes. Our conscious and subconscious minds perform in an analogous manner. The conscious mind creates an idea with the best intentions of designing a plan and getting results. The subconscious mind, on the other hand, interjects its own agenda causing many ideas to not manifest at all, much less as they were conceived. Our achievement rates can be greatly increased by using affirmations and visualization.

Our motivation to be positive will increase when we recognize that we live in a negative society that dwells on the adverse effects of all aspects of life. You'll need some protection from this onslaught. Devise a plan to reduce your exposure to daily negativity. First, however, you need to address the many negative messages you carry within.

Our training in negative thought patterns begins in early childhood. I'm sure you can remember a few admonitions from your parents: "Don't make a mess." "Don't bump over that chair." "You're clumsy." "You can't play ball as well as your sister." As children we believed these things because our limited experience gave us few accurate comparisons and because no one was counteracting them. Nagging and criticism only make us feel inadequate and bad about ourselves. Having little or no training for parenting, most parents are unaware that the most effective means of changing behavior is to praise desirable behavior. Supporting positive actions builds self-worth and confidence, which are the foundations of further positive actions.

Fortunately, as adults we are not bound to the negative images we learned as children and can reverse ingrained negative images. We can systematically displace them with accurate, positive statements of our worth, skills, and abilities. We can begin by reviewing past experiences and feedback received from thoughtful individuals we respect. We can remind ourselves of our successes in coping with challenging situations in the past. Repeatedly reminding ourselves of these successes can persuade our subconsciouses that the messages of childhood are not valid and that we are capable and lovable.

Another tactic is to consciously avoid negative people and negative discussions. Next time a friend or stranger burdens you with their unsolicited litany of grievances, notice how it leaves you exhausted and in a bad mood. Learn to turn such conversations toward possible solutions and avoid contact with such people whenever possible. If you are forced to work with whiners, learn to be amused by their unfortunate attitudes and perspectives. When discussions deteriorate into complaint sessions, ask yourself if the generalizations of doom and gloom actually do affect your quality of life and if so what you can do to improve things. I'm not suggesting that you become a smiling fool but that you not engage in non-productive recitations of misfortunes and poor judgments. Sharpen your critical thinking by accurately evaluating the circumstances and by focusing on solutions. Avoid reciting everyone else's contributions to the problem.

Be selective in your choice of media, entertainment, and news sources. Distinguish between sensational reporting that creates a sense of hopelessness and thoughtful reporting that includes glimmers of hope and stories of similar situations where individuals made positive changes. Make a pact with yourself to find one positive news story every day.

Where will you find it? Look for publications that strive to inform rather than sensationalize. My favorite is the *Christian Science Monitor* because it gives a consistently accurate worldview.

The next step is to unburden your mind of distractions. Accurate perception of reality requires that you make a conscious effort to remove clutter from your mind and your life. Use the same discerning criteria to choose your activities as you do to select your friends, news, and entertainment sources. Avoid continually chasing after new experiences and social contacts that distract your attention from meaningful goals.

Learn to appreciate yourself and you will find it easier to let go of activities that distract you from achieving your goals. Identifying your priorities requires that you understand yourself. Self-knowledge is more important than all the facts you memorized in school. Take time to recognize your strengths and weaknesses and fully accept yourself just as you naturally are. As you work toward change, be gentle and forgiving. Embrace unexpected results and pitfalls along the way, realizing that they are part of an imperfect process.

Retraining your mind empowers you to influence your subconscious; heal and direct your body; increase your self-love and self-worth; improve your professional and physical performance; brighten your attitude; and build nurturing, productive relationships.

The conscious mind addresses the subconscious. The more forceful and vivid the communication, the more effective it is. Contemporary research demonstrates that your brain communicates with the rest of your body and is effective in making changes. (Sarno 1998, p. 145) You must invest time and effort in consciously choosing the direction you want to go if you are to affect change. Rather than thinking, "There is no way I can get over this virus before the bike tour," identify your priorities, affirm your direction, and take action. Try saying, "I am going to get adequate sleep, fluids, and nourishment, and recover in time to enjoy the tour." Feelings of helplessness exacerbate emotional stress and weaken your resolve to affect healing and change. You will have more confidence in your success by acknowledging that you are not alone in your problem but that many people have faced this particular problem. This recognition relieves stress and empowers you to solve your problems. Empowerment is strong medicine.

Make a habit of thinking positively of yourself. Negative self-talk is sure to sabotage your efforts. Instead of saying, "I have really poor stamina," try saying, "I am improving my stamina with adequate sleep, food, and frequent exercise." Rather than saying, "I can't learn to use toe clips," say, "I'm learning to use toe clips to increase my stamina and muscle symmetry." Then proceed to learn and feel confident that you will succeed.

You will improve your performance in all realms of your life by affirming your ability to achieve desired results. Rather than dwelling on the fact that you have undertaken a task that is over your head, tell yourself that you can creatively find a solution even when that means finding the appropriate person or resource to help you learn the needed skills. Recently I was challenged by trying to create a chart on my word processor and was not making any headway. As I rode to work I thought, "I'm in over my head." I caught myself thinking this limiting thought and displaced it with, "I'm going to think of some creative solution or redesign the chart." Promptly, I remembered I hadn't liked the layout when my designer first created it and visualized another design that I was confident I had the skills to create. I wasted no time stewing about my inadequacies but moved directly on to a solution.

Affirmations are magic for adjusting attitudes. Instead of repeating daily that a work associate is driving you crazy, tell yourself that he or she is the fool in a play or the clown at the circus. Assure yourself that you can be the spectator and respond to your associate's ire or poor judgment without getting sucked in emotionally. I once found myself getting irritated with people who used poor judgment in maintaining their bicycles. That made it increasingly difficult for me to be gracious and help them learn how to care for their bikes. I resolved to change my attitude and examined what made me out of sorts. I began using the affirmation, "I am amused by poor judgment (mine as well as others')." Within a couple days I had no problem being cheerful when riders brought their negligently damaged bikes in for service. I have also enjoyed more frequent laughs at myself when I make poor decisions.

How often we sabotage relationships by negatively characterizing someone important in our lives. By releasing that person from the negative hold we have on them, we can create an honest and positive image in our minds causing relations to spontaneously improve. After many years as an employer, I was startled to discover a disturbing pattern. When I burned out from too many hours at work, I unconsciously began to blame my employees for my self-imposed fate. Rather than searching for solutions within my control, I harbored ill thoughts about certain employees. That is not to say that my discontent with their work was not initiated by inadequate performance but that by directing my negative emotions toward those employees, I sabotaged their ability to perform satisfactorily. It was no wonder that those employees' performance progressively declined until I let them go. Now I understand that the negative energy I directed toward them weakened them and limited their ability to perform up to standards. When I develop a negative characterization of someone, I now take time to identify the origins of my feelings and think of something positive about the person. Otherwise that relationship will spin into a downward spiral.

The first step in using affirmations and visualizing to transform your life is to define your goals and ambitions. Be sure to include your health and fitness goals as well as your life goals. What do you want to add to your life? What do you want to subtract? Removing clutter from your life is an essential step in concentrating your focus on fewer goals. You will achieve your goals twice as fast when you are dividing your energy among three goals rather than six. Your energy goes where your mind goes. When you define your goals and give them your attention, you will achieve them.

Schedule a time without distractions to identify your priorities and define your goals. I recommend a solitary bicycle ride to a quiet place with an inspiring view. Ask yourself what you want to become and what you want to achieve. Take along some paper so you can record your ambitions.

Visualizations are images you create of you achieving your goals. They focus on the process of reaching your goal or on your achieving them. They help you conceptualize the details. They help your mindbody perceive just what you want. Performance imagery involves mentally rehearsing a task while you are relaxed. When the time comes to perform, each step feels familiar, and you will do a better job. Visualizations optimize your performance in strength training, retraining your riding technique, mitigating pain, directing body energy during acupressure, and facilitating healing during Qigong practice. Create an image for body energy that is effective for you. You might imagine healing energy as cleansing spring water or pure, white light.

After you have defined your goals, carefully write out appropriate affirmations. I recommend the system described by Dr. Alan Zimmerman in his CD GOALS: *Good Intentions Are Never Good Enough*. (www.drzimmerman.com/tools/productinformation/cd3.htm) As you formulate your affirmations use these three rules:

1. Use the present tense. Your mind takes information at face value. Although your subconscious may balk at first, be firm and convincing, and it will accept your assertion. Say, "I practice my stretching fifteen minutes every day."

2. Make it personal. These are to transform you; you cannot wish changes into other people. Say, "I have an excellent memory with clear and instant recall."

3. Express a positive direction. Use only positive words. Instead of saying, "I don't tense up when I ride narrow trails," say, "I remain relaxed in challenging riding situations."

Other qualities to include in your affirmations that will make them more fun and effective:

4. Be as specific as possible. Rather than saying, "I am losing weight by exercising daily," say, "I weigh a trim 145 pounds."

5. Include feeling words. Say, "I am amused by poor judgment."

6. Use modifiers such as, "I love myself unconditionally."

You should feel good saying your affirmations. If you feel consistently poor when you say one, it is probably not a good choice for you. Replace it with a different form or an entirely different idea. Your mind can handle 10 to 15 affirmations at a time but effectiveness is increased by concentrating on six or eight.

You will need to be consistent in your practice. Say them each four or five times, three times each day. You can recite them silently or aloud. The more senses you can involve the better. Visualize your result. Create drawings or cut out pictures to remind you of your goals. Write them down when time permits. Use flash cards. Choose a time when you are relaxed and without distractions. Attach your practice to certain activities during each day. Say them morning and evening and maybe before meditation or stretching practice. I always say mine at the same place on my ride home each night on a bike path where I am not concerned with traffic. It is important not to miss a single practice so you might find it helpful to record them and play them to yourself when you are feeling low on motivation.

How long will it take to see results? Dr. Zimmerman says it could be two days or two years. It takes 21 days to get them into the subconscious. Characteristically around day 10 to 14, you will start making excuses for not practicing. This is your mind resisting change. Make up gimmicks to get through this period. Bear in mind that habitual thought patterns will take longer to change.

Optimize your progress. Select goals that are physically possible. Affirmations are not miracles but they are a means to focus all of your resources on achieving results. Be discrete and share them only with positive people, not with skeptics. Be persistent. Don't be fooled when you observe some progress and then slack off or you will lose ground quickly. Continue saying each affirmation for months until it is fully ingrained and part of your basic nature. Beware of self-limiting thought patterns. Dr. Zimmerman calls these "mind binders." They will consume your energy. Whenever an old mind binder comes up, just tell it, "Get off my back," or "I'm awesome and can handle this!"

Using affirmations and visualizations is really fun. They are personal pep talks that strengthen your personal outlook and empower you. They banish the victim mentality. Surely we would all benefit from some basic ones:

"I love myself unconditionally." "I am worthy." "I am patient, skillful, and understanding in dealing with coworkers and family." "I am full of enthusiasm."

Affirmations heal us physically, mentally, emotionally, and spiritually. "It may sound too good to be true. But the evidence is quite clear. A thought or a goal held firmly, repeatedly, in the conscious mind will eventually seep into the subconscious and become part of your operating system." (Dr. Zimmerman's Tuesday Tip, 4/21/03) I recommend that you subscribe to the *Tuesday Tips* for weekly support in becoming a consistently positive and can-do person. Sign up free at www.drzimmerman.com/free_resources/newsletter/tuesdaytip.htm

Journaling for Reflection and Quieting Your Mind

Journaling will help you get your thoughts and concerns out of your head and down on paper. Writing crystallizes thought.

- Begin by reflecting on your thoughts, feelings, and experiences. How did your day go? What did you accomplish? What would you do differently? How would you like to handle tomorrow? Or if you journal in the morning before meditation, you might ask: What did the quality of sleep indicate about my degree of contentment? Do my dreams provide any insights (amusements or fears) for me? What challenges does today's schedule provide and how can I address them creatively?

- Think through the challenges and make a plan. Make a list to take with you the following day.

- Nebulous worries sap your strength and accomplish nothing. Try to identify the source of your concern. Determine if there are solutions for this problem. If there are, your worries are not necessary. You'll deal with it at the right time. If solutions are not readily apparent, you can't fix the problem by worrying about it. Put this challenge on your list until you can give it your full attention. Once you focus your energy on any task you will be able to identify appropriate options. Either the solution will become clear or you will discover the next step toward resolution. You might even *enjoy* working toward resolving the challenge.

- Try reading some of your journal entries from previous days. You can monitor the progress you have made and look for patterns in your behavior and responses to circumstances and challenges. Consciously developing new attitudes and choosing new behaviors is a great way to get off the treadmill of life. As a friend so wisely says: the goal is to live 365 unique days each year and not the same one over and over again.

A Testimony to the Benefits of Journaling

A dear friend, Wilma, was traumatized by the suicide of her teenage step-grandson. They had shared a close and loving relationship, and Wilma had delighted in supporting him in his many achievements. The task of sorting out his possessions and cleaning his room had fallen to her while her heart was heavy with grief. During the process, she discovered things that were so emotionally devastating that she decided she could not share them with anyone else. The burden weighed heavily on her and interfered with her sleep and digestive process. Her doctor of many years picked up on her anxiety and emotional burden and prescribed medication to help her sleep and to relieve her indigestion.

Wilma shared this story with me after suffering for months. I suggested she might try to write down her feelings and then destroy her writing if she was fearful someone would discover her secret. The next day she left to return to the state where the suicide had occurred. It would not be an easy journey. She would visit her step-grandson's family and support another daughter during heart surgery.

Six weeks later upon her return, Wilma volunteered the information that she had taken up journaling, and the release was so much more effective than the medication that she had discontinued taking it. She had frequently taken time to herself to journal and protected her little book as a companion in her suffering and healing process.

I recommend you also keep a **fitness journal**. Keep it in a separate book from your mental health journal. Record your observations of the influence of rest, nutrition, and integrated health practices on your performance. As you examine the patterns of your performance, you will become more sensitive to the relationship of your health practices to your sense of wellness. Progress is not just linear so enhance the depth and breadth by keeping tract of subtle changes as well as measurable changes. Be sure to record the number of reps and amount of weight used during strength training so increases can be appropriately gradual to ensure steady progression without injury or other setbacks. If you are inclined to take your pulse upon waking or record ride distances, your fitness journal will consolidate all this information and make it more useful. In any case, have fun and keep your focus on the larger picture of your personal wellness and contentment.

Beginning a Meditation Practice

Meditation has been practiced for thousands of years and is gradually finding greater acceptance in the U.S. The reasons to meditate and the benefits are many and varied. Perhaps the most helpful description in a predominantly Christian culture is that:

Prayer is talking. Meditation is listening.

Another description is: **Meditation is being, not doing**. Avoid judging, conceptualizing, or pursuing intrusive thoughts. Simply breathe consciously, let go of intrusive thoughts, and quiet your busy mind. When your mind chatter stops, revelations will come to you. These revelations may be creative ideas, a welling up of inner strength, a flood of compassion, or an uncovering of hidden emotions. Or perhaps you will simply experience tranquillity and clarity of mind. If you have not practiced meditation, you might benefit from the many books on the subject. Beware of methods that engage you in *doing* things. Here are just a few tips to encourage you to get started.

- Find a peaceful place away from distractions.

- Make yourself completely comfortable. You may choose to sit in a traditional position. I recommend you avoid the full lotus and Zen position with feet folded back under your buttocks. The full lotus strains your knees, and the Zen position cuts off circulation to your lower legs. Try the half-lotus or the cow pose, p. 187, which is especially beneficial for cyclists. Sit in a straight-backed chair if that is more comfortable.

- Begin by closing your eyes to shut out visual stimulation.

- Keep your back and head erect to promote the flow of energy up your spinal column. Support an erect spine by holding your hips vertical. Regularly stretching your hamstrings will make this easier. If you begin to slump, visualize pushing energy up your spine with each exhalation. With practice, this technique will make sitting erect quite effortless.

- To get started, simply observe your breathing. Gradually move into SELF breathing — controlled, diaphragmatic breathing that is Slow, Even, Long, and Full. If that is helpful but not adequate, try three-part or 1:2 breathing. Books on Yoga and meditation will provide many more breathing exercises.

- Whenever your mind wanders, gently release the thoughts and draw your attention back to a peaceful quiet. Initially you may find that visualizations, like imaging an oscilloscope with a flat line on it, help. Imagine that each thought causes the straight line to become wavy and release the thoughts by returning to the straight line. Or coordinate your breathing with an imagined tracing up and down the contours of your body. With each inhalation, begin at the coccyx, trace up the contours of your spine, and over the top of your head. On the exhalation, trace down the front surface of the center line of your body to the perineum.

- When you are compelled to engage in a high-pressure schedule, you may have difficulty settling into meditation and getting in touch with yourself. Try searching your being for your *essential self*. You may look for your essence in a part of your body or just scan your consciousness for the true you. Finding your essential self, however you image that, is wonderfully grounding and mind clearing.

- Chanting a classic mantra or singing can change your breathing with calming rhythms.

- If strong emotions well up, gently breathe into them wherever they seem to manifest in your body.

- Be accepting of what you experience and remain open, free of expectations.

- Continue each session as long as you appreciate the experience but avoid prolonged practice sessions. Ten minutes is a good beginning practice. Your meditation experience should be effortless and revealing.

- Journaling before meditation can get projects and concerns on paper and help clear your mind.

Meditation techniques are vehicles to help you explore and discover yourself. The techniques do not ensure a change in consciousness but do increase the likelihood of emerging insights. These exercises allow you to personally discover that there are different moods, attitudes, and states of consciousness from your everyday state of chronic low-grade stress. They can enable you to be more aware of your feelings and condition and your *ability to control* them.

Maintaining a regular practice for several weeks will help you experience benefits sooner. Another function of practice is to have the skill available in difficult times. The more we practice the easier it is to initiate meditating when we feel low, vulnerable, highly emotional, or scattered. It may be more challenging to quiet our minds, calm our emotions, and integrate our mind and body during these times, and meditating can help. Transformations during meditation may release worries, reduce vulnerability to life's pressures, or increase compassion. It is quite remarkable that as you practice over the months and years, the ability to quiet the mind and emotions becomes easier. From the initial experiences of spending most of your practice time letting go of intrusive thoughts, you can progress to enjoying an ever-increasing quiet and effortless feeling of inner calm.

I would not be honest discussing integrated cycling and health while ignoring spiritual development. Surely individual spiritual experiences vary widely. I observe that some people possess a compelling drive for spiritual growth, some are nonchalant in their interest, some are indifferent, and still others strongly deny the spiritual aspect of their human nature. I encourage you to make space for your spiritual nature. It can be a reliable source of inner strength. If you have not tapped this resource, it is worth some practice to find and develop it. It can bring balance to your life, increase your energy and contentment, improve your performance in all activities, and increase your joy in all your relationships. Spiritual growth developed through study and meditation can be fulfilling. The cravings and drives manifested in food obsessions, extreme sports, and the consuming pursuit of career or wealth can be symptoms of unfulfilled spiritual practice and development. Balance, both physical and mental, both intellectual and emotional, is a manifestation of continuing enrichment of spirit, body, intellect, and emotions.

In recent years the medical community in the U.S. is acknowledging the relationship of spirit and healing. Increasing evidence brings to light that meditation has a strong healing effect on imbalances in the autonomic nervous system (the involuntary nervous system). Regular practice can influence such disorders as high blood pressure, anxiety disorders, pain, and gastrointestinal problems. Developing a regular, daily meditation practice is a vital tool for maintaining wellness and facilitating healing. (Weil, *Self Healing*, April, 2001)

Responding to Seasonal Change

Seasonal variations are dimensions you can use to integrate your wellness. Since intimacy with nature is diminished by large houses and comfortable cars, we tend to disregard the changes in the seasons. If you'll thoughtfully observe the differences in your moods and activity levels between July and November, you'll surely discover a contrast. Consciously adapting to these changes can contribute to your health and your pleasure in each season. Try selecting foods that are harvested during the current season. Savor the soft fruits of summer in the summer and relish winter squashes or make some pumpkin custard or bread in the fall.

Fall is a healing season, and you will be wise to respond to the natural urge to slow down, eat more, and sleep longer. The task of fall is to renew yourself from the summer's exertion and excitement and store up energy for the demands of winter. (My apologies to riders in the Southern Hemisphere who must adjust the months mentioned here.) It is natural to eat more when the weather turns cooler, and you need more calories to keep warm. Just avoid overindulging. Spend more time relaxing and getting adequate sleep but keep exercising so you don't lose the fitness you developed in summer. Take time to create an exercise plan that will keep your spirits *and* energy level up during shorter days. Perhaps sharing a fitness class with friends will appeal to you. If you enjoy quiet time at home when the streets are messy, develop your Yoga or Taiji practice. Be sure your winter cycling clothes are ready, and your bike is in good repair (maybe add fenders) so you can ride on sunny, warmer winter days when the streets are clear. It is especially worthwhile to maintain your fitness level from September to the start of ski season if you are a skier.

On the other hand, use your good judgment and restraint to avoid burnout in the summer. Riders often commit to summer riding events, train too intensely, and are burned out by mid-summer. Pace yourself in training for any multiple-day cycling events. Vary the length, energy level, and route of your training rides to keep it fun. Constantly compelling yourself to train increases the likelihood of burnout. Select events that are within your grasp each season. If you have never done a week-long tour, start with a relaxed, three-day tour and take time to build up for a longer tour the next season. It is difficult to maintain balance and pace yourself if you must pressure yourself to prepare.

In the spring, temper your yearnings for warm, dry weather by inspecting your equipment and making sure it is ready. Be especially thoughtful about gradually building up your tolerance to your bike seat. Frequent rides of 10 miles or less will help you condition your butt without damage.

Variety is the spice of life, and the changing seasons can be an inspiration for change.

Some Basics on Massage

Massage aids healing and recovery and increases knowledge of your body and your awareness of its condition. It rejuvenates and integrates your mind and body. The resulting relaxation creates a fresh perspective. Increasing evidence shows that the condition of your musculature reflects the state of your mind and nervous system. Bodywork can improve both and is another route to reach the subconscious mind.

Massage can be performed for you or you can do it yourself. Of course, it is wonderful to have a massage from a professional therapist who is technically trained and whose skills are heightened by years of experience. Regular visits to a nurturing massage therapist will support your effort to care for yourself. However, you can also learn and develop the skills for self-massage and to share the joys of human touch with friends and family. Certainly the most accessible massage is self-massage. You are always available to yourself. You know just where your discomforts are and how you would like to treat them.

How does massage work? Through the activity of manipulating the skin, tissue, and joints, massage increases blood flow, improves range of motion, and warms and softens tissues. This manipulation can be sports-specific when you focus on those muscle groups worked hard by a particular sport. While prolonged activity causes muscles to shorten, massage relaxes and lengthens them, restoring flexibility and comfort. *Cautionary note:* massage should never be expected to take the place of stretching. Stretching lengthens muscles more effectively than massage.

Using your fingers or a massage tool, you can identify tight muscles by locating tender places. When you find those sore and tender spots, you can massage them before complications arise. The increased blood flow caused by manipulation not only facilitates healing but also helps flush out chemicals that cause muscle stiffness and soreness. Manipulation can help open those invisible channels of energy flow in the body called meridians and utilize acupressure points.

Here are some tips to help you:

Gradually increase pressure while working on each muscle group. Begin by brushing your hand over your muscles. Gradually increase pressure as you sense the condition of the muscles and as they relax. Be sensitive to the amount of pressure you apply as well as to the tightness of the tissue you are working on. Superficial muscles must be loosened before it is possible to manipulate deeper muscles. When you first touch the muscles you want to massage, you may not feel any knots. Patiently continue gentle massage until the superficial muscles have released, enabling you to determine the condition of the muscles below. Try this easy experiment. Close your eyes, place the fingers of your hands on your temples, and gently rub them making small circular movements. Do they feel smooth without tenderness? Continue massaging them and the surrounding area for a couple minutes while you direct your breath to them. Now can you feel firm lumps and tenderness below the superficial muscles?

Use a caring touch. Healing benefits can be increased if you focus affirmations of wellness and appreciation on the part of the body being worked. To facilitate the opening of tight muscles, breathe deeply and mentally bring your breath into the area being manipulated.

Seek out and experiment with massage tools. You probably have some stray tennis balls around the house. They are excellent tools for reaching tight back muscles that are difficult to reach with your hands.

Tennis ball massage — Put two tennis balls in a stocking or sock and tie it off so the balls are held adjacent to each other. Lie on your back on the floor. Select a surface that is soft enough to allow tolerable pressure by the tennis ball. Place the balls under your neck at the base of your skull and progress down your spine to your sacrum. Relax onto the balls and breathe into any discomfort created by the balls. Enjoy the progressive relaxation for two minutes or less and then roll on top of the balls moving them down another inch or two. Gradually work down the back or across your trapezius muscles, applying this relaxing pressure anywhere that you would like to massage. If you have two tender areas, work one or two balls along the line between them. Repeating this in the morning and evening can greatly relax your shoulders, neck, and back. It will also help you discover tender and tight places you may never have reached. Refer to further details under "Exercises to Condition Your Back," Chapter 5, p. 225.

For more details on massage, refer to the many books available on this subject. Joan Johnson's *The Healing Art of Sports Massage* is a concise resource.

Pressure Point Therapy

Acupressure is an ancient Chinese system of applying pressure to key points on the skin to stimulate the body's natural healing abilities. Pressure on the designated points releases muscle tension, relieves pressure on nerves, stimulates circulation, balances vital energy, and inhibits transfer of pain messages to the brain. It supports your ability to understand and participate actively in caring for yourself and the healing process. The purpose of acupressure is to aid and encourage your body to correct its own imbalances.

You are probably familiar with acupuncture that uses tiny needles to stimulate the same acupoints. Acupressure preceded acupuncture in development and continues to be the more effective method of self-treatment for tension-related ailments. Because it uses your hands for treatment, it is available and safe to use any time and any place. Acupressure has no negative side effects but some restrictions are appropriate for people who have specific medical conditions or who are pregnant. You should also avoid applying pressure on bruises, scars, or injuries.

When you are choosing among the tools presented here in this chapter, pressure point therapy is a good practice to begin with. It is easy to learn to do effectively and the beneficial results are immediate. Fifteen minutes a day will be more transforming than the weekly use of massage or stretching. Daily practice is essential to optimize results. To begin, select an area of your body that is particularly tight or causing discomfort and apply acupressure to several points over that area. In addition to opening this area to health and healing, this attention to your needs will nurture you psychologically.

Acupressure points are usually located on or near some anatomical feature that will help you find them such as a muscular cord, a tension knot, or on the indentation or protrusion of a bone. These points are especially sensitive to bioelectrical impulses and conduct those impulses readily. Descriptions of the acupoints will get you close to the point, but the exact location varies among individuals and must be found by touch. You will experience tenderness at the precise point, which you might describe as achy, burning, or tingling. You may also experience referred sensation, for example, pressure on acupoints on the forearm may give a sense of warmth or create movement in your hand.

All points are located on energy pathways known as *meridians*, which run lengthwise along the body and are paired on both the right and left sides of your body. Meridians connect every aspect of physiological and anatomical function. To function well, every part of the body must be in balance and work in harmony with the entire system. If these channels are healthy, the entire system works harmoniously. If they are damaged or inefficient, messages are not clear or not in sync, and the entire system suffers. The Chinese identified this system more than 2,000 years ago. Today, modern medicine has been able to confirm this network using sensitive electrical measuring devices.

You might think of meridians as the routes by which the mind pervades the body. When you feel a certain emotion, body and mind are transformed simultaneously as predictable chemical processes at the cellular level are elicited by the emotions. You need not ask whether the mind or body initiates the response or restricts the mind to the brain or some invisible mysterious realm. Emotional and physical health are tied together by one system. Western science attributes these phenomena to neuropeptides while Chinese science attributes them to vital energy or qi. (Cohen, p. 224-226)

Most meridians are named after internal organs. Rather than referring directly to the physical organ, the names refer to bodily functions. For example, according to traditional Chinese medicine the health of the immune system is governed primarily by the condition of the kidney, liver, lungs, and spleen. Stimulating acupoints along these meridians

A Key to the Standard Names and Abbreviations of Meridians

B	Bladder
CV	Conception Vessel
GB	Gallbladder
GV	Governing Vessel
H	Heart
K	Kidney
LI	Large Intestines
Lu	Lung
Lv	Liver
P	Pericardium
SI	Small Intestines
Sp	Spleen
St	Stomach
TW	Triple Warmer

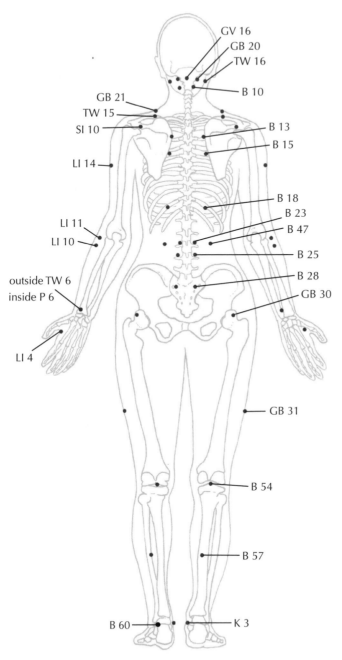

GV 16
GB 20
TW 16
B 10
GB 21
TW 15
SI 10
B 13
B 15
LI 14
B 18
B 23
LI 11
B 47
LI 10
B 25
outside TW 6
inside P 6
B 28
GB 30
LI 4
GB 31
B 54
B 57
B 60
K 3

As you practice acupressure using the points given under each body part in Chapter 5, refer to this anatomic chart to help you locate them. To simplify organization, acupoints are listed with the body part where they are located. You will also find descriptions of their broader benefits and effects on distant parts of the body.

does fortify these organs, but also recharges the body to increase resistance to the inevitable stresses and strains of daily life. (Gach, p. 53) Each acupoint has a poetic name but I will use the letter-numeric designation. For example, a point key to the entire nervous system is Heavenly Pillar or B10. (Gach, p. 22) That designation means it is the tenth point on the bladder meridian.

Three meridians have names that are body functions unfamiliar to Westerners. The triple warmer's function is to regulate the balance of heat and moisture in the body. The upper warmer is the head, chest, heart, and lungs. The middle warmer is the solar plexus, including the spleen and stomach. The lower warmer is the lower abdomen including the liver and kidneys. (Cohen, p. 166) I hope this description of an ancient system will make it feel familiar and more accessible to you.

The benefits of acupressure will be optimized when you select a quiet and relaxed environment. Use SELF breathing and bring your attention to the healing point. Visualize increasing the strength and flexibility of the area, and if pain is present, visualize it leaving your body. Avoid practicing after a heavy meal when your blood is diverted to your digestive system or when you are especially hungry. Wait for about an hour after eating. If time and place permit, enjoy a hot herbal tea or a period of deep relaxation after practice.

Cultivate an appreciation for good **technique**. Direct pressure toward the center of your body but you can experiment with the angle of approach to find the most sensitive point. Before applying pressure, massage the area surrounding the point. Unless the area is extremely tight or painful, probing for the exact location will be adequate. This massage warms and relaxes the superficial muscles increasing access to deeper tissue. Gradually apply pressure, hold a steady, penetrating pressure, and then release gradually. Time lapse might be five to ten seconds to gradually apply pressure, thirty or more seconds to maintain pressure, and release gradually over five to ten seconds. You will generally experience an aching or "good hurt," but if it hurts a great deal, use a lighter touch. You may use your middle finger, thumb, or three longest fingers but the middle finger on each hand is the strongest and most sensitive. Limit practice on any area of the body to 15 minutes since the effects can be quite strong. If you stimulate several points on your legs, avoid exerting them the rest of the day. In addition to direct pressure, you can experiment with using a slow kneading motion, brisk rubbing to create warmth, or repeated patting with finger tips or a loose fist.

As you gain experience, you can customize your practice to your needs. You will notice as you apply pressure to each point that the tenderness subsides with time. You can begin to release pressure as the tenderness diminishes. As you become familiar with the response of each point, you can concentrate on the more sensitive points that need attention and skip ones that are not sensitive. However, be sure to foster energy balance by applying pressure to the corresponding points on both sides of the body. If the point on one side of your body is more sensitive than on the other side, give it more attention. Use the variations in sensation as a guide to your current state of health and physical condition. As you work any area, begin closest to your head and work away, opening the channels of communication from your central nervous system. When you are finished working an area, brush your hand over the area with gentle strokes to draw excess energy out of the area.

Treatment can benefit muscles and nerves at the site of pressure as well as muscles and organs distant from that point. These are referred to respectively as *local* and *trigger* points. If you have an injury, do not apply pressure directly to the sensitive, injured area since the stimulation could increase inflammation.

There are many resources to guide your practice. I have drawn the suggested exercises in Chapter 5 primarily from Michael Reed Gach's *Acupressure's Potent Points: A Guide to Self-Care for Common Ailments* and Marc Coseo's *The Acupressure Warm-Up for Athletic Preparation and Injury Management.* You may also choose among Shiatsu books. Shiatsu developed in Japan from Chinese origins. It applies firm, rhythmic pressure along a series of points on one meridian. Reflexology is another pressure point therapy developed in the U.S. that activates points that correspond to body parts and organs. The points are primarily in the feet and secondarily in the hands. Still another system coordinates points in the ears with muscles, joints, and organs.

Acupressure benefits athletic performance by promoting properly balanced physical, mental, and psychological attitudes. Competitors often achieve a personal best performance following acupressure or acupuncture. They benefit from increased circulation warming muscles and joints, improved coordination resulting from adequate communication between brain, nerves, and muscles, stronger muscles, complete range of movement, and stable joints.

Acupressure can be used with stretching as a warm-up. Refer to Coseo's *The Acupressure Warm-Up* for stretches beneficial to each meridian. You can custom design a warm-up to stimulate joints and muscles that are used heavily in cycling or whatever activity you are beginning. You can give attention to parts of your body that are susceptible to injury or have been injured previously. Try this sequence of acupoints designed for over-all warm-up. Apply pressure with your thumb on the palm side of each joint of your ring finger on both hands. Then use GB 34 and St 36 just below the knees. Pressure point therapy can also be used as a cool-down to reduce stiffness or soreness and speed recovery.

On long rides or multiple-day tours, you can use acupressure while taking a break to increase comfort, energy reserves, and relaxation.

Vital Energy

The condition of your vital energy is an important determinant in your well-being. This energy is distinct from the rejuvenating energy of sleep, the metabolic energy from food, and the power of conscious awareness. It should not be difficult to understand this subtle energy since there are many energetic processes in your body. They include the beating of the heart, peristalsis, and the manufacture of hormones and enzymes. (Weil, 1983, p. 151) Sadly neglected by Western allopathic medicine, this component of human nature is described, cultivated, and valued by other cultures around the world. The Chinese know vital energy as *qi*, the Japanese as *ki*, and Yogis as *prana*. Qi is the vital force upon which many ancient Asian healing arts and martial arts are based. It is a life force that influences your vibrancy. Recognized by the Chinese since before 2000 BC, the concept and practice of cultivating qi is not confined to one philosophy or religion. Practicing Qigong is no more Buddhist or Daoist oriented than taking vitamins is Christian oriented. (Zi, p. 165-166) I will draw on the Chinese tradition for concepts and terminology because the Chinese have recorded their understanding of qi for thousands of years, and I have studied it in greater depth than other traditions.

It is easier to describe the benefits of qi than to define it. Qigong is the practice of cultivating qi and its application to healing and harmony of mind and body. Taiji Quan is one form of Qigong practice developed for martial applications. It uses slow, graceful, choreographed movements. The primary benefits of Qigong are that it:

- Increases awareness of your body, your energy and energy distribution, your mental condition, and your spiritual dimension
- Balances your body, mind, and spirit into an integrated whole
- Regulates your immune system
- Promotes healing
- Facilitates digestion
- Warms the body
- Mitigates pain
- Heightens creativity
- Heightens self-defense skills

So what is the nature of this remarkable energy? The Qigong discipline divides qi into prenatal or original qi and postnatal qi, which is absorbed from nature, nutrients, air, and water. Qi is the life energy that flows through all living things. A dead person has no qi. A healthy person has more qi than an ill one. Health implies more than an abundance of qi. In a healthy person, qi is clear rather than turbid. It flows smoothly throughout the body rather than being blocked or stagnant. You might think of qi as an inner energy supply. Every day you draw on this energy, and the supply is diminished with age if you do not recharge it through proper nutrition and healthy mental and physical activities including meditation, exercise, and abdominal breathing. Qi is dissipated rapidly by excessive indulgences in food, sex, substance abuse, and other unhealthy activities. When you are young, qi is abundant and circulates freely without much effort. As you age, qi is less abundant and circulation is impeded by muscle tension. As qi withdraws, it first leaves your extremities: the fingers, toes, hands, feet, head, arms, legs, and so on.

Qigong is the art and science of regulating internal energy to improve health, calm the mind, and condition the body for optimum performance in sports and the arts. The practice involves healing postures, movement, self-massage, breathing techniques, and meditation. You will derive the best benefits from daily practice. An early morning session of 20 to 40 minutes should focus on maintenance and self-nurture. Another session later in the day would emphasize learning and developing new skills. Qigong is fun, economical, and requires no special equipment. It is easy to practice on business trips, bike tours, or in your back yard. It can be done standing, sitting, or lying down so it is ideal for the differently-abled. Classes, books, and video tapes of Qigong exercises are readily available. I recommend Kenneth S. Cohen's *The Way of Qigong: the Art and Science of Chinese Energy Healing*. See www.qigonghealing.com.

To appreciate the function of vital energy within your body, you need to understand some intangible features. In the Qigong discipline, energy circulates through *meridians*. Refer to p. 139. The primary center of energy is the *dan tian*, which is in the center of the body, half way between the navel and the pubic bone. Notice how this corresponds to your center of gravity, of movement control, and the muscular movement of abdominal breathing. This is where the Qigong practitioner plants the seeds of health, longevity, and wisdom (in the heart-mind). The *bubbling spring* is on the bottom of each foot, one-third of the way from the base of the middle toe to the back of the heel. Earth qi passes through this point to enrich your qi. It is an acupuncture point as well as a focal point for grounding your being. The Qigong classics state that qi begins at the feet, is controlled by the waist, and manifest in the hands. If this sounds strange to you, shake yourself, loosen up, and remember that the most important things in life are intangible.

The principles of Qigong practice require an unfamiliar use of your body. In Qigong, the body sinks, lowering the center of gravity and energy level. Knees and hips are slightly flexed, and the abdomen muscles are loose. The feet are rooted, increasing balance and stability. Shoulders are dropped, and the neck is empty, letting energy rise to the top of the head. Generally, the body below the waist is heavy and above the waist is buoyant. The attributes of Qigong are awareness, tranquillity, effortlessness, sensitivity, warmth, and rootedness. The resulting use of your body is remarkably different from Western habits. I am fascinated to discover that this style of movement is characteristic of the natural grace of small children and the goal of the teachings of Yoga, Alexander Technique, Feldenkrais, and Rolfing. With deep abdominal breathing vital to their foundation, these techniques appear to be universal, intercultural, and timeless. Why are they not widely appreciated in the West? Probably because we believe we must exert effort to acquire a new skill. The idea of sinking our energy and surrendering to a deeper wisdom beyond our conscious control causes us to fear some mysterious meltdown.

If you study Yoga, you may be familiar with another organization of vital energy. In Yogic tradition, energy gathers along the spine, moving up to the *third-eye* (above the nose, in the center of the brow), and the crown of the head. These energy centers, or *chakras*, are vertically aligned along the spine and extend from the base of the spine to the crown of the head. They are not physical like nerves but are a series of energy centers that regulate and control the neuro-hormonal system that in turn controls the mindbody functions. (Kriyananda, p. 197) The purpose of practicing Yoga postures, *asana*, is to align and cleanse the body and to balance the lunar and solar energies, enabling energy to freely travel up the chakras to higher states of consciousness.

My Personal Experiences with Taiji Quan

I first became familiar with Taiji as a graduate student in the early sixties. My

Taiwanese house mate, Betty Chao, practiced her form every morning in our living room. I was fascinated by her discipline, serenity, and focus. We were close friends, and I asked her to teach me what she was doing. She told me it was a form passed down through the family and taught to her by her father. Every morning she would show me another move, and I learned the entire form my mimicking Betty. For two years I practiced faithfully every morning. I was motivated by the grace of the movement, the sense of well-being, and the clarity of thought that filled me during practice and stayed with me most of the day. When I was drained while studying for exams and writing research papers, a 10-minute break to practice my form would restore my focus and revitalize my energy. It was actually better than sleep. Wow! It cost nothing, was legal, fun, and satisfying!

After graduate study in textile chemistry, I married, lived in Germany for two years, completed an M.A. in German, and bore two sons. Twenty years later, I resumed my Taiji studies in Golden, knowing I needed the benefits of my practice. Since 1986, I have started each day with Taiji and until 2000 I attended weekly correction classes. Since I began studying Yoga in 1996, I have added several Yoga postures and seated meditation and additional Qigong exercises to my morning ritual. That is a 20 to 40 minute investment in the quality of my life and my daily performance. My motivation remains high. If I miss a practice due to poor planning, the quality of my day is noticeably diminished. Why would I choose to set myself up for a fatiguing and scattered day?

On several occasions I have experienced remarkable benefits from my practice. One day I had a failed root canal. In the process, a nerve was mangled, leaving me in considerable pain. As I went to class that evening, I wondered why I wasn't going to bed instead. During class I managed to focus on my practice and much to my astonishment, the pain completely dissipated. What joy and relief!

Early in my practice I was taking a cross-country ski clinic, and my hands became uncomfortably cold. This day was windy and cold, and the ski suit I was wearing constricted circulation at my elbows. I put on all my mittens but my hands remained miserable. As I stood waiting for my turn to practice the demonstrated technique, it occurred to me that I might be able to move my qi into my hands and get some relief. I concentrated on moving my energy into my hands. Within seconds my hands became vibrantly warm. With that success, my dedication to Taiji ratcheted up another notch.

More recently I was having some plumbing done at my house and needed to locate the sewer. A Taiji friend suggested that her husband would be willing to come over with his divining rods and search for it. After Taiji class that night, Michael, his 10-year old son, and I had fun walking around my yard each with our wire coat hangers bent in L-shapes. We held the short end in the loose fists of each hand and delighted in watching the wires move freely in our hands crossing each other at specific places in the yard. The problem was that they were too active, and we couldn't decide which spot might be the sewer.

Months later after I had located the sewer by another means, I decided to take my divining wires out again and see how they responded to the known sewer location. I was disappointed when the wires hung motionless in my loosely closed fists. Perhaps my qi was weak. After all, my previous success had been directly after Taiji class. So I did my form and tried again. To my delight, the wires moved actively once again. These are experiences where qi has helped solve specific problems or its effect has been demonstrated physically.

The Contribution of Vital Energy to Integrated Wellness

Integrated wellness depends on developing the awareness and skills to maintain the quality of your vital energy and to ensure its even flow and distribution. Your body holds tangible and intangible blockages. The most common blocks are muscular tension created from overuse, misuse, and stress. You can usually identify them during massage as hard, tender places. Other blocks are more subtle and result from unresolved emotions and psychological pain, either from abuse, denial, or a sense of vulnerability. You may assume a protective posture as a sort of character armor. This unnatural and imbalanced carriage is maintained by the chronic contraction of certain muscles. Vital energy is blocked by this tension. Hips and shoulders are the most common areas of stored tension. When you consider the critical relationship of the hips and shoulders to the spine, you may have a new appreciation of the negative impact on back health caused by muscle tension and misalignment in these areas. Refer to the discussion on hips in Chapter 5, p. 190.

There are many video tapes and books on various vital energy techniques but the guidance of an experienced teacher can help you avoid mistakes and provide inspiration. Weekly classes are a good beginning and can help you develop the discipline to practice daily. Try this exercise from Kenneth Cohen as an example of how you can center yourself and tune in to your energy flow.

1. Sit in an upright chair with the soles of your feet flat on the floor and close your eyes.
2. Let your weight sink downward so you are supported by the floor and the seat of the chair.
3. Open your spine by letting it feel spacious with each exhalation.
4. Release your sternum and let it float upward and forward.
5. Release the back of your neck so your chin drops down about a quarter on an inch.
6. Release your jaw and let your tongue rest loosely and flat on the bottom of your mouth.
7. Release any tension in your eyes and let your eyes be lightly closed.
8. Relax your abdomen so it is completely free and open.
9. Create room for breath and shift your position to release any tension.
10. Rest your mind to your dan tian.

Part of the wisdom of internal Qigong is the discovery of emptiness and the cultivation of awareness of quiet, peacefulness, and the mind free of concepts.

When energetic flow is established, you feel "connected all over." In contrast, notice how you lose touch with any part of your body that holds tension. As tension spreads, and body sensation diminishes, mental activity increases until you may believe your thought process *is* your entire self. Cultivating vital energy integrates your mind, body, emotions, and spirit, thereby increasing your integrity. You will also enjoy a greater interconnectedness of your body parts.

The ability to guide the movement of vital energy enables you to energize yourself at will. Practicing the following exercise will help you discover that fatigue is strongly influenced by attitude and the condition of your vital energy.

1. Sit on a bench (with your knees lower than your seat bones) or sit Indian style on the floor. You'll want to remove your shoes and may want to sit on a towel or blanket to raise your seat bones above your feet.

2. If your chest is collapsed, you can open it by clasping your hands behind your hips, putting your palms together and straightening your elbows. Enjoy that open-chested feeling. Then put your hands back in your lap and relax.

3. Hold your back as erect as if it was suspended from the top of your head. Release your shoulders downward. Now focus on your back to find its natural curvature. Use only the muscles necessary to support yourself.

4. Begin at your tailbone and visualize gradually lifting energy up your spine.

5. Use SELF breathing and take a few minutes to relax and enjoy the feeling of natural alignment.

6. If you begin to slump, visually push energy up your spine with each complete exhalation. With each inhalation visualize opening the flow of energy through each extremity one at a time and draw it to your spine.

You may be surprised to find yourself feeling energized and renewed. This exercise is helpful for centering at the beginning of meditation. You can use it to energize yourself any time you find yourself slouching. Erect posture is essential to effective breathing since slouching confines your chest and diaphragm and inhibits free movement of the abdominal muscles.

Daily practice of Qigong increases your general sense of well-being and promotes healing of illness and injury. You can facilitate healing yourself as well as seeking the help of Qigong healers. Qigong is especially effective in increasing circulation, reducing inflammation, mitigating pain, and soothing digestive disorders.

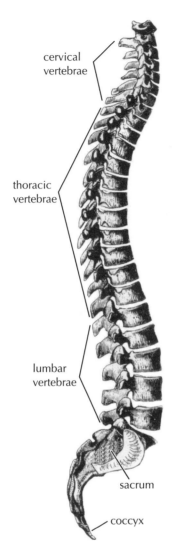

cervical
vertebrae

thoracic
vertebrae

lumbar
vertebrae

sacrum

coccyx

A side view of the vertebral column

Usually the first four bones of the spine are fused and form the coccyx or tailbone. The next five vertebrae are fused to form a large triangular bone, the sacrum. The lumbar spine is the next five vertebrae, which are the largest moveable portion of the spine. The thoracic spine is formed by the next twelve vertebrae. The neck or cervical spine has seven small vertebrae. (*Anatomy of Hatha Yoga*)

When qi is projected externally, it enhances your sensitivity to others and your ability to communicate. In Chinese traditions, cultivation of qi and creative performance are intertwined. Qi contributes to releasing creative energies and projecting outstanding performance by calligraphers, painters, singers, and martial artists.

Regular practice cultivates fluid and efficient movement. Through conscious intention and movement of qi, you can learn to release contracted muscles and organs. This subtle freedom enhances agility, balance, and relaxation. Vital energy gives a new meaning to relaxation. By drawing on your vital energy, you can enjoy relaxation while supporting your body in an upright position. You may have learned at an early age that pouring on more energy will optimize your performance. Sometimes less energy is more effective. Now you can rediscover how the skillful use of your body optimizes performance. Your increased sensitivity and control will enable you to respond to your body messages that tell you which movements and energies improve your performance. Both your skills and stamina will improve.

The emphasis on strength and power in sports focuses attention on muscle contractions in movement. Releasing tension in non-working muscles is just as important! In retraining your riding technique, you will learn that releasing your old style is a crucial step in establishing a new riding form. Subtle changes can be more easily manifest by directing your energy through conscious intention rather than by muscle contraction.

Contrast the energetic level of these two riding postures. The slouched rider on the right has relaxed the muscles needed to support her for efficient riding form. The rider on the left is using energetic intention to extend her back. By releasing the muscles that pull her down, she frees the appropriate muscles to let her float up. Alexander Technique refers to this as our natural "anti-gravitational force." This example of intention is more efficient, maintains a healthy spinal curvature, reduces neck strain, and can be sustained for prolonged periods without fatigue.

Which of these riders is more energetic and having more fun?

Practicing Tools for Integrated Wellness Will Improve Your Cycling Performance

Over-training, injury, and central fatigue are caused by excessive activity. You may ride beyond your comfortable stamina level, overuse a misaligned joint, or work too long at the office or on a pet project. Frequently the resulting exhaustion is not followed by sound sleep. In fact, immoderate activity usually distracts the mind and results in further excesses. You may even continue to careen out of balance until you become ill, injured, or emotionally agitated or depressed.

Tranquil exercise is grounding and can establish an equilibrium that reduces the risk of wide energy swings. Rather than focusing exclusively on physical fitness and sport, devote time and energy to emotional, spiritual, and vital energy fitness.

Ken Cohen recommends the following tranquil exercise sequence. Practice every morning for 40 to 60 minutes. Exercise between five and seven o'clock before eating. Perform 10 minutes each of seated meditation, Yoga, Qigong, and Taiji or other tranquil exercise. After practicing this routine for several months, I am able to work longer without fatigue, maintain a more compassionate disposition in difficult situations, and ride with more stamina and improved technique.

Upon rising you might try these exercises:

1. The cat

2. Two repetitions of downward-facing dog, upward facing-dog, and child's pose

3. Ten minutes of seated meditation (I like to sit in cow pose for five minutes on each side. Be sure to choose a position that is comfortable for you.)

4. Yoga postures: seated spinal twists, preparation for the elephant, and triangle or sun salutation

5. Qigong exercises to cleanse impure qi, gather qi from nature, and move qi throughout the body

6. Taiji: Yang short form

As your skills improve, you will observe increases in your stamina, your pleasure, and your ability to stay in the moment.

Even though I have practiced Taiji and meditation each morning for years, this extended morning preparation for the day and investment in integrated wellness enables me to maintain my equilibrium and release inner energy I didn't know I had. My five-day workweek ends Saturday evening. Saturdays are demanding with the need to be attentive to many customers. Often I don't get to eat lunch until late afternoon or even after closing. Being so drained on Saturday evening, I sometimes still feel dragged out on Sunday mornings, even after nine hours of sleep. My Sunday morning routine is to ride 10 miles to the Kriya Yoga Center for meditation. I ride the same route and know just how each hill feels and what gears I use. Some Sundays I'm pretty pooped and drop into my lowest gear for minor hills.

The first Sunday after taking a Qigong workshop with Ken Cohen, I instituted the above tranquil exercise routine. I had wakened that morning feeling low energy and sore. I knew I needed all the help I could get in order to enjoy my ride. About an hour after breakfast I set out on my bike. As I climbed the first hill about three miles into the ride, I was amazed at my stamina. No small chainring for me that morning! To my delight, my energy and focus remained high even as I completed my 20-mile loop. Here was tangible evidence of the transforming effects of cultivating and integrating my vital energy. My sleep and fuel were the same as many other Sundays, but the new ingredient was the extended exercise to cleanse and open the flow of qi throughout my body.

I have been fortunate to have developed these component exercises over the last two decades and can draw on them for immediate results. If you are not practicing tranquil exercise now, begin with the Yoga, meditation, and acupressure described in this chapter and begin Qigong classes.

Conclusion

Western cultures have dissected, analyzed, and isolated each aspect of human nature. This has distracted us from integrating all parts of our lives. Fortunately we have opened our doors to the East and are benefiting from healing traditions that focus on maintaining health by balancing the body, emotions, intellect, and spirit. Combine these energy-centered wellness practices with the Western fitness and training techniques and you can design programs that will maintain balanced fitness and health and result in contentment in the midst of turmoil.

The physical and intangible parts of our nature respond similarly to caring maintenance. When we massage tight muscles, they may feel smooth and relaxed initially. As we continue to warm and stimulate them, the superficial surface muscles relax. After a few minutes, we gain access to the deeper tissue and can feel its true condition and loosen it up. The same sequence occurs when reflecting on our emotions. When we search for the causes of feeling glum, the first feelings to surface are related to recent events and superficial emotions. When we take time to embrace those emotions, accept them as our own, and release them, we can discover gradually the underlying causes of our current mood swing. When we observe these personal patterns regularly, we may be fortunate enough to correlate the tight muscles with the knotted emotions and work on releasing our retained tension by controlled breathing, stretching, acupressure, and reflection.

Increased awareness is essential to maintaining a healthy equilibrium. Using the techniques introduced in this chapter, you can begin a program of life-long wellness that will heighten your sensitivity to how you use your body and to imbalances in your mindbody, emotions, spirit, and social life. Effective breathing and quieting your mind are the first steps to heightened awareness. We react to the inevitable daily stresses and strains by becoming imbalanced. These specific fitness techniques are selected to help you develop an awareness of equilibrium rather than the more common approach of physically manipulating your body by force. Stretching, massage, acupressure, and Qigong open your body's natural lines of communication, helping you develop greater sensitivity and control essential to optimum fitness and health.

No matter what your circumstances or health inheritance, the choices resulting in abundant well-being are yours. Set your goals and use affirmations and visualization to empower yourself to change. Work through difficult decisions with your family, employer, and friends so you are able to care for yourself. Everyone will benefit by your transformation. Recognizing that you are the only one who can substantially change your circumstances and improve your wellness will help you invest time and energy into caring for yourself.

Take time to reflect and experiment with the tools I have described in this chapter. You will be rewarded in proportion to the time and energy you invest. Begin with small steps in preventative maintenance. Then, when you recognize the first signs of health imbalance, take responsibility for regaining equilibrium by cutting down on non-essential expenditures of energy, adjust your food and drink intake, and pay more attention to your physical, mental, and emotional needs. Take control of your health maintenance and personal fitness and become a participant in your healing process.

chapter 5

Riding Style Modifications Optimize Comfort, Efficiency, and Wellness

- Your Feet
- Your Ankles and Calves
- Your Knees
- Your Hips
- Your Diaphragm

- Your Back
- Your Shoulders and Neck
- Your Arms and Hands
- Your Head and Face

The significant problems we face cannot be solved at the same level of thinking we were at when we created them.
~Albert Einstein

What factors increase your riding efficiency?

Preoccupation with bicycle equipment makes it difficult to identify the elements of riding technique that actually increase your efficiency and riding pleasure. Preparing your body and mind — tactics that are available to everyone for free — will actually cause the greatest improvements in your stamina. Perhaps that is why building a strong fitness foundation is undervalued. Pay attention now, I am giving you the secret handshake of bicycling bliss!

Riding stamina and pleasure are dependent on the following elements:

Pedaling technique that moves the bike forward — Your bike is propelled only when force is applied perpendicular to the crankarms. Developing a fluid, circular pedaling technique can increase your efficiency dramatically.

Relaxed torso, arms, and hands — Relax your grip on the handlebars, flex your elbows downward, and use only those upper body muscles that stabilize your torso. Learn to eliminate unnecessary muscle involvement even at high exertion levels. Significant movements of your torso, except when you are sprinting to the finish of a race or beating your buddies up a steep mountain trail, will make you unduly tired without contributing to the forward propulsion of your bike. You'll be delighted to discover that relaxation will allow you to go farther before fatiguing, and it also will help you recover faster. Your ability to generate power efficiently depends on your ability to relax ineffective muscles.

Remember that relaxation also facilitates skillful bike handling. Avoid muscling your bicycle!

Diaphragmatic breathing — This facilitates relaxation and effectively oxygenates your blood to feed your muscles. Although your current breathing technique keeps you alive, your quality of life and general performance will improve as you learn to breathe consciously.

For fun and simplicity, we'll begin our discussion of body mechanics at the feet and progress up the body to the head. For each body part we will consider:

- Its function
- Its optimum technique
- How you can develop optimum form
- Its common problems
- Exercises to correct your current habits and to benefit each body area

Although it is convenient to discuss individual body parts, they do not function in isolation. Full integration of all body parts, in fact, integration of body *and* mind, optimizes efficiency. As your awareness of body use increases, you may notice the predictable influence of one body part upon another. For example, the carriage of your neck and head strongly influences the curvature over the entire length of your spine. Proper alignment of your hips reduces knee and foot strain. Tension in your hands or feet will spread into your arms and legs. I hope that by learning to optimize the use of each body part, you will heighten your awareness of how you use your entire body and that this awareness will lead you to a fully integrated riding form.

Let's get started!

Your Feet

The function of your feet is to transfer power to the pedals.

What is Optimum Pedaling Technique?

Biomechanically, your power is transferred to the pedals most efficiently by keeping your feet close to horizontal from the two- to five-o'clock portion of the pedal stroke. Then you need to gradually lift your heels through the remainder of the pedal stroke. Your heels reach their highest point when each pedal is at the ten-o'clock position. Placing the ball of your foot within half-an-inch of the pedal spindle will increase efficient use of your lower leg.

Apply power to the pedals throughout the full pedal stroke. Rather than resting each leg alternately as it moves up the back of each stroke, keep your legs powering your pedals throughout the entire stroke. Everyone has a powerful downward push, and now you can also concentrate on pulling back across the bottom, pulling up around the back, and

Placing the ball of your foot within half-an-inch of the pedal spindle will increase efficient use of your lower leg.

pushing across the top of the stroke. Apply force to the pedals perpendicular to the crankarm at every point in the pedal rotation. Now you can understand why some system to attach your feet to the pedals is necessary for efficient technique.

Next time you are on your bike, examine your pedaling technique. Surely you will discover that you are slacking off during some part of the pedal stroke. How did your current pedaling style evolve? As a child, you probably started riding a single speed bike with big, broad pedals. Like the bikes most kids ride today, your seat was too low, and the crankarms were relatively long. Efficiency and healthful body use were the least of your concerns — you just wanted to cruise around the neighborhood with friends.

Your childhood pedaling technique had a dominant downward stroke. When the going got tough, you moved the pedals slowly or stood up because you had no gears. The low seat position caused great stress on your knees at the top of the pedal stroke, so you wisely coasted whenever possible. You probably didn't ride much during the years when you were bonding with automobiles. The next time you rode, you had an adult body, many more demands on your time, and a much more sophisticated bike. Your bike had gears, some form of foot attachment to the pedals, and a wider range of seat post adjustment. Speed and distance were more interesting to you. Most likely you enjoyed your improved equipment but continued using your childhood riding technique.

Let's contrast the power transfer of your early, untutored pedaling technique with that of optimum technique. During the untutored pedal stroke, the greatest power transfer is from the two- to four-o'clock part of the rotation. However, from the six- to one-o'clock positions, power transfer is negligible. This means that power is transferred on less than half the pedal stroke! If you only use a strong downward stroke, you basically coast around the rest of the pedal rotation to the next downstroke. Worse still, if you don't pull up through the six- to eleven-o'clock portion of the pedal stroke, your opposing leg must work against the counter weight of the leg moving through the upstroke! Do you see how the untutored pedaling technique results in wasted energy and premature fatigue?

Retraining for Optimum Pedaling Technique

Rather than shopping for a more expensive bike to make you faster, take time to transform your pedaling technique to maximize your power output. The most basic training technique is to visualize moving each foot in a full circle. You will need to practice at about 80 revolutions per minute (rpm) of the pedals. See cadence information on pp. 158-159. Concentrate on equalizing your exertion throughout the pedal stroke. This means you will exert less force on the downward stroke to better balance your power on the upward stroke. Probably your downward stroke is so strongly established that you will only need to focus on the six- to one-o'clock portion of the pedal stroke. Visualize making circles around the circumference inscribed by each crankarm. It often helps to develop power at the bottom of the stroke by imagining that you are wiping your feet on a doormat. Your old pedaling technique probably used angular exertion. The visualization of these contrasting pedaling techniques might look like this:

Contrasting visualization to facilitate retraining your pedal stroke

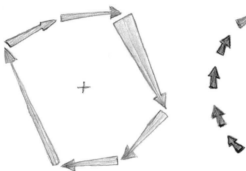

Untutored, angular movement   Retrained, fluid circles

Once you are comfortable with the circular movement, gradually increase your power to avoid regressing to your earlier, angular style.

Using a fluid and balanced power stroke will help balance the strength of both extensors and flexors of the hips and knees. You will be delighted to discover that once you begin using both legs to power throughout the entire stroke, the under-developed muscles will strengthen quickly. This balance contributes to healthful joints and general agility. In contrast, using only the muscles that push the pedals downward causes the hip extensors to become significantly stronger than the flexors. This imbalance increases strain on the lower back, contributing to discomfort or even to injury. Refer to the illustrations of hip flexors and extensors on pp. 188-189.

You can use a couple of methods to analyze your pedaling technique. This first method is used in spinning classes or on any stationary bike. You can try this technique outdoors if you find a safe place away from traffic. Pedal briefly using only one foot and evaluate your power on the full rotation. Then contrast that with solo pedaling with the other foot. Do you find difficulty maintaining momentum through the back of the pedal strokes? You might also observe that one leg moves throughout the pedal stroke with relatively uniform power while the other leg moves awkwardly.

Another evaluation technique that works especially well on a mountain bike with high-volume tires is to reduce your tire pressure leaving just enough air to protect your inner tubes and rims. If your bike bounces up and down with each pedal rotation, it indicates that you use a pulsating stroke. If you move forward without bouncing, your pedal stroke is balanced and fluid. This same experiment can be made with rear suspension or a Soft Ride® beam and by observing how much pogo stick action you create.

Retraining yourself in this new technique will take time and vigilance. After so many years of using a powerful downward stroke, it will take time to get the feeling of the new style. Experiment to discover what tricks help you focus on improving your form. Perhaps emphasis on pushing through the top of the stroke will seem to come naturally. Maybe pulling up on the back side of the stroke will help you feel the greatest transformation. You may find that increased resistance makes you more conscious of your performance, so observe your style when climbing hills or carrying a heavy load. You may be able to bypass the step-by-step evolution of new pedaling technique by moving directly into fluid, full-power circles with each foot. Visualize how that will feel, affirm that you can succeed in the transformation, and let go of your old habits in one step.

It is all too easy to lapse back into the old pulsating pedaling style. Be especially watchful when you are tired or when the terrain requires more power. It is under these circumstances that you can benefit the most from the increased power of optimum form.

Understanding and Utilizing the Benefits of Spinning and Pushing

Spinning is the fluid, circular pedaling form characterized by long-distance, high-energy road bikers. **Pushing** uses a dominant downward stroke much like the untutored form of childhood. Pushing is popular among mountain bikers during technical riding because it gives a burst of power when needed to overcome obstacles. It also diminishes rider weight on the saddle to minimize impacts and to facilitate moving the bike over bumps. Both styles are appropriate in certain situations. Pushing increases power output and can be useful for short bursts over rocky, uneven terrain where exertion levels vary widely. Spinning will increase your speed and endurance on pavement or during more uniform riding conditions. Choose the style that optimizes your performance in each riding situation and avoid pushing all the time. Pushing is another cause of lower back strain that will increase discomfort and risk of injury.

Crankarm length is a consideration for each technique. Relatively short crankarms facilitate spinning, and longer crankarms increase leverage for pushing. That is why it is common for a rider to use 170 mm crankarms on a road bike and 175 mm length on a mountain bike.

Pushers often position their saddles farther back on the seat post. You may have done that if you felt you just couldn't get far enough off the back of your saddle to feel comfortable. Your powerful downstroke was pushing you off the back of the seat. Rather than purchasing a new seat post with greater setback, I recommend that you cultivate spinning most of the time and use pushing to help you overcome obstacles. Then return to spinning when the terrain permits. Or feel free to be a true pusher and get off and push your bike. This will give your butt, knees, lower back, and lungs a rest and enable you to enjoy the scenery. In any case, select a saddle position that meets your needs for most of your riding. Refer to "Saddle Position," pp. 194-198, and use a plumb line to access the relationship of your saddle to your crank.

Many mountain bike riders train extensively on the road to develop their spin and efficient form without the constant challenges and distractions of technical riding.

Maintaining a Minimum Cadence of 80 rpm

Whether you spin or push, cadence is important. **Cadence is the revolutions per minute (rpm) of the pedals.** You can measure it with a cycle computer or by counting how many times one foot comes over the top of the pedal stroke in 15 seconds. A count of 20 strokes in 15 seconds equals 80 rpm. Eighty rpm is a good target cadence for recreational riders at moderate exertion levels. Avoid bogging down below 80 rpm on short ascents or spinning above 110 rpm on short descents. Shift your gears with each change in terrain to achieve a constant cadence. Refer to "How to Use Your Gears for Optimum Health and Performance for 21 or More Speeds," Chapter 6, pp. 283-284.

Riders sometimes resist increasing their cadence. "But I like to ride at 50 rpm. I feel I am getting a better work out." It is true that you are working harder: low cadence emphasizes leg power and builds leg strength. But you are sacrificing endurance and unnecessarily increasing stress on your body. Let's look at an analogy from weight training. Riding at cadences below 80 rpm is similar to performing 10 repetitions with 100 pounds of weight. You will work harder using more muscles but you will run out of fuel and stamina sooner. Your intense workout makes it more difficult to remain fully oxygenated, increasing production of undesirable byproducts including lactic acid. In contrast, riding at a minimum of 80 rpm is similar to performing 100 reps with 10 pounds of weight. It is more efficient, uses fewer muscles, generates less heat (wasted energy that is hard on joints), and enables you to ride longer with less fatigue. You will be able to oxygenate your muscles fully, avoiding the burning discomfort of lactic acid build up. If you want to achieve a fitness-building workout in a short time at 80 rpm, carry an additional load on your bike, climb hills at moderate speed, or combine these two.

Low cadence is appropriate under certain conditions. It generates more power in the short term, making 60 to 80 rpm useful on steep, off-road climbs. If you choose to ride at low cadence to develop your leg strength, good pedaling technique is even more critical to maintain balanced strength of opposing muscle groups. So experiment and see if you can pedal with good form at low cadence. Low cadence is also suitable for cruising slowly around the neighborhood or riding with small children. But when you want to ride more than five miles at moderate and high energy levels, a minimum cadence of 80 rpm will increase your endurance. You may even find that at increased exertion, you naturally increase your cadence to 90 to 100 rpm.

Riding at more than 80 rpm is as important in reducing wear and tear on your bicycle as keeping it free of grime. Higher cadence reduces chain tension, increasing the longevity of drive train components. It also reduces stress on the spokes of the rear wheel and wear on the rear tire.

Your Body is More Efficient When Your Technique is Uniform

Continuously pedaling and maintaining steady cadence increases your efficiency. Coasting frequently will slow your forward progress and your fitness development. Some years ago when I was riding my bike on an errand about 10 miles away, I became impatient with my slow progress homeward. I observed that whenever my bike would roll forward without my pedaling, I let it coast. I don't know when I fell into that habit but I decided right then to retrain myself to pedal continuously. I was surprised to discover how frequently I caught myself slacking. When I was attentive and pedaled constantly, I was pleased to notice how quickly I progressed toward home.

Now I find that even after years of riding with good form, I occasionally regress into ineffective technique. When I'm tired, I catch myself lapsing into a slow cadence or slacking off on the upstroke. Once you have established good form you too will be wise to focus your attention on your technique on every ride to catch yourself when you lapse into poor technique. If you have fallen into the habit of intermittent pedaling, remember that you can go farther, faster with less effort by pedaling constantly. Other benefits will be better aerobic capacity and increased leg strength.

There is one important exception: about every 15 minutes take advantage of a downhill or tailwind to stop pedaling and lift off the saddle to let your circulation improve in your saddle-contact area.

Cycling Vocabulary Limits Our Perceptions of Riding Styles

Just think of the wide variety of words describing pedestrian styles. Some people stroll or saunter, others tramp, traipse, or trudge. Most commonly people walk or hike. During high exertion, athletes race walk, jog, and run. "Bike riding" does not give any clues about the energy level or purpose of the ride. How would you describe your riding style in walking terms?

Your bike setup and riding form increase in importance as your energy level increases. If you are a stroller, proper bike setup will increase your pleasure but cadence and fluidity of pedaling style are less critical. If you are a hiker — purposefully moving along your route — or a jogger — picking up speed — you will want to optimize all aspects of your riding technique.

The Benefits of Cycling-Specific Shoes

While your legs and buttocks generate most of your power, your feet transfer it to your bike. Power enters your feet at the heels, transfers to the balls of your feet, and then goes into the pedals. During this transfer, the rigid sole of cycling-specific shoes support the longitudinal arches of your feet. If you ride in running shoes or flexible walking shoes, your feet work harder as the shoe flexes on each pedal stroke. Remarkably, supporting your feet with stiff-soled shoes reduces strain on your knees as well as your feet.

A second benefit of cycling-specific shoes is that they provide easy access to the pedals. Take care to select a tread pattern appropriate for your pedals and walking style. If you use toe clips and straps, select a tread that will allow you to tip the pedals up easily and slide across the pedals without resistance. Look for a low profile tread. If you ride with clip-in (commonly called "clipless") pedals, the shoe sole must accommodate the cleat. Since you will not need to slide your foot across the pedal, your tread choice should be based on the

High-end road shoes with substantial cleats result in an awkward walking style with an increased risk of slipping. They do give maximum stiffness and can eliminate the discomfort caused by the pressure of the pedals under the balls of the feet.

High-end mountain bike shoes with recessed cleats enable you to walk normally. The spiked tread increases traction in soft earth but limits traction on rocky ground. Most recessed-cleat models allow road riders to walk comfortably. Again, maximum stiffness can eliminate discomfort from pedal pressure.

Recessed-cleat recreational shoes provide the greatest comfort and ease in walking without sacrificing much stiffness. The tread makes it easy to access pedals with toe clips and straps and increases traction due to greater contact surface.

More economical recreational shoes can be used with clip-in pedals, toe clips, and straps or Power Grips®. Though they may not be as stiff as more expensive shoes, they usually provide greater support than running or walking shoes.

terrain where you will walk. While spiked soles are popular with shoe manufacturers, most recreational riders will appreciate cycling shoes with good walking treads that provide traction on hard surfaces.

Proper fit is more important than style when shopping for cycling shoes. The numerical size of shoes is only a starting point. Fit shoes to the length of your longitudinal arches rather than to the overall length of your feet. You will have greater comfort and reduce foot strain by ensuring that the balls of your feet are directly over the flex-points in the shoes. While trying on shoes, be sure your heels are firmly back in the heel cup and then secure the laces and/or Velcro®. Now stand up to evaluate if the flex point coincides with the balls of your feet. Bear all your weight on each shoe to determine if they are comfortable even with your foot spread out under your weight. Before installing cleats or riding with the shoes, wear them around home for a couple hours to be sure they are satisfactory. By protecting them while you test them, you can return them for a different size or style if necessary. Cycling-specific shoes are so critical to cycling performance that I recommend buying them after a helmet, but before cycling gloves, shorts, or jerseys.

Attachment to Your Pedals

Attaching your feet to the pedals will increase your cycling pleasure and provide worthwhile health benefits. Though riders love to tell horror stories about falling over when they couldn't extract themselves fast enough from their pedals, don't let other people's comic tales deter you. Just laugh at these stories and then go right ahead and learn to use a pedal attachment system. The choices include: mountain bike toe clips with or without straps, Power Grips®, and various clip-in pedals.

The most basic attachments are **mountain-bike toe clips**. These are easier to enter and give more support than the single pronged road-bike toe clips. They hold your feet on the pedals so they do not slip off at high cadences or in rough terrain. When you select the correct toe clip size, your feet are held on the pedals with the balls of your feet within a half-inch of the pedal spindles. You can gradually build your confidence with toe clips, adding the straps after you have learned to tip up the pedals with your feet. During this time, you will derive some benefit while still allowing you to step off the side of the pedals in an emergency. When you do add the straps, tighten them enough to provide support but

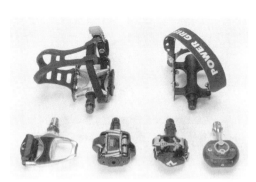

Some popular choices of pedal attachment. Clockwise from upper left: toe clips and straps, Power Grips®, Speedplay Frogs® Shimano SPD®, Time ATAC®, large platform road clip-ins.

not so tightly that it is difficult to remove your foot. When you want to take your foot off the pedal, concentrate on pulling your foot straight back off the pedal. Initially select non-technical rides to reduce demands for quick footwork. You might note that toe straps are still manufactured with the traditional clasps. Thread the strap under the roller and through the top of the buckle but leave the end free. This allows you to tighten the strap with one hand by pulling the strap up. To release the tension on the strap, just push down on the top of the buckle. Transferring power on the upstroke to pedals with toe clips and straps requires that you keep your feet close to horizontal and lift up from the toes to prevent slipping out of the clip. If your seat is too high, and you tend to point your toes at the bottom of the pedal stroke, you will derive minimum benefit from the pedal attachment.

Power Grips® are another option. You enter by tipping the pedals upright and sliding your toes in toward the bike frame. As you rotate your heels into pedaling position, the straps snugly secure your feet. Power Grips® are economical and excellent problem solvers for riders with feet larger than size fourteen or smaller than size seven. The length of the straps is adjustable to accommodate almost any size or style of shoes. So you can ride in boots or other unconventional riding shoes. It is convenient to buy pedals with Power Grips® already installed since they can only be installed on pedals with bolt-on cages.

Clip-in pedals provide delightful freedom and efficiency. Are they worth the investment? How long will it take you to get used to them? Most cyclists who use them love them. But others have rejected them and returned to standard toe clips and straps. What should you do? Here are some helpful comparisons:

Clip-ins	**Toe clips and straps**
Great freedom	Cumbersome
Easier starts on steep ascents & stop signals	Some struggles on challenging starts
Best power transfer available	Power transfer limited to about 75 percent of the pedal stroke
Compact, will not gouge your shins	Bulky, may bang or gouge your shins
More skill needed getting out	More skill needed getting in
Significant financial investment ($55 and up)	Economical ($10)
Necessity of wearing cycling shoes	Choice of any footwear for spontaneous cruises
Greater awareness of your pedaling technique	

Note: If you ride at temperatures below freezing, the cleat attachment through the shoe sole draws the heat out of your foot and into the mass of the metal pedal. The composite body of Speedplay® pedals won't draw as much heat away from your feet as entirely metal models. You may find that for cold weather riding you appreciate the insulation provided by your intact sole on conventional pedals with toe clips and straps.

Manufacturers have designated clip-in pedals as designed for either a mountain bike or a road bike. The type of pedals you select will determine the style of shoes you can use with them. I recommend that you base your choice of pedal on the style of shoes you want to use and not on the style of bike you will put them on. The cleats of mountain bike clip-ins recess into the soles of the shoes allowing you to walk normally. The cleats of road bike clip-ins protrude under the balls of your feet making walking awkward. Recreational riders usually appreciate the versatility of recessed cleats for road and off-road riding. It is great to be able to take a stroll at a picnic or go grocery shopping with little risk of losing your footing. You will notice a slight loss of traction with the cleats under the balls of your feet. If you like to jump from rock to rock while off your bike during a bike outing, a little more caution is required. You can simplify your cycling life by using the same type of pedals on all your bicycles. Just put on your shoes and ride any one of your bikes.

How do clip-ins work? A cleat is screwed to the sole of the cycling-specific shoe. The compact pedal grasps the cleat as you step firmly onto it. The cleat releases from the pedal when you rotate your heel out and down, away from the bike. All clip-ins have some means to adjust the ease of release.

The health of your legs depends on your feet being able to work in the direction they naturally point. Over the next few weeks, observe the orientation of your feet while walking. This is most dramatic when your footprints are recorded in snow or when you walk with wet shoes on dry pavement. You may be surprised by their lateral alignment, and that the alignment changes with time due to tension and fatigue.

The variations in foot alignment probably originate in your hip and knee joints. Perhaps you have observed cyclists' knee action while riding behind them. Their knees may flare out to the side on each upstroke or one knee inscribes figure eights. These actions are convincing proof that not all knees work as perfect hinges. I recommend that you use stretching, Yoga, Taiji Quan, massage, and Rolfing to optimize the alignment of these joints and their surrounding muscles. These will improve your efficiency and general health as well as reduce the risk of injury.

With so many variables in foot, knee, and hip alignment, selection of the specific brand and model of clip-in pedals is worth careful consideration. The retention mechanism of many clip-ins limits the lateral rotation, or **float**, of your feet on the pedals. The range of float among brands varies from four to more than twenty degrees. **Clip-ins with less than eight-degrees float put chronic stress on your knee joints** while clip-ins offering more than eight-degrees float will accommodate the intricate movements of your joints. For this reason, if you have sensitive knees that are vulnerable to stress, you would be wise to choose Speedplay®, Time®, or Bebop® pedals, all of which offer adequate float to protect your knees.

Clip-ins are available at a wide range of prices. Avoid the temptation of saving one hundred dollars on pedals while putting your knees at risk. How much medical care for your knees can you buy for that amount of money? Other factors to consider are the availability of shoes compatible with each pedal model, durability, ease of maintenance, and the convenience of having the same pedal system on all your bicycles.

You release your feet from all clip-ins by twisting your heel out and down. If considerable force is required to free your feet, you are contributing more strain to your hard working leg joints. Shimano Pedaling Dynamics® (SPD), SPD® copies, Time ATAC®, and Crank Brothers® pedals require that you work against the retention spring to release. Twisting your knees against lateral resistance is hard on them. Only the mechanism of Speedplay® and Bebop® pedals do not require exertion to release from their pedals. Cyclists with experience on different clip-in pedals report that Speedplay Frogs® are the most knee-friendly and user-friendly pedals. The entry to Frogs® is also easy. You press your feet down or slide them across the pedals rather than having to catch the front of the cleats in the pedals and press your heels down.

Many new bikes come with clip-ins or no pedals at all. Unfortunately the stock clip-ins are usually economical copies of Shimano SPD® pedals. They have less than five-degrees float. Some riders report that these are more difficult to enter and release than SPD® pedals. When you buy a new bike, be sure to evaluate whether the stock pedals suit your needs, just as you will need to evaluate the stock saddle, shifters, stem, handlebars, and crankarm length. Ask the retailer what price adjustments will be made for these modifications.

Once you have selected your clip-in pedals, take time and care installing the cleats on your shoes. The performance of each leg and the agility of each foot are different and may require different adjustments of right and left cleat and pedal if they are spring loaded. Observe how each foot is aligned when you walk and try to accommodate the natural orientation of each foot when you position your cleats. The fore-aft position of the cleat on the shoe should place the ball of the foot as close to the pedal spindle as possible.

The risks and cautions of cleat installation vary with different brands of pedals. For Speedplay®, Time®, and Bebop® pedals, the risks are minimal due to knee-protecting float. However, casual installation of SPD® and SPD® copies can result in knee strain and injury, causing you to stay off your bike while your knees recover. I recommend you get help with the cleat installation for pedals with minimum float. If you like to tinker and have healthy feet and knees, refer to cleat installation in *Zinn and the Art Of Mountain/Road Bike Maintenance*. Otherwise, go to a bicycle retailer who offers the Fit Kit RAD® (Rotational Adjustment Device) cleat positioning system and pay an experienced operator to evaluate the performance of your feet while riding and to help you optimize the cleat position on your shoes.

Consider this summary of pros and cons of attachment to your pedals before you abandon the idea of choosing a new system in order to avoid change.

Benefits of Attachment to Your Pedals

1. Attachment holds your feet onto the pedals so they don't slide off, especially at high cadences and in rough terrain.

2. Your feet are held in optimum fore-aft position on the pedals with the balls of your feet over the pedal spindles.

3. You can power the pedal throughout its entire rotation allowing:
   a. The full use of more muscles at all parts of the pedal rotation.
   b. Transfer of forces tangential to the pedals at the top and bottom of the pedal stroke.

4. Attachment increases your stamina and endurance as the workload is distributed over more muscles.

5. Off-road, you can enjoy quick and effective response to prevent a pedal from colliding with obstacles in your path.

6. For urban riding, pedal attachment makes it easier to reposition your pedals for a strong start in traffic.

7. Clip-ins make you more aware of the use of your feet and can help you improve your pedaling technique.

8. Attachment allows you to tell your own stories about your ineptitudes while learning to use your new pedal attachment system!

Detriments of Attaching to Your Pedals

1. You will need to do some research.
2. You must learn a new skill.
3. You must spend some money.
4. You will want to ride in cycling shoes most of the time.
5. You're going to look foolish occasionally but can enjoy a good laugh while accepting your own miscalculations!

Here are some suggestions for **learning to use clip-ins**. On your first rides, cruise around in your neighborhood or in an empty parking lot. Avoid technical single-track or heavy traffic. Be attentive to the use of your feet. Clipping-in on many models requires that you catch the front of the cleat in the pedal and bring down your heel firmly to engage the back of the cleat. Speedplay Frogs® do not require as much agility of your feet to clip-in. Generally you just slide your foot across the top of the pedal, then press down to engage the elastomer-loaded plate at the front of the cleat. When Frog® cleats are new, they have a breaking in period. I find it helpful to use another technique for effortless entry. Basically I reverse the release movement. Place your foot on the pedal, rotate your heel out about a quarter of a turn and listen for the cleat to click in. Then let your foot return to its natural orientation.

When you want to click out, visualize making a fluid movement of your heel out and toward the ground. This will help you keep your heel down and increase the leverage you exert on the cleat. Be sure to practice with both feet even though most riders tend to prefer one foot for stopping.

Take care to shift your weight *toward* the foot you are releasing. You can do this by leaning in that direction or by pressing down on the handlebars on that side. These movements will ensure that you can catch yourself with your free foot. You will rarely be successful in trying to release your second foot when you are already starting to fall away from the foot you want to release. Your confidence will probably suffer a bit during the transition to clip-ins but you will soon delight in your new-found freedom and power.

Common Foot Problems and Discomforts

Even though it is convenient to discuss each body part separately, remember that optimum performance depends on your using your body as an integrated, coordinated whole. The dependency of each body part on the health and efficient use of all other parts is particularly clear in discussing foot problems. Some discomforts that manifest themselves in the feet actually originate in the pelvis and knees. You will need to refer to the sections on the hips and knees for corrective exercises that benefit your feet. Refer to pp. 211-214 and pp. 182-188, respectively.

Numbness or Burning at the Balls of Your Feet and Toes

Numbness is generally the result of prolonged compression of the nerves that give sensation to the affected areas. The nerves that innervate the feet originate in the lower back at the lumbar and sacral vertebrae. Because the nerves of the lumbar and sacral plexuses are connected and go primarily to the lower limbs, they are frequently described together as the lumbosacral plexus. The nerves of the lumbar plexus lie on the inside of the posterior abdominal wall and are embedded in the psoas major muscle before passing into the lower part of the anterior abdominal wall or into the thigh. They are especially vulnerable to compression as they pass through the groin of riders with a forward lean of more than 45 degrees. The nerves of the sacral plexus supply the musculature of the buttock the back of the thigh and all the muscles below the knee. The sciatic nerve forms from several nerves originating on the front of the sacrum but passes laterally behind the ischial tuberosity. It continues down the back of the femur and branches into the common peroneal nerve that swings around the outside of the knee in a vulnerable position to supply the calf and foot. (Jenkins, pp. 239, 240, 255-257)

Lumbosacral Plexus - anterior view

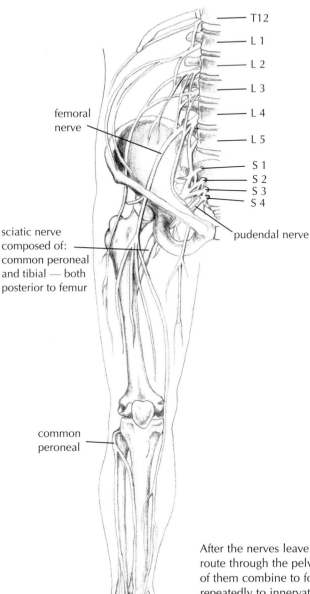

T12
L 1
L 2
L 3
L 4
L 5
S 1
S 2
S 3
S 4

femoral nerve

sciatic nerve composed of: common peroneal and tibial — both posterior to femur

pudendal nerve

common peroneal

The distribution of these nerves passes through and under many of the muscles used in pedaling. Sensation can be impaired by impingement between muscles, between muscle and bone, and by pressure against the saddle. The sciatic nerve is especially vulnerable to compression as it passes around the ischial tuberosity, under the gluteals, and among the lateral rotators of the thigh. If you have experienced the distinctive discomfort of sciatica, you know that compression of nerves in the lower back, hips, and knees can cause pain or numbness in the feet. In fact, sciatic nerve problems have become increasingly common, leading me to believe that the hips are another favorite location for tension from unresolved, past and present trials of life.

If you ride off-road and on-road, you may have

After the nerves leave the spinal column, they follow a complex route through the pelvis and legs to the feet. In the pelvis, some of them combine to form the sciatic nerve and then branch repeatedly to innervate all areas of the lower extremities. Nerve impingements are caused by chronically tight muscles, misalignments, and compression of the buttocks, perineum, and thighs against the saddle. Sciatic discomfort can be relieved by stretching, by postural improvements, by reducing life stresses, by modifying riding position and technique, and by minimizing pressure against the saddle.

noticed differences in foot comfort. Riding technical trails means you are out of the saddle often. You may use a softer, wider seat, a suspension seat post, or rear suspension to help absorb impacts. You may even get off your bike more often to negotiate challenging terrain. These aspects of off-road riding style relieve pressure on the nerves and vessels that feed the feet and result in greater comfort even with the same pedals and shoes. On the road, you are more likely to ride for prolonged periods at high intensity with little change in body position. You may use a narrow and less padded saddle or not yet make a habit of lifting off the saddle frequently to relieve pressure and impacts. All these factors make it more likely for you to experience foot numbness or discomfort on your road bike. Just adjust your style to reduce discomfort.

What precautionary measures can you take to prevent foot numbness or referred pain from the hips and legs?

1. Get professional help to ensure that your hip and knee alignments are not causing problems.

2. Practice the exercises recommended in the sections on hips and knees to improve and maintain optimum alignment.

3. Select a saddle that provides adequate support to the ischial tuberosities, eliminates pressure on the perineum, and reduces pressure to the insides of the thighs. Good luck! It may be difficult to find a saddle that does all of these things if you have bulky thighs.

4. Lift off the saddle regularly to allow adequate circulation through the large blood vessels that feed the legs and feet and through the system of lymphatic tubes that also pass through the groin.

5. Experiment with moving your feet forward on the pedals to mitigate pressure directly under the balls of your feet. This can be accomplished by moving the cleats back on your shoes or by installing larger toe clips.

Other Simple Measures to Increase Circulation and Foot Comfort

• Be sure your shoes fit well. Provide adequate space at the balls of your feet to allow for circulation. There is a balance between adequate space of circulation but not so loose that your feet move excessively in your shoes. Check your shoes for protrusions under the balls of your feet, especially where the cleats attach. Be sure that the shoe closure allows adequate adjustment for your feet contours and for relief from swelling.

• Some riders' feet swell on long rides and especially in hot weather. Try drinking more water and diluting your energy beverage. Foot swelling is generally caused by fluids (both blood and lymphatic fluids) not moving up out of the legs. Pressure on the saddle contributes to this problem so be sure to lift off the saddle often and try walking occasionally to see if that helps.

- Select socks and insoles that provide adequate cushioning to prevent nerve compression and to allow circulation at the soles of your feet.

- Wear shoes that provide support on the pedals. Even if you have cycling-specific shoes, you may need to invest in the rigid-soled models to dissipate pedal pressure.

- You might also benefit from custom foot beds (available at Alpine ski stores) or orthotics. Most of these shoe inserts are designed for walking or running and do not provide adequate support above the pedal and cleat. Be sure they extend beyond the balls of your feet for protection. If you suffer from discomfort at the joints at the base of your toes (the transverse arch behind the metatarsal heads), a slight lift in the foot beds at this point can provide space between the metatarsal heads and facilitate blood flow to the toes. This diminishes the risk of nerve and circulation impairment at these joints.

- Develop your upstroke on the pedal stroke to provide relief from constant downward pressure on the soles of your feet.

- On extended, high-energy rides, numbness in your feet may be unavoidable after about an hour. You can usually find relief by walking your bike for several minutes.

Preventing General Foot Fatigue

Reduce the work your feet do by wearing cycling-specific shoes. Discard old cycling shoes when they are no longer rigid through the longitudinal arch of the foot.

Tensing your feet will also cause premature fatigue. You may be holding your feet rigid or gripping the soles of your shoes with your toes. You may be gripping with your toes because your feet are behind the pedal spindle, which causes inadequate foot support. If this is the case, install larger toe clips or move your cleats back on your shoes.

Preventing Sore Toes

Pressure on the toes can be caused by too small shoes that jam your toes or by too large shoes that allow your feet to slide forward until they hit the front. You may be able to salvage these shoes by changing your insoles to a different thickness or by cutting the insole out under your toes. Usually you just need to get new shoes that fit properly. Take personal responsibility for fitting your shoes since most sales staff are untrained or have limited experience. Learn to value your feet since they are so critical to your mobility and greatly influence the condition of your entire body, your carriage, and your mood.

Cautionary note: Some people are installing wedges between the shoe sole and the cleat to change the angle at which the feet contact the pedals. While some riders have found such wedges useful, in most cases the problem originates in the alignment of the hips or knees. Placing a wedge under the foot could cause damage to the ankles and/or knees. Before having wedges installed, consult with a qualified professional to determine whether wedges would actually solve the problem or just treat the symptoms and result in further damage.

Exercises to Correct and Benefit the Feet

Giving special attention to foot care can rejuvenate you quickly when you are tired or feeling restless or glum. The following exercises can be done on the floor or while enjoying a warm bath.

Foot-hand clasp — Sit on the floor with your legs outstretched in front of you. Keep your pelvis and back erect. Cross your left foot over your right thigh. Place your right palm and left-foot sole together. Begin with your pinky finger and toe and interlace your fingers with your toes. Initially this can be quite challenging. Once you have interlaced them, make gentle circular motions with your hands. Then gently bend the toes forward and back. Now remove your fingers from your toes and compare the spread of the toes on your left foot with those on your right foot. Repeat this exercise with your left hand and right foot. This is especially beneficial if you have been experiencing numbness or burning in the toes or balls of the feet.

Foot-hand clasp

Massage the longitudinal and transverse arches of your feet.

- You can massage your arches by sitting in the same position as foot-hand clasp. Apply pressure with your thumbs along your arches.

- You can also incorporate a longitudinal arch massage with this kneeling exercise. Kneel with your hips above your knees and your knees and feet hip-width apart. As you slowly sit back onto your feet, press your calves out to the side to reduce strain on your knees. Grasp your kneecaps with each hand and lift them upward to effect a gentle release. If this position places too much strain on your knees, place a blanket under your buttocks rather than sitting on the floor. Breathe consciously and let your legs and feet relax fully. Stroke down the longitudinal arches of both feet moving from the heels to the toes, applying firm pressure with your thumbs or the knuckles of your fist.

- While standing or sitting in a chair, place a tennis ball under the sole of one foot and roll it around applying firm pressure. Give special attention to the length of your longitudinal arch. You will likely experience tenderness just in front of the heel cushion and at the base of your middle toe.

Acupressure - K 1 Bubbling spring — *Benefits* - It is the source of earth's qi and a primary balance point for the entire body. It relieves postural alignment imbalances and the muscle cramps that result. *Location* - It is one-third of the way from the base of the second toe to the heel. *Application* - As described in the previous massage, apply pressure with your thumb or with a tennis ball. You can use a golf ball if you desire more pressure. You can relieve fatigue and improve relaxation by rolling the ball slowly along the length of your longitudinal arch.

Foot circles — Sit with your back against a wall (or sit upright in the bath tub). Extend your legs straight out in front of you. Now make circles with your toes initiating movement at your ankles. First bring the soles of your feet so they face each other, gently circling your toes back toward your knees. Continue outward so your soles face out and away from your knees. Complete the circles by pointing your toes and finally bringing your soles to face each other again. Now reverse the circles. Orient your soles away from each other toward the outsides of your calves. Circle outward away from your knees. Pull the

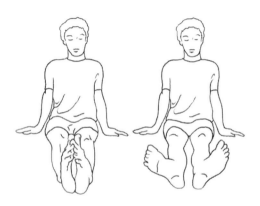

Foot circles

pinky-toe back toward your knees and gradually rotate your feet inward so the soles are again facing each other. Move on to pointing your toes and back to the starting position. Perform this exercise slowly and *gently*. Excess zeal can result in cramping in your shins, calves, or peroneal muscles.

Your Ankles and Calves

The function of your ankles and calves is to keep your feet at effective angles for maximum power throughout the pedal stroke relative to the position of your knees over the crank.

Your ankles are the joints that adjust the orientation of your feet to the position of your knees. Your lower legs do most of the work in maintaining the ankle and foot position.

What is the Optimum Technique?

All joints function best close to the middle of their range of movement. They are more efficient there and are less likely to suffer strains. Take a moment to observe the full range of movement of your ankles. Sit on a chair and cross your legs. Flex and extend your foot and observe how far the ankle can move. Now walk around and observe the extent of your ankle movement. Although your ankles are probably quite flexible, your feet remain perpendicular to your lower leg most of the time while walking. This is the position where your ankles are strongest and most efficient. Now try walking or riding using an exaggerated movement of your ankles. They fatigue quite quickly and you may even be able to feel your calf muscles working more than usual.

These observations will help you discover the importance of using your ankles and calves to maintain your feet at about 90 degrees to your lower leg throughout the pedal stroke. This means keeping your feet close to horizontal from the two-o'clock to five-o'clock portion of the pedal stroke and gradually lifting your heels through the upward pull on the pedals. Your heels should be highest as the pedals pass through the nine- to eleven-o'clock portion of the stroke.

Avoid keeping your heels above your toes on the downward stroke or more than 30 degrees above horizontal on the upward stroke. This extreme position diminishes your power transfer and engages your calf muscles without contributing to the propulsion of your bike. Keeping your feet close to horizontal has the added benefit of causing a healthy hamstring extension.

What Should You Look for in Retraining Your Ankle and Calf Use?

Begin by evaluating your ankle and foot position while riding. Have a friend give you feedback or use an indoor trainer and mirror to observe your own style. You may discover that you are pointing your toes at the bottom of the stroke, using exaggerated movements, or holding one or both ankles rigid. What considerations will help you retrain your ankles and calves?

Whether you point your toes at the bottom of the pedal stroke or not is simply a matter of personal style. It was probably influenced by your choice of seat height. The mechanics of power transfer of the crankarm determines the efficient use of your ankles and calves. If you point your toes more than 30 degrees at the bottom of the stroke, most of the power applied to the pedal is downward, as if to elongate the crankarm and not to propel the bike forward. Rather, keep your heels lower than 30 degrees above horizontal and you can efficiently draw your feet back, perpendicular to the crankarm, and propel your bike more efficiently. These two styles use different muscles. Calf muscles are used to point the toes and make little contribution to propulsion. Pulling the foot backwards against the resistance of the pedals uses primarily knee flexors (primarily hamstrings) and hip extensors (dominantly gluteus maximus). Experiment with these two different directions of exertion and see if you don't notice a difference in efficiency.

When you ride with toe clips and straps rather than clip-ins, the horizontal position of your feet is essential to power on the upward stroke. You need to emphasize lifting with your toes against the toe clip and strap using shin muscles, the strongest being the tibialis anterior, the prominent superficial muscle of the shin. (Calais-Germain, p. 258)

If you are holding one or both ankles rigid, you need to release tension and cultivate an efficient and fluid flexing of your ankles. This habit is fairly common and will result in premature fatigue and tension spreading to your feet and legs. It may be caused by fatigue or lack of attention to technique. It might also result from an imbalance in leg strength. On my first bike tour, I experienced a knife-like pain at the outside of my left knee. It was severe enough that it really got my attention. Since bicycle touring provides plenty of time to observe my riding technique, I began to study the workings of my left leg. I discovered that my right leg was much stronger than my left leg. After fatigue had set in, my left leg struggled to keep up, and my left ankle became rigid. The discomfort was diminished by helping my left ankle relax and by flexing fluidly throughout each rotation of the crank.

Common Discomforts in Your Ankles and Calves

Problems that manifest in the ankles and calves may originate in other parts of your legs. Refer to common problems of the feet, pp. 166-170, and knees, pp. 181-182.

The most common problem is premature fatigue of the ankles. This is usually due to tension and rigidity in your ankles. This is likely to be a problem with your non-dominant leg on long rides. Just as I discovered, you may be pushing your weaker leg beyond its endurance level, and it is compensating by tightening up. You will probably find relief by walking a short distance or relaxing and stretching your weaker leg. When you return to riding, give attention to your form, flexing your ankle naturally, and letting your thigh muscles work uniformly throughout the full pedal stroke.

Ankle fatigue can also be caused by your pedal attachment system. If your clip-ins restrict the lateral movement of your feet on your pedals, your pedals may be forcing your ankles to work at an awkward angle. Reposition your cleats if your pedals have less than eight-degrees float or change to new pedals with more float.

If one of your legs is longer than the other, one ankle could be straining to extend that foot farther. Placing a shim under the cleat of the shorter leg can solve this problem. Before using a shim, consult with a professional to determine if your difference in leg length is skeletal and permanent or muscular that can be corrected by realigning your hips or back. It is important to correct the actual problem and not the apparent one. Casually using a shim when the problem is actually misalignment will only add a new problem on top of the old one.

Exercises to Benefit Your Ankles and Calves

All these exercises can be done on the floor or while enjoying a warm bath.

Foot circles — See the description under exercises for your feet (p. 171).

Kneel — This will stretch the front of your ankles. Refer to the description under exercises for your feet, p. 170.

Toe raises — Refer to strength training, pp. 124-125.

The squat — This benefits many parts of the body and is a popular alternative to sitting in chairs in many parts of the world. People with low body bulk will perform this with greater ease. Follow these instructions, and if they are too challenging, try the alternatives described below. Place your feet shoulder width apart and parallel to each other. Squat down, keeping your heels on the floor. Maintain the natural curvature of your back and lift through the top of your head. Let your chest open and come forward between your legs. You can strengthen your inner thigh muscles by pressing outward against your thighs with your upper arms while squeezing your knees together. Breathe and relax into this position.

Alternatives to the basic squat — Place your feet shoulder wide and point them out 45 degrees from parallel and squat down. Does that feel better? If you tend to tip over backwards, position yourself facing a door frame or heavy piece of furniture. Hold on for support as you squat down. Another option is to let your heels come off the floor and support yourself only on your toes. Breathe consciously and relax into the position. If you practice this daily, you will progress toward the classic squat.

Acupressure — These two acupoints can be used simultaneously. **K 3 Bigger stream** — *Benefits* - It relieves swollen feet and ankles and strengthens the ankle joint. It also relieves toothaches and ringing in the ears. Do not use this acupoint during pregnancy. **B 60 High mountains** — *Benefits* - It relieves sciatica, thigh pain, headaches, and lower backaches as well as relieving pain in general. *Location* - Both points are on the indentations midway between the anklebones and the Achilles tendon. K 3 is on the inside of the ankle and B 60 on the outside. *Application* - Place your thumb on the inside of your ankle and your fingers on the outside. Hold firmly for one to two minutes. Angle the pressure forward aiming just below the anklebones. You will feel increased tenderness when the angle is correct. Release gradually and end by lightly brushing your thumb and fingers over the acupoints.

Shiatsu for the calves and Achilles tendons — This quick massage relieves fatigue, chronic tension, and muscle spasms in the calves, ankles, and feet. *Position* - Sit on the floor (or in bed when you get cramps at night). Extend both legs in front of you, flexing your feet back toward your knees and drawing your kneecaps up. Then place one foot on the floor in front of you about 14 inches from your seat bone. *Location* - These eleven points are along the bladder meridian at the middle of the calf (gastrocnemius muscle) and Achilles tendon. *Application* - Use firm, rhythmic pressure with both thumbs. Begin just below the back of the knee at the top of the calf. With thumb tips together or overlapping, gradually press into the fleshy muscle on a slow exhalation and slowly release the pressure on the inhalation. Move down the muscle about one inch and repeat. Coordinate your breathing as you move down your calf, applying pressure to eight points. Continue through three points on the Achilles tendon. Observe the tenderness at each point for comparison with the other leg and with the subsequent massages. Repeat on the other leg. To increase the benefits, apply pressure to each point for one or more breaths.

Your Knees

The function of your knee is to bend and move back and forth through an arc of about 70 degrees in a plane parallel to the bicycle frame (sagittal plane).

Most hip and foot movements are limited to the sagittal (front to back) plane by their placement on the saddle and pedals. This not only minimizes lateral stress but also makes it easier to understand effective technique for propelling the bike. The leg muscles concerned especially with extending and flexing the hips and knees contribute most to propulsion. As explained in Chapter 4 under strength training, cyclists must not neglect the muscles concerned with adduction, abduction, and lateral and medial rotation. These muscles play important roles in stabilizing movement on the bike and play a supporting role as synergists. Because the thigh muscles act on both the knees and the hips, the muscles of the legs that make the greatest contribution to propulsion or are most likely to cause problems will be discussed separately. For example, the ITB that originates at the iliac crest and inserts at the top of the tibia is discussed under common knee problems since that is where discomfort is most likely to reveal problems.

Cyclists are justifiably concerned about their knees since they flex and extend repeatedly through a wide range of movement. However, cycling is kinder to the knees than many other sports since cycling minimizes impacts, weight bearing, and lateral stress. With these attributes, cycling is often recommended as therapy during knee and hip rehabilitation.

The knee works like a hinge and is the largest and strongest joint in the body. It enables the femur (thigh) and the tibia (lower leg) to change angles in the sagittal plane, protected by the third bone of the knee, the patella (kneecap). The knee is held together by *ligaments* that connect bone to bone and *tendons* that attach the controlling muscles to the bones. These ligaments and tendons along with the synovial membrane form the *joint capsule*. It is filled with *synovial fluid* that lubricates knee parts and nourishes the cartilage of the joint. C-shaped collars of cartilage or *menisci* cushion movements of the bones against each other. *Bursae*, small, fluid-filled sacs, reduce friction and enable muscles and tendons to glide across bones.

The protuberances at the ends of the femur and tibia, or the *condyles*, move against each other. The condyles of the femur are convex, and those of the tibia are concave. The patella slides across the femoral condyle and is held in place by the quadriceps femoris and patellar tendons.

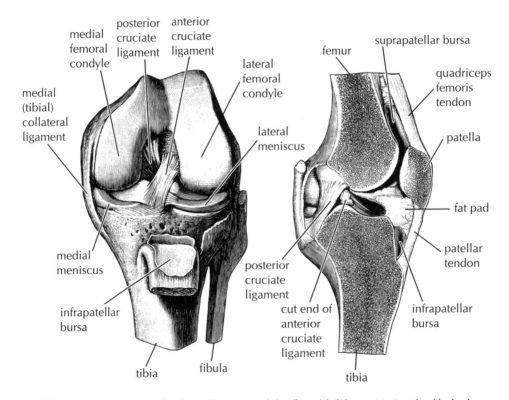

On the left is an anterior view of a deep dissection of the flexed left knee. Notice the fibula that runs parallel to the tibia on the lateral side is not involved in the knee joint capsule. On the right is a sagittal cut of the extended knee joint. (*Anatomy of Hatha Yoga*)

The principle extensors of the knee are the quadriceps. They move the shin forward, pulling the tibia in line with the femur. The principle flexors that move the lower leg back are the hamstrings. The knee is stabilized laterally primarily by the vastus medialis on the inside of the leg and the iliotibial band on the outside of the leg. Because the knee is more "open" on the inside (medial aspect), it is important to keep the muscles that stabilize the medial aspect of the knee strong. Refer to the acupoint locator on p. 140 where you can see that the angle formed by the femur and tibia is close to 170 to 175 degrees rather than 180 degrees. (Calais-Germain, Lamotte, p. 194)

Knees perform strongly under heavy use as long as their components are balanced and aligned. Problems arise when the hinge action is subjected to excessive lateral stress due to trauma or to stresses caused by misalignments or imbalances in the surrounding tissue and hip and ankle joints. Unlike the elbows, the bones of the knee do not limit the range of movement. Healthy knees depend on balanced strength and flexibility of the muscles as

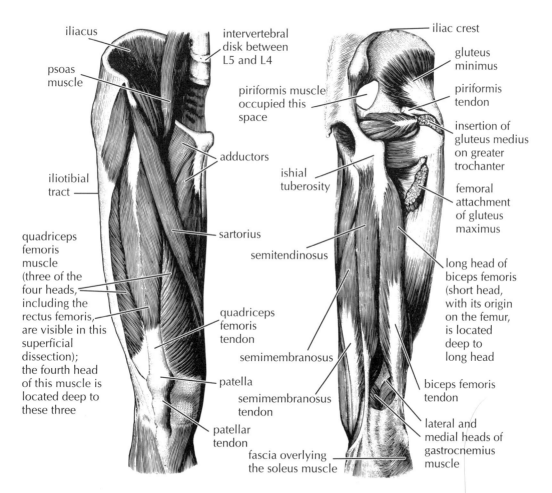

The right side of the pelvis (deep dissection), and the outer muscles of the right thigh and knee, as viewed from the front

A posterior view of the right side of the pelvis, thigh, and knee. This hip dissection is deeper than the one on page 189 and reveals the gluteus minimus. The piriformis and gluteus medius are now removed except for their tendons of insertion on the greater trochanter, and the only remaining part of the gluteus maximus is its femoral insertion. (*Anatomy of Hatha Yoga*)

well as ligaments and tendons of the thigh and lower leg. Imbalances result from misuse, biomechanical irregularities, and compensations from injuries.

Routine maintenance will sustain healthy knees and balance the strength and flexibility of the surrounding muscles, tendons, and ligaments. I recommend Dr. Coulter's routine to resolve minor knee problems. (Coulter, pp. 311-312) Begin with five minutes daily and gradually build up to fifteen minutes. Stand in mountain pose (p. 101) with isometric contraction of the muscles surrounding the knees. This brings all parts of the knees together in anatomically correct alignment. Contract the primary extensors and flexors of the knee by lifting the kneecaps to engage the quadriceps and move the tailbone forward to engage the hamstrings. Maintaining this firm base, alternately shift your weight forward and back. Twist to the right and then to the left. Hold in each position for a count of two to seven breaths. To adjust the workload, change the position of your hands and arms. If your knees are sensitive, place your hands on your hips or grasp your elbows, crossing your arms behind you. Progressively increase your workload until you can reach overhead and clasp your hands behind your head or cross your forearms above your head and grasp your elbows. Gradually these exercises will strengthen the knee capsule.

Optimum Knee Use on Your Bike

Knee performance problems originating from cycling are solved by correcting your bike setup as well as by correcting the way surrounding tissues and joints function. Your knees should move consistently in a vertical plane parallel to the bike frame. However, it is fairly common for cyclists' knees to wobble in and out in arcs, ovals, or figure eights as the feet move through the complete pedal stroke. These inefficient patterns of knee movement are generally caused by problems outside the knee joint. Optimum use of your knees depends on correcting these problems, beginning with a careful evaluation of the use and workings of your feet, ankles, knees, and hips. Problems in any of these joints cause complications in other parts of the legs. Optimum knee use depends on correcting performance of the entire leg and foot rather than the knee alone.

Improving your knees' performance requires a two-pronged approach. First you will need to modify your bike setup and your pedaling technique to minimize knee strain on your bike. Secondly, you will need to perform exercises to maintain healthy knees or to correct strength and flexibility imbalance. If you have biomechanical asymmetries, like different leg lengths, you will need to address these issues. Start by correcting the easy things first. Use this checklist to identify equipment and style changes you can address yourself.

1. Maintain your cadence at more than 80 rpm. See cadence information, pp. 158-159.

2. Check your seat height. For details in establishing the optimum height see "Saddle Height," pp. 194-196. If you are experiencing discomfort at the front of your knee, the saddle is probably too low. If the discomfort is at the back of your knee, the

saddle is probably too high. To avoid sore muscles, make any seat height adjustments in small increments over a period of time.

Having the saddle too low causes your knee to bend at an acute angle at the top of the pedal stroke. As you begin downward pressure on the pedal, the tendon of your quadriceps pulls strongly on your knees. Knee strain is reduced when the angle of your knee is not so acute. You might ask, "If the angle of the knees is more critical at the top of the pedal stroke, why is it customary to set saddle height by evaluating leg extension at the bottom of the stroke?" It's simply because it is easier to see the correct oblique angle of the extended leg.

3. Check the fore-aft position of your saddle. Riding with your saddle too far back forces the hip joint to work at one end of its range of movement. It makes it difficult to pull up on the pedals and balance the downward stroke. The resulting muscle imbalance pulls forward on your lower back and transfers stress to your knees. Refer to "Forward Position of the Saddle," pp. 196-197.

4. Avoid overuse and over-training. Respond to extreme fatigue and discomfort by reducing your exertion and shortening your ride. Rest is as important to building fitness as working out. Be sensitive to your need for rest when you have ridden a lot of miles during the week or when other demands make you unduly tired. At birth you are given only one pair of knees. All additional knees are expensive and inconvenient to install. Protect your knees by responding to discomfort: change your pace, your position, or your riding goals. Avoid that compelling urge to keep up with or surpass your riding companions when your knees hurt. Drop back, suggest a break, eat energy food, or drink a beverage. In other words, take care of yourself. There will be other days to excel.

5. Position your feet on your pedals with the balls of your feet within a half-inch of the pedal spindle. Change the size of your toe clips or move your cleats on your shoes to reposition your feet.

6. If you use clip-in pedals with less than ten-degrees float, your cleat alignment may hold your feet in an unnatural lateral rotation, putting strain on your knees. This is the likely problem if you are experiencing discomfort in the iliotibial band at the outside of your thigh and knee. Refer to the "Iliotibial band friction syndrome", p. 182.

7. Convert to Speedplay® pedals that do not require exertion against resistance while twisting your knees to exit. Although the leg and foot movements to get out of the pedals are the same as other pedals, there are no springs holding your feet in place that must be overpowered to exit. Exiting is accomplished by aligning the shoe cleat with the prongs on the pedal.

8. Select a crankarm length that is appropriate to your leg length. Most riders under 5 feet 3 inches will benefit from road bike crankarms of 165 mm and mountain bike crankarms of 170 mm. Riders taller than six feet three inches will benefit from longer crankarms, at least 175 mm for road bikes and 180 mm for mountain bikes.

9. Avoid holding your knees in a locked position even when coasting. Just let your knees relax. If you choose to extend one leg while coasting, consciously alternate legs. Try coasting with both crankarms horizontal and alternating your lead foot. Take this opportunity to stand up and give your butt relief. Treat you knees to their anatomically correct position. Straighten both legs and momentarily tighten the knee flexors and extensors to renew your knees. You can also bend forward, pivot at the hips, and stretch out your hamstrings.

10. If you are having soreness in one or both knees, observe your heel use while walking or running. During stressful times you may strike the ground too hard with your heels. You can correct this by imagining that while you are walking, your legs are energized by strings attached to the fronts of your kneecaps and gently pulling on you horizontally. Walk lightly, lifting from the top of your head. This will eliminate stress on your knees and feet and can relieve knee soreness as long as you maintain a gentle stride.

11. Cycling is a fine activity for people with one leg more than half-an-inch longer than the other. As body alignments change, leg length differences can also change. This is especially noticeable when these differences are caused by muscular misalignments. Have a professional measure your leg bones to determine if your leg-length difference is permanent and what the magnitude of that difference is. If your leg-length difference is permanent, shims under the cleat or the entire sole can help you avoid muscle strain and saddle discomfort.

Protect your knees from chilling in temperatures below 60 degrees Fahrenheit. The synovial fluid and bursae are more effective in reducing friction when they are warm. Carry leg or knee warmers or wind pants to slip on when weather or riding conditions change unexpectedly. Avoid the foolishness of spending all your cycling funds on your bike rather than spending some on clothing to protect your health and increase your comfort and cycling performance.

Correcting Misalignments and Muscular Imbalances is the Means for Improving Knee Use

The next step is to develop an exercise routine to build balanced muscle strength and flexibility and alignment of legs and joints. Although our discussion has progressed from the feet up, leg performance is strongly influenced from the hips down. Time invested in building strength and flexibility for cycling is well spent since the muscles of the hips and thighs that are important to propulsion and stability during cycling are the foundation of erect posture, agile movement, and healthful breathing for all activities. For this reason I recommend you start your practice with the exercises to benefit the hips, beginning on p. 211.

Professional help is essential in retraining your habitual movement patterns. It requires a trained, experienced observer to analyze the movements that have become second nature to you after years of use. Refer to Chapter 4, "Tools for Integrated Wellness" and the discussions of Alexander Technique, pp. 92-96. Also consider Rolfing and other forms of bodywork that help you learn to realign your body for balanced and effortless use.

Common Problems of the Knees

Give special attention to small problems when you first become aware of them. When you recognize symptoms, eliminate them by appropriate rest, stretching, strengthening, or by modifying your form. Responding to body feedback before damage is done requires patience and restraint. Foregoing high exertion exercise for a few days is surely better than ignoring early signs of strain, sustaining injury, and then enduring the expense and pain of medical treatment in order to get back to normal functioning.

It is beyond the scope of this book to diagnose knee problems. Refer to Dr. Michael J. Ross's *Maximum Performance* for easily understandable explanations of knee problems common to cyclists and possible solutions. Let me give a brief description of two of these so you might recognize them in their early stages and take preventative measures.

Patellofemoral syndrome is often referred to in cycling circles as chondromalacia. Pain in the front of the knee is characteristic of the poor tracking of the patella over the grooves of the femoral condyles. Like other knee problems, this can be caused by muscle imbalance, biomechanical problems, or overuse. Pain worsens with and after activity, especially under increased load. It may also occur with prolonged periods of sitting. Imbalances in muscle strength or flexibility pull the patella to one side. The most likely muscles are those that stabilize the patella. The vastus medialis on the inside of the thigh may be weak, or the iliotibial band (ITB) on the outside of the knee, thigh, and hip may be chronically tight. The patella may also be held too firmly against the femoral condyle by tight muscles at the back of the thigh and calf. Biomechanical problems can also stem from foot position. Overpronation (flat feet) or oversupination (too high arch) affect lateral tracking of the patella as does too narrow placement of the feet on the pedals relative to hip width. This is referred to as the Q factor and can be corrected for wide-hipped riders with pedal shaft extenders. You can purchase Knee Savers® online from www.bikescor.com. Refer to the following exercises to stretch and strengthen the quadriceps and stretch the ITB and hamstrings. Refer to exercises to balance foot and ankle muscles on pp. 171, 174.

Iliotibial band friction syndrome (ITBFS) is the second most common overuse injury among cyclists. (Ross, p. 167) The ITB is a fibrous tendon that runs from the hip along the outside of the thigh and attaches just below the knee. The muscles of the ITB are the tensor fasciae lata, embedded in this sheath and the gluteus maximus. When the knee is straight, the ITB is in front of the femoral condyle. When the knee flexes beyond 30 degrees, the ITB slides over this prominence. When the IBT is chronically tight the constant friction can cause irritation and inflammation. The symptoms worsen with increased load and impact. ITBFS is associated with overpronation, oversupination, bowlegs, pigeon toes, and leg length difference of more than half-an-inch. It can be aggravated by excess leg extension on the bike. Although pain is usually felt on the outside of the knee, a similar irritation can occur at the hip where the ITB slides over the greater trocanter of the femur. Since there is no swelling or limitation of movement of the knee, it may be difficult to motivate yourself to reduce activity to affect healing. Remedies are to reduce overuse of knee; to adjust the bike seat down and forward (as described on p. 194 and 196); to correct biomechanical problems; to stretch the ITB, quadriceps, and calf muscles; and to strengthen the gluteus medius on the upper, outside of the buttocks.

Exercises to Benefit Your Knees

Acupressure applied to the points along the feet, legs, and hips is an ideal practice to begin improving the balance of strength, flexibility, and energy in the knees and surrounding muscles, tendons, and ligaments. The illustration shows selected, key acupoints but you will find more in Marc Coseo's *The Acupressure Warm-Up* and other books among the recommended readings. Twenty minutes a day on these nine points will change the condition of your legs in a week or ten days. Refine your technique by using the guidelines in Chapter 4, p. 141. Anticipate a transformation in your legs.

GB 30 Jumping circle — *Benefits* - This is the most important acupoint for relieving hip problems: sciatica and lower back discomfort. It relaxes tendons and restores joint mobility. It also relieves frustration and irritation. *Location* - It is in the center of the buttock about one-third of the distance from the tailbone to the greater trocanter (the prominence at the hip joint). This is on the inferior gluteal and sciatic nerves and the gluteus maximus and piriformis muscles. *Application* - The many layers of muscle in this area require firm pressure and preliminary massage to relax them. Press on the point with thumbs, fists, or by lying on a tennis ball. During a bicycle ride, you can have fun pressing the horn of your saddle into GB 30 while you stand astride your bike with one foot on the ground and the other on the raised pedal as you might at a stop signal. Pressure is applied to the buttock of the raised leg.

GB 31 Wind market — *Benefits* - This point strengthens tendons and bones, regulates qi and blood and relieves thigh discomfort. It also dissipates wind and cold. *Location* - It is on

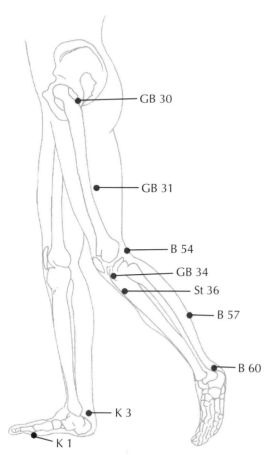

Key acupoints on the hips, legs, and feet

the vastus lateralis, the quadriceps muscle on the outside of the thigh, about seven inches above the crease of the bent knee or where the middle finger tip extends on the thigh with the arm along the side. The lateral femoral nerve and artery cross this point. *Application* - Press firmly with the index and middle finger. You can also lie on a tennis ball or pat GB 31 with the soft fist.

B 54 Bend middle — *Benefits* - Applying pressure to this point opens the knees and back and releases stiffness, sciatica, and arthritis in the knees, back, and hips while promoting circulation. *Location* - This is easy to identify at the back of the knee in the popliteal space. *Application* - Sit on the floor cross-legged, then lift one leg and place that foot flat on the floor about 14 inches in front of your seat bone. Place your fingers on your kneecap and press your thumbs firmly into the popliteal space. You can apply steady pressure or massage. You may prefer to extend your legs in front of you with the back of the knees on the floor and then apply pressure with a tennis ball. From a standing position, you can bend at the hips and pat the popliteal space with the thumb side of your fists. Repeat on both knees. You can enhance the benefits of this application by warming your knees by vigorous rubbing with the palms of your hands on each side of the kneecap. Then breathe deeply, relax, and appreciate the warmth and openness of your knees.

GB 34 Sunny side of the mountain — *Benefits* - It relaxes the muscles of the lower leg, helps prevent shin splints, and promotes healing of sprained ankles. It activates strength and endurance, especially in the hips, and nourishes tendons and joints. *Location* - It is just below the knee, slightly to the outside in the depression between the heads of the tibia and fibula. *Application* - You can apply pressure to GB 34 and B 54 simultaneously. In the seated, bent leg position, place your thumbs in the popliteal spaces and your index and middle finger tips on GB 34.

St 36 Run three miles — *Benefits* - This is a powerful point for revitalizing the qi and blood of the entire body. It strengthens the entire body, especially the immune and digestive systems. It tones muscles and relieves fatigue. *Location* - Find it four-finger widths below the lower edge of the kneecap and one finger width outside of the shinbone. You've found the correct place if the muscle below your fingers moves when you flex the foot. *Application* - Traditionally this is rubbed briskly with the heel of the other foot but it can also be pressed firmly with the fingers.

B 57 Support the mountain — *Benefits* - It helps prevent calf cramps and tight Achilles tendons. It relieves foot swelling and lower back discomfort. *Location* - It is right at the bottom of the bulge of the calf muscles (gastrocnemius and soleus), about halfway from the crease at the back of the knee to the heel, in the center of the leg. *Application* - This is among the points activated during the Shiatsu massage of the back of the calf, pp. 174-175. Sit in a chair and cross one leg on top of the thigh and press with both thumbs. Several key nerves cross this point so it is normally quite sensitive. Carefully apply pressure for about one minute. If you prefer to stand, bend forward and apply pressure with your fingertips.

K 3, B 60, and K 1 — Refer to pp. 174 and 171 for these points in the feet and ankles.

For the Feet and Ankles

Page numbers refer to the instructions under "Exercises to Correct and Benefit the Feet," and "Exercises to Benefit Your Ankles and Calves."
The squat — p. 174
Foot circles — p. 171
Acupressure K 3 and B 60 — p. 174

For the Calves

Toe raises — Refer to pp. 124-125
Ankle rockers — Refer to p. 125
Shiatsu for the calves — Refer to "Exercises to Benefit Your Ankles and Calves," pp. 174-175.
Acupressure of K 3 and B 60 — Refer to "Exercises to Benefit Your Ankles and Calves," p. 174.

For the Hamstrings

Preparation for the elephant — Refer to p. 102.
Downward-facing dog, upward-facing dog, and child's pose sequence — Refer to pp. 103-104.

Supine, lateral twist — This sequence benefits many aspects of the legs and trunk. It flexes the feet and ankles, stretches the hamstrings and pectorals, aligns the hips and spine, and strengthens your abdominal muscles. Because this is performed lying down, it is thoroughly relaxing when you are tired. Lying down protects your back as well.

a. Lie on your back, arms extended out to your sides at shoulder level, palms up. Breathe evenly and align and lengthen yourself from head to toe.

b. Slowly, to the count of seven, raise your extended left leg as you alternately point the toes away and then toward you on each count.

c. When the leg is vertical, continue to move your left foot, first forward and back, then side to side. Then inscribe two to three circles with your toes, using the entire foot and moving from the ankle, first clockwise and then counterclockwise.

d. Now grasp your left leg with both hands, keeping the leg vertical. Gently flex the knee and alternately press your heel toward the ceiling, straighten the knee, and give a strong hamstring stretch. Repeat four to five times.

e. Release your grip on your leg, bend your knee, and bring your thigh to your chest. Clasp both hands around your knee and lift your head toward your knee. Hold this position briefly while breathing consciously.

f. Now bring your head and arms back down to the floor. Return your outstretched arms to shoulder level with palms up. Bring your left knee toward your right side, rotating your spine. Rest your right hand on the top of your bent left knee, producing a light downward pressure. Hold the position and with each exhalation let your left knee drift farther toward the floor.

g. When you feel that the rotation is complete, return your right arm to its position on the floor, bring your left knee to your chest, clasp it with both hands, and lift your head toward your knee.

h. Reverse the steps until your left heel is again on the floor.

i. Now repeat on the right side.

j. When completed, bring both knees to your chest, clasp them with your hands and release your tailbone and sacrum toward the floor and breathe consciously. How do you feel?

For the Quadriceps

Classic quadriceps stretch — Stand with your feet together, supporting yourself for balance with one hand on a wall. Bring your right arm to shoulder height in front and make a large horizontal circle, stretching away from your shoulder (to open it up). Bend your left leg at the knee, reach across your back, and grasp the top of your left foot. Pull your foot up

Quadriceps stretch

The camel

gently with your arm. Keep your thigh facing forward and avoid letting it rotate out to the side. Relax and breathe. To intensify the stretch, push your left foot back away from your buttocks, continuing to hold it in your right hand. This further opens your left groin and right shoulder. Repeat on the other side.

The camel — Kneel with toes pointed into the floor, body upright. With your palms on your hips, place both thumbs into your lower back. Raise your left arm to shoulder level in front of you and with a sweeping, circular motion of your outstretched arm, bring your left hand onto your left heel. Now repeat the arm movement with your right arm so both hands are on your heels. Press your hips forward and contract your buttocks. If you are free of neck complications, let your head lean backwards. Breathe and hold this position. To come out of the posture, reverse the sequence. If you want to intensify the stretch to your quads, place the tops of your feet on the floor to increase your backward bend. If your knees are sensitive to pressure, place some padding under them.

For the Inner Thigh Muscles

Full knee extensions — This exercise strengthens the inner thigh muscles especially the vastus medialis that is usually the weakest quadriceps. Sit on the floor with your legs straight out in front of you. Point your toes back toward your head. Tighten the muscles of your legs while trying to roll your feet, knees, and thighs inward. Hold this position briefly, focusing on the effort of your inner thighs. Release and repeat a few times. To increase the workload, place a pillow or rolled bath towel under your knees and straighten your knees completely and hold. Perform several repetitions.

Inner-thigh lifts — These strengthen the inner thigh and hip adductors. Refer to p. 124.

Inner-thigh stretch — This stretches the inner thigh muscles, especially the gracilis, and increases the mobility of the hips. Sit on the floor with your knees out to the side and the soles of your feet together. With your fingers pointing backwards, place your hands comfortably behind your hips for support. Press your heels firmly together but spread your toes outward like the pages of a book. Sit upright, release your knees toward the floor, breathe deeply. When you have completed the stretch, lift your knees upward and together using the strength of your arms. Rest a moment and observe the sensations in your legs.

Inner-thigh stretch

For the ITB and Piriformis

Piriformis stretch — Use this as a warm-up for the cow pose. It improves hip flexibility and stretches hip abductors (on the outside of the thigh) and deep back muscles. It is safe for sensitive backs since your back is stabilized against the floor. Lie on your back with your feet on the floor and knees bent. Raise your left leg so your knee is bent 90 degrees, and your shin is parallel to the floor. Cross your right ankle across your left knee. Reach your right hand between your thighs, your left hand around the outside of your left thigh, and clasp your hands around your left thigh. Gently draw your left thigh toward your chest. Breathe into your right piriformis. Return your feet to the floor and repeat on the other side. If you have good flexibility and would like to increase the stretch, move your right foot down your thigh closer to your hip and clasp your hands around your left knee.

Cow pose - lower limbs — This stretches the piriformis and increases flexibility in the hip joints. It is traditionally valued as a meditation posture. Begin by kneeling on all fours, move your right knee to the center and cross your left knee behind it on the right side of your right knee. Now gently sit back between your feet. Be sure to place your feet out wide and spread to the sides so there is space for you to sit between them. If at first this is uncomfortable, place a blanket or pillow under your seat bones so you don't have to sit back so far onto the floor. Hold this as long as you are reasonably comfortable, breathing consciously into each hip joint. Come out of the posture the same way you got into it and repeat centering the left knee to start. When I first tried this posture, my left hip was very uncomfortable with the left knee on top. I practiced every morning until I could sit on each side for 5 minutes during meditation. This practice has profoundly improved my hip and

Cow pose

lower back mobility and balanced hip use! The upper portion of the cow posture is with shoulder stretches, p. 237.

ITB stretch — Notice that we rarely use the hip adductors in our daily activities, that is moving the extended leg across our midline. These exercises are beneficial to both the ITB and piriformis muscle. Lie on your back on the floor. Loop a strap or rope around your left foot and hold it taut with your right hand. Extend your left arm out at shoulder height on the floor. Lift your leg so it is perpendicular to the floor. Keep your right hip and leg on the floor while you bring your left leg across your body to your right side until your left hip begins to roll up. Use the strap to help bring your leg into position and keep it straight. Breathe into your ITB and piriformis. Return your leg to vertical and lower it to the floor. Repeat with the right leg.

Outer-thigh lifts — Refer to pp. 123-124.

Your Hips - Positioning and Using Your Pelvis Effectively

The function of your hips is to maintain an angle of forward tilt that optimizes the performance of your thigh muscles, the curvature of your back, and the health of your perineum and genitals. The hips also play a key role in controlling your bicycle.

This posterior view of a dissection of the pelvis and lower abdomen reveals the iliacus and psoas. Collectively they are referred to as the iliopsoas and are the primary flexors of the hips. They are active on the upward stroke of the pedals. Notice that the psoas originates at the lumbar vertebrae and the iliacus at the front of the iliac crest. They insert on and below the lesser trochanter of the femur. Chronic tension in these muscles is difficult to identify since they are deep within the pelvis and lower abdomen. (*Anatomy of Hatha Yoga*)

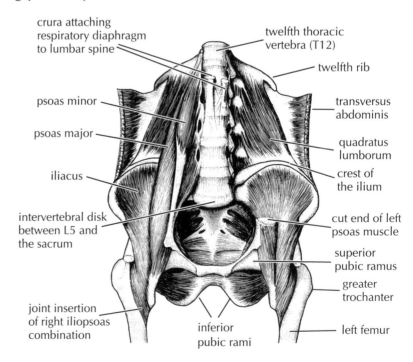

crura attaching respiratory diaphragm to lumbar spine

twelfth thoracic vertebra (T12)

twelfth rib

psoas minor

transversus abdominis

psoas major

quadratus lumborum

iliacus

crest of the ilium

intervertebral disk between L5 and the sacrum

cut end of left psoas muscle

superior pubic ramus

greater trochanter

joint insertion of right iliopsoas combination

inferior pubic rami

left femur

Just as the bottom bracket is the heart of your bicycle, your hips are control central for your body. Every postural shift of the pelvis affects your spine and the posture of your entire body. The pelvis is the connection between the thighs and the upper body and the foundation of the torso. Its principle role is to stabilize your back and legs.

In lay terms, "hips" refers to the entire pelvic region. It is made up of the pelvic bowl, hip joint, lumbar spine, sacrum, coccyx, and the muscles, ligaments, and tendons that attach to them. More specifically, "hip" refers to the hip joint. It is a ball and socket joint where the femur attaches to the acetabulum of the pelvic bowl. Flexibility of the hips depends primarily on the mobility of the hip joint and elongation of the resisting muscles. Range of movement is limited by ligaments and bone stops that need to be protected to maintain the stability of the joints.

The hip flexors and extensors are the strongest muscles in your body. Balancing their

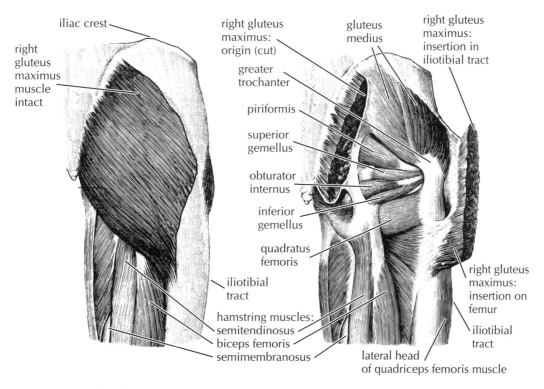

A posterior view of a dissection of the muscles of the right gluteal region and upper thigh. On the left are the outer muscles and the primary hip extensors: the gluteus maximus, semitendinosus, biceps femoris, and semimembranosus. On the right are the deep muscles and indication of the origin of the gluteus maximus on the iliac crest and its dual insertion to the femur and iliotibial tract. The flexors are active on the downward pedal stroke. Notice the piriformis and other parallel deep muscles that rotate the hip laterally. They do not contribute to powering the pedal stroke but chronic tension in these muscles contribute to sciatica. (*Anatomy of Hatha Yoga*)

strength and flexibility is essential to the comfort and health of the lower back and legs. This balance is achieved by a combination of optimum pedaling techniques and regular practice of maintenance exercises. Let's look at the influence of pedaling technique. During optimum pedaling technique, the downward stroke is balanced closely by the upward stroke. That develops both the extensor of the hips (gluteus maximus and hamstrings) and the flexors (iliopsoas, rectus femoris, and tensor fasciae lata). The extensors pull on the back of the iliac crest (top of the posterior pelvis), and the flexors pull on the front (anterior). When their relative strengths are imbalanced or they hold chronic tension, lower back discomfort usually results.

Optimum Use of Your Pelvis

Your **hip activity** should be limited to subtle movements when your hips are stabilizing your back and legs while pedaling. The exertion to propel your bike forward should leave your seat bones relatively still on the saddle. Of course, you will see movement of the buttocks and thigh muscles but you should observe no side-to-side rocking on the saddle. In contrast, your hips can be quite active while controlling your bike, especially on technical trails. Bike handling control will be achieved primarily by weight shift and pressure on the sides of your saddle. Your control skills will be enhanced by a supple back and limber hips. So, you may ask, what are the handlebars for? Are they strictly decorative? No, they are quite handy for directing your bike through sudden, sharp turns to avoid unexpected obstacles on the street or trail.

The **position** of your pelvis is key to the performance and health of your back and legs. Your choice of **anterior tilt** depends primarily on how upright you like to sit on your bike. The farther forward you lean your torso, the more you need to tilt your pelvis to maintain your lumbar curve. Avoid bending your upper torso forward while keeping your pelvis upright. Arching your back in this manner impairs diaphragm movement and reduces power output. Select a comfortable saddle so you will not compromise a healthy back in order to maintain healthy perineum and genitals. If you ride completely upright, sit erect and maintain your natural spinal curvature. Other factors to consider in selecting your forward lean are the comfort of your neck, shoulders, arms and hands. These factors are discussed later in this chapter under the appropriate body parts. Circulation through the groin is a problem for riders who maintain an anterior pelvic tilt of more than 45 degrees. In this position it is important to sit up every 15 minutes to allow blood and lymph fluids to nourish and cleanse the legs.

Your **lateral** position should center you over the mid-line of your saddle. This will eliminate the need to compensate for asymmetries in your weight distribution while controlling your bike. It will also minimize the risk of injury due to the resulting asymmetric use of your legs and back. Some riders find comfort on traditional, narrow saddles by sitting a bit to one side. If you are doing this, I encourage you to test saddles with a cut-out section in the center to relieve pressure on the perineum. Eliminating the increased risk of strain or injury from riding asymmetrically far outweighs the perceived benefits of riding on a marginally comfortable saddle.

The **fore-aft** position of your hips on the saddle should place your ischial tuberosities (seat bones) on the widest part of the saddle where they are well supported and can rest securely. This usually will result in your buttocks being flush with the back of the saddle or protruding one or two inches off the back. Shifting your position on the saddle is not necessarily an indication of improper saddle or body position. It is a healthful opportunity to shift pressure points. The position of your buttocks on the saddle and the position of the saddle on the bike are interrelated. We will discuss this in detail in the following section on saddle comfort.

Since your hips are in the middle of your body, many factors influence optimum hip performance. Let's consider the following factors in depth:

- Comfort on the saddle and protection of the genitals
- Controlling your bike with your hips
- Common problems of the hips
- Exercises to improve the alignment, strength, and flexibility of your hips

Comfort on the Saddle and Protection of the Genitals

The saddle is the base of support for the pelvis, and your degree of comfort on the saddle strongly influences your posture and the use of your entire body on your bike. You may be limiting your riding performance by allowing your saddle choice to determine your riding posture and diminish your ability to generate power. Your choice of saddle also affects your bike handling abilities. If your saddle allows you to sit comfortably and relax you can more skillfully control your bike. If it creates tension you will have trouble responding quickly to control issues and may over-react. All riders should address these issues. Thanks to an ever-increasing variety of saddle designs and a better understanding of how to protect the saddle contact area, most riders can be comfortable without injury to the seat bones or the genitals.

You should reconsider your riding style and saddle choices if you have casually tolerated discomfort on the saddle. This is especially challenging on long, high-energy rides. Saddle selection is not just a matter of comfort but also a matter of protecting your genitals from injury and eventual sexual dysfunction. We'll consider two sets of factors: bicycle setup and body use and preparation.

Factors to consider is saddle selection and bike setup that contribute to comfort and health:

- How to evaluate saddle design and make a selection

- How to determine your optimum saddle position
- How to select pants for cycling that meet your personal needs

Factors to consider in body use and preparation:
- Tone the muscles of the perineum.
- Select a forward tilt of your pelvis that ensures comfort and health of your back and genitals.
- Relieve constant pressure on the saddle that compresses blood and lymph vessels and nerves.
- Diminish impacts through the saddle from the riding surface.

All these factors should be optimized to ensure comfort and freedom from injury on the saddle.

Saddle Selection and Design

Riders experiencing saddle discomfort often want assurance that a specific saddle model will be best for them. To select the best saddle for you, you must test ride and compare several models. One rider's experience does not transfer to another. You are each different in anatomy, riding style, tolerance to discomfort, and comfort expectations. Literally, riders range in tolerance from "hard ass" to "princess who slept on a pea." For a conclusive test, you will need to ride each saddle about 10 miles. Take the tools needed to adjust the saddle on each test ride and experiment with saddle tilt, height, and forward position. Find a bicycle retailer who will let you test ride saddles before making a final purchase.

The purpose of a bike saddle is to support rider weight on the seat bones, to protect the perineum from pressure, and to provide control of the bicycle using legs and buttocks. (A saddle with no horn severely limits the rider's ability to control the bike.)

One of the most important factors in saddle comfort is the contour of the top surface. It also

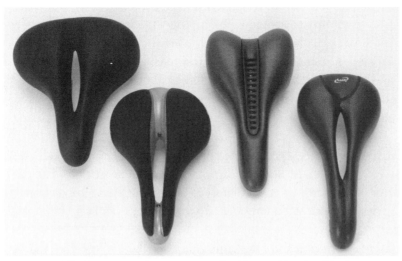

Cut-out saddle designs vary in contours and width, making it critical to test ride them to find the most comfortable one for you.

Evaluate saddle contours when selecting a saddle.

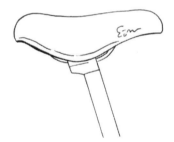 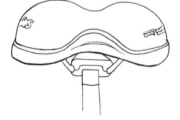 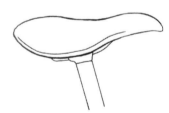

Flat top-contour

Back of saddle with pronounced bulges

Saddle with dip midway up the length

needs to be sufficiently wide and cushioned to support the seat bones without bruising the tissue under them. On the other hand, it should be narrow enough to allow ease in movement off the back of the saddle and to prevent chafing or pressure on the inner thighs. Finding this balance is a challenge for riders with wide pelvic bowls and bulky thighs. The center of the length of the saddle should be depressed or cut out to prevent pressure on the perineum. Many riders appreciate a reasonably flat saddle. Riders weighing less than 150 pounds will have trouble resting securely on saddles that bulge under the seat bones. If there is a dip across the saddle midway up the horn, the rider tends to slide into the dip and to experience pressure on the front of the perineum and pubic bone. These are general observations, however, so don't shy away from a saddle you like just because it does not conform to these guidelines.

Much ado has been made of gel saddles. This high tech material developed to simulate human tissue has given comfort to many riders. However, the term "gel" means only that the saddle contains *some* gel. Often a thin film of gel is placed over foam, giving the saddle the characteristics of foam while the benefits of the gel are lost. All-gel saddles spread the pressure on the seat bones over a larger area, while foam causes the greatest pressure where the seat bone presses deepest into the saddle. You will especially appreciate the distribution of pressure afforded by gel when you ride multiple-day tours and if you weigh 200 pounds and more. However, gel saddles are heavier and may not be contoured for comfort.

If you are considering a gel saddle pad, bear in mind that they have limited value because the top-surface contour of gel saddle pads is poorly defined. In fact, they tend to apply pressure equally to the entire perineum, which may quickly cause numbness to the entire saddle contact area.

The material that covers a saddle strongly influences comfort. You may consider buying a saddle with a durable, weather- and abrasion-resistant cover of leather or leather-like material. Most of these materials are fairly stiff and increase pressure under your seat bones.

Lycra® and other supple materials are pliable and generally will be more comfortable. You can increase their durability by protecting them with decorative or water-resistant slip-on covers.

Saddle Position

Three important aspects of bicycle saddle position are height, forward position, and tilt. Selecting an optimum position for you will probably require a compromise between comfort and body mechanics.

Saddle Height

This is based on proper leg extension while pedaling. Sit on the saddle as if riding, hips centered on the saddle, and seat bones supported on the widest part of the saddle. Wear your cycling shoes and place the balls of your feet over the spindle (or clip into your pedals). Push one pedal to the bottom of the crank rotation, keeping your knee slightly flexed. Align the crankarm with the seat tube of the frame. That leg should be extended 85 to 90 percent or bent at 25 to 30 degrees.

A few cautionary notes in establishing saddle height:

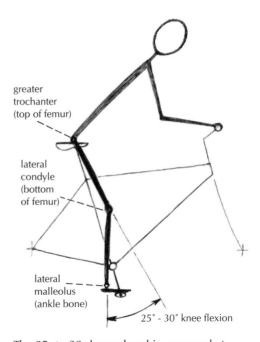

The 25- to 30-degree bend is measured at the knee between lines formed by the greater trocanter (hip joint), lateral femoral condyle (protrusion on the outside of the knee), and by a second line formed by the lateral femoral condyle and the lateral malleolus (bump on the outside of the ankle).

1. Be sure that your leg is flexed but not hyper-extended.

2. Be sure that your hips do not rock from side to side on the saddle when you ride. Have a friend ride behind you and observe your hips. Such rocking can cause severe saddle discomfort and inefficiency. Lower the saddle until you are able to reach the pedals without tipping your hips or pointing your toes.

3. Make changes in your saddle position gradually. Rapid change can result in sore muscles. If you are a high-mileage road biker, modify the height by one-eighth-inch increments every four to five rides.

Situations where it is appropriate to *lower* your seat post a little:
- You are setting up your mountain bike for technical riding.
- You are uncomfortable on the saddle and are seeking greater comfort.
- You have just moved your saddle back on the rails.
- You have installed a new saddle of greater height between the top surface and the rails than the one used for the measurement.
- You have changed cycling shoes or pedals, and this has decreased the distance between your foot and the pedal spindle.

It is appropriate to *raise* your seat post a little if:
- You point your toes at the bottom of the pedal stroke rather than keeping your feet close to horizontal.
- You are using a suspension seat post (or other form of suspension that varies the seat height).
- You have just moved your saddle forward on the rails.
- You have installed a new saddle of less height than the one used for the measurement.
- You have changed cycling sole thickness or pedal platform height.

If we asked you to walk with extremely deep knee bends you would know that this is exhausting.

You might like to compare the height you have set up with a calculated height described in Chapter 6, p. 262. Many riders need to install a longer seat post to accommodate proper leg extension when the bike is properly fitted to rider proportions.

Avoid being tricked by two misconceptions about saddle height that result in too low a saddle placement.

Misconception I: "I want my feet to touch the ground easily when I'm seated on the saddle. I'm just going to lower it." This is okay if you are getting used to a new bike and plan to ride a few miles on flat terrain. As you gain confidence on the new bike, gradually move

But many riders sabotage their pleasure and endurance by riding with their seats too low.

the saddle up to proper height. Practice getting off the saddle as described under "How to Get on Your Bike While Benefiting Your Hips," pp. 206-207.

The highly repetitive nature of pedaling a bike makes it critical to establish a saddle position for easy pedaling, not for ease in sitting on the seat while stopped. A saddle that is too low stresses your knees. Try this convincing demonstration of how damaging it is to your knees to ride with the saddle too low. Walk around the room with your knees bent at 90 degrees. Notice how quickly your legs fatigue. Knee discomfort is usually an indication that something is wrong, not that you are getting a good workout.

Misconception II: "I like my saddle lower than the handlebars so I can sit more upright." This rationale will cause you to sacrifice your knees to protect your neck. After raising the saddle as calculated above for correct leg extension, observe the relationship of your saddle to your handlebar height. Most riders like to have their handlebars at least as high as the top of the saddle. Once you have established the proper seat height, does your handlebar position cause you to ride with too much forward lean or too great an arm reach to be comfortable? If so, correcting the problem will require some research or advice from your bike mechanic. Most traditional stems are too short to raise. Look for the marks on the vertical portion of the stem and place them at the headset locknut. This is the maximum, safe stem height. If this position does not bring the handlebars high enough to make you comfortable, you will need a new stem and/or stem extender. Refer to the illustrations of these components on p. 269.

Forward Position of the Saddle

The forward position of the saddle determines whether the hips and knees work at the middle or edge of their range of motion. The efficiency and endurance of these joints is strongly influenced by the relationship of the seat bones to the crank. **This relationship is the foundation of bike setup, and handlebar position should be established after seat height and forward position are established.** Rather than setting the forward position of the seat based on the middle of the seat rails, establish the correct position based on your femur length and pelvic structure.

Here is a simple test to establish the best position for you. With the saddle at the correct height and the crankarms horizontal, drop a plumb line from the shinbone just below the kneecap (this is the head of the tibia) of your forward foot. The plumb should come within a half-inch of the pedal spindle with the ball of your foot centered above the spindle. This allows the best biomechanical advantage for uniform power on the full pedal stroke. If this saddle position leaves you farther from the handlebars than you would like, modify the handlebar position with a different stem rather than by sliding the saddle too far forward on its rails.

If the correct forward position of the saddle places the seat post clamp at the extreme front end of the rails, they will probably bend over time, forcing you to replace your saddle. You can avoid the risk of damaging your saddle or having it break during a ride by selecting a different seat post. Some seat posts clamping mechanisms are located farther behind the center of the seat post. These are designed to accommodate riders with a *pushing* style of pedaling but they will provide a greater range of forward adjustment for riders with longer than average femurs.

Saddle Tilt

Base your choice of saddle tilt on perineal comfort, back comfort, ability to generate power, and freedom of movement of your diaphragm.

Saddle comfort is generally improved by positioning the top of the saddle nearly horizontal or by tipping the front of the saddle slightly upward. Bearing your weight on your seat bones relieves pressure on your perineum. If you have tipped the front of your saddle down, be aware of the resulting problems. First, this shifts more weight forward onto your hands, which can contribute to numb hands and sore shoulders. Second, it causes you to slide forward onto the narrow part of the saddle. In this position your perineum bears most of your weight rather than your seat bones.

A plumb line dropped from the head of the tibia should fall within a half-an-inch of the ball of the foot and the pedal spindle when the forward position of the saddle is correct.

How does tilting your saddle affect your back? Tilting the front of your saddle up will probably cause you to shift your pelvis toward a more vertical position. Unless you sit completely upright, the vertical pelvis causes you to round your lower back, diminishing your

Tilting the front of the saddle up will probably cause you to ride with a vertical pelvis, losing your lumbar curve while arching your back.

Selecting a comfortable saddle that enables you to maintain your healthful S-curve and will reduce strain on your spine.

lumbar curve and your ability to generate power. It is healthier for your back to maintain its natural S-curve. The classic "flat back" of road riders means that the spine is in a healthy alignment but it will probably cause unacceptable pressure on the genitals. I recommend you select a cut-away saddle to eliminate pressure on your perineum. This will give you the option to tilt your pelvis forward, maintain the natural S-curve of your spine, breathe diaphragmatically, and output more power.

However, if you choose to ride with a forward lean greater than 45 degrees, you will limit your comfort and health choices. Refer to "The Influence of Your Pelvic Tilt on Your Diaphragm Function," p. 215.

Rider Clothing

For the last 20 years, cycling clothing has been dominated by Lycra® jerseys, shorts, and tights. Now the greater variety of choices should help you find just what you desire in cost, style, and function. Before shopping, you may even find suitable cycling clothes in your current wardrobe. Here are some critical factors to consider in choosing riding clothes to optimize comfort on the saddle:

1. Eliminate seams and elastic under the seat bones because they cause bruising and inflammation of your sebaceous glands (known as saddle sores) and often lead to painful infections. Major offenders are blue jeans and underwear elastic. If you do not have cycling specific clothing and are beginning to ride regularly, you may find that sweat pants or wind pants provide freedom from chafing and bruising.

2. You may also want to invest in cycling undershorts known as liner shorts. They are less expensive that cycling shorts and convert much of your leisure wardrobe to a cycling wardrobe. This is an especially good choice for very large and very small riders since bicycle clothing manufacturers have a limited understanding of the diversity of human body size.

3. Cycling-specific shorts have been the norm among dedicated cyclists for years. They are worth considering and are now available in form-fitting Lycra® or loose-fitting casual shorts with padded liner. The loose-fitting shorts of Supplex® or twill may be more enjoyable when your ride includes a picnic, hike, or shopping. The function of the crotch-insert is to cushion the seat bones and to protect the genitals from pressure and chaffing. Just as with saddles, there are many varied designs, and the only way to be sure a particular crotch-insert will increase your comfort is to ride in them. Unfortunately, you will need to purchase them to make this experiment.

4. There are several things you should know when fitting Lycra® shorts. You should see wrinkles of fabric across the buttocks when you stand upright. The shorts are tailored to be smooth when you bend forward in a traditional riding position.

Consider this while trying on shorts and avoid buying them too small. If the shorts are too tight, they will be less durable, and the insert can be pulled up tight against your perineum, causing increased discomfort. Try on several sizes of the same short design to determine the best fit.

5. Proper care of cycling shorts will reduce the likelihood of saddle sores and prolong the life of the garment. Wash them after every wearing. The moist, dark environment of the crotch-insert makes it an ideal medium for bacterial growth. On multiple-day tours, especially at temperatures higher than 70 degrees, select shorts that dry overnight or take enough pairs to change them daily. Personal hygiene is also important. Regular bathing of the area that contacts the saddle is recommended. If your overnight facilities do not allow bathing, wiping the skin under the seat bones with rubbing alcohol or antiseptic first aid fluid is good insurance against saddle sores.

6. Some riders find comfort with no padding. If you weigh less than 150 pounds and have a well-contoured and cushioned saddle, try riding without crotch padding. Bulky padding can contribute to pressure on the perineum, and you might feel more comfort without it. Liner shorts without padding or with thin padding can eliminate elastic and seams under your seat bones.

Sooner or later everyone gets saddle sores. They usually start as inflamed sebaceous glands and mature into pimples. The sooner you treat these the better. Before they progress into boils, clean them carefully with clear, low-oil bath soap. Rinse and dry carefully, then apply rubbing alcohol, antibiotic ointment, or tea tree oil. Determine what works best for you. You may find that alternating disinfectants is effective. Be sure to remove ointment or oils completely with each bathing or reapplication. If you ride a lot of miles or have sensitive skin, warm sitz baths in Epsom salts can prevent infections and facilitate healing.

Riding Style

Let's face it. The human butt was not designed for riding on a little bicycle saddle. For that reason, all aspects of riding must be optimized to be comfortable on the saddle and protect the genitals on long rides. The more intensely you ride, the more vulnerable you will be to saddle area problems. Keep your body supple and stretch often, both on and off the bike. Change positions regularly and take a little walk from time to time.

Diminished circulation in the saddle area is a common cause of discomfort and numbness in the perineum and lower extremities. Major blood vessels, nerves, and lymphatic vessels, which feed, cleanse, and innervate the lower extremities, pass through the groin where they are compressed between your body weight and the saddle. Even if you don't stop and dismount, raise your weight off the saddle several times each hour to let these nerves and vessels continue normal function. Give special attention to this while climbing hills. During bicycle tours, take a water or snack break or even a brief walk to give yourself a "circulation break." This will improve blood flow and enable nourishing blood to flow amply into your legs and depleted blood to return to your heart and lungs. Such a break will also diminish impingement of the nerves in your hips and on the saddle and reduce the likelihood of numb feet. The unimpaired flow of lymph fluids can more effectively cleanse cellular waste products from your legs and feet.

Whenever you are off the bike for several weeks, begin conditioning gradually. Several five- to ten-mile rides will give you some base of conditioning before setting out on 25- to 50-mile rides. If you ride a long distance without preparing your saddle-contact area, you may have to give up riding while you allow your damaged tissue to heal.

To avoid abuse, rise off the saddle while riding over rough surfaces, whether potholes in the street, or a long, rough descent on a mountain trail. One bad impact to the perineum can be very painful and damaging. Suspension seat posts, which are both economical and effective, are an excellent addition to saddle comfort. You might also test ride saddles with elastomers or coil springs built in to absorb impacts.

If you are not inclined to buy new equipment, you can increase your comfort by regulating your tire pressure carefully. Many riders place more value on efficiency than on personal wellness. Consequently, they inflate their tires to excessively high pressure, thus preventing their tires from absorbing a lot of impact. Try lowering your tire pressure. If you weigh less than 150 pounds, keep your 100 psi tires at 90 to 95 psi. Mountain bike tire pressure is more comfortable between 35 to 40 psi. If you weigh more than 150 pounds, you will need to increase your tire pressure to protect your rims and inner tubes. Experiment. You may be delighted! Refer to the section on tire pressure on p. 278.

Special Saddle Comfort Notes for Men

Fortunately, media attention to penile numbness among cyclists has made it easier to discuss this delicate subject. For years, the cycling community has discussed this subject, as well as the potential for impotency caused by long hours of high-energy riding on hard, narrow bike saddles. More public debate has been led by urologist Irwin Goldstein, M.D. Like all crusaders, he has taken an extreme position. His study of male impotency related to cycling indicates that the major cause is falling on the top tube of the bicycle during childhood and adulthood. (This is further reinforcement for the importance of proper bike fit at all ages.) The resulting debate has renewed concern about impotency among male cyclists. Prolonged compression of the vascular bundle can cause arterial scarring and reduce blood flow into the penis. This problem is intensified for riders who weigh more than 180 pounds and older men with general circulation problems and enlarged prostates.

The solution to the problem is *not* to stop riding, because the general health benefits of cycling are too significant. Here are some suggestions:

1. Ride less intensely. When you experience discomfort or numbness, change your position, get off and walk, and shorten your ride.

2. Optimize your comfort *before* a problem develops since symptoms are not always present.

3. Bear your weight on your seat bones and not on the genitals.

4. Wear cycling shorts to help dissipate pressure on the vascular bundle.

5. Lift your weight off the saddle as frequently as every fifteen minutes to let the blood flow.

6. Minimize impacts transmitted from the rear wheel through the saddle by shifting your weight off the saddle onto your pedals in anticipation of bumps. Here is a great excuse for a suspension seat post or saddle with shock absorbing elastomers or coil springs.

7. Determine your optimum weight distribution between saddle and handlebars and modify your bike to accommodate this.

8. Work with qualified professionals to make sure your bike fits properly and to establish a riding position that optimizes your comfort and minimizes pressure on the genitals.

9. Experiment with several saddles until you find the right one. Don't get stuck on how trendy the saddle looks when you are off your bike. You won't feel very trendy at mid-life with erectile dysfunction.

Historically, men take two different approaches to relieving pressure on the vascular bundle:

a. Most men "dress right or dress left." That means placing their genitals slightly right or left of center. For lean men with a preference for one side, riding a reasonably narrow saddle with a ridge down the middle allows them to sit slightly off center and minimize compression to the urogenital vessels. Again, bear in mind that this asymmetric riding position increases your risk of strain or injury due to prolonged imbalanced body use.

b. For stocky men and those whose genitals are centered, a wider, amply padded saddle can help them bear their weight on their seat bones and dissipate pressure on the vascular bundle.

In any case, support your weight on your seat bones and test ride as many saddles as necessary to find complete comfort.

Special Saddle Comfort Notes for Women

A woman's pelvic floor has limited support. When the pelvic floor muscles are well toned, the abdominal organs are held higher in the pelvis. This reduces pressure on the soft tissue contacting the saddle. Use the Kegel exercise to tone and maintain your perineal muscles. Learn to contract the pelvic floor muscles by pretending to shut off the flow of urine. With your abdominal muscles relaxed, tighten the pelvic floor muscles, hold for five seconds and then release for five seconds. If you have not been practicing the Kegel exercise regularly, perform three sets of 10 daily. Lying on your back to practice shifts the weight of your abdominal organs off the pelvic floor and reduces pressure on the perineum. This position may help you as you develop your skill and strengthen your perineum. As a maintenance routine perform 10 repetitions daily while standing or sitting to increase the workout. These exercises not only develop the integrity of the pelvic floor but can reduce bloating and improve bowel comfort and function. Practicing this exercise daily for the rest of your life reduces your risk of urinary incontinence, diminished sexual function, and genital prolapse as you get older.

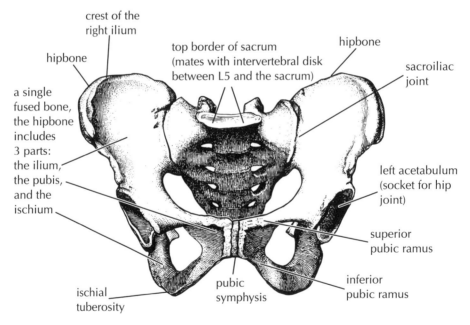

The female pelvis is broader and flatter than the male pelvis and has a larger cavity for child bearing. Notice how a narrow bicycle seat that does not support the ischial tuberosities presses directly into the urogenital triangle formed by the ischia and pubis. In this position it is possible for the saddle to apply excess pressure to the inferior pubic ramus and increase risk of compression to the pudendal nerves, arteries, and veins. Choosing a saddle wider than your ischial tuberosities that is flat or depressed through the longitudinal center can diminish damaging pressure to the perineum and genitals. These observations are true for men and women. (*Anatomy of Hatha Yoga*)

Women must give special attention to hygiene because vaginal infections are likely to result from casual care. Avoid abuse to the perineum by stopping your ride before you damage that tissue. Just tell your riding companions that you need to take a break or stop riding for the day. Everyone has experienced severe saddle discomfort and will understand your need to change plans.

Women riders have more "favorite" salves and lotions than I can count. I suggest avoiding greasy ointments since they are difficult to wash off, retain infection-causing bacteria, and interfere with normal sebaceous gland function. You might try applying a little Baby Magic by Playtex® or another light emulsion between your inner labia after bathing. Post-menopausal women can increase comfort by occasional application of estrogen vaginal creams.

Even though female and male genitals are distinctively different externally, the blood vessels that feed them and the nerves that give them sensation follow the same route under the inferior pubic ramus. This bone connects the ischium with the pubic bone. Pressure exerted by the bike seat against this bone can cause compression of the pudendal vessels and nerves critical to genital health and function. If you weigh more than 180 pounds or delight in riding pounding descents, you need to give special care to selecting a saddle and suspension in the seat post or rear triangle of your frame. Consider further that a typical bike saddle provides one fifth of the support of sitting in a chair and pressure per square inch is greatly increased on the bike seat. It is clear that finding comfort on the saddle is not just a matter of comfort but is critical to your health and sexual pleasure.

Skillful Bike Handling Begins with the Hips

Keeping your hips relaxed and supple is the secret to quick and effective bike control. Supple hips depend on relaxation of the entire torso and on fluid, lateral movement of your spine.

Consider unicycle riding technique. Even though riders have no handlebars, they are capable of maneuvering unicycles in tight curves. Riders turn their unicycles by dipping their hips in the direction they want to turn. Without handlebars to turn or a frame to push against laterally, the movement of the hips combined with weight shifting causes the rider to turn the unicycle when desired. These skills transfer well to bicycle handling. You can increase your balance and bicycle control skills by practicing riding without using your hands. Select a time when you are relaxed and in a place free of traffic. Ride at a moderate pace with no hands, striving to control your bike with your hips, anchoring your sight on a distant point, and shifting your weight. More subtle movements can be achieved by moving individual knees to one side or the other for lateral corrections.

Finesse is Riding Lightly on Your Bike

Learning to ride lightly on your bike will reduce abuse to your body and your bicycle.

Letting your bike dance beneath you will increase your technical finesse and efficiency. Again, relaxation is essential.

Contrast these two styles on a fast, steep descent. First imagine that you are tired after a long day. Your hands grip the brakes, and your arms, shoulders, and neck are tight with tension and fatigue. You lose focus and are unable to avoid a hole in front of you. Blam! You hit it square on. Due to your rigid body, all your weight is forced onto your front wheel. Although you maintain control, the impact to your front wheel leaves a permanent flat spot in your rim and probably a flat tire.

In the second scenario, you are relaxed and focused. Your hands grip the brakes firmly but your arms, shoulders, and neck are relaxed. Your elbows are flexed, and you float downhill. When a large pothole appears, you ease off the saddle and drop to an easy, loose crouch. As your bike drops into the hole, your legs and arms absorb the impact. Smoothly, you sit down on the saddle and fly on down the hill with ease without abusing your bike or body.

While suspension increases your comfort level in all technical situations, it is not a replacement for riding skill. Avoid becoming careless on a bike with suspension by bashing into obstacles. It is hard on your bike as well as on your body and complicates interactions with other trail users.

Find your balance point by locating your center of gravity on your bike. You can do this by rolling forward slowly and shifting your weight to the side until you start to fall over. Now try this off the saddle and notice how quickly you can correct your bike from this position. Riding in a relaxed crouch off the saddles allows you to move your bike freely beneath you to respond quickly to obstacles.

Pedaling primarily propels your bike but it can also be used advantageously to help you relax and to increase traction. Of course you pedal on the ascents and high-speed flats but pedaling on descents as well facilitates relaxation and reaction time. Coasting with your legs in a locked position usually causes tension to build up. If the surface you're riding on is smooth, sit on the saddle and spin your pedals for relaxation. If it is rough, get out of the saddle and flex your legs in a relaxed crouch. Either of these positions also allows you to respond quickly with your feet to avoid hitting obstacles with your pedals.

Pedaling on descents also gives you increased control through improved traction with the rear wheel. A freely rolling wheel can't be directed as quickly as one under power, and a locked-up wheel can only skid. If you are in loose gravel or snow and pedaling on the descent causes you to go faster than you feel safe, pedal for control while you steadily apply the brakes to reduce your speed. Try it; you may be surprised!

I learned this counter-intuitive lesson years ago while watching a mountain bike race. I was watching at the top of a near-vertical slope about 100-feet long. Goodness knows I would have walked my bike down this slope by balancing it on the rear wheel while controlling the speed with my rear brake. However, this is what I observed. The novice-class riders began riding tentatively down this slope, locking up their rear wheels with their brakes and skidding wildly this way and that. Dust flew everywhere, and several of the riders flew off their bikes before reaching the bottom. To my amazement, the expert-class riders never stopped pedaling. Yes, they did ride at higher speeds, but by pedaling all the way down the slope, they arrived at the bottom in control. Wow!

This technique can also be used in snow, ice, sand, or mud. Riding under these conditions is excellent for improving bike handling skills and confidence. Be especially supple and relaxed but ready to apply power to pull out of a skid and regain control. Body tension diminishes traction by preventing your bike from gliding to the most stable surface.

Breath control and bike control are interwoven. On trail or road, when the challenges of navigation increase, it is easy to become anxious, breathe erratically, tighten up, over-react, and fail to negotiate technical challenges successfully. Use a conscious, prolonged, exhale to return to relaxed control and successful completion of a demanding section. Try this technique on unexpected ice and when you experience a loss of confidence during stream-crossings or a rapid sequence of obstacles on single track. This is a very rewarding way to turn a deteriorating situation around. Rather than trying to power your way through technical single track, ride more slowly, relax, and be ready and able to respond appropriately to each obstacle.

If you are having an off-day, and your repeated blunders are rattling you, try this technique used by professional athletes. First, take three, controlled diaphragmatic breaths. It is physically impossible to remain anxious or tense while breathing abdominally. Next, say a simple, unarguable statement like: "Today is Wednesday" or "The sky is blue." This sets your mind in a positive mode and helps you let go of your poor performance. Letting go of the past is as important as getting back to the present. Forget the blundering performance you have just demonstrated and look ahead to riding on with finesse. (Hendricks, p. 161)

To ride with finesse requires that you ride within your focus and energy level on all occasions because focus is paramount to control. Your energy — and consequently your bike — will go where you direct your visual focus. Avoid looking at an object you want to avoid. Instead, look at the line you want to ride. Lead with your chin when you need to make a sharp turn, such as negotiating a switchback. Lift through the top of your head, pivoting your neck on the spinal column, and look back into the turn. Your body and bike will execute the turn skillfully.

You will also control your bike with greater ease if you keep your head upright and look down the trail 20 to 30 feet or down the road 100 feet or more, depending on your riding speed. This visual rudder helps stabilize you much as a physical rudder would. It also gives you more time to pick the line for your tires, anticipate moves, respond to obstacles, and be more relaxed in general. Remember that relaxation is what enables you to stay supple and to respond to challenges ahead. Because many novice trail riders remain preoccupied with the details right in front of their bikes, they are doomed to continual panic response. Try to stay aware of the quality of your mental focus, which changes from day to day and from moment to moment. If your mind is scattered and your body weary, slow down. Beware of the challenge of group rides, where riders tend to concentrate on group dynamics rather than on their own condition. While you develop basic skills, ride alone or with friends who will accommodate each other's needs.

Improving Your Bike Handling Skills with Practice Exercises

You can have fun improving your skills at any level. Try some of these exercises out of the way of traffic.

1. Set up a low-speed slalom course of small stones. Practice weaving around the stones both on and off the saddle. Increase the challenge by placing the stones progressively closer together.

2. Practice skidding on snow, sand, or gravel to build confidence and a relaxed style. Select a construction site or other place where skidding will not cause erosion and deterioration of a trail.

3. Achieve control by riding along a two-by-four-inch board placed flat on the ground.

4. Develop your weight-shifting skills by riding slowly up a curb without pedaling. Shift your weight back and pop the front wheel up for an easy wheelie over the curb. Then shift all your weight to the front wheel and let the rear wheel roll up onto the curb.

There is no need to swing your leg over the high saddle. Just step over the top tube while holding your handlebars and saddle.

5. Set yourself up for success by riding when you are relaxed, energetic, and confident. Back off when you feel tense, tired, or puny.

6. Try other conditioning activities such as unicycling, skiing, footbag, Taiji, and Yoga.

7. Learn to ride like a child: be sensitive to your body's feedback and your bike all the time.

How to Get on Your Bike While Benefiting Your Hips

Abandon the childhood practice of running and taking a flying leap onto one pedal while swinging the other leg over the saddle. This can be stressful to your bicycle frame (since you weigh more than 60 pounds

Simple Steps to Starting to Ride with Control

Begin with one pedal at the two-o'clock position.

As you bear your weight on the raised pedal, the bike begins to roll forward.

From this increased height, sit back onto the saddle.

Reverse this Process to Dismount with Control

Shift your weight onto the lowered pedal and lift your buttocks off the saddle.

Slowing your speed with the hand brakes, lower your second foot to the ground.

Shift your weight onto the ground and complete your controlled stop.

now) and will create imbalances in your hips if you habitually mount your bike from the same side.

A more controlled way to start riding is to stand facing your bike with one hand on the handlebars and one on the saddle. Just step over the top tube so that you are straddling the bicycle frame. Now place one foot on your pedal and raise it to about the two- or twelve-o'clock position. Place your weight on this pedal and as the bicycle begins to roll forward (controlled skillfully with your hand brakes), rise back onto the saddle and bring your other foot onto the second pedal. After you have gained momentum, place your second foot in your pedal attachment system. To dismount, reverse this process step-by-step.

What are the benefits of this technique? It allows you to reach the ground easily while mounting and dismounting *and* to use a correct seat height for effective pedaling. It is an excellent opportunity to increase your hip flexibility. Most of us

Riders with limited hip movement can mount their bikes by laying the bike down on the ground and stepping over the width of the frame. Then just lift the bike up so you are straddling it.

Bike Friday®'s top tubes are so low they are easy to mount and fun to travel with, folded into their suitcase/trailer. Both Rex at six feet two inches and Mary Lou at five feet two inches can ride this frame with confidence and control.

mount our bikes from a favorite side. Here is a chance to make your non-dominant side as flexible in the hip and strong and stable in the leg as your dominant side. Consciously mount your bike from the "other" side, until it feels comfortable and you can do it with confidence.

If you have an impairment in your hips or knees, you can mount a bike that seems too high by tipping it over toward the ground, letting it down by the handlebars, and then stepping sideways across the width of the frame. From this wider stance, pull your bike up between your legs so that you straddle it. If neither of these techniques is possible, don't give up cycling. Seek out a frame design or bike style with an unusually low top tube. Step-through frames are available in some economical models. If you want a more expensive bike, a splendid option is a Bike Friday® by Green Gear®. They are built on 20-inch wheels and fold for transport. Another winning aspect is that their top tubes are about 21 inches high measured seven inches in front of the seat tube. Many riders have been able to mount a Bike Friday® with enough ease to continue enjoying cycling even after hip replacement.

Common Problems of the Hips

Problems originating in the hips are common and difficult to diagnose. The challenge arises from the complexity of the pelvis and the tissue, organs, blood vessels, and nerves that are located in or attached to it. Let's look at the structure and functions of the pelvic region that are important to cycling:

- The skeleton of the pelvic region includes the pubis, seat bones (part of the

ischium), hip joints (part of the ilium), tailbone (coccyx), sacrum, and lumbar spine.
- Muscles of the thighs so active in cycling originate in the hips.
- Muscles of the pelvis stabilize the trunk and legs.
- Muscles of the abdomen support breathing.
- Organs in the pelvic bowl process digestion, elimination, and reproduction.
- Many of the nerves that innervate the legs and feet originate at the lumbar spine and travel through the pelvis.
- The floor of the pelvis includes the perineum and genitals.

All of us have some degree of asymmetry in the hips. For many of us that means our right side is stronger, less flexible, and slightly forward of the left hip. Two factors contribute to this condition: most people are right dominant and spend a lot of time driving. Because the right foot operates the accelerator and the brake, we tend to hold the right leg and hip chronically tight and somewhat forward of the left hip. If you are left dominant, this problem may not be so dramatic. These tendencies are compounded by continued misuse of your bodies when you are not driving. You may find yourself consistently using your right leg whenever strength and balance are required, making it still stronger and tighter. This asymmetry contributes to lower back problems and other imbalances throughout the body. In addition to regular stretching and strengthening exercises, remember to balance daily use of your legs to reduce the likelihood of strain and injury.

The pelvic region is a common site of retained emotional distress. To work on improving your well-being and reducing problems originating in the hips, examine both physical and emotional elements. Because resolution of problems originating in the hips may not be as simple as stretching daily, I have great compassion for riders who labor over saddle discomfort, numbness or pain in the inner thighs, and lower back pain. These nagging problems require commitment to treatment, changes in life style, and retraining to use your bodies naturally.

Search your emotions and try to discover if you dislike parts of your pelvis, especially those that cause you problems. Changing your attitude toward these parts will contribute to their improved function and your general well-being. I discovered the importance of changing my attitude about my digestive and eliminative organs after fasting in preparation for an examination of the sigmoid colon. I asked myself why I had unpleasant feelings toward the exam and the preparation. I was surprised to discover that I disliked my colon. Probably these feeling began 30 years earlier when my mother died of colon cancer. I realized that disliking a vital part of my body would surely contribute to its ill-health. By studying the structure and function of the intestines, I developed a special appreciation and affection for them and subsequently I noticed they worked better.

If you have already experienced problems centered in the hips and have never sought professional help, this might be a good time to do so. Most of these problems stem from tension, misuse, and misalignment in the hips and lumbar spine. Professional counseling will help mend old emotional wounds and calm anxieties. Seek out the care of a massage therapist, chiropractor, osteopath, Rolfer, or other bodywork specialist. They can help you increase your awareness of your body-use habits and help you discover misalignments and chronic tension. Instruction in Alexander Technique and Qigong are other methods to help you achieve healthful equilibrium and effortless movement.

If you have been blessed with comfort and good function of your pelvis and its contents, you will benefit by regular exercises to maintain your continued well-being. Use the exercises listed below and the exercises for the abdominal muscles, pp. 227-228.

You have probably experienced some of the most common hip problems cyclists experience. Discomfort on the saddle leads the list and is discussed in detail beginning on page 191. Foot numbness or pain usually originates in the hips and is discussed under "Common Foot Problems and Discomforts," pp. 166-170.

Sciatic nerve impingement causes pain or numbness anywhere along the path of the nerves that innervate the hips, legs, and feet. The sciatic nerve is the largest nerve in the body and is actually a group of nerves. It originates in the lower back at the confluence of some of the sacral and lumbar nerves that originate from their respective vertebrae. They are the conduits for sensation from your lower extremities to your brain. As the components of the sciatic nerve travel down your legs, they divide at your knees into a complex network that gives sensation to your calves and feet. Although many people experience some discomfort in the buttocks and thigh, true sciatica is pain or numbness the length of the leg and into the foot. In severe cases the cause may be damaged disks. Here is a case where prevention is the best approach. Routine stretching and strengthening exercises for the muscles of the abdomen and lower back can prevent this painful problem that is usually initiated by pressure, overuse, and stress. Refer to the discussion of Dr. Sarno's treatment of TMS, pp. 62-63.

Piriformis syndrome is a condition in which the piriformis muscle irritates the sciatic nerve. The piriformis originates at the sacrum, connects to the top of the femur, and runs horizontally deep beneath the gluteal muscles of the buttock. (Refer to the illustration on p. 189.) It rotates the thigh laterally and will become tight and shortened when you sit cross-legged and in other positions that rotate the thighs and knees outward. Cycling and other activities that result in tight hamstring and buttock muscles also aggravate it. Usually the sciatic nerve runs beneath the piriformis but in about 15 percent of people it goes directly through the piriformis muscle, making them more prone to this condition. (Harvard Women's Health Watch, March 2001) This condition is best prevented before it develops. Use the piriformis stretch and cow posture for the lower limbs described on p. 187 to establish and maintain flexibility and mobility.

Iliotibial band friction syndrome can also cause pain at the hip joint. Refer to the causes and remedies for this common injury on p. 182.

Exercises to Improve the Alignment, Strength, and Flexibility of Your Hips

Maintenance exercises for the hip flexors and extensors focus on stretching chronically tight muscles. Heavy use while pedaling means these muscles are shortened in cyclists. Long hours sitting in chairs flexes both knees and hips and results in chronically shortened hamstrings, quads, and iliopsoas.

Intense side stretch — From mountain pose, widen your stance to about three feet. Turn your left foot out 90 degrees to point to the left. Point your right foot inward at a 45-degree angle to your left foot. Bring your left heel so it is in line with the arch of your right foot. Rotate your hips so that you face the left looking over your left foot. Standing erect, cross your forearms across your back, grasping your elbows. Draw your shoulders back to open your chest. Lifting from the top of your head and keeping your hips turned to the left, bend forward from your hip joints until your torso is horizontal. Keep your right heel anchored, stretching out the right hamstring. If that is not possible, shorten your stance or let your right heel come off the floor. Align your left knee so the knee cap is in line with your foot and gently draw your knee cap up without hyper-extending that knee. Engage the quadriceps of both legs and lift your seat bone upward to stretch your hamstrings. Breathe consciously and hold this posture, giving attention to how your hips feel. With an inhalation, raise your torso and pivot at your hip joint to your starting position. Let your arms hang relaxed at your sides and notice differences in sensation between your left and right sides. Turn and repeat to the right side.

Intense side stretch

Warrior — This is one of several warrior poses and addresses many aspects of body strength and flexibility. Begin again in mountain pose and widen your stance to about four feet. Your ankles should be directly under your wrists when your arms are

Warrior

Locked gate

fully extended at your sides at shoulder height. Turn your left foot out 90 degrees and your right foot in about 45 degrees. Line up the left heel with the instep of your right foot. Keep your hips facing the original direction, at right angles to the left foot. Raise your arms to shoulder level, stretching out through your fingertips. Turn your head to face left, lifting from the top of your head. Bend your left leg until your knee is directly above your left ankle (your knee is bent at 90 degrees). Drop your scapulae and relax your shoulders. This can be achieved by rotating your palms upward, checking your scapulae, then rotating your palms downward again. Keep your torso erect as if being pulled back gently at your right shoulder. Breathe and hold. As strength and flexibility permit, widen your stance and drop your weight until your thigh is parallel to the floor. Come out of the posture by reversing the process. Repeat on the other side.

Locked gate — This posture is excellent for digestive organs. Kneel on the floor with your hips above your knees. Place your left leg straight out to the left with your foot pointing forward. The toes of your left foot should align with the right knee. If it is more comfortable, place your left heel on the floor at right angles to your left shin and in line with your right knee. Keep the right thigh vertical and raise your arms to shoulder height, extending out through your fingertips. Rotate your palms upward. Bend to the left at the waist, letting your left hand rest on your left leg. Raise your right arm over your head, above or touching your right ear. Look up to your right elbow. Breathe, hold, and repeat on the other side.

Preparation for the pigeon — This stretches the perineum, piriformis, and iliopsoas. Start on your hands and knees and straighten your legs as you come up onto your feet. Bring your left knee forward, placing it mid-way between your hands with your left foot placed under your right groin. Move your right foot from resting on the toes to resting on the top of the foot and knee. Gently let your hips down toward your left foot. Look forward and lift through the top of your head, elongating your back and opening up across your chest. At first, rock your

Preparation for the pigeon

hips easily from side to side. As you become more limber, ease your weight down onto your pelvis and breathe deeply, letting your hips settle down.

Bridge — This supine stretch helps release the iliopsoas, stretches abdominal organs, and strengthens the inner thigh muscles. Lie on your back with your arms along your sides, palms down. Bend your knees and bring your heels about six inches from your buttocks. Lift your hips up as high as is comfortable by pushing your feet against the floor and by using your quadriceps. Do not work your back. Extend through the top of your head keeping your throat and neck soft. Keep your knees hip width apart. To come out of the pose, lay each vertebra on the floor beginning with the thoracic spine. To release your back from this back bend, draw your knees to your chest and place one hand on each knee. Roll sideways, elbow to elbow, and enjoy the massage across the rim of the pelvis.

Bridge

Shooting bow — You will stretch your hamstrings and groin muscles while stretching and strengthening your shoulders. Sit with your legs outstretched flat on the floor in front of you, toes drawn back toward your knees (dorsiflexed). Keep your pelvis upright, your back straight, and lift from the top of your head. Bring your hands forward to reach your shin or feet, wherever you can reach without sacrificing a flat back. Flex your knees slightly if necessary. With your left hand, grasp your left foot from the outside. As you exhale, lift your left foot back toward your left ear as far as possible by bending your left elbow and knee. Breathe consciously. When it becomes difficult to hold your foot by your ear, release your left arm and leg, placing your foot back on the floor keeping hold of your foot. Your left shoulder will benefit from stretching it while you securely hold your left foot as you place it back on the floor and straighten your knee. Visualize breathing into your shoulder and give attention to relaxing it. When you are satisfied with your shoulder stretch, release your hold on your foot and sit upright again. Repeat on the right side.

Shooting bow

Hip opener — This stretch complements the cow pose and increases lower back comfort by opening your hips (stretching

Hip opener

Maintaining Healthful Posture While You are Sitting

Are you sitting more and enjoying it less? By sitting with your pelvis tilted slightly forward you will maintain your lumbar curve, allow your diaphragm to perform well, and eliminate compression of the disks in your lower back. You will need to be selective in your choice of chairs. This distinction eliminates all overstuffed furniture. Instead, choose chairs that have high enough seats to place your knees lower than your seat bones. Few chairs are designed to do this but you can correct your desk chairs by placing a folded towel under your seat bones at the back of your chair seat. If you must sit in a chair that is too low for your size, move to the edge of the seat and place your feet under the chair or extend your legs out in front of you. Either technique will place your knees lower than your buttocks.

Avoid furniture that causes you to slouch or lean on the backrest. If you are tired, and back support feels good, you will probably cause an increase in your sense of fatigue when you flatten your lumbar curve. If you act exhausted, you will feel exhausted. Slouching compresses the diaphragm and limits effective breathing. The deficiency in your oxygen supply makes you even more fatigued and lethargic.

If you need to sleep, forget chairs and go lie down or put your head on a desk or table and catch a quick nap. The benefits of power naps are once more gaining attention.

hip abductors and lateral rotators). Sit cross-legged on the floor. Place your shins as close to parallel to each other as possible by bringing your feet under your knees. Lift through the top of your head to establish your natural spine curvature. Place the palms of your hands on the floor in front of your legs. Pivot at the hips without diminishing your lumbar curve. Gradually walk your hands out in front of you as far as possible without arching your back. Breathe deeply into your hips and lower back, and as they release, move your hands farther away.

Piriformis stretch — These last three exercises are in Chapter 5 on pp. 187 and 188.

Cow pose - lower limbs

ITB stretch

Acupressure — Refer to the acupoints for knees, thighs, hips, and lower back on pages 182-184 and 225-226.

Your Diaphragm

The function of the diaphragm is to support expansion and contraction of your lungs.

These muscles are controlled by the autonomic nervous system but you can also control them consciously to optimize breathing performance and psychological condition. For further details on the mechanics of active breathing refer to information in Chapter 4, pp. 76-77.

The Influence of Your Pelvic Tilt on Your Diaphragm Function

Sit on your bicycle in your usual riding position. Take a few full, diaphragmatic breaths in this position. Are you able to move your diaphragm effectively? Now try tilting the top of your pelvis forward (anterior pelvic tilt) while flattening your back and opening your abdomen and chest. Again, breathe several full, diaphragmatic breaths. Do you notice increased movement of your abdomen and chest? You can release confined diaphragm and abdominal muscles either by increasing the anterior tilt of your pelvis or by sitting more upright. These changes may necessitate selecting a more comfortable saddle or moving your handlebars closer to your shoulders. On the other hand you may discover that increasing your anterior pelvic tilt effectively lengthens your torso making your shoulders more comfortable with your existing handlebar arrangement.

Although you may like to wear a small pack around your hips for hiking, it will restrict the movement of your abdomen when you are breathing abdominally on your bike. I recommend you use a cargo rack and pack to carry supplies on your bike.

The significance of pelvic tilt is another example of how each part of your body plays a complex role in riding form. The classic, low, aerodynamic position of bicycle racers does reduce wind resistance and increase potential power output but it can also impair breathing. Extra lean bike racers may breathe effectively in that extreme position but riders with extra weight around the waist will breathe more easily and fuel their entire bodies with more oxygen if they sit with their backs and pelvises at less than a 45-degrees forward lean.

Exercises to Benefit Your Breathing Components

Acupressure

B 13 Lung associated point — *Benefits* - It releases the shoulder, neck, chest, and lungs and improves breathing. *Location* - It is on the back between the spine and scapula about a finger width below the upper tip of the collarbone. *Applications* - You can treat this acupoint sitting up or lying down. While sitting, reach over your right shoulder with your left hand and locate the bony ridge along the top of the scapula. Follow down toward your spine. You'll find a depression between muscles between the end of the ridge of the scapula and the spine. Find the achy place and apply pressure for several deep (SELF) breaths. Repeat on the left side. You can also apply pressure with a tennis ball while lying on your back. Refer to p. 138 for details.

TW 15 Heavenly rejuvenation — *Benefits* - It relieves tension and pain in the neck and shoulders, calms nerves, relieves nervous tension, increases resistance to colds and flu, and is good for the lungs. *Location* - It is located midway between the neck and outside of the shoulder just behind the highest point and above the shoulder blade. It is just below GB 21. *Applications* - Again reach across your chest with the left arm to the right shoulder and

Yoga swing

Taiji bear

curve your fingers into the sensitive spot. Maintain pressure for three SELF breaths, then release, relax your hands in your lap, and take three more breaths before repeating it on the other side. You can also pat these points on either side by alternately swinging your arms across your chest and patting yourself on the shoulders.

Lu 10 Fish border — *Benefits* - Pressure applied here relieves breathing difficulties, swollen throat, wrist pain, and tendonitis in the thumb extensor that may be aggravated by high resistance in thumb operated shifters. *Location* - It is on the palm-side of the thumb in the center of the fleshy pad at the base of the thumb. *Applications* - Lay your right hand palm up in your lap and apply pressure with the thumb of your left hand. You may also rub the area briskly.

Shiatsu points in the delto-pectoral crease — *Benefits* - It relieves breathing difficulties, chest tension, congestion, and tension due to emotional distress. *Location* - The three points are in the crease at the front of the shoulder between the deltoid and the major pectorals. The highest point is just three finger widths below the collarbone (Lu 1 Letting Go). *Applications* - Reach across your chest and with your fingertips press into the tender pectoral on the exhalation, hold about 15 seconds, gradually release on the inhalation, and move to the middle point less than an inch below. Repeat and move to the lowest point. Shiatsu will help you maintain a rhythmic action that is coordinated with your breathing. Repeat on the other side.

To Limber Your Diaphragm Area

Yoga swing — Stand with your feet spaced at shoulder width. Raise your arms and keep them at shoulder level. Rotate your arms and shoulders 90 degrees to the left, looking over your left shoulder. Your right heel may lift off the ground to facilitate this rotation. Then swing back 360 degrees to the right, look over your right shoulder, and allow your left heel to lift off the floor. Swing freely. Relax your chest and diaphragm and notice how air involuntarily moves in and out of your lungs. Breathe gently from your diaphragm.

Taiji bear — Again, stand with your feet spaced at shoulder width but plant them firmly and evenly weighted on the floor, keeping your knees flexed. Imagine yourself as a bear. Gently move your shoulders with your hips and let your arms swing limp from side to side. Avoid twisting your shoulders beyond the movement of your hips. Your hips and abdomen will receive a gentle massage as your forearms bump against them with each turning of the hips. Breathe diaphragmatically.

Spinal twist

Exercises to Improve Respiration

Spinal twist — This tranquil exercise massages the abdominal organs, releases the diaphragm area, and opens the chest. Sit on the floor with your legs stretched out in front of you while dorsiflexing your feet. Bend your left knee and bring your left foot back to your left buttock, placing the sole of your foot on the floor. Keeping your knee vertical, place your left hand close behind the center of your hips, with your fingers pointing straight back. Keep your left elbow straight and your spine elongated upward. Stretch your right arm out at shoulder height, bending your right elbow. Bring it across your chest and place your bent elbow on the left side of your left knee. Point your outstretched right hand upward. Continue to look over your right shoulder while you settle into the spinal rotation. Then turn your head to look back over your left shoulder. With each diaphragmatic inhalation, elongate upwards. With each exhalation, relax your torso into the twist. Hold the position, breathing deeply and evenly as long as you are comfortable. Then reverse the sequence to release the posture. Repeat on the right.

Triangle — This posture benefits many parts of the body and is worthy of daily practice. It is included here because of the fine stretch it gives the rib cage, diaphragm area, chest, and shoulder. Stand with your feet about three to four feet apart, facing the direction your feet are pointing. Your stance should be wide enough that your ankles are just below your wrists. Now turn your left foot 90 degrees to the left and your right foot 45 degrees toward the left. Keeping your hips facing the original direction, inhale and raise your arms to shoulder height

Triangle

with palms forward, gently stretching out toward your fingertips. Exhale and bend to the left over your left leg, pivoting at the hip joints. Let your left hand come down along your left leg or to your foot, wherever it is comfortable. Your right arm should point up, forming a straight, vertical line with your left arm. Extend through the top of your head, aligning your cervical spine with your thoracic spine, and then rotate your head to look up toward your right hand. Breathe deeply and evenly. Refinement points: Keep your right arm stretching straight up toward the ceiling. Rotate your right shoulder back and your right hip back in line with your left leg. Strive to make your body flat as if it were held between two pieces of parchment. Keep your right heel anchored, and thigh muscles gently engaged. Reverse the sequence to come out of the posture and repeat to the right.

You can open your chest further with a dynamic variation. Move your raised arm back as far as is comfortable. On the exhalation, move your upraised arm over your head above your ear. On the inhalation, move the same arm back to its backward position.

Cobra — This posture opens the chest, extends your spine backwards, and strengthens spinal erectors and triceps of the upper arm. It is also an excellent massage for abdominal and reproductive organs while aiding digestion. It helps to practice cobra regularly to build arm and shoulder strength – especially if your arms fatigue when you keep your elbows flexed on long rides.

Cobra

Lie face down. Place your palms on the floor with your hands aligned forward and your fingertips just under the top of your shoulders. Keeping your arms relaxed, lift your head and shoulders up with your back muscles. When you are as high as possible, use your arms to raise your shoulders farther. Lift from the top of your head, open your chest, and keep your shoulders relaxed, with your elbows close to the sides of your trunk, and elbow creases facing forward. Avoid lower back discomfort by pressing your pubis into the floor and squeeze your buttocks together. Strive to keep your feet together. Breathe deeply, hold and release gradually, letting down your mid-section, then your shoulders, and finally your head. Let your breathing return to normal and repeat several times.

Your Back

The function of your back is to stabilize the movements of all the rest of your body. A strong back is essential to efficient and healthful riding technique.

We have already discussed some aspects of back stability because the lumbar spine is part of the pelvic region but here's some more information to go on.

Optimum Use of Your Back

When riding skillfully, you use the back muscles that are necessary for balance and propulsion and relax the ones that do not contribute. Although the muscles of the back do not directly move the pedals, they do stabilize the pelvis for efficient leg action. Relaxation and the ability to distinguish between active and passive muscles are truly the secret to increased power and stamina as well as skillful bike handling and control. So why is it so difficult to relax and activate only those muscles specific to each task? It's probably because few riders breathe diaphragmatically and practice relaxation skills. Their cluttered minds interfere with biofeedback. They know they want to ride stronger so they pour on more power activating *all* muscles available, not just those specific to propelling the bike.

The anatomic illustrations in Appendix D, pp. 405-413, clarify the layered structure of all muscles including those of the trunk. The *deep muscles* are short and act precisely. They work constantly to maintain and recover proper anatomic alignment. In the back they act between adjacent vertebrae to maintain and recover proper stack of the vertebrae. The deep muscles are strengthened by movements that are close to vertical. We are more familiar with the outer or *superficial muscles* since we can see them move, often know their names, and can more readily move them voluntarily. Since they are larger in mass and length, they are more powerful and less precise than the deep muscles. Their actions are intermittent, and they are responsible for large ranges of motion such as extension of the spine and rotation of the trunk.

By identifying the primary muscle groups used for riding, you may be able to increase your awareness of the working muscles. The latissimus dorsi starts at your waist and extends along your spine, forming a large fan that ends up on your side, below your armpit. They insert on the humerus (bone of the upper arm) and act on your arms. The spinal erectors, just as the name says, run the full length of your back on either side of your spine. Their three component parts flex, extend, and laterally bend your back. The external obliques run from the back of the ribcage down to connect in the front of your pelvis. These abdominal

Outer and Intermediate Layers of Muscles of the Back

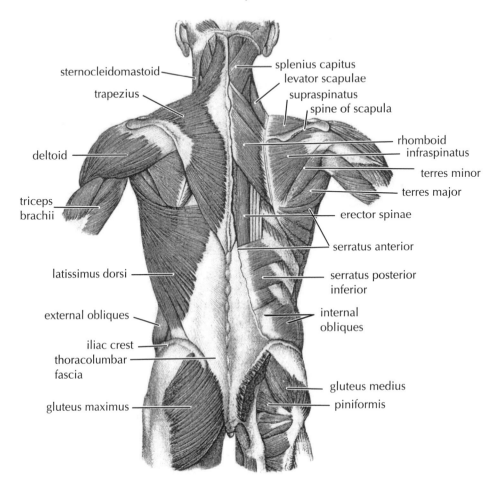

sternocleidomastoid

trapezius

deltoid

triceps brachii

latissimus dorsi

external obliques

iliac crest

thoracolumbar fascia

gluteus maximus

splenius capitus

levator scapulae

supraspinatus

spine of scapula

rhomboid

infraspinatus

terres minor

terres major

erector spinae

serratus anterior

serratus posterior inferior

internal obliques

gluteus medius

piniformis

The intermediate (and deep muscles) muscles of the back operate between the torso and lower extremities to stabilize the back and support the upper body. The superficial muscles of the upper back originate at the spine and manipulate the scapula and upper limbs. The spinal erectors are not shown here. They are the deep muscles of the back that hold the back erect. (Sappey)

muscles play an essential role in stabilizing and moving the upper body. When they are poorly developed, they shift undue load onto the back muscles making the back more vulnerable to fatigue and injury. **Strong abdominal muscles are essential to a healthy back.**

Optimum use of your back muscles will stabilize your body for efficient use of your limbs, open your chest, free your diaphragm for effective breathing, and diminish stress to your vertebrae and disks. Visualize extending from your tailbone through the top of your head and manifest that action by energetic intention rather than muscular force. At the same time, broaden across your scapulae without collapsing your chest. These are subtle actions that primarily use your deep muscles. They will help you avoid hunching your back and scrunching your shoulders. This riding posture will make you light and responsive and improve your bike handling skills and your breathing capacity.

Maintain your natural spinal curvature for a healthy spine. The mass of the body of each vertebra is designed to bear weight. Hold your torso and head erect and avoid slouching. Whatever forward lean you choose on your bike, maintain the S-curve of your spine. That will reduce asymmetric compression of your disks, avoid stressing your spinal ligaments, reduce fatigue, and reduce the risk of injury.

The profile of your back on your bike strongly influences your riding performance but it is limited to some degree by characteristics of your back. Three aspects of individual body proportions influence back profiles:

1. **The relative proportion of the height of your pelvis to the length of your upper back**
2. **The flexibility of your back**
3. **Weight distribution**

Keeping the pelvis vertical while riding with a forward lean causes compression of the vertebral disks and stress on the spine due to loss of the natural curve.

You may be aware of the **height of your pelvis** when you shop for pants. Because women characteristically have higher waists than men, women's pants are designed with longer rise. If you have a tall pelvis, arching your back on your bike has the effect of shortening your torso. If you sit with a forward lean of more than 15 degrees, you may be surprised to discover that increasing your pelvic tilt has the effect of lengthening your back. It will shorten your reach to the handlebars and increase power output. Again, I encourage you to tilt your pelvis forward, maintain the natural curvature of your spine, and use a saddle that is comfortable in this position.

Your individual mobility, possible impairments, and the range of movement possible at different parts of your spine determine the **flexibility of your back**. Daily practice of spinal rotations and forward and backward bends will optimize the flexibility of your

Contrast that with this healthful spinal curvature made possible by tilting the pelvis forward and engaging the deep muscles along the spine to energetically extend through the top of the head.

back. If you have had back injuries or have sensitive places in your spine, you will want to proceed slowly and gently with exercises. These may cause some parts of your spine to be permanently limited in mobility. However, by design, the spine is more flexible in some areas. Mobility is greatest between the sacrum and rib cage and in the neck. The structure of the pelvic bowl and the rib cage limits movement. Some points are so mobile we might refer to them as "hinge" points. They are at the base of the skull, the top of the thoracic spine (at the base of the neck), the base of the thoracic spine at the waist, and at the top of the sacrum. (Calais-Germain, Lamotte, pp. 18-21) Their greater mobility makes them more vulnerable to injury and increases the importance of supporting them with strong surrounding muscles.

Weight distribution plays an important role in your choice of riding position. If you carry substantial weight in your shoulders and upper body, you will probably want to lean forward less than 30 degrees. The more upright position will reduce the work of your shoulders, arms, and hands. On the other hand, if most of your weight is in your hips, leaning forward will require less effort. If you have a stout mid-section, leaning over can impair the use of your diaphragm. Weight distribution also influences your bike-handling style. Heavier shoulders facilitate forward weight shifts for control. Heavier hips require bolder movements to move your weight forward but facilitate lateral control with the hips.

Back profile plays a major role in your ability to generate power and in bike handling skills. Refer to "The Influence of Riding Position on Your Cycling Experience" in Chapter 3, pp. 53-55.

Sitting completely upright does have drawbacks because it is a static position. Your body responds as if you were sitting in a lounge chair and may, as a result, favor low energy riding. You will probably do most of your steering with the handlebars rather than with your hips. Your center of gravity is over the saddle rather than over the pedals. When you need to lift your weight off the saddle to avoid an impact from the trail or road, you must first lean forward to bring your weight over the pedals. Only then can you rise slightly off the saddle. Unfortunately, your response may be too slow to avoid a painful impact through the saddle. Your spine is also more vulnerable to vibrations and impacts from the road or trail that pass up through each vertebra and disk. A suspension seat post can reduce this problem. Suspension seat posts with a parallelogram design change the direction of the impacts and may protect the spine more effectively than a simple spring or elastomer that is designed to dampen the shock. You may need to adapt to suspension seat posts since they vary the distance between the saddle and the crank.

Leaning forward 30 to 45 degrees is a dynamic position. It places your center of gravity over the pedals so you can shift your weight off the saddle onto the pedals simply by straightening your legs. This enables you to respond quickly and effectively. This style of riding requires more upper body strength so you can take this opportunity to develop the needed strength or sit more upright to avoid the workout. The forward-leaning position does have some drawbacks. It applies more pressure to the front of the perineum, and your neck works more to hold your head upright.

Make your choice of forward lean freely, responding to sensitivities in your neck, shoulders, and hands. Avoid clinging to traditional riding positions that may cause you to be uncomfortable, risk neck injury, or even stop you from riding. Bicycle riding is for fun as well as for fitness. Select a position that satisfies your current needs and let your position change as your style evolves.

You will want to give special attention to the way you use your back in the following riding situations:

1. When you move left across traffic, check your mirror for traffic approaching from the rear and then *physically* turn around and scan all traffic movement. To do this, place your left hand on your left thigh to free your left shoulder and reduce the risk of swerving your bike during this maneuver. Turn around by initiating this spinal rotation from your lumbar spine and extending it upward into your neck. Relax into the rotation to enable you to turn as far as possible. Check your neck rotation to be sure you are rotating on the vertical axis of your cervical spine and not cranking your neck around with your head dropped forward.

2. When you ride technical single track, keep your spine supple so you can respond quickly with the appropriate movements.

3. When you are climbing, stay seated and use your gears to maintain your cadence close to 80 rpm. Climbing seated is more efficient than standing since less upper body work is needed. If you need to call on extra reserves to climb and do stand up, a strong upper torso will help you put your extra power into moving the bike forward.

4. When you are riding into a strong head wind, drop into a low forward tuck to reduce wind resistance.

Retraining Yourself to Use Your Back Effectively

You can increase your power output and endurance by holding your upper body relaxed and by avoiding bobbing. Observe yourself as you ride past large windows or have a friend watch you ride to see if your upper body bobs up-and-down or side-to-side. The information will make it easier for you to retrain your body while riding on the road. The more predictable and uniform nature of road riding makes it easier to concentrate on efficient riding technique. The ever-changing demands of single track make it more difficult to focus on cadence, fluid power stroke, and breathing. If riding single track is your passion, commit some time to developing your biomechanical skills on the road. When these new skills become habitual, you can transfer them to single track.

Use the following techniques to help you relax your back while riding:

1. Ride lightly with a resilient spine. If you feel that you are tensing up, check your relaxation by tipping your hips from side-to-side.

2. Be agile and respond quickly to bumps and obstacles along your line of travel by transferring your weight onto your pedals to absorb impacts with your legs and arms rather than your spine.

3. Breathe diaphragmatically and rhythmically.

4. Keep your cadence above 80 rpm.

5. Develop a fluid power stroke, being sure to pull up at the back of the crank rotation.

6. Look ahead on the road or trail more than 15 feet in front of you. Turn your head in the direction you are turning and let your chin serve as a rudder.

7. Try singing while you ride. This encourages deep, controlled breathing, improves your bike handling, and raises your spirits. It may also amuse your riding companions.

8. Develop strength in your back and abdomen with maintenance exercises.

9. Stretch daily to increase your flexibility.

10. Make it a priority to avoid crashing. Riding with finesse does not include crashing.

A strong, relaxed back reduces tension in your upper limbs. One of the benefits of riding technical single track is that you exercise your entire body while controlling your bike. Tension is less likely to creep into your back when your movements are varied.

Common Back Problems Experienced on Your Bike

For many riders, a comfortable riding position *is* the riding experience. Forcing yourself into a stressful riding position on a particular bike is like trying to force your feet into shoes that don't fit. You may succeed but you will be miserable and could injure yourself in the process. Bike setup plays an important role in how you use your body. If, for example, your handlebars are too far away from your saddle, they may cause you to straighten your elbows, tense up your shoulders, and over-extend your back. Riding in this position for prolonged periods can stretch your back muscles excessively, making them weak and vulnerable to injury.

Cyclists seem to be troubled as often by discomfort in the lower back as in the upper back. As described in the section on hips, fatigue and soreness in the lower back are usually caused by an imbalance in strength and flexibility of the hip flexor used on the upstroke and hip extensors used on the downstroke. Refer to the sections on optimum pedaling technique and cadence on pp. 154-159.

Lateral movement of the hips also causes premature fatigue. Be sure your seat height is correct to prevent rocking your hips on too high a seat or straining your hip extensors with too low a seat height. If you ride with a forward lean of more than 45 degrees, experiment with your pelvic tilt and with sitting a little more upright to reduce back strain.

You may want to review the causes of cycling discomfort in Chapter 3. For details of optimum use of the upper back, shoulders, and neck, refer to pp. 230-232.

Exercises to Condition Your Back

A strong, flexible, and relaxed back and abdomen will increase your athletic performance, improve your posture, and make life more fun. Cycling uses a limited range of movements making it important to stretch and strengthen the synergists of your torso. Select a variety of exercises for your back and abdominals and do them faithfully every day. Using a variety of exercises builds balanced strength and flexibility over more muscles. Ten minutes a day invested in your back goes a long way toward preventing back problems.

If you have a back injury or impairment, consult with your physical therapist before doing the following exercises. You will also need to experiment to find a riding position that reduces stress on the sensitive portions of your back. Riding in an upright position on smooth surfaces is usually comfortable, and since most impacts can be avoided, cycling provides a unique opportunity for aerobic exercise for those with more serious back injuries.

Tennis ball massage for your back — Long haul bicycle tourists have lots of tricks for keeping themselves strong and comfortable during days or weeks of riding. Wanda's trick is to carry a tennis ball on tour. After each day's ride, she uses it to relax her back. This promotes quality sleep and prevents back problems as the days of riding extend into weeks. The mechanism is simple: discretely applied pressure releases tension.

This relaxing practice "awakens" the deep muscles of the back and increases energy flow along the spine. The details of this technique are in Chapter 4, p. 138. The bladder meridian parallels the spine on both sides, so tennis ball pressure massages many acupoints including the following key ones: GB 20, B 10, B 13, B 15, B 18, B 23, B 25, and B 28.

Acupressure

B 13 Lung associated point — Refer to p. 215 under "Exercises to Benefit Your Breathing Components."

B 15 Row the boat — *Benefits* - This acupoint eases breathing, opens the chest and releases the trapezius, rhomboids, and sacrospinals. *Location* - It is located about two inches below B 13 toward the lower edge of the scapula. *Application* - You will need to reach it with tennis balls since it is in the middle of your upper back. If the pressure causes too intense discomfort, you can support your shoulders with pillows or books.

B 18 Twisting around — *Benefits* - Pressure applied here relieves stooping and soreness from twisting exercises. *Location* - It is approximately two inches below your scapula, in the muscular trough on either side of the spine. *Application* - Continue the progression with the tennis balls.

B 23 and B 47 Sea of vitality — *Benefits* - This is the most important point in the back for releasing lower backache and sciatica. (Coseo, p. 38) It also relieves fatigue associated with tension and discomfort as well as sexual and reproductive problems. *Location* - Both points are at the back of the waist. B 23 is on either side of the spine and B 47 is about an inch-and-a-half farther out. *Applications* - B 23 is easily reached lying down with the two balls in a sock. Or you might tightly roll up a towel and lie on it. From a seated position you can rub both points vigorously with the knuckles of your hands held in soft fists. B 47 is right on the ropy muscles at the back of the waist. It is convenient to apply pressure toward the spine with a thumb on each side and fingers pointing forward on the hips. Another application that relaxes much of the back is to lie on your back with your knees drawn to your chest. Gently rock side to side from elbow to elbow massaging your hips and upper back. After any of these applications, breathe deeply and relax and enjoy the benefits for two to five minutes.

B 25 Arching the back — *Benefits* - It is good for imbalances anywhere in the body but especially between the lower back and abdomen. The more tender the point, the greater the imbalance. It also releases the psoas and relieves irregular bowel function. *Location* - It is in the trough at the side of the spine at the level of the iliac crest. *Applications* - You can move down from B 23 and continue pressure with your thumbs in a seated position or with tennis balls while lying on your back.

B 28 One of the sacral points — *Benefits* - This is especially good for cyclists since it relaxes the gluteus maximus and increases fluid hip and thigh movement. It also strengthens reproductive organs, relieves menstrual cramps, and expedites the labor of childbirth. *Location* - It is among sixteen points that form a V on either side of the sacrum. It is on the upper inner edge of the gluteus maximus. *Applications* - You can use the same seated and lying techniques as described for B 23 and B 47.

Cat — Get down on hands and knees, making sure your hands are directly under your shoulders, and your knees are directly beneath your hips. Begin movement at your tailbone and tuck it in while tightening your buttocks muscles. Like a cat, arch up the small of your back. Tighten your abdominal muscles and draw them up toward your spine. Arch your shoulders and let your head relax down toward your chest. During this sequence, exhale slowly and completely. During the inhalation, rotate your tailbone upward, pulling your navel toward the floor, making your back concave. Expand your chest with air, raise your head up, and look toward the ceiling. Visualize these two reverse arches as waves starting at the tailbone and progressing toward the head. Repeat 4 to 6 times coordinated with your breathing.

Cat

Variations on the cat — This strengthens the stabilizing muscles that run diagonally across the back.

a. Again, begin on hands and knees. Lift and extend the right arm and left leg level with your back. Elongate from the tips of your fingers down through your toes. Position your head so you are looking to the tips of your extended fingers or at the floor. Lift from the top of your head, extending your neck. Hold this as long as you can maintain it comfortably while continuing controlled, diaphragmatic breathing. When you are ready, bring this hand and knee back to the floor and lift the other ones. Repeat at least twice on both sides.

Variations on the cat

b. Use the same movements as in "a" but coordinate movements with your breathing. As you lift the opposing arm and leg, inhale and then exhale while returning them to the floor. On the next inhalation, lift the other arm and leg.

Cobra — Refer to instructions for this posture on pp. 218-219.

Abdominal roll-ups — Refer to strength training for the abdominal muscles, p. 116. When you finish, stretch out your abdominal muscles with a full-body stretch, extending your arms over your head and elongating your legs through your

Leg lifts

Plow

heels. Enjoy this complete stretch while breathing abdominally.

Leg lifts — They strengthen the muscles of the lower abdomen. Only perform these if you are free of back problems. Lie on your back with your arms along your sides, palms down. Keeping the small of your back pressed against the floor, slowly raise your extended legs off the floor until they are perpendicular to it. Lower your legs gradually to the floor, giving special attention to the positions where your legs are 30 and 60 degrees above horizontal. Remember to breathe diaphragmatically and regularly throughout the lift. Try a variation with your hands under your buttocks. For a more challenging workout, lift your head and shoulders off the floor and repeat several times. Remember that this is a strong workout so don't overdo and regret it.

Supine lateral twist — Refer to pp. 184-185.

Cross-country skiing — Both classic and skating techniques are excellent, especially for your triceps and muscles that cross your back diagonally.

Plow — This is a good exercise to balance backbends. Lie on your back with your hands palm down beside your hips or extend your arms over your head. On an exhalation, lift your feet slowly until your legs are vertical. Lift your pelvis off the floor and continue bringing your feet over your head. Keep your legs as straight as possible unless they need to flex a bit as your toes touch the floor above your head. Extend your neck, striving to keep the back of your neck on the floor. As you come out of the pose, place each vertebra one at a time on the floor. *Variations* - If this is too hard on your neck, you can place a folded blanket under your shoulders to raise them and release pressure on your neck. If it is difficult to bring your toes to the floor over your head, you can place your head about 20 inches away from a wall perpendicular to your torso and rest your toes against the wall. As this becomes easier you can gradually move away from the wall.

Your Shoulders and Neck

The function of your shoulders is to provide a stable and relaxed platform of support for your neck, arms, and hands.

The function of your neck is to support and control your head to optimize perception and breathing.

Your shoulders and neck are considered together in this section since their muscle structure and function are so intimately interrelated.

Shoulder and Neck Use to Optimize Comfort and Efficiency

The musculature of the shoulders and neck is complex. The heaviest muscles of the neck are the upward continuation of the back muscles, primarily the spinal erectors of the neck and head. Two actions position your head when you are riding with a forward lean of 45 degrees or more: the extension of the neck and the tipping of the head at the top of the vertebral column (the occipital-atlas and atlas-axis joints). (Germain, pp. 58-60) The muscle groups of primary interest to cyclists are the trapezius, the spinal erectors of neck and head, and the levator scapulae. Refer to the illustration of the back muscles on p. 220. The sternocleidomastoid (SCM) and suboccipitals (deep muscles at the base of the skull) are active in tipping the head back. The trapezius is a broad, flat, triangular muscle that extends from the base of the skull to the lower part of the upper back. It fans out from the vertebrae and comes together at the outer edge of the collarbone, then covers the shoulder blade. It is divided into three parts: the upper, middle, and lower trapezius. The upper trapezius attaches to the collarbone (clavicle). The middle attaches to the acromion and shoulder blade (scapula). And the lower trapezius attaches to the spine of the scapula and extends down at an angle to the vertebrae at the level of the 12th rib. The trapezius elevates the shoulder and moves the scapula. The longissimus muscles run from the back of the skull (mastoid process) to the vertebrae of the neck and upper back and draw the head backwards. The levator scapulae extends from the upper vertebrae of the neck downward diagonally to the scapula. When the neck is fixed, it raises the shoulder blade and shrugs the shoulders. When the shoulder blade is fixed, the levator scapulae draws the neck and head back.

Cycling requires that these muscle groups be *strong* to support the head during long rides and yet *flexible* to allow the range of movement required to watch traffic and survey the scenery. If you ride in a traditional position with a forward lean of 45 degrees or more, tension in these muscles builds from the strain of hyper-extending the neck: holding it back beyond a neutral position. Prolonged contraction causes muscles at the back of the neck to shorten and tighten. For this reason you will probably appreciate a more upright torso position that is more healthful and makes riding more fun.

Proper use of the muscles of the shoulders and neck can reduce strain and delay the onset of fatigue. Begin with your head and lift upward with the spinal erectors to diminish the curvature of your neck and lengthen the upper trapezius and levator scapulae. Relax the muscles that are not holding up your head. Usually the muscles at the front of the neck, especially the SCM, are chronically shortened from carrying the head in a dropped forward position. This requires that the spinal erectors work against them. You can help release the SCM by turning your head to one side and grasping the prominent, ropy muscle on the other side of your neck. Hold it gently for a minute or two. This is a good activity while you are driving. The SCM is also stretched during any of the back bends where your head drops back to lengthen muscles at the front of your neck when your mouth is shut.

The shoulder joint is made up of two joints and is supported by the sternum, ribs, and spinal column. The bones of the shoulder region form the shoulder girdle: the clavicle (collarbone), the scapula, and the head of the humerus. The only attachment of the shoulder joint to the core skeleton is by the clavicle at the sternum. The shoulder joint is highly mobile due to this distant attachment to the core skeleton and because the actual joint attaches to the highly mobile scapula. The head of the humerus attaches to the outside edge of the scapula at the glenoid cavity. At the top of this joint you can feel the acromion process of the scapula that supports the shoulder end of the clavicle. The shoulder has two more joints at each end of the clavicle where it attaches to the acromion and the sternum.

Many muscles move the clavicle, scapula, and humerus. In addition to the muscles already mentioned, the serratus anterior below the arm pit on the back of the rib cage (Refer to the illustration on p. 220) is another important working muscle for cyclists. It helps support your weight on the handlebars as you lean forward and can be strengthened by upper body push ups. Refer to strength training, pp. 119-121.

It is necessary to consciously release and elongate non-working shoulder muscles while riding since the shoulders are often a repository for tension and stress. Begin at the base of your skull then drop and broaden your shoulders to release these muscles. Visualize opening up your shoulder joints and broadening your upper back without collapsing your chest. This will increase circulation to your hands and decrease pressure on the nerves in your shoulders that innervate your hands. This relaxation and visualization will help you avoid numb hands. Refer to "Common Problems of the Arms and Hands," pp. 244-247.

Solving Common Problems by Optimizing Use of Your Shoulders and Neck

Upper back, shoulder, and neck discomfort usually converge and concentrate in the region of the upper thoracic spine. It results from chronic tension in all the surrounding muscles rather than distinguishing the working muscles from those that should be inactive.

The main contributors are the extensors of the neck holding the cervical spine at an extreme curvature, permanently shortened and sensitive trapezius muscles, and scrunched shoulders. You can resolve this discomfort by optimizing your technique as described above, customizing your bike setup, avoiding misuse and overuse, and maintaining a daily exercise routine to strengthen and stretch your upper body. We have already discussed how to resolve general discomfort in Chapter 3.

Use this comparison of healthful and painful riding postures to evaluate your own form.

Healthful use of the upper body	**Painful use of the upper body**
Lift through the top of the head, release the chin downward, relax and drop the shoulders, and bend the elbows downward. Hold your wrists neutral and your hands loose on the grips.	The head is slung down between the shoulders, the neck is hyper-extended, the shoulders are drawn up. The wrists are bent and braced against the handlebars and the hands cling to the bars with a death grip.

Once you determine what you need to change, you will probably need months to build strength in weak muscles and make your new posture feel natural to you. First you will need to make needed changes to your bike. Then be patient and work on retaining one aspect of your form at a time. Start at your head and work down to your hands.

It is safe to assume that you will need to change your bike to create the experience you desire. Riders only question their bikes' componentry and setup when problems arise. When you critically evaluate what you want from cycling, you may discover that the solutions to your problems require that you depart from traditional norms. If you want cycling to help you build a healthy body, a cheerful outlook, and an enjoyable exercise routine, you will probably need to make some changes to your bike.

Upper back discomfort usually indicates that you are straining to reach the handlebars.

This is not because their placement is wrong, but because they are not where you would like to have them. Once you have repositioned your handlebars within comfortable reach, you can relax your shoulders and extend through the top of your head to prevent scrunching your shoulders and causing a tension knot in your upper back. Refer to Chapter 6 for factors to help you determine how to customize your bike.

The placement of your elbows strongly influences your ability to relax your shoulders if you lean your torso forward more than 15 degrees. Your upper trapezius must contract to extend your arms forward to reach handlebars that are low and far forward. When you flex your elbows and bring them back toward your hips where they are nearly below your shoulders, it is easier to relax your shoulders and upper back. If you do not want to change the position of your handlebars, lean farther forward.

If you experience upper body discomfort during a ride, here are some techniques to bring relief. Change your head position often to give relief to your trapezius and levator scapulae. When you are stopped, bring your chin to your chest and relax the supporting muscles at the back of your neck. Limber up your shoulders by inscribing circles with your shoulders backward and forward. This will help open your pectoral muscles and shorten the latissimus dorsi to counteract the hunched-over position common among cyclists. Change the position of your hands on your handlebars often. Keep your jaw slack and free from tension. Stop every 30 to 60 minutes to evaluate your condition. Then take this opportunity to do some of the stretching exercises that follow. The *umbrella* is especially easy to do along side the road or trail.

Exercises to Benefit Your Shoulders and Neck

Self-Massage Techniques

Acupressure — Work these acupoints as a sequence starting at the back of the head and progressing to the hands to open energy flow and communication from the head down. Activate all points on both sides of the body and respond to differences in sensitivity. You can adapt activation of all these points to be done while lying in bed. It will take less than 20 minutes and will begin your day with a cheerful attitude. Performing this routine daily for ten days will transform your upper body. Refer to the acupoint locator in Chapter 4, p. 140.

GB 20 Gates of consciousness — *Benefits* - This point has many benefits and is especially beneficial for cyclists. It improves neuromuscular coordination and relieves tension in general. It also increases flexibility in the neck and shoulders and reduces headaches, insomnia, trauma, irritability, and head and neck pain associated with colds and the flu. *Location* - There is one on either side just below the base of the skull in the depression created by the two large neck muscles on each side of the spine. *Application* - Place the fingers up on the back of the head and the thumbs on the acupoints. Direct the pressure upward and inward. Close your eyes and breathe deeply for about a minute. Gradually tilt your head back. (This is not to easy to do lying down.)

TW 16 Window of heaven — Drag your thumbs directly from GB 20 to TW 16. *Benefits* - This acupoint also relieves headaches and tension in the neck and shoulders. *Location* - It is located in an indentation at the base of the skull about an inch and a half behind the earlobes. *Application* - Immediately follow pressure on GB 20 by dragging your thumbs across and down slightly. This point is often sensitive so adjust your pressure gradually. Direct the pressure upward into the base of the skull.

GV 16 Wind mansion — This is the place where the spinal cord enters the cranium. *Benefits* - It relieves mental stress, insomnia, and any problems with the ears, eyes, and nose, including nosebleeds. *Location* - It is at the center of the back of the head in the large hollow under the base of the skull. *Application* - Press with the tips of the fingers of both hands. Slowly tilt the head back and forward while breathing deeply with eyes closed. Pressure on GV 16 can be combined with pressure on the third eye point (GV 24.5) between the eyebrows at the top of the nose to clear the mind or with pressure on the center of the upper lip (GV 26) to stop nosebleeds. You can also pinch the bridge of the nose for neck pain.

B 10 Heavenly pillar — *Benefits* - It relieves burnout, exhaustion from over-exertion, insomnia, and eyestrain. This is an important point since it relaxes the neck and increases circulation of blood to the brain. *Location* - It is a half-inch below the base of the skull on the ropy muscles on either side of the spine. *Application* - You can apply pressure with the fingers of both hands or grasp the back of the neck with one hand and apply pressure on one side with the heel of the hand and on the other side with the fingers.

GB 21 Shoulder well — *Benefits* - It relieves nervousness, irritability, and fatigue as well as neck tension and discomfort. *Location* - It is on the highest point of the shoulder on the trapezius, halfway between the neck and outer edge of the shoulder. Pregnant women should press lightly. *Application* - This is chronically tender. Place your fingers over the top of your shoulder and let the weight of your arm apply pressure. Close your eyes and imagine healing energy flowing into your shoulders. You can also pat this point gently by alternately swinging your arms across your chest and slapping the top of your shoulder.

TW 15 Heavenly rejuvenation — Refer to instructions under acupressure for the breathing components, pp. 215-216.

SI 10 Shoulder valley — *Benefits* - It relieves the posterior deltoid active in supporting your upper body on the handlebars. *Location* - It is above the crease between the body and upper arm on the back. *Application* - You can reach this with a tennis ball or reach around the head of the humerus and press it with your middle finger.

Shiatsu points in the delto-pectoral crease — Refer to acupressure to benefit the breathing components, p. 216.

LI 14 Outer arm bone — *Benefits* - It relieves toothaches as well as relaxes the arms, neck, and shoulders. *Location* - It is about one-third of the way between the shoulder and the elbow at the base of the deltoid slightly toward the back of the arm on a wiry muscle band over the arm. *Application* - Massage the area briefly while you search for the tender point. Then apply pressure and gradually release. This is especially beneficial when combined with GB 21 on the top of the shoulder. From this point, begin **Shiatsu massage of the upper arm** by following the tender line from LI 14 down to the elbow. Remember to use rhythmic applications of pressure about every two inches, finding four points before the elbow.

LI 11 Crooked pond — *Benefits* - This is another key point. It balances the immune system, relieves cold symptoms, and regulates intestinal activity. It also relieves tension in the upper limbs. *Location* - It is at the top of the crease of the elbow on the outside of the joint. *Application* - Fold one arm across your lap with the thumb up. Place the fingers of your other hand around your elbow bone and apply pressure with your thumb at this tender acupoint. You may also enjoy rubbing it briskly to generate warmth.

LI 10 Arm three mile — *Benefits* - This is another key point that revitalizes the entire body, balances immune function, benefits digestion, and strengthens and tones muscles throughout the body. For cyclists and people who have tight forearms it relaxes the forearms, wrists, and hands. This point has the same benefits for the forearm as St 36 has for the lower leg, ankles, and feet. *Location* - It is two thumb widths below LI 11 at the top of the forearm. *Application* - Fold one forearm across your lap. Place the other thumb inside the elbow joint and grasp the forearm just below the elbow joint with your fingers. From here you can proceed with **Shiatsu massage of the lateral forearm** by following the line of tenderness to the wrist and applying pressure about every inch.

Shiatsu massage for the medial forearm — *Benefits* - Use this is especially if you have wrist or carpal tunnel sensitivity. *Application* - Rest your elbow on your waist and extend your forearm away from your torso with palm up. Probe with your thumb on the inside of your forearm to locate the tender point just below the elbow crease on top of the radius. Again, follow the line of tenderness to the wrist. Gently brush over the area you have treated when you have finished.

TW 5 Outer gate — *Benefits* - This is another key point that regulates and relaxes the entire body and relieves allergic reactions, rheumatism and tendonitis. It also relaxes the upper limbs. *Location* - It is on the outside of the wrist, two thumbs width above the wrist in the depression in the center of the arm between the two bones. *Application* - Hold one arm in your lap with the thumb up. Apply pressure to TW 5 with your fingers while applying pressure to the next point, P 6, with your thumb.

P 6 Inner gate — *Benefits* - It calms the spirits and balances the internal organs, relieving indigestion, insomnia, and wrist pain. *Location* - It is on the palm side of the wrist on the other side from TW 5. *Application* - Apply pressure at the same time as to TW 5 using your thumb.

LI 4 Joining the valley — *Benefits* - This is a key point that must be avoided during pregnancy. It balances energy between the upper and lower body and balances the gastro-intestinal system. It also relieves frontal headaches and depression. *Location* - It is in the valley between the thumb and index finger in the middle of the webbing. *Application* - Place one hand palm down in your lap. Draw the thumb of that hand beside the index finger. Place the other thumb in the middle of the fleshy mound between the thumb and index finger and then release the thumb to access the point. Direct the pressure to the middle of the hand.

Lu 10 Fish border — Refer to p. 216.

Stretching Exercises to Benefit Your Shoulders

I am offering a variety of shoulder and neck exercises because riders have so much shoulder and neck discomfort. Select several that you enjoy to practice daily and then rotate through the others regularly. Perform these first three exercises in sequence to provide a progressive warm-up for the shoulders.

Opening your shoulders and chest using a doorway — Stand facing into an open doorway on the side without the door. Bring your arms out from your sides far enough to contact the door frame with your wrists. Take a step forward if you like. Keep your arms straight and relaxed and lean into the doorway gently, opening your shoulders. Take four to six SELF breaths in this position, release, and then move your arms about ten inches up on the door frame. Repeat this in about four to six arm positions. If the door frame will support your weight, you can complete the routine by hanging from the door frame when your arms are vertical.

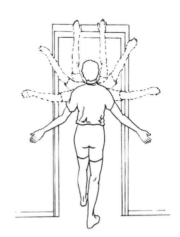

Opening your shoulders and chest using a doorway

Arm circle against a wall — Stand beside a wall with your left shoulder close to it and your feet six to twelve inches away from it. Align your body in mountain pose (see p. 101). Keeping your arm extended and the back of your hand against

Arm circle against a wall

Opening your shoulder
against a wall

Umbrella

the wall, move your hand forward and upward to inscribe an arc. Stop when your hand is just above your shoulder, and it feels right to turn your palm toward the wall. Hold this position with your palm against the wall for about eight SELF breaths and feel the warmth increase in your shoulder as the blood from your arm floods into your shoulder. Then continue the arc toward your back, completing a circle with your hand. Keeping your palm against the wall, pause in mountain pose and bring your attention to your left shoulder. Turn and repeat this sequence with your right arm and shoulder.

Opening your shoulder against a wall — Facing the wall, extend your left arm at shoulder height. Place your palm against the wall and spread your fingers wide apart. Now turn back to your right so your torso is at right angles to the wall and align your body in mountain pose. Place your feet six to twelve inches from the wall. The closer you stand to the wall, the more intense the stretch. Keep your left elbow straight. You will probably feel the nerves that extend through the armpit and down your arm and perhaps even into your hand. This is a convincing demonstration of the route of the nerves from your shoulders into your hands. Repeat with your right arm.

Umbrella — This posture lets your neck relax completely, opens your chest, and increases your mental and visual acuity through improved flow of blood to your head and upper body. Begin in mountain pose. On the inhalation, clasp your hands behind your back, interlacing your fingers with your palms together and keeping your elbows straight. On the exhale, bend forward, pivoting at the hips. Keep your back straight, maintaining the natural curve of your cervical spine. When you are bent as far forward as is comfortable, release your back and neck and let your head hang freely. Now raise your arms and hands high over your head. Keep your knees as straight as possible to stretch your hamstrings. Continue breathing and maintain this position for six to eight breaths. Inhale as you straighten up. Release your clasped hands and relax.

Eagle - upper body — This pose elongates the middle trapezius. Raise your arms to shoulder level, extending them to your sides. Swing them forward in a sweeping motion until your right elbow crosses above your left elbow. Now bend your elbows so your forearms are vertical and intertwine your forearms until your palms face each other. On each inhale, raise your arms from the elbows. On each exhale, extend your hands away from your forehead, broadening your upper back. Breathe into this strong stretch of the shoulders. Disentangle your arms, bringing them again to your sides at shoulder level. Repeat with your left elbow on top.

Eagle - upper body

Cow - upper limbs — This upper torso portion of the cow posture stretches your triceps and opens your shoulder joints. Begin in mountain pose, consciously moving your scapula back and down. Extend your right arm forward and up, inscribing a large semi-circle with your hand with your palm facing left. When your hand is above your right shoulder, bend your elbow and bring your palm down onto your scapula. Now raise your extended left arm up in the front to shoulder height, palm facing the side. Bring your left hand down toward your left hip. Bending your arm at the elbow, move your left hand up to the middle of your upper back. Stretch to try to bring the fingertips of both hands together. Breathe deeply and enjoy the sweet stretch in your right triceps and the opening of your left shoulder. Keep your back and neck erect. If you are unable to touch fingertips, try this variation: hold a hand towel or sock in your right hand. As you bring your left hand to mid-back, grasp the sock and move your grip up it to position your arms for a comfortable stretch. This is a good aid to use while you are developing greater flexibility in your shoulders and arms. Repeat with your left elbow raised. Repeat twice on each side.

Cow - upper limbs

Shoulder scrunches — This tensing and releasing of the shoulder muscles increases blood flow and relaxation to the upper trapezius. Forming both hands into tight fists, draw your shoulders up as high as possible toward your ears and contract all the muscles in your shoulders. Then drop your shoulders open, stretch out your hands, and enjoy the sense of relaxation. Breathe evenly and regularly throughout this exercise. This too is a discrete exercise to do mid-ride. Repeat several times.

Shoulder scrunches

Stretching Exercises to Benefit Your Neck

Gentle warm-up sequence — This will rotate and flex your neck in all directions. When your neck muscles are tight, be especially gentle and breathe into each stretch. If you have had a neck injury, select only those portions of this sequence that will not stress your neck. Sitting or standing, lift gently through the top of your head. This sequence can be done with each position held 30 seconds while breathing consciously or with your breath coordinated with each movement. For example, with the first movement, rotate your head and neck to look over your left shoulder as far as is comfortable and hold while breathing into the posture. Then repeat on the right side. Or you could exhale as you look over your left shoulder and inhale as you face forward and then exhale as you look over your right shoulder.

Next, bring your chin to your chest and tip your head back so you are looking upward. Try both breathing options to see which you prefer. Repeat several times.

Finally, inscribe circles with the top of your head, moving your head through your full range of movement. First, inscribe your circles clockwise and then counter-clockwise.

Levator scapulae stretch — Begin sitting or standing with head facing forward. Gently bend your head and neck to the side, bringing your ear toward your shoulder. Rotate your head downward, bring your chin to your chest, and look down your right side. Reverse the sequence. Repeat on the other side. Remember to continue to breathe, exhaling as you rotate your chin to your chest.

Upper trapezius stretch — To stretch your right trapezius, place your right arm behind your back, bending at the elbow. Bring your chin to your chest and turn your head so that you are looking toward your left hip. Inhale. As you exhale, relax your right shoulder and let the stretch lengthen. Reverse the movements and repeat on your left side.

Elongation of the trapezius and the levator scapulae — Lying on your back on the floor, clasp your hands behind your head at the base of your skull. Lift up your head, bringing your chin to your chest. Lifting toward the top of your head with your hands to elongate the back of your neck, gradually lower your head to the floor while keeping your chin on your chest. This will help prevent "forward head posture" and counteract the prolonged contraction of the trapezius and levator scapulae while riding.

Preparation for the elephant — Refer to instructions in Chapter 4, p. 102 for this posture.

Strengthening Exercises for the Neck and Shoulders

To strengthen the upper trapezius — Repeat the shoulder scrunches while holding weights in each hand and raise and lower your shoulders. Breathe consciously and concentrate on the sensations of your shoulders.

To strengthen the cervical spinal erectors — This exercise will enable you to feel the work of the spinal erectors and strengthen them. Sitting upright, clasp your hands on top of your head. Let the weight of your arms apply pressure to your head. Resist this downward pressure with your neck muscles and push up with your head. Hold for about a minute and then release your hands. Notice how your head floats upward. This is the work of your spinal erectors. By stretching, using acupressure regularly, and minimizing stress in your life, you can learn to release the voluntary muscles of the neck allowing your head to float effortlessly like the sensation after you released the weight of your arms.

To stretch and strengthen all sides of your neck — This sequence is done lying across a bed. Place your shoulders flush with the edge of the bed so your head is hanging off the edge. Begin lying on your stomach with your arms at your sides. Keeping your chin tucked under toward your chest, lift the top of your head upward. Slowly and gentle inscribe a circle with your chin. When you have raised your head as high as is comfortable, move your chin away from your chest, out and down, as you lower your head to its relaxed, resting position. Repeat this a total of three times. As your neck becomes stronger, and three repetitions seem too easy, increase to four repetitions.

Now turn onto your right side, keeping your shoulder at the edge of the bed. Again, let your head relax completely off the side of the bed. Raise your head up toward your left shoulder as far as is comfortable. Repeat a total of three times.

You guessed it. Now roll onto your back and let your head hang back off the edge of the bed. Exercise special care if you sense any tenderness in your neck, especially in this position. Raise your head three times.

Finally, on your left, still keeping your shoulders flush with the edge of the bed, let your head hang off the edge of the bed and lift it three times.

To facilitate a symmetric alignment of your neck, shoulders,

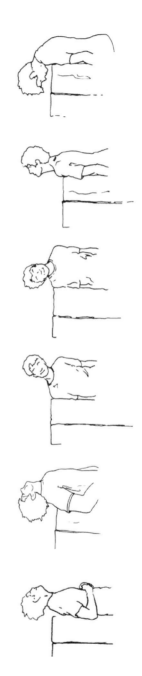

To stretch and strengthen all sides of your neck

and back, repeat the first step of the sequence on your stomach.

You will notice your back muscles working gently through this sequence. It is also a good opportunity to give your neck a gentle massage. In each relaxed position, feel your neck for sensitive places and massage them.

Downward-facing dog, upward-facing dog, and child's pose sequence — See Chapter 4, pp. 103-105 for instructions on this sequence.

Your Arms and Hands

The function of your arms and hands is to support the forward lean of your upper body; to absorb impacts; and to control the handlebars, brakes, and gears.

Occasionally, you use your hands and arms to increase your power output while climbing standing up and for controlling your weight over the front wheel.

How to Use Your Arms and Hands to Optimize Control and Minimize Discomfort

Your arms and hands have a lot of work to do. They control the handlebars as well as the brake levers and shifters. Improving your technique will help you become a more skillful bike handler and will reduce some of the most common discomforts of cycling.

Keep your elbows flexed. As you create a gentle bend in your elbows, let your elbows drop toward your hips. Avoid letting them stick out to the sides. The dropped-elbow position may feel awkward when your hands are on the horizontal grips but you will benefit from learning to keep your elbows down whether they are on the horizontal grips or the bar ends. When you let your elbows bend out to the sides, your deltoids and supraspinatus (another abductor of the arm connecting the scapula and humerus) contract and increase tension in your shoulders without benefiting your performance.

Your elbows have two important jobs to do: flex to absorb impact and bend to adjust your forward lean.

Optimize your arm and hand use by keeping your elbows flexed downward toward your hips and your wrists nearly straight. Mary Lou appreciates an intermediate forward lean of about 30 degrees. Strive to use your elbows and wrists like this whether you sit upright or lean forward more than 45 degrees. Placing her hands on the bar ends makes it easier to keep her elbows in.

Elbows are the original front suspension. With a gentle flex, they can absorb front-end impacts, protecting your neck and shoulders. If you ride with a rigid fork, flexed elbows reduce the incidents of pinch flats by absorbing your body weight with your arms instead of with your front tire and rim.

There are many occasions when you can benefit from leaning forward on your bike. Drop to a lower position when riding into a strong head wind. You can generate more power by leaning forward to engage your gluteus maximus. This is especially important while climbing. Bringing your torso forward also increases the weight over your front wheel and keeps it on the ground while climbing or riding humps. Holding your elbows rigid increases the risk of tendonitis in the elbow.

Riding with a forward lean of more than 15 degrees with your elbows flexed works your triceps and supports your upper body weight on the handlebars. You'll enjoy this position more with strong triceps. So practice the strength training exercises recommended in this section. If you carry substantial weight in your shoulders or breasts, you may find a more upright position more comfortable.

Hold your wrists in a neutral position while keeping them supple and relaxed. A neutral position is stress-free. To determine the natural angle of your hands on your forearms, hold a pencil loosely in your fist and let your arms and hands hang fully relaxed at your sides. Observe your hand orientation. The pencil will point about 45 degrees inward toward your torso mid-line. This indicates that holding the handlebar grips places your forearm and wrist in a 45-degree rotation beyond neutral. A wrist position 45 to 90 degrees above horizontal minimizes strain. **Your choice of handlebar arrangement is essential to healthy wrists and hands.** The classic drop handlebars of road bikes have been favored for their many hand and wrist positions. If the elbows are flexed, the positions on the drops provide a neutral wrist position. Rotating the handlebars up slightly from the traditional low position can also provide another neutral position on the control levers. Take care to adjust the rotation of drop bars to give you several favorable positions.

Notice the natural position of the hands on the forearms.

It is not the type of handlebars you use that protects your wrists but the attention you give to setting it up right for you and then maintaining flexed elbows and nearly straight wrists. You will also need to give attention to the rotation of your control levers on flat handlebars. Rotate the controls so you can apply the brakes with your wrists nearly straight and position the gear control levers so you can operate them without straining your thumbs.

Position control levers to minimize wrist strain.

Equally important for optimum hand and wrist use is the choice of **control levers**. Hand strain will be reduced by ergonomic controls that utilize the greatest strength of your hands. In other words, do the brake and gear controls use your hands in a stress-free, efficient manner? Certainly the control levers designed for flat handlebars make the best use of hand strength and function. The dual control levers of drop bars (both STI® and Ergo®) require large hands for efficient use, and the reach cannot be adequately adjusted for medium- and small-sized hands. The lateral wrist movements required for braking and shifting are rarely used for other activities and consequently use muscles that may not be well-developed. Take extended test rides with various controls on flat and dropped bars to determine which combination serves you best. The ability to adjust the angle of bar ends on flat handlebars independent of the control levers makes this combination versatile in meeting individual preferences.

Bar ends are essential to stress-free use of flat handlebars. If you don't use them already, this would be a good time to start. Bar ends are frequently referred to as "climbing bars" due to their popularity for gaining power when you are climbing standing up. They also provide an alternative hand position, a neutral wrist position, and are of value to all riders who use flat handlebars. If you choose to lean farther forward for greater power or for a more aerodynamic position, the acute bend in your elbow reduces the blood flow to the forearms

Ted demonstrates holding bar ends at 45 degrees using a bent elbow and a straight wrist.

Some riders prefer to lay their outstretched hands across bar ends at 15 degrees.

Bending your elbows will enable you to use your 45-degree bar ends for occasionally riding while standing.

The 15-degree bar end rotation is easy to reach if you enjoy the workout of climbing out of the saddle.

and hands. Combine this with the twist in the forearm on horizontal grips and the effect is so dramatic that the position can be maintained only briefly. Surely bar ends are necessary to sustain this forward position on flat bars.

Adjust the rotation of your bar ends on your handlebars to provide the greatest comfort for your favorite arm and hand positions. Evaluate whether their current position actually meets your needs. Bike stores tend to install bar ends with a rotation of 10 to 15 degrees above horizontal. Try riding with them like that and observe your elbow and wrist positions. Are you flexing your elbows and holding your wrists neutral? If you prefer to close your fist around your bar ends, you may need to rotate them up closer to 45 degrees above horizontal. Notice that this position will still allow you to pull on them for climbing while you're standing up. Just bend your elbows a bit more. In addition to personalizing the angle of rotation of the bar ends, be sure that the diameter of your bar ends also provides comfort in the grip of your hand. For further discussion of the relationship of hand and wrist use and handlebars, refer to Chapter 6 and the sections on choice of handlebars and control levers, pp. 270-275.

You may feel uncertain with your hands on the bar ends away from the control levers. In heavy traffic or on technical single track, you may choose to keep your hands on the horizontal grips next to the controls. But for the majority of your riding you can learn to move your hands quickly down to the control levers. If you practice moving from the bar ends to the horizontal grips, you will restore your confidence in reaching your controls when needed. Practicing with one hand at a time, move your hand from the bar end to the controls. Repeat this movement several times and focus on planting this movement in your brain. This may seem elementary but it works.

Practicing moving your hands from bar ends to the handlebar grips will encourage you to ride most of the time on the bar ends and enable you to use your brakes and gears appropriately.

The more you can relax your forearms, wrists, and the grip of your hands, the better control you will have of your bicycle. A loose grip allows the front of your bike to respond to small variations in the riding surface. This reduces impacts and strain on your hands and arms. The only time you need to maintain a firm grip on the handlebars is on steep, rocky descents. Then a firm grip is important while squeezing the brake levers and controlling the handlebars. You can get some idea of how successful you have been in relaxing your grip by looking at your handlebar grips or tape. Are your grips distorted and torn? Is your tape sliding down your drop bars? These are indications that you need to relax your grip.

Consider that rigid and tense hands, wrists, and arms transmit impacts that travel up your arms as far as there is tension. If your elbows are straight and your shoulders are tense, impacts will travel all the way up to your neck and head. Again, use the muscles that hold up your torso and control the bike and let your other muscles relax.

Common Problems of the Arms and Hands

Probably the most common problem is numb hands. While riders often search for heavily padded gloves to prevent hand numbness, the root cause is compression of the nerves that give sensation to the hands. These nerves originate at the vertebrae of the neck, pass through the shoulders and armpit, and progress down the arms to the hands. The ulnar nerve generally innervates the fourth and fifth finger of the hand. The median nerve passes through the carpal tunnel and

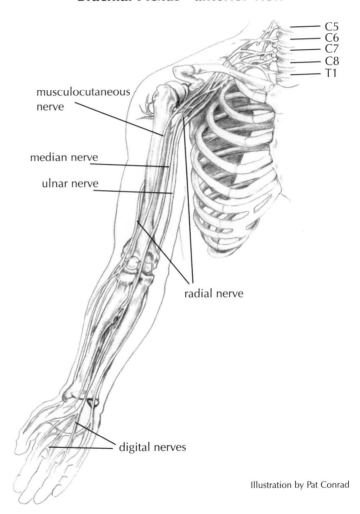

Brachial Plexus - anterior view

C5
C6
C7
C8
T1

musculocutaneous nerve

median nerve

ulnar nerve

radial nerve

digital nerves

Illustration by Pat Conrad

The nerves of the brachial plexus originate at vertebrae C5 to C8 and T1. On their route to the arms they branch to supply the shoulder muscles and then pass between the clavicle and the first rib to enter the delto-pectoral crease. In so doing, they converge to form four main branches: the musculocutaneous, the median, the ulnar, and the radial. As these pass through the arms, they branch in a complex pattern giving sensation to the muscles and skin of the arms and hands.

innervates the thumb, index, and middle fingers. Compression of these nerves by muscle or by bone, at any point along this path, can cause hand numbness. Because the paths of the two nerves are similar, one or both nerves may be affected.

How can hand numbness be prevented? Padded gloves alone will not solve the problem that originates anywhere along the brachial plexus. The most common cause is tension in the neck and shoulders. Be sure that your riding position is optimized for your comfort. If you must strain to reach the handlebars, there is tension in your shoulders. Try this demonstration of muscle function in the shoulders: stand upright and place your left hand over the upper trapezius muscle on your right shoulder. Slowly reach forward with your right until your arm is fully extended. Now repeat this experiment with your torso leaning forward at 45 degrees and observe the difference in activity of the upper trapezius. Now lean forward at the angle you normally ride and extend your hands forward to the position where you usually grasp the handlebars. Do you notice that the farther forward you lean and the more your arm is extended, the greater tension you create in your shoulder as the upper trapezius and other muscles contract to move your arm forward?

To reduce the likelihood of compression on these critical nerves, you must optimize both your bike setup and your body use. You need to modify your bicycle to bring the handlebars to a position that allows you to relax your shoulders. If your bicycle's top tube is too long, it may not be possible to bring the handlebars close enough to your shoulders to give you complete comfort. On the other hand, even if your bike fits properly, and you desire a more upright riding position, straining to reach that position creates tension in your shoulders, arms, and hands. Fatigue plays a role in the problem and may cause you to hunch your upper body and to collapse your shoulders forward, compressing the nerves between your collarbone and first rib. Refer to the section on handlebar position, pp. 266-268.

Shelley is a high-mileage commuter who visits Self-Propulsion often. About three times a week she makes a 38-mile round trip from downtown Denver to Golden. She rides her mountain bike so she can be confident in all traffic and weather conditions. Unfortunately, her hands were going numb at the beginning of each trip, which must have been quite unnerving. She finally sought help, and we were able to help her maintain normal sensation in her hands by making three changes. First, we installed a taller stem to raise her handlebars to the same height as her saddle as well as bringing them closer to her shoulders. In addition to hand numbness, she was having pain high between her shoulder blades. The new handlebar position would permit her to relax her upper back and shoulders. We also observed that her handlebar grips were torn and distorted. After replacing them, we encouraged Shelley to give attention to holding her bars loosely, with a relaxed grip. These two changes helped, but she was still bothered by occasional numbness. As a last step we suggested that she try giving up her hydration system pack to determine if the straps were causing enough pressure on her shoulders to impinge her nerves. Sure enough, with that last suggestion, she was able to ride free of hand numbness. It was the combination of changing her handlebar position *and* her willingness to modifying her riding style that brought success.

Use this checklist to help you optimize your riding style and bicycle setup to prevent **hand numbness.**

1. Relax your grip on the handlebars and practice riding with a loose hold. This actually increases your control and helps you avoid fighting the handlebars.

2. Check the tilt of your saddle to ensure that it enables you to bear most of your weight on your saddle. Sloping the saddle horn down shifts more weight onto your hands.

3. Rest your thumbs while riding by bringing them up beside your palms and index fingers occasionally. Many people have thumb injuries and impairments, making selection of shifter type worthy of careful consideration. Test ride both lever and twist operated controls to determine which are kinder to your hands and wrists.

4. Consider whether a different diameter grip or bar wrapping on both handlebars and bar ends would reduce strain. Riders with especially small or large hands should give careful attention to this detail.

5. Add bar ends to your flat handlebars. This will give you an alternative hand position and a neutral wrist position.

6. Change the angle of rotation of the bar ends on the handlebars for optimum comfort in *your* favorite riding position.

7. If you ride with drop bars, rotate them so that your hands rest comfortably on the control levers. You may find greater comfort and ease of control if the lower part of the bar points back toward the rear hub even though tradition has established that the lower part of the bar should be horizontal.

8. Select riding gloves that do not constrict circulation in your hands at any point of pressure. Give special attention to the bulk and position of the seams.

9. If your brake levers have a reach adjustment, shorten the reach so it eliminates hand strain. The brakes should be adjusted so that the levers are inside the middle knuckle of your hand when the pads contact the rim.

10. The rotation of your control levers on flat handlebars should also be customized to your needs to reduce strain during frequent use.

11. Your decision to ride with drop bars or flat bars should be based on your comfort and your confidence in using your control levers. Refer to the discussion of flat versus drop bars, pp. 272-273.

Adjust the reach of the brake lever close enough to the handlebar grip that the first knuckle of the fingers can reach it with enough strength to apply the brakes.

Set up the brakes with a loose enough pull cable to bring the lever into the middle knuckle of the fingers before the brake pads contact the rim. Your hand grip is much stronger in this position than if you grip the levers with the tips of your fingers.

12. A suspension stem can be an economical modification that reduces shock to your hands, arms, shoulders, and neck.

Elbow use is key to upper body health and bike control. It is unfortunate that cyclists rarely appreciate their elbows until they hurt. Occasionally cyclists experience tendonitis in the elbow. It is usually caused by bracing their torso against the handlebars while riding or from misuse in racket sports, golf, and baseball. In these sports, tenderness can occur on the inside of the elbow from bending the wrist too hard toward the palm of the hand. In cycling, soreness is more likely to occur on the outside of the elbow and is caused by gripping the handlebars too tightly. Tense hands and rigid wrists and elbows cause all impacts to the front of the bike to be transmitted up the arm. (Harvard Women's Health Watch, August 2000)

Of course preventive measures are best to protect your elbows from injury. Warm up gradually for all physical activities before increasing your energy output. Regularly practice some of the following stretching and strengthening exercises. What can you do when you notice discomfort? Reduce the intensity of your riding both in miles and energy level. Keep your arms, wrists, and hands supple when you do ride. Apply pressure point therapy to your arms and hands. Applying ice is remarkably effective during the early stages of tendonitis.

Exercises to Benefit Your Hands and Arms

Use all the exercises to benefit the shoulders and neck to prevent hand numbness.

Stretching Exercises

Cyclists' reverence — This will restore and strengthen your hands when they have been

Cyclists' reverence

weakened by extensive braking on long descents. Place your palms together in front of your chest in the traditional prayer position. Raise your elbows to shoulder height so your fingers point inward toward your chest. Keeping your hands pressed together, gently push the heel of your hands away from your chest. Hold briefly, release, and drop your hands to your sides to let the blood flow into them. Breathe deeply and focus on releasing and stretching the muscles on the inside of your forearm. Repeat as needed.

Umbrella — Refer to the shoulder exercises, p. 236.

Strengthening Exercises

Cross-country skiing — Proper poling technique strengthens the triceps and elbows. It also helps you learn to relax your wrists and hands. Power with your arms only as they pass your hips. Keep your hands open and relaxed, holding the poles in your hands by properly adjusting the straps.

Pumping up tires with a manual pump

Push ups — Refer to strength training, Chapter 4, pp. 119-120.

Cobra — This is primarily to strengthen the back which will enable you to reduce the weight your hands and arms bear. When you assist your back with your arms, you strengthen your triceps, wrists, and hands. Refer to the breathing exercises, pp. 218-219.

Downward-facing dog — Refer to p. 103.

Squeezing a ball — Select a ball that's about two-and-a-half inches in diameter and reasonably squishy. A tennis ball is too stiff. First squeeze the ball with your full hand, repeating until your hand begins to tire. Complete each session of squeezes by stretching your hand open wide and spreading your fingers as far apart as possible. You may also like to work each finger individually, opposed by the thumb on the other side of the ball. If you rarely do manual labor this will give you additional strength to resist fatigue while riding and to close your quick release levers properly.

Wrist rolls with weights — p. 121.

Wrist forward and back bends with weights — p. 121.

Self Massage

Acupressure — Refer to the sequence under shoulders and neck, pp. 232-235. For elbow pain, give special attention to LI 11, TW 5, and LI 4.

Triceps massage — This will relax the triceps muscles and increase the healing flow of blood to the area. Place your right forearm across your waist. Stroke firmly or knead the triceps from your shoulder down to the elbow with your left hand. Repeat on your left side.

Your Head and Face

The function of the head and face is to act as control center for the central nervous system and to optimize sensory perceptions and good judgment.

Triceps massage

The Optimum Use of Your Head and Face

As we discussed with neck use, maintain the natural curvature of your cervical spine by letting your spinal erectors lift your head upward and relax your chin downward. If you lean forward more than 30 degrees, lift your gaze rather than straining your neck to pull your head into a more upright position to see.

Experiment with the tilt of your head so your neck and eyes share the work of looking ahead. You may discover you don't need to hold your head so vertically to see where you are going. Adjust your helmet and visor to provide protection without interfering with your sight. Since most adults impact the front of their heads in a crash, keep your helmet about one inch above your eyebrows for maximum protection.

Tension in the neck muscles at the back of the head can easily intensify tension in the adjacent muscles of your tongue and jaw. Or if you habitually carry tension in your tongue or jaw, it can spread to your neck muscles. When you breathe through your mouth, avoid holding your jaw open and rigid. Let it hang slack and softly place the front of your tongue against the back of the top teeth. This will help keep your mouth moist. Let the rest of your tongue settle at the bottom of your mouth.

Your ears give important sensory information about traffic, other trail users, and approaching animals. Enhance those clues by turning an alert ear toward the sounds. Use your earphones when you are not on your bike. Earphones increase the risk of mishap on your bike and are illegal when you're operating any vehicle, including your bike.

Two other points about head movements are worth mentioning. Move your head freely and often to keep your neck flexible. Remember to pivot on the erect cervical spine and not contort your neck from a forward head position. Use your chin as a rudder by turning your head in the direction you want to go. If you are relaxed, your body and bike will follow.

Tips to Help You Retrain Your Head and Facial Riding Habits

Begin by evaluating your current habits of holding and moving your head and face both on and off the bike. Before changing your movement patterns, consider how it affects the curvature of your entire spine. If you try to pull your head to a new position with your muscles, you will probably compound problems. The following exercise can demonstrate the risks of forcing a new movement style. Sit on your bike with your usual forward lean (holding on to some stable support with one hand). Now release your neck and shoulders and let your head float upward. Take a moment to observe how this feels. Now tip the top of your pelvis forward and lengthen from your tailbone through the top of your head. Take a few conscious, diaphragmatic breaths. Hopefully, the second position feels more natural and sustainable because it originates from the pelvis and lengthens the entire spine.

Using energetic retraining techniques will be more lasting and healthful than imposing a localized, muscular correction. Controlled breathing and visualization are key tools to energetic retraining. Bike riding and working at a desk cause many riders to carry their heads too far forward. This carriage collapses your chest, tightens neck muscles, impairs your balance, and influences the curvature of your entire spine. Without guidance, you may try to pull your chin back and elongate the back of your neck, introducing new tensions. This technique of retraining body use is the essence of Alexander Technique. Refer to the discussion of Alexander Technique in Chapter 4, pp. 92-96.

Common Problems of the Head and Face

1. **Tight and sore muscles at the base of the skull across the head between the ears —** The solution is to quit your job and move to Hawaii. Oh, short of that, lift through the top of your head while riding. Take frequent breaks during long, high-energy rides to stretch out using the umbrella and the triangle postures. Modifying your bike to allow a more upright riding position will also help relieve this tension.

2. **Tired jaw muscles —** This can be caused by holding your jaw in a rigid position while riding. It may just show up during riding but is aggravated by chewing too vigorously or clenching your teeth in your sleep. You may overlook this tension but it is important to identify it because it contributes to neck and head strain. Evaluate your jaw by applying light pressure with your fingertips, starting in front of your ear lobes. Now move your fingers diagonally downward just in front of your jawbone. Relaxing these muscles will help if the area is tender to the touch. A gentle massage will help release this tension. Try tensing all these muscles by clenching your jaw and then completely releasing. Or try making slow gentle circles with your jaw first in one direction and then the other. Tough energy bars fatigue the jaw so select softer ones. Most energy bars will soften if you carry them next to your body during cooler weather. Notice how you chew while

eating a meal. You may need to slow down, chew more gently, and savor your food more.

3. **Tension in your tongue** — Tension in the tongue, jaw, and base of the skull are interrelated because your tongue is attached at the back of your neck. While you ride, consciously relax your tongue in the bottom of your mouth. Cultivate releasing your tongue by practicing the lion posture in the following exercise set.

4. **Tired eye muscles** — You may notice this when you are practicing a new head position. Exercise your eyes to strengthen *and* lengthen the muscles. Try the following exercises. Eye fatigue can also be due to dust and drying while riding. *Always* wear protective eyewear. Gray, amber, and clear, interchangeable lenses are convenient for sun, dim light, rain, and night riding. Your eyes are too precious to neglect. Protective eyewear will also reduce the risk of something flying into your eye and causing you to crash while you are reacting to the discomfort. The frequent adjustment of focus from close in front of the bike to the distance farther away provides beneficial exercises for your eye muscles.

Exercises to Benefit Your Face, Eyes, and Head

Lion — This relaxes your face, tongue, and jaw as well as the grip of your hands. It floods your larynx, throat, face, and hands with healing blood.

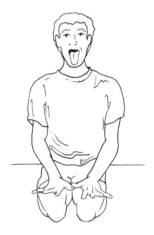

Lion

Sit on your heels with your feet folded back under your buttocks. Increase your comfort by rising up to a kneeling position and pressing your calf muscles out to the sides as you sit back down. Place your hands over your kneecaps and lift them up gently to release the patellar tendon. Stroke firmly down the tops of your thighs to release your quadriceps. Now place your fists on your thighs above your knees with palms down. Hold your back erect from the top of your head, and close your eyes. Take a long, slow inhalation. Clench your fists, tightly scrunch up your face, and contract as many muscles as possible. Release everything at once. Make a loud, fast, and energetic exhalation to fully empty your lungs. Extend your fingers from your fists, spreading them out wide. Open your eyes wide and look up as far as possible. Open your jaw wide and stick your tongue far out and down. Be sure you are opening the back of your throat. Enjoy that wonderful release of hands and face. Swallow to moisten your throat before each repetition. This is a funny posture and will lighten your mood.

Scalp massage — This feels really good after sweating in a helmet for hours. Give attention to tender areas. By massaging your scalp regularly you will discover the areas where you tend to store tension and can massage those areas more thoroughly.

Focus your mental energy — This is a trick that will remove scattered energy from your mental process. Use this when you need to concentrate at work or before a bike ride. Sit upright and close your eyes. Place the fingers of both hands in vertical formation on your forehead just above your nose. Firmly and slowly draw them across your forehead to your temples. Now lift them from your temples and shake the scattered energy off your fingertips. Return your fingers to your forehead at the hairline. Again, draw your fingers across to your temples and shake the energy off your fingers. Continue this procedure, each time returning your fingertips to an imaginary line running from the bridge of your nose to the base of your skull. Each time draw your fingers out to your ears and shake off the scattered energy. When you are finished, put your hands in your lap and sense the peace and quiet in your mind.

Facial massage — This is another renewing exercise you can do anywhere, anytime. You are going to inscribe circles with the fingertips of both hands on each side of your face. One pair of circles is on each side of your forehead, one pair on your cheeks, and finally a pair on your chin. Begin on your temples, move your fingers toward the center of your forehead above your eyebrows, up the mid-line, and across the hairline back to the temples. Repeat several times, observing tender places. From the temples move down to the jaw joint, across to the upper lip, up the sides of your nose, and out beneath your eyes back to the jaw. Repeat several times. Finally follow the jawbone across to the middle of your chin, up to your lower lip, and back to the jaw joint. When you complete several repetitions of this final pair of circles, place your hands in your lap and feel the warmth and observe the healthful color of your face.

Exercising your eye muscles —

a. Close your eyes and *gently and slowly* move your eyes through these patterns.

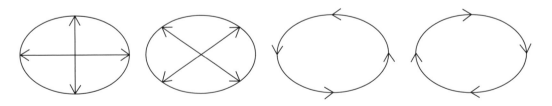

b. Try this random head tilt exercise to help you separate your head movements from your eye movements. With your eyes open, pick a point less than 10 feet in front of you. Focus your eyes on that point and tilt your head, rotate it, and nod up and down while keeping your eyes on the target. It is interesting to note that people past 50 years of age find it most difficult to raise their eyes up. So, senior riders, be sure to keep practicing these exercises and overcome this weakness.

Conclusion

Bike riding is more fun when you feel capable and in control. You can increase your pleasure in riding and improve your riding skills with the following practices:

1. Ride several times a week so the use of brakes and gears becomes automatic and does not require your attention. Building confidence in your skills is the foundation to having fun and the gateway to developing agility and power.

2. Give your full attention to the experience of riding. Tune in to your physical needs and comfort level and the beauty of things around you.

3. Commit to a daily practice of stretching and diaphragmatic breathing so your riding performance will be balanced and free.

4. Use conscious breathing to foster relaxation while you ride. Relaxation is the magical key to controlling the movement of your bicycle and cycling fun.

5. Practice optimum technique throughout each ride so you will feel alive and renewed at the end of the ride.

Practicing good riding technique is more important to your physical fitness than power output. The unfortunate preoccupation with developing strength often causes people to continue riding long after they are tired. Fatigue causes you to regress to old, less efficient, and often harmful patterns. Instead of building fitness, you are damaging yourself physically and psychologically. Riding through fatigue without adequate fuel or using poor breathing technique usually results in sore muscles. This soreness is an indication that your muscles have suffered micro-tears. Instead of becoming stronger, your muscles have actually been damaged. Building fitness demands careful attention to the quality of your exercise and sensitivity to your stamina level.

Optimizing your riding technique requires thoughtful evaluation of your current form. You will be more successful learning a new technique by consciously letting go of your old habits. Trying to apply the new form over your old form makes learning complex and slow. As you take up a new technique, visualize it in accurate detail. Then redirect your energy and intention into creating it.

You will need to ride often to achieve noticeable results and to stay motivated. During retraining, you will need to ride several times a week, giving your attention to optimizing your technique. Select a distance that is short enough to avoid fatigue and long enough to warm up completely. The benefits of regular practice will be easily apparent while you develop your stretching practice. Select one Yoga posture and practice it daily with attention to the quality of your form and your breathing. In ten days to two weeks you will notice how much easier it is to perform the posture and changes in your body dynamics.

Be realistic. Achieving results requires commitment to your practice. This is true not only of making time in your schedule but also of staying mindful throughout your practice. Correcting dysfunctional breathing habits will probably take years but the benefits to your general health, productivity, and disposition will reward you many times over.

I hope you will return to this text regularly as you refine your understanding of your body mechanics and riding technique. Have fun and enjoy the adventure of learning! When it comes to learning new skills, you can't start any sooner than right now.

chapter 6

Customized Bicycle Setup
Supports Riding Style

- Fitting Your Bike Frame to Your Body Proportions
- Steps for Personalizing Your Riding Position
- Questions and Answers About the Effects of Bike Setup on the Rider
- Understanding Gearing with Three Chainrings

Fitting a Bike Frame to Your Body Proportions

Your **bicycle fit** and configuration are as essential to your cycling pleasure as the skillful use of your body. Bicycle fit involves matching the bicycle frame proportions to your body proportions and is the single most important factor in selecting a bicycle. If you select a bicycle that is too large or too small, and the distance between the stem and the seat post is not right, your pleasure and performance will always be compromised regardless of the quality of the bicycle. Many would-be cyclists buy a bicycle that looks great and shifts and handles well. But when they go for a ride, they tire quickly and develop sore muscles. If the bike is too tall, the negative impact on the rider's performance can be quite subtle. Every time riders dismount, the risk of hitting themselves on the top tube diminishes their confidence. This uncertainty makes it difficult to focus awareness on technique and makes them hesitant to pour on full power. When they have difficulty keeping up with friends, they usually conclude they are out of shape and don't realize that the cause of their fatigue is a poorly fit bike. So they are likely to return home disappointed by cycling and hang up their bikes forever.

Bicycle fit and riding position are separate but related issues. **Riding position** is a personal choice that should change and evolve with your riding style. It should meet your immediate expectations, enable you to relax comfortably, and ride at an enjoyable exertion level. Don't be persuaded by well-intended friends or sales staff to try to adapt to the way a bicycle was designed. Experiment with various riding positions and bicycle components until you are delighted with the results and eager to get on the bike. If you try to adapt to something less, you will probably quit riding before your style has a chance to adapt. When you are buying a new bike, find out if the modifications you want are mechanically possible. Some design aspects limit custom options. The bicycle modifications you choose will cost time and money. Overcome your hesitancy to invest more in a bike by weighing the cost of customizing it with the cost of medical care to treat injuries resulting from chronic stress or misuse. The investment in adapting your bicycle is an investment in **your health and fitness**.

This distinction between bicycle frame fit and setting up a bicycle for your desired riding position means that you **select a bike by fitting the frame dimensions to your body proportions and then change the seat post, stem, and handlebars to create the position you desire**. These are two critical steps that will make it possible to adapt the bike to meet your evolving riding style and changing position simply by changing components. You will not have to buy a new bike just to ride in a more casual or more dynamic position.

Common Factors that Complicate Bicycle Fitting

The most common error new bike buyers make is to select a bicycle that is too large. When in doubt, you are **better served by a smaller frame**. Usually this error results from selecting a bike that provides an upright riding position rather than determining frame fit by top-tube length. A smaller bike permits better control and reduces the likelihood of crashes and severe injury. For each person's body proportions, an optimum frame fit can be found, independent of riding style. Your choice of frame size should be based on your body proportions and not on your riding style. Don't limit your potential to develop sophisticated bike handling skills just because your initial plan is to ride sedately around your neighborhood or to ride casually along an urban bike path. Your fit should allow you to ride any technical level of trail should you fall in love with cycling. In any case, you will have more fun and be more confident if you fit your bicycle so you can control it skillfully.

Smaller frames are stronger than larger frames. This is unfortunate for tall people but the longer each frame tube, the weaker the entire frame. Therefore, it is especially important for tall people to ride as small a frame as possible that allows them optimum performance.

Bicycle **manufacturer's frame size measurements** are not standardized. They all measure from the center of the bottom bracket spindle along the seat tube to an undefined point in the seat cluster, the place on the frame where the seat tube, top tube, and seat stays converge. Listed frame size measurements can vary as much as two inches on two frames with the same dimensions! Even different models from the same brand will be measured differently. For that reason, shopping for a 21-inch frame road bike is only useful as a starting reference point.

To complicate matters further, **frame sizes used by manufacturers are not relevant in fitting** the frame to rider proportions! We will discuss in detail selecting an optimum frame fit by determining the appropriate top-tube length and stand-over height. Then you can measure the critical dimensions of any frame to identify bikes that might fit you.

Wheel size is another factor complicating bike sizing. Frame sizes listed for bikes with 700c or 26-inch wheels do not correlate to frame sizes of bikes with either one or both wheels smaller.

If you are **shorter than five feet two inches or taller than six feet four inches** you will have a limited choice of stock bikes that fit. If you are close to these heights and have unusual proportions of torso length to leg length, you will also have limited choices. The added research and patience required for you to find a good fit will be well worth it in the long run. Most riders five feet two inches and smaller will find that at least a smaller front wheel is necessary for safety, control, and comfort. Terry Precision Bicycles® does an excellent job of meeting the needs of smaller riders. If you are taller than six feet six inches, a bike with wheels larger than 700c or 26 inches would create proportions better for you. Unfortunately, larger wheeled bikes are uncommon.

When you are shopping for a new bike **expect to customize it to meet your needs**. This chapter examines in detail the pros and cons of common modifications. We'll give special attention to seat and handlebar position and their relationship to each other. Follow the "Steps for Personalizing Your Riding Position" on pp. 261, 263 to give you an idea of what you need to modify to make you comfortable and efficient.

Bicycle Measurements That are Useful in Evaluating Fit

Using standardized measurements will help you accurately evaluate bike frame sizes. Effective top-tube length and the stand-over height are the two basic measurements used in bike fitting. Using these frame measurements along with your body measurements will give you an objective means of evaluating bicycle fit for your needs. You can use these comparative numbers in the following situations:

1. Use when you would like to evaluate your current bike fit. If you are comfortable and ride with reasonable stamina on your bike, it may fit you well. By measuring your bike and then yourself, you can calculate fit guideline measurements that will suggest whether you could benefit from modifying your bike. If your current bike is close to your fit guidelines, you can use it for comparison when you shop for a new bike. If the guideline numbers you calculate are substantially different from your bike, you have probably adapted to a fit and position that diminishes your performance and efficiency.

2. If you have one bike that is comfortable and another that causes nagging aches, measure them and compare. This should help you decide whether the uncomfortable bike can be modified to fit or is simply the wrong size and will always be uncomfortable. It is wise to set up all your bikes with the same riding

position. This will diminish the chances of sore muscles when you switch from one bike to the other.

3. When shopping for a new bike, take your calculated fit guidelines and a measuring tape with you so that you will only test ride bikes in your fitting range.

Although these numbers are not fool proof, they will give you standardized measurements that make accurate comparisons possible. Since both metric and English units are used by the bicycle industry, use the one that is meaningful for you. Expect to find mountain bikes measured in English and road bikes in metric units. Your task will be simplified by purchasing a tape measure with English on one edge and metric on the other.

Make the following measurements on your current bike(s) or any new bikes you are considering. Use the illustration to help measure accurately. Then record the measurements on the form provided on p. 262 to use in reference to frame fit.

Effective top-tube length (TT) — Place the bike on a level surface. Measure along a horizontal line from the center of the stem to the center of the seat post. The stem (and head tube) and seat post (and seat tube) are usually parallel so you can measure at any point along the tubes. Be sure your measurements are precisely horizontal. You would be wise to invest in a string-mounted bubble level or a ruler with a level built in.

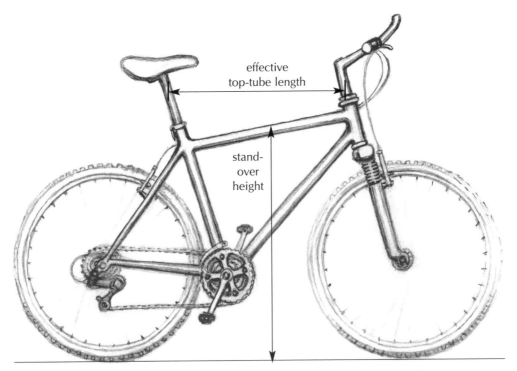

Measurement of stand-over height (SO) and effective top-tube length (TT)

Stand-over height (SO) — Hold the bike upright and measure the distance from the floor to the top of the top tube, ten inches in front of the seat tube.

Wheel base — Align the front wheel with the frame and measure from the center of the front axle to the center of the rear axle. This is a useful measurement for explaining bike handling characteristics.

The following measurements are useful for comparing riding position:

Floor-to-center of the handlebar at the grip — This measurement allows you to directly compare the heights of handlebars on various bikes. If you want an upright riding position, you can determine how much you would have to raise the handlebars. Take care to hold the bike upright for this measurement.

Seat-to-handlebar extension — This distance reflects the "reach" of your riding position: how far forward your torso leans and how far your arms extend. Measure from the top of the saddle above the seat post center forward to the center of the handlebar at the stem. If you have a comfortable bike, you can use this measurement for comparison. If you like a different bike and need to shorten the reach, this measurement will tell you if the desired modification can be made with a different stem or if the top tube is too long for you to be comfortable even after modification.

Relative height of handlebar and seat — Are the handlebars above the top of the seat or below it? Place a yard stick horizontally across the top of the saddle just above the seat post center. Measure the distance between the yardstick and the handlebar grip height. Sight from the grip to the yardstick and measure the difference in height between them. Record this as a negative number if the handlebars are lower than the seat. This relationship is critical to comfort. Most riders appreciate the handlebars at the same height or higher than the top of the saddle. On a new bike, this measurement is only meaningful if you first position the seat at the optimum height for you. Refer to pp. 194-195 for establishing the optimum seat height. If you are comfortable on your current bike, measure this relationship before adjusting the seat height so you will know how you like this relative position.

The reliability of bicycle fitting systems depends on the skill and experience of the evaluators. Most are based on the experiences of bicycle racers and may not be useful for you. Because many of these systems are designed for custom-built frames, you might pay for a lot of information that is not useful when you buy a stock frame.

The bike frame fitting system offered here will provide you with guideline measurements. They are only guidelines because linear measurements of the body are only part of the fitting story. Other factors you should consider are:

1. Weight-to-height ratio — A stocky rider may benefit from a slightly larger frame than a thin rider. If riders are large around the waist they may need more space between the seat and stem.

2. Weight distribution — Riders with bulky upper bodies generally need larger frames than riders with most of their weight in the hips.

3. Bone size — Large-boned riders may need larger bikes than small-boned riders. The experienced eye can usually make this distinction by observing wrist diameter. Head, hand, and foot size can also give some indication of bone size. If you wear large shoes for your height, larger than usual helmet, and extra large gloves, you may need a slightly larger frame than the guideline numbers indicate.

4. Riders who are older than 60 years usually lose some height. They should fit their peak size because their bone lengths have probably not changed. The loss of height is usually the result of reduced cushioning in the joints. They may need a larger bike than seems apparent initially.

5. The riders' current or anticipated riding style — Experienced and skillful riders will appreciate a smaller bike that will increase their sense of power, maneuverability, and control.

Selecting the optimum fit from stock bicycle sizes usually requires some compromises and problem solving skills.

Body Measurements for Calculating Fitting Guidelines

Three body measurements will be helpful: floor-to-crotch, torso length, and arm length. In order to calculate valid guidelines, these measurements must be taken precisely as defined and accurately. You will need the help of a friend to make these measurements. Remove your shoes to make the measurements.

Floor-to-crotch — Measure from the bottom of your pubic bone to the floor. Use a dowel or one by two inch board about 20 inches long. Place it up in your crotch. Holding it in front and in back of your pelvis, pull it tightly up into your crotch against your pubic bone. This will not be comfortable but don't injure yourself. You are trying to simulate sitting on the bike seat. The dowel must be horizontal for this measurement to be accurate. Use a carpenter's level if you have one. If not, you can buy a cheap little level at a hardware store. Or have your friend set the dowel level and measure from the *top* of the dowel to the floor along a vertical line.

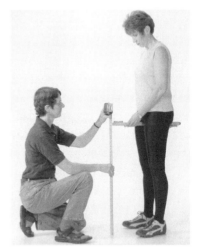

Measure the floor-to-crotch using a level to accurately determine the distance from the pubic bone to the floor. You will simplify the calculations if you take these measurements with your shoes off.

Measure the sternum notch-to-floor by resting a level dowel or pencil in the indentation at the top of the breastbone, the sternum notch.

Measure arm length from the end of the acromion at the top of the arm to the center of the prominent wrist bone on the pinky side. Hold the arm out at a 45-degree angle while measuring this.

Sternum notch-to-floor — The sternum notch is the soft spot at the base of the neck, at the top of the sternum (breastbone), between the collarbones (clavicles). Place the end of the dowel or a pencil in the sternum notch and again bring it accurately to horizontal. Now have your friend measure from the *bottom* of the dowel to the floor along a vertical line.

Arm length — Take care to measure the arm exactly as defined, from the tip of the shoulder bone (acromion) to the middle of the wrist bone on the pinky finger side of the hand. Measure this while you hold your arm at 45 degrees straight out to your side. To find the bone at the tip of your shoulder, relax your arm down along your side. This will relax the muscles of your shoulder and make the (acromion) easier to locate. If you have a bulky shoulder, you may need to hunt for this bone. The acromion is the most prominent, horizontal bone at the outside tip of your shoulder at the top of your arm. Follow your collar bone out to the tip of your shoulder. The acromion is right at the end of it, at the back of your shoulder joint. Or you can find it by following the spine of the scapula to the end of the shoulder. Now raise your arm to 45 degrees in a line with your shoulders with your palm down. Measure from the outside end of the acromion along your arm to the center of the prominent wrist bone at the back of your wrist.

Steps for Personalizing Your Riding Position

After you have established the appropriate frame size, you will want to determine what modifications are needed to achieve the riding position you desire. Begin with the relationship of the pelvis to the pedals to minimize stress on hip and knee joints. This procedure will be easier with the help of a friend. You can do this by putting your bike on an indoor trainer or by supporting yourself against a stable object while demonstrating your riding position.

1. Position your hips squarely on your saddle and sit on your bike in your typical riding position.

continued on page 263

Record of Body and Bike-Frame Measurements
and Calculation of Fitting Guidelines

Bicycle frame measurements for reference:

Effective top-tube length: _____ inches   **Stand-over height:** _____ inches

Wheel base (center hub to center hub): _____ inches

Floor-to-center of the handlebar at the grip: _____ inches Bottom-bracket height: _____ inches

Seat (from center of seat post)-to-handlebar at the grip (along a horizontal line): _____ inches

Difference between the height of handlebars (at the grips) and the top of the saddle: _____ inches

Floor-to-crotch _____ inches

- Calculation of appropriate *stand-over height* of the bike:

    Mountain bike - subtract 3-6 inches from floor-to-crotch measurement _____ inches

    Road bike - subtract 2-4 inches from your floor-to-crotch measurement _____ inches
        Use the smallest value if you are five feet tall and the greatest value if you are
        six feet four inches tall. Pro-rate the distance for intermediate heights.

- Calculation of *top-of-seat to center-of-pedal spindle length*, pedal down,
    aligned with seat tube: (floor-to-crotch) x 1.09 inches = _____ inches
    This number will help you establish an appropriate seat height.

Sternum notch-to-floor _____ inches

- Calculation of your *torso length*:
    (sternum notch-to-floor) – (floor-to-crotch) = _____ inches

Arm length _____ inches

- Calculation of appropriate *top-tube length*:
    (torso length + arm length) x (forward-lean factor) = _____ inches
    The forward-lean factor takes into account your riding style and your torso position. The smaller
    the factor, the more upright the riding position and the shorter the calculated top-tube length.
    Mountain bike factors: upright: 0.48, 15-29 degrees: 0.495, 30-45 degrees or more: 0.51
    Road bike factors: upright: 0.47, 15-29 degrees: 0.485, 30-45 degrees or more: 0.50
                (These angles use vertical as zero degrees.)

Top-tube length = (_____ + _____) x _____ = _____ inches
            This number will range from 18-25 inches. Most top tubes are between 20 and 24 inches.
            The shortest top-tube lengths on Terry Precision Bicycles® are 19 inches.

2. Set the proper saddle height as calculated above or by using the angle of the knee bend as described on p. 194.

3. Establish the proper forward position of the saddle by dropping a plumb line from below the knee cap on the head of the tibia. The saddle position varies among riders depending on the distance from the rider's seat bone to the knee joint. Refer to Chapter 5, "Forward Position of the Saddle," pp. 196-197 for details.

4. Place your hands on the handlebar grips of flat handlebars or on the control levers on drop bars. Observe how you are using your hands, arms, and shoulders as an indication of comfort with the current setup. If you are touching the grips with the tips of your fingers, andyour elbows are straight or your shoulders are drawn forward, you probably would like to sit more upright or bring the handlebars closer to your shoulders. If you have drop bars and prefer to hold the bars on the top of the horizontal portion of the bars, that is also an indication you might like the bars closer to your shoulders.

5. Now demonstrate what you think would be an optimum position by leaning forward the way you would like to ride and reach forward as if to grasp imaginary bars.

6. If you would like to make changes, record your conclusions by measuring the floor-to-center of grip distance and the center-of-seat post to center-of-grip distance.

7. Consult with your bike mechanic to determine if that position can be achieved with your frame size and components. The following discussion of component choices will help you understand what possibilities are available to you.

I hope these guidelines will enable you to evaluate your bicycle fit and riding position with confidence. You will need to experiment to achieve an optimum setup for your current style.

Questions and Answers About the Effects of Bike Setup on the Rider

Let's look at the key factors in setting up your optimum riding position. We'll consider each component of the bicycle that influences comfort and performance.

As we consider bike modifications, the importance of the stem to riding position will become obvious. The effective top-tube length is critical in fitting the bike frame to your body proportions. However, stem choice is the primary means for setting up your bike for your desired riding position. Using an adjustable stem enables you to adapt the handlebar position to your evolving riding style. If you select a frame with a top tube more than one inch longer than your guideline top-tube length, you will probably limit future options for customizing your bike.

How does saddle height affect your knees and your comfort?

This is the most important adjustment for health and endurance.

- The saddle height is one of two parameters that are the basis for all other adjustments for rider comfort. The height is based on leg length. All other relationships in rider position evolve from the saddle position.

- The optimum saddle height allows for a 25-30 degree bend in the knee with the foot at the bottom of the pedal stroke. Refer to the illustration on seat height on p. 194 to see what angle is measured.

- Raising the saddle slightly, reduces stress on sensitive or impaired knees.

- If you are a novice building confidence on a new bike, you may feel more secure with the saddle low enough that you can easily touch the ground. However, the low saddle position puts added strain on your knees and makes you work harder. Avoid riding more than a few miles at a time with the saddle in this position. You will want to raise the saddle gradually to the appropriate height as you become accustomed to the new bike. Keeping the saddle too low is a common mistake. For details on establishing the optimum saddle height, refer to "Saddle Height" p. 194.

How will moving the saddle forward to get closer to the handlebars affect pedaling performance?

The stem is the place to change your relationship to the handlebars, not the saddle.

- The horizontal relationship of the saddle to the pedals should be considered along with seat height as the basis for all other adjustments for rider position.

- Forward seat position varies among riders depending primarily on femur length and the total distance from the seat bones to the knee joints.

- Evaluate the optimum position for you by using a plumb line described in "Forward Position of the Saddle," pp. 196-197.

- After establishing the saddle to crank position, you may find the handlebars are too far forward to reach comfortably. Changes greater than three-eighths-of-an-inch should be made by changing the stem.

- Sliding the saddle close to the end of the rails may cause the saddle rails to bend. Once the rails bend, replace the saddle immediately before it breaks.

- There is no standardization of the saddle placement relative to the length of the rails. The offset of seat posts varies also. If you are at the limit of adjustment with your current saddle and seat post, look for different ones that provide the adjustment you need.

- The forward position of your saddle strongly influences your pedaling style. Make this choice consciously by referring to "Understanding and Utilizing the Benefits of Spinning and Pushing" on pp. 157-158.

How critical is the top-tube length to bike fit?

It determines whether you can be comfortable on the bike and whether you can control the bike skillfully.

- Refer to your guideline top-tube length as calculated on p. 262.

- The top-tube length should be considered together with the horizontal length of the stem. This distance between the saddle and the handlebars determines the comfort of your upper torso, neck, shoulders, arms, hands and genitals. It also influences your bike handling skills.

- When the horizontal length of the stem cannot be shortened enough to provide the comfort and control you desire, the top tube of the frame is too long. Conversely, the top tube is probably too short if you require a stem longer than 130 mm.

- Body proportions, flexibility, and personal preference will determine the appropriate distance between saddle and handlebars. It should be long enough to achieve the forward torso lean you desire when you are holding the farthest reach on the handlebars: the end of the bar ends on flat handlebars or the control levers on drop bars. Remember to keep your shoulders relaxed and your elbows bent toward your hips when you test this position. For further details refer to "Optimum Use of Your Back," in Chapter 5 on pp. 219-223.

- The distance should be short enough that you can move your buttocks off the back of the saddle while holding the farthest reach on the handlebars. This "off-the-back-of-the-saddle" position is a control maneuver for steep descents or emergency stops.

What are the advantages of the sloping top tube compared with a horizontal one?

All other factors remaining constant, the sloping top tube creates a smaller main triangle and a stronger frame.

- The sloping top tube gives a slight increase in straddle clearance. However, this is deceptive.

Sampson demonstrates a controlled descending technique. Moving your buttocks off the back of the saddle also enables you to stop quickly at high speed without going over the handlebars.

The height of the top tube directly behind the head tube is substantially higher than at the seat tube, increasing the risk of landing on it during sudden dismounts, especially on an incline surface.

- Sloping top tubes are the norm on front suspension bicycles. To accommodate the movement of the lower legs of the fork, the clearance of the fork crown over the tire of suspension forks must be greater than on rigid forks. This causes the head tube and the front of the top tube to be a minimum of 32 inches high on a 26-inch wheeled bike regardless of the frame size.

What benefits will you gain from raising the handlebars?

Raising the handlebars will increase comfort and reduce upper-body strain.
- The higher you raise the handlebars, the less strain there will be on your hands, arms, shoulders, and perineum. However, the more upright your position, the greater the weight on your seat bones, and the slower and less dynamic your bike handling. You will need to bend and drop your elbows to lean forward for increased power output and to reduce resistance in a strong head wind.

- Your choice of handlebar height will determine the position of your center of gravity over your bicycle. If your center of gravity is over the pedals when you are seated *and* your arms are not fully extended, you will have optimum control and mobility on your bike. If your center of gravity is over the saddle when you are seated, and your arms are fully extended, you will diminish mobility and control but you can enjoy riding with less upper-body strength and use. What you choose depends on your personal preference. Refer to the diagram of the influence forward lean has on performance, p. 55.

- There are many ways to optimize your riding position, even for the same riding style. Your choices will be influenced by your center of gravity, body weight distribution, and arm length in relation to torso length.

- Refer to the discussion below on the mechanical limitations to changing handlebar position.

- The benefits and detriments of handlebar height will depend on the horizontal and vertical relationship of your handlebars to your saddle at optimum height. Let's consider the effect of vertical change with the horizontal extension remaining constant.

Pros and Cons of Placing the Handlebars More Than Three Inches *Above* the Height of the Top of the Saddle

- Most of your weight is on the saddle.
- Pressure is reduced on the front of your perineum.
- Less upper-body strength is needed.
- People with back and upper-body impairments may be able to enjoy cycling.
- Upper-body workout is diminished by this more static riding position.
- Weight shifts for bicycle control or comfort are slow since riders must first shift their weight off the saddle to move it forward over the pedals.
- Steering is primarily with the handlebars since lateral hip movement is limited.
- The gluteals are less active in this position.
- This position requires that you lower your shoulders on steep ascents to hold down the front wheel or to fully utilize the gluteals.

Pros and Cons of Handlebars *Within* Three Inches of the Saddle Height

- This distributes the rider's body weight more evenly between saddle and handlebars, at about 60/40 percent.
- The rider can be more agile for better control and faster weight shifts.
- Although it shifts some weight off the seat bones, it puts more pressure on the front of the perineum and hands.
- This position requires greater upper-body strength and results in increased strength.

Pros and Cons of Handlebars More Than Three Inches *Below* the Top of the Saddle

- Weight can be more evenly distributed over both wheels most of the time.
- It gives an excellent workout for the upper body, while requiring greater upper-body strength.
- This is a highly dynamic position with fast response times.
- The back is close to horizontal for an aerodynamic position and requires an extreme anterior pelvic tilt to maintain a healthy spinal curvature.
- Riders must shift their body weight back to prevent endos on steep descents.
- It places steady pressure on the hands and front of perineum even while weight is reduced on the seat bones.
- It increases stress on hands, arms, and shoulders.
- The gluteus maximus performs at maximum power output when the pelvis is tilted forward.
- Riders must focus on developing a strong pedal upstroke in order to balance the output of the powerful gluteals and reduce lower back strain.

In general, what are the effects of changing the horizontal stem length?

Horizontal stem length affects rider position and bike handling response.

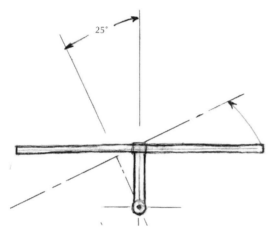

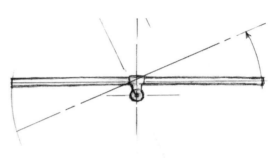

Handlebar movement with different stem lengths

While turning with a long horizontal stem, both hands move forward to affect a turn.

While turning with a short horizontal stem, one hand moves forward and the other backwards.

The Effects of a Short Horizontal Stem (60-90 mm) on Steering Performance?

- It shortens the distance between the saddle and the handlebars to achieve a more comfortable riding position.
- It changes steering characteristics, requiring that you move opposite ends of the handlebars less distance to affect change in wheel direction. See the illustration above.
- It shortens the steering response time.
- It allows use of your bar ends with less forward reach and shoulder fatigue.

The Effects of a Long Horizontal Stem (100-150 mm) on Steering Performance?

- It increases the distance between the saddle and the handlebars to achieve greater horizontal extension.
- It slows steering response time, requiring less attention to holding a line.
- It moves the handlebars farther from the axis of rotation of the fork steerer. This results in more complex steering.

Are there mechanical limitations to changing handlebar position?

Yes, the type of stem on your bike will determine your options.

- These modifications are achieved by installing a taller, traditional stem; a clamp-on stem extender; a more upright clamp-on stem; and/or handlebars with rise. The combination you will need depends on how much height you need and the current components on the bike you want to modify. These illustrations will help you determine the components you will need.

- Using the full range of choices among stem extenders, stems, and handlebar curvatures, you can move most handlebars to the desired position if the top tube is short enough.

Types of Stems

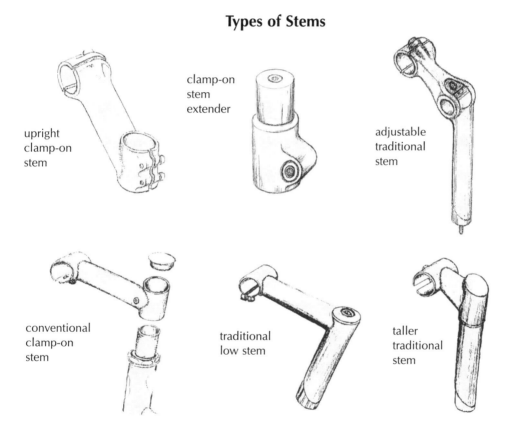

upright clamp-on stem

clamp-on stem extender

adjustable traditional stem

conventional clamp-on stem

traditional low stem

taller traditional stem

- As we have already discussed, extreme changes have a marked affect on bike handling. Of course, that could be just what you want.

- If you have the unusual fork steerer diameter of 1 1/4 inches, it may require the use of a shim in the steerer to accommodate a 1 1/8-inch stem. These shims do not appear to compromise the security of the stem installation.

- It may be more challenging to find an understanding mechanic than it is to find the parts required for your modification. Quality Bicycle Products® and Delta® stock the parts needed for most modifications.

- Take your bike with you to discuss modifications so that the bicycle retailer can see whether you have a traditional or clamp-on stem, the steerer diameter, and other mechanical details.

What are the effects of the length of flat handlebars and the width of drop bars on bike handling?

Shorter flat handlebars require less movement for the same response of the front wheel. The bike handles more quickly.

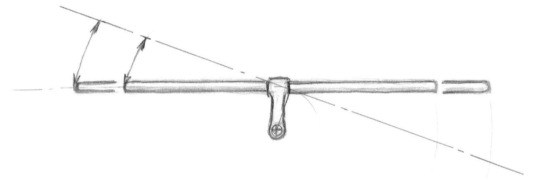

As the hands move closer to the stem, less movement is required to effect the same change in front wheel direction. Handlebars shorter than 20 inches will probably make the bike squirrely.

- A shorter flat handlebar is another means for bringing the grips closer to the rider's shoulders, increasing comfort as well as control.

- For average shoulder widths, 21-inch length flat bars handle well. You may choose wider bars if you have especially broad shoulders. The use of bar ends positions your hands at the ends of the bars and makes the 21-inch bar a better handling choice than the stock 23-25 inch bars. They can easily be cut shorter.

- Drop-bar width is more closely related to the rider's shoulder width. The control levers should be close to the width of the shoulder joints, making 44 cm (17 1/2 inch) the norm.

- The diminished leverage of drop bars requires more upper-body strength than 21-inch flat bars. Certainly that is one reason riders appreciate the stability and control of flat bars.

Would handlebars with rise provide a more upright position?

Yes, but they have some drawbacks.

Handlebars with rise are also known as riser or downhill bars.

- Riser bars limit control lever position along the bar and consequently limit the choices of length of the bars. Shimano Rapid Fire® shifter bodies must not contact the handlebars if they are to perform properly.

- Rotating the bars also changes the angle of the grip.

- Flat handlebars allow control levers to be placed anywhere on the handlebar at the rotation that is most comfortable for you. Refer to the photo of reduced hand strain, p. 242.

- If you want to raise the handlebars for a more upright position, you can maintain greater variety and adjustability of hand positions by keeping flat handlebars and gaining height with a taller stem or clamp-on stem extender. Bars with rise can be used to gain additional height when the stem extension or tall traditional stem are not adequate to achieve the desired height.

- Bars with rise sometimes result in the bar ends pointing out to the sides of the bike. This usually does not create a stress-free position for shoulders, arms, wrists, and hands. Refer to "Your Arms and Hands," pp. 240-244.

Are bar ends on flat handlebars just for climbing?

No, bar ends will increase comfort on any terrain.
- They provide an alternative hand position.

- They provide a neutral wrist position that does not rotate the forearm inward 45 degrees as the hold on the horizontal grip does.

- This neutral wrist position opens up circulation to the hands and wrists by reducing stress on hands and wrists so it is not transmitted to the arms, shoulders, and neck.

- They enable you to ride for longer periods of time with a forward lean of 45 degrees when strong winds or steep terrain make that advantageous.

continued on page 273

Flat Handlebars on Road Bikes Can Provide the Comfort and Control of a Mountain Bike with the Efficiency of a Road Bike

If you want to ride greater distance on the road or want more efficiency on urban trails, you probably would enjoy a performance road bike with flat handlebars. Or you might enjoy converting your current road bike with drop bars to flat ones. Consider these influential factors:

- **Your pelvic tilt determines your potential power output.** Arm and hand position is simply a personal choice. Refer to pp. 54-55.

- **Handlebar style does not determine the rider position.** You can select a stem that gives you the desired position with either flat or drop bars. When the handlebars are easy to reach you can easily change your forward lean by bending your elbows.

- **Your handlebar choice should be based on how you like to use your hands.** Having more than one hand position helps reduce strain on your hands and forearms. One position should provide a neutral wrist position, and bar ends will provide that on flat bars. A hand position that allows you to hold the bars with a relaxed grip is a healthy one. You can lean into bar ends with bent elbows and not have to grip them tightly to maintain your hand position. Reducing hand strain is more important than the total number of hand positions a handlebar provides.

- **Choose handlebars that use control levers you can operate with ease.** Dual levers (Ergo® or STI®) make gear shifting more convenient on drop bars. However, the hand movements required for shifting are not used much in daily activities, and often riders' hands are not strong enough to shift without straining. For riders with average-to-small hands and bikes with three chain rings, the dual levers are especially demanding to operate. By contrast, controls on flat bars use the well-developed strength of the hand's grip.

- **The upper trapezius muscles contract to hold the arms extended in the forward reach characteristic of drop bars. This aggravates chronic shoulder and neck strain.** Riding bikes with relatively long top tubes and stems have increased the problem of shoulder strain for cyclists. Add to that the chronic tension most people carry in their shoulders from stress and riding in an extended position on drop bars can be quite miserable. Refer to p. 245.

- **Bars positioned more than three inches below the seat require the rider to hyperextend an already tight neck and may result in hip strain.** If the resulting anterior pelvic tilt is more than 45 degrees, the hip joints operate at the edge of their range of motion. In addition, a horizontal back position can cause circulatory problems in the groin.

- You can rotate the bar ends on the handlebars to accommodate your favorite riding position. If you bend your elbows and grip the bar ends in your fist, you may like your bar end at about a 45-degree angle. If you ride with your open palm across the handlebar and bar ends, you may like the bar ends lower at about 10-15 degrees above horizontal. Refer to the illustrations on hand strain in Chapter 5, p. 242.

- They are often called "climbing bars" because they can give increased leverage while climbing at high exertion levels but all riders' hands and wrists will benefit from using them regularly.

- Access to control levers is limited when your hands are on the bar ends but you can practice moving your hands down onto the handlebar grips for quick access to the controls.

- Refer to the discussion on hand use on p. 243.

What factors influence the choice of drop bars or flat bars on a road bike?

Drop bars have been the norm on road bikes for several reasons:

- For road riding, drop bars provide a great variety of hand positions while holding the torso relatively motionless.

- When the drop bars are positioned with the top of the bar lower than the saddle, they provide a more aerodynamic position that allows greater power generation even with arms outstretched and elbows extended.

There are reasons why you may prefer flat bars on your road bike:

- Flat bars can result in a more upright position, which is healthier for your neck, shoulders, and hands.

- If you have small hands and find it difficult to operate the dual control levers on drop bars with confidence, flat handlebars can give you better control with less fatigue.

- Adding bar ends to flat handlebars can give you alternative hand positions and reduce forearm and wrist fatigue.

- Flat bars with bar ends allow you to bend your elbows and drop down into a lower position for reduced wind resistance and increased power generation.

- Flat bars are available with several choices of bends. Most flat bars have a bend of about 5 degrees. A few are available with a 15 degree bend that is just right for the angle of the human fist on the forearm. This small difference makes a noticeable difference in comfort.

Compare the subtle difference between the common 5 degree handlebar bend and the more ergonomic 15 degree bend pictured on the right.

What considerations influence your choice of shifters?

This is primarily a matter of personal preference. Make your decision based on test riding experience.

- If you have sensitive thumbs, twist shifters may reduce stress on your thumbs.

- If you have sensitive wrists, you may find levers less fatiguing.

- Riders with small hands will want to evaluate their control capability carefully on dual-control levers on drop bars. Flat bars with bar ends may be easier to operate.

- Be sure to select shifters that are compatible with the derailleurs on your bike.

- If gear indicators contribute to your riding pleasure, be sure to select shifters with indicators.

- SRAM's Dual Drive® puts all the shifting into the right hand, and the internally geared rear hub makes it possible to shift while standing still, while coasting, as well as when pedaling!

How should riders position their brake levers?

Position them for optimum control and minimum strain on hands and wrists.

- You can determine this position by extending your arms forward to hold the handlebars from your favorite forearm angle. For flat handlebars, you will make this adjustment by rotating the brake levers on the bars. For drop bars, you can adjust the rotation of the handlebars in the stem. This will vary: from the straight portion at the bottom of the bars being horizontal to about 20 degrees above horizontal. On drop bars the brake-lever tip should align with the bottom of the handlebar's lower edge or a half-inch higher for dual levers.

- Brake reach on flat bars is usually adjustable. That means you can shorten the distance between the lever and the grip. Better control can be achieved if both levers are between the first and middle knuckles of most of your fingers when the brake is fully released. Adjust your brake cable length so that the lever comes inside your middle knuckle when the brake pads contact the rim. This will utilize the strongest grip of your hand and will reduce strain.

Is it worthwhile to upgrade my brake mechanism?

If you have a hand impairment or you are vulnerable to hand strain, you may benefit from new brakes. We will not consider the more expensive options of mechanical or hydraulic disc brakes.

- The road bike dual pivot brakes and mountain bike V-brakes are powerful and require less hand strength to operate skillfully than cantilever brakes and older styles of caliper road brakes. If you ride often in mountainous terrain, in heavy traffic, or with a heavy load where controlled stops are critical, it is worth your while to invest in V-brakes or dual pivot road bike brakes.

- Often brakes that seem inadequate in design simply need proper maintenance. Preventative brake maintenance is critical for *any* brake model. Many brake pads are glazed and provide inadequate friction on the rims either from aging or because they are made of a poor compound. Check them often for glazing, wear, and position on the rim. Note that some pad/rim combinations are incompatible: they either don't stop effectively or screech even with adequate toe-in. Replace troublesome pads.

- Skillful brake use will also improve the performance of any style of brake. Use both brakes simultaneously. The front one has better stopping power. It is more effective because when you apply your brakes, your weight shifts forward onto the front wheel increasing traction on the riding surface. It responds faster with less resistance because the cable and housing are shorter. Using the rear brake will help you avoid going over the handlebars but if used alone can cause the rear end to slide out from under you.

- Practice the emergency stop for situations when you must stop suddenly, especially at high speed. Put your pedals in the horizontal position, lift your buttocks off the saddle, and slide back over the rear wheel while extending your arms to full length. This important technique can bring you to a controlled stop even in an emergency. See the photo on p. 265.

What determines appropriate crankarm length?

You will want to consider your leg length, bicycle type, the terrain you usually ride, and pedaling style.

- Crankarm length determines the diameter of the circle the pedals move through on each stroke. It influences leverage and cadence. For average-sized riders (five feet nine inches), 170 mm crankarms are considered the norm for road bikes and 175 for mountain. Even though there is indecisive research on crank-arm length, we can make some generalizations.

- Riders with longer legs should use longer cranks than short-legged riders.

- Shorter crankarms allow you to spin better (ride at higher cadence in lower gears), since they result in a smaller pedal circles, and require less flexion of the knees and hips. They are more desirable on the road.

- Longer crankarms give greater leverage and are better for pushing higher gears at lower cadence. These conditions are more common off-road.

- If you are five feet two inches or shorter, take care to have 165 mm cranks for road and probably 170 mm for dirt. If you are taller than six feet four inches, you may want 175 mm cranks on the road and 180 mm or more off-road.

Is the traditional obsession with lightweight bikes justified?

I'm so glad you asked! If you are a bicycle racer or competitive in nature, bike weight is a legitimate concern. If you ride with friends who always challenge you to keep pace, weight is important. For fitness riders, added weight provides a better workout. Let's look at some facts.

- A lightweight bike allows you to ride farther with less exertion and greater endurance. It is an asset when accelerating, decelerating, climbing, or lifting your bicycle for storage or transport.

- A heavier bike is an asset while descending or riding at constant speed. It builds strength faster and allows a better workout independent of distance or pace.

- Weight training is used in most sports. It can improve your stamina without your having to go to the weight room. Isn't it amusing to observe friends who ride lightweight bikes for recreation but drive to the gym to work out with weights or resistance trainers? It is true, weight training does give different benefits and perhaps in a more efficient way.

- Some riders, including self-contained tourists, actually like the stability and performance of a heavy bike (or heavily loaded bike). When you hit deep sand at moderate speed, a loaded front end will probably enable you to ride right through the sand without crashing.

- Bikes weighing less than 27 pounds cost more. The frame is only a fraction of the total weight of a bicycle. The components, wheels, and tires weigh much more than the frame. Although aluminum frames have a reputation for being lighter weight than chromoly steel frames, they will weigh about the same at the same price and with the same components. It is necessary to buy a bike well over $1,000 to get a bike under 25 pounds in weight. It is worth noting that manufacturer's listed bike weights are usually wishful thinking.

Feel free to evaluate what works best for you.

Should I experiment with different tires to increase my riding enjoyment?

Certainly: tire materials, tire construction, tread design, volume, and air pressure can make a significant change in your own comfort and in your bike's handling.

- Pay for a quality tire if you are looking for performance and durability. You are cheating yourself when you buy a cheap tire (less than $15). Although many brands are available, years of experience demonstrate that Continental®'s German-made tires are premium tires using natural rubber, polyamide cord, and carefully researched designs.

- Improved traction depends on tire materials, tread design, and inflation pressure. A natural rubber compound with carbon black provides excellent traction. Synthetic "rubbers," colored tires (without carbon black), and recycled rubber just won't grip the riding surface or provide the durability of natural rubber. Continental®'s colored tires with activated silica provide colors, as well as lower rolling resistance and better traction with only slightly less durability.

- Resist the temptation to transfer car tire technology and experience to bicycle tires. Because of the vast differences between vehicle weights, tire widths, and air pressures, comparisons are usually not valid.

- Select your tread design based on the types of surfaces you ride on most or where you want the best performance. On road bike tires, small variations in tread pattern are inconsequential. Whether a tire is slick, has siping (narrow groove patterns), or a fine texture is purely academic because contact surface area is the primary determinant of traction. A smooth tire measuring 22-25 mm across at 100 psi will provide good traction under most circumstances. If you want good traction on poor pavement or gravel, a tire measuring 25-30 mm width at 80 psi will give the desired stability and comfort. For mountain biking, the traditional big tread-blocks are effective on surfaces they can penetrate: loose dirt, mud, and snow. On decomposed granite, so common in the Rocky Mountains, wider spaced, lower profile blocks provide better contact area, improved traction, and control.

- Rolling resistance is a function of tire carcass construction, tire pressure, and tread design. A supple tire that conforms to some extent to surface contours will have less rolling resistance than a stiff tire that requires that the bike and rider be lifted over even small bumps on the riding surface. Tire stiffness is increased by thorn resistant tubes or plastic tire liners. Avoid these common products.

- Tube sealants are outstanding products for eliminating worry about flats with minimum effect on bike performance. Sealants are products not designed for the mechanically inept but for riders who enjoy riding more than repairing flats. It is a kindness to fellow riders during group rides not to interrupt everyone's progress for your flat repair. There are many beautiful riding locations on the western U.S. plains and deserts where you simply cannot ride without sealant. You can prolong the useful life of sealants that function by fiber plugging the puncture hole by adding one-two ounces of water after 1,200 miles or five years. Sealants are not magic so learn how to make them work and make flat repair a distant memory.

- Tread design is best evaluated by test riding the tires in the conditions where you desire optimum performance. Tire treads are generally made popular by the media and not by actual performance testing.

Tire Pressure Guidelines			
Loaded bike/ rider weight	High pressure road tires	Cross tires	Mountain bike tires
Under 160 lb.	90-105 psi	70-85 psi	35-50 psi
Over 180 lb.	105-120 psi	75-95 psi	45-60 psi

- Optimum tire pressure depends on the weight of the total bike load and on the riding surface. Change your tire pressure often to optimize performance under different circumstances. Above is a tire pressure guide based on weight. Riders (combined with load weight) over 180 pounds must take care to use enough pressure to protect their rims from unexpected impacts on rocks and potholes.

- Reduced tire pressure increases traction, rolling resistance, and rider comfort. You may work a little harder but will gain better control and more comfort (as well as more exercise).

- Increased tire pressure reduces rolling resistance but you will gain greater efficiency at the price of less comfort. Decide on the balance of trade-offs by experimenting with different pressures. This means that you will need to carry a functional frame pump to add air during rides.

- In selecting optimum tire pressure, weigh your personal priorities. Many riders tend toward higher pressures. Try using lower pressures and enjoy the comfort, stability, and a better workout!

- Rim width rarely limits the choice of tire width. A wide tire on a narrow rim increases the likelihood of pinch flats (cuts in the tube due to the compression of the tire and inner tube against the rim during impact on an edge or corner on the riding surface). The limiting factor is more likely to be frame clearance, and the best test is to install the tire and see if it clears the frame at the rear triangle stays and the fork blades. Tire widths marked on the tires themselves do not accurately reflect the true width of the mounted, inflated tire. These numbers are only of relative value. They are the second number of size designations like 700 x 28c, 27 x 1 and 26 x 2.125. This is also true of inner tubes. Check the product visually to find the width you desire.

Do Presta (French) valve stems enhance wheel performance?

No, they too are a burden of tradition that I disparagingly refer to as nuisance valve stems.

- A few aero rim designs do not accommodate the larger diameter Schrader (American) tube valve stem and require longer valve stems only available in Presta. All other rims can be converted to Schrader valves by drilling and filing the valve hole to the larger diameter. After converting thousands of rims to Schrader valve holes, we have found the common concern about substantially weakening the rim to be unsubstantiated.

- Schrader valves are more durable because they are larger diameter, familiar to Americans, facilitate pump attachment, and simplify installing and maintaining tire sealant in the tubes.

- If you like Presta valves, go right ahead and enjoy them.

Understanding Gearing with Three Chainrings

It would not be possible to write a book on cycling without some discussion of gearing. I will stay away from gear charts and lengthy digressions about the virtues of specific gearing systems. Gearing is surely an area where tradition has burdened the thinking of many cyclists. For how many decades did cyclists strain their knees through the use of classic road bike gearing with only two chainrings? The advent of mountain bikes brought the gearing enlightenment, and Shimano® took the lead in developing user-friendly, high precision shifting.

Understanding the Effect of Cog and Chainring Size on the Ease of Pedaling

The chainrings and front (left) shifter affect the major ranges in gearing. The smallest chainring gives you your easiest (low) gears, and the large chainring the hardest (high) gears. You will probably use your middle chainring most of the time for rolling terrain. The small chainring is for climbing and the large one for descending.

In each of the three gear ranges, the rear cogs and shifter (right) provide the small steps that make it possible to maintain a constant cadence over varied terrain, fatigue levels, and wind conditions. Refer to cadence, on pp. 158-159. Shift often, have more fun, and preserve your knees! The number of cogs you have is not as important as the manufacturers and popular press would have you believe. It is not worth investing in upgrades unless you have seven or fewer cogs or need to replace worn out shifters or the rear wheel. Refer to the discussion on using your gears for details on skillful shifting technique, pp. 283-284.

Modifying stock gearing seems to be an irrepressible urge for cyclists. Fortunately, many stock bikes are designed with adequate gearing, especially bikes in the middle- to high-price range. Some situations make gear modification worthwhile:

1. If you ride frequently in mountainous areas
2. If you carry loads for touring or commuting
3. If you have leg or hip impairments or other physical conditions that reduce your stamina

The calculation of "gear inches" is helpful in evaluating gear range and for comparing gearing on various bicycles. It considers all the factors that influence the ease of pedaling: chainring size, cog size, and wheel size. The only correlation between gear inch and mechanical function is when the gear inch number is the same as the wheel size. For example, a 26-inch gear on a mountain bike means that one pedal stroke corresponds to one wheel rotation. That is also true for a 27-inch gear on a 27-inch wheeled road bike.

The calculation is simple:

$$\frac{\text{number of teeth on the chainring}}{\text{number of teeth on the cog}} \quad x \quad \text{wheel size in inches} \; = \; \text{gear inches}$$

For bikes with 700c wheels, use 27 inches for the wheel size to end up with the units in inches.

Here are some comparisons to give meaning to calculated gear inch values. The gear range on traditional 10-speed bicycles is a low of 40-inches and a high of 100-inches. This is inadequate unless you ride only on flat terrain or average more than 100 miles per week. These parameters also hold for all bikes with two chainrings. Oh yes, people do ride these inadequately geared bikes under other circumstances but their knees are at risk. Currently, high quality road bikes with two chainrings still have low gears around 40 inches but the high end has moved up to 108-130 inches, great for riding down steep mountain passes under constant power (if you have the nerve). Road bikes with triple cranks designed for road use offer a low of only about 30 inches. Classic road touring bikes offer a 27-inch low. These are fine for day trips or supported tours but if you want to carry a load for self-contained touring, you will benefit from at least a 22-inch low. Bicycling bliss is achieved on- or off-road with a 17-inch low gear. You can add lower gears to road bikes by two approaches. The more economical is to select larger cogs in the rear and install a new long-cage rear derailleur and longer chain. The second option is to select a mountain bike crank and front derailleur that will usually reduce your high gear to about 100 inches as well as giving you easier gears for climbing. Front derailleurs for triple cranks generally have a maximum performance range of 22 teeth, which means that the difference in number of teeth between the largest chainring and smallest should not exceed 22 teeth. Choosing a greater difference will result in poor shifting precision.

If a 100-inch gear was at one time the norm, is it still a valid choice? Probably not. If you are riding a road bike on the road, you will probably run out of gears at the high end on descents (also referred to as "spinning out the top"). If you like to coast, that is fine, but it is alarming to spin out the top in traffic. It greatly reduces your ability to keep up with traffic and limits your ability to control your bike. A 108-inch gear will probably be adequate except on the steepest descents. As mentioned above, 108-130 inches will allow you to ride at unreasonable speeds on straight mountain descents. Gearing needs on mountain bikes are different from road bikes. Mountain bikes, even with low profile tires, roll more slowly on descents. Close to a 100-inch high will probably be adequate on

Summary of Gear Inch Values

Load means ballast of more than 15 pounds or bike and load greater than 45 pounds.

	On-road without load	On-road with load	Off-road without load	Off-road with load
17"	Excessive	Sweet	Sweet	Sweet
22"	OK steep terrain	Sweet	OK	Inadequate
30"	OK rolling terrain	Inadequate	Inadequate	Forget it!
40"	• • • • • Totally Inadequate • • • • •			
100"	Inadequate	Inadequate	OK	OK
108"	OK	OK	Excessive	Excessive
>108"	For steep descents	Lows are important	Excessive	Excessive

pavement, but you will need high gears only rarely off-road. Especially for technical off-road riding, it is fine to sacrifice some high gears for easier low gears.

Any bike has some duplicate (or close to duplicate) gears. A 27-speed drive train has more redundancy than a 14-speed one. Whether this bothers you or not depends on how you conceptualize gearing. If you imagine your gear range as a continuum from easiest to hardest, the redundancies will probably bother you. But if you observe your gearing mechanism closely, you will see that using your gears in sequence actually requires complex and inefficient shifting patterns. If instead you visualize your gears as three major ranges with multiple small increments in each range, the repeat gears become an asset. (Refer to the illustration.) It means that you have some of the same gears in different gear ranges: you can reach the same inch gear from the small chainring as from the middle chainring without having to change gears both front and back. Wow, did you notice that beautiful clump of yellow columbine in the ravine?

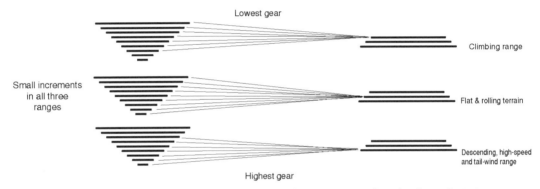

Gearing with three chainrings can be easily understood if you conceptualize the three chainrings as the three gear ranges and the cogs in the rear as the incremental changes available in each range.

When buying a new bike, give careful consideration to cost effectiveness. It is usually more economical to buy a more expensive bike with the gearing you want than to buy a more economical bike with a narrower range of gears and then upgrade it. Be sure that your desired upgrade is possible. Generally, it is more economical to make gear changes in the rear cogs than on the chainrings since they are expensive and not replaceable on many bikes, either by design or lack of availability. Changing chainrings usually results in some loss in shifting precision.

There are challenges to altering your chain drive. As gearing technology has become more sophisticated, compatibility of components has become a complex issue. Before you start buying new components, consult with a trustworthy mechanic or with Shimano®, SRAM®, or Campagnolo®. Campy still does not offer as wide a choice of gearing as Shimano® does.

Internally-geared hubs offer many benefits not available with derailleurs. They minimize maintenance by eliminating front derailleurs and multiple chainrings. Gear shifting action is independent of pedaling making for carefree riding. They can be shifted while standing still, while coasting, and while pedaling. It is purely delightful to be able to shift into an easier gear while sitting at a stop signal enabling you to accelerate easily through the intersection. SRAM®'s Dual Drive and many Shimano® internally-geared hubs are combined with rear derailleurs providing a wide range of gearing. Even used alone, the gear range of seven-speed hubs is adequate for most applications. In mountainous terrain you will probably want the smallest chainring available to shift the entire gear range to easier pedaling. New gear technologies are developed every few years so be sure to evaluate what works best for you before buying.

How to Use Your Gears for Optimum Health and Performance for 21 or More Speeds

1. With numbered gear indicators, 1 is the easy (low) gear for climbing and 3, 7, 8, and 9 are the hard (high) gears for descending.

2. Use your front shifter (left) to make major changes in range, 1 (or far right on the indicator) for ascending, 2 (middle) for rolling terrain, and 3 (far left) descending.

3. Use your rear shifter (on the right grip) to change gears in small increments within each range in order to maintain constant cadence.

4. Both derailleurs change gears by pushing the chain over to the next cog or chainring. This can only succeed when the chain is moving by your pedaling. The front derailleur requires skill in shifting for two reasons: the derailleur operates on the chain where the chain is under tension and the difference between chainring sizes is substantially greater than between cog sizes.

5. The front derailleur will shift with greater precision if you let up pressure on the pedals just as you change the shifter. This is especially important between the middle and small chainrings. You can ensure smooth shifting from the middle to large chainring by making that shift only at cadences greater than 80 rpm.

6. For Rapid Fire shifters, take care to move the shift levers through the full range of movement to the next click with each shift. While shifting to a larger chainring, hold the shift lever until the chain settles securely on the large chainring for dependable shifting every time.

7. Choice of appropriate gear is determined by your cadence rather than the gear indicators. They tell you what gear you are in but the appropriate gear enables you to maintain a cadence greater than 80 rpm at a sustainable exertion level.

8. Avoid "cross-over" chain positions. Those place the chain in the largest chainring and largest cog or the smallest chainring and smallest cog. These positions put undue stress and increased wear on your chain. Your indicators will show 3 (left) and 1 (right) or 1 (left) and 7, 8, or 9 (right) when you are in a cross-over position You will also be warned by a grinding noise as your chain drags on the front derailleur or adjacent chainring. You can ride in similar gears with the chain on the middle chainring and one of the middle cogs.

9. When shifting between your middle and large chainrings, you should already have your chain on the smaller cogs (5, 6, 7, 8, and 9). This means you would already be in your harder cogs before moving into your hardest chainring.

10. When shifting between your middle and small chainrings, you should already have your chain on the larger cogs (1, 2, 3, 4, and 5). You should make small-increment shifts, gradually moving into easier gears before making a major range change with your front shifter into the easiest chainring.

11. Avoid chain slap (when the chain hits the chain stay) off-road by shifting into the middle chainring before descending. If you stay in the small chainring you used for climbing the hill, your chain will take little nicks of paint off your frame on bumpy descents.

Conclusion

Fitting the bicycle to your body proportions is so critical to enjoyment that it is worth your time and energy to make measurements of your body and the bicycles you want to ride. Variations in frame design and measurements warrant your use of a standardized system for understanding what you need and for making comparisons among bicycles.

Once you have studied your current bike or selected a new bike, expect to make some modifications to personalize it to your needs. When buying a new bike, it is most economical to buy a stock bike as close to your expectations as possible. The areas where your body contacts the bike are most likely to require modification. Select pedals, saddle, controls, and handlebar position and type that are efficient, comfortable, and easy for you to operate.

Make your choices based on your own objective evaluation from test riding. It is fine to stick with tradition when you make the choice consciously. It is unfortunate, however, to follow the traditional route simply because you didn't know there were options.

One of the great attractions to cycling is the ability to establish your unique style of riding and support your style with appropriate equipment. Have fun with the equipment as long as it provides you with comfort and supports good health. But remember that the joy of the ride is in the attitude and perspective of the rider.

chapter 7

Sustained Riding Performance Depends on Balanced Resources

- Oxygen
- Fluids
- Food
- Sleep
- Freedom from Infection
- Conservation of Your Resources
- Muscle Recovery

- Focus
- Balanced Development of Confidence, Strength, and Skills
- Selecting Compatible Riding Companions
- Introducing Someone Special in Your Life to Cycling

Elements that Contribute to Optimum Physical Performance

Discussions of athletic performance often focus on how to develop muscular strength. However, there are many factors that contribute to stamina. You can probably remember a ride when your body was well-toned but you felt like a bucket of lead. Each pedal stroke seemed to require all the exertion you could rally. Why do you experience these periods when exertion is unpleasantly laborious? Most likely, the reason is simple: you were not properly fueled. It is difficult to identify the specific causes of low-energy levels when riders first begin building fitness. Novice riders often attribute poor stamina to inadequate muscular strength. As fitness and experience increase, you will learn to recognize other reasons for a low-energy day. Now, however, is a good time to optimize energy sources so you can ensure adequate stamina most of the time.

Seven key energy sources strongly influence your stamina: oxygen, water, food, sleep, freedom from infection, muscle recovery, and focus. Maybe you're inclined to attribute all fatigue to inadequate muscle strength. If so, recognizing that each of these resources is essential to optimize riding performance will literally give you more to go on. You will benefit from abandoning the "tough it out" mentality and by giving attention to nurturing yourself as an athlete.

Many new-bike buying customers at Self-Propulsion are motivated to purchase new bikes because they want to be able to ride faster with less effort. The search is usually initiated by a riding companion who is tired of waiting for their slower pace. Companions generally reason that a lighter bike will help their friends keep up. And maybe it will. But first I inquire about their current bike and then I caution them that equipment makes less difference than riding priorities and total energy reserves. Often the faster rider is exhilarated by speed and distance, and the slower rider wants to enjoy the scenery, the pleasure of movement, and renewal. New equipment may not change those priorities or even make the slower rider faster. I can assure you that adequate sleep and eating fresh vegetables and fruits seven to nine times daily will make more difference in performance than moderate upgrades in equipment.

In addition to clarifying your riding priorities and optimizing all your resources, learning to be sensitive to individual health factors can help riders be more accepting of differences in stamina. I recommend a checkup with your family doctor and getting the appropriate blood chemistry tests. Such factors as low hemoglobin and thyroid levels can make a substantial difference in individual performance levels. Some of these physiological factors can be improved while others are just basic to our individual natures and require acceptance. One of the reasons I enjoy riding alone is that I can ride at my relatively slow pace and not have to explain to anyone that my hemoglobin levels are low and that I don't oxygenate myself as well as most riders.

Oxygen: Your Most Basic Resource

We are entirely too casual about one of our most vital resources — oxygen. It surrounds us every day. We breathe it without much awareness yet it is essential to the health and function of every cell in our bodies!

Learning to **breathe consciously**, using your diaphragm in a slow, controlled manner, can give you greater control over your attitude, your mental acuity, and your stamina. As your awareness of breathing as a tool increases, you may notice that involuntary, shallow, chest breathing limits all aspects of your performance and satisfaction in life. Refer to Chapter 4, pp. 72-86, for the discussion on breathing. To more fully utilize Ayurvedic breathing and understand its value during athletic performance, refer to John Douillard's *Body, Mind and Sport.*

Experiment with controlled, diaphragmatic breathing while cycling and you will be surprised by the remarkable benefits. It helps you maintain a moderate-intensity exertion level. Hill climbs and descents blend more graciously in your thinking. This kind of breathing helps warm your entire body as well as reduces the risk of overheating during extreme temperatures. Your stamina will be increased by the natural, self-pacing effect. It will draw your focus to the moment and slow down your mind when it is racing with the demands of life. You can return from your ride renewed and rejuvenated. Controlled breathing can help you stay tuned to your body feedback. The resulting self-awareness is essential to improving your technique and optimizing performance.

What is the **condition** of the air you breathe? If you are prone to respiratory infections, you may appreciate the healthy function of your nasal passages, throat, bronchial tubes, and lungs. Let's consider some ways to protect your respiratory system while riding. In high winds or in temperatures below freezing, you can warm and humidify the air by breathing through your nose or through a fleece face mask. The cilia in your nasal passages can also remove some of the airborne, particulate matter. Particulate pollution can be especially high in winter in arid climates. I have been astonished to observe the high concentration of particulates in the beam of my helmet-mounted light.

Air **purity** is a constant concern in urban riding. But what about the high concentration of dust inhaled while riding on dirt roads and trails? Once silicon particles get into your lungs they stay there forever. Let's not suffer the debilitating illnesses of miners of the past. Cycling masks that filter out urban pollutants are a wise investment for cyclists who ride frequently in heavy traffic. Less sophisticated filters can be used to reduce dust intake but filters used during high exertion must permit abundant airflow. The deep breathing of high exertion increases your risk of respiratory damage by pollution. Both ozone and carbon monoxide reduce athletic performance. If you have not found a suitable air filter to wear, what can you do to reduce the health hazards of air pollution? Avoid riding near heavy traffic or on main highways during peak traffic hours. Be aware of wind patterns. Moderate winds can help clear the air of toxic fumes but they may increase the hazards of particulates in dusty places. Exercise indoors on high pollution days.

Riding at **elevations above 6,000 feet** limits available oxygen and requires some special precautions to minimize the effects. Your body requires less oxygen-carrying hemoglobin at lower, more oxygen-rich elevations. There is less oxygen at higher elevations, and it takes time for your body to produce more red blood cells to oxygenate your muscles and brain adequately. You may hope you can avoid being slowed down by the fatiguing symptoms of less oxygenation but it's one challenge you can't overcome by forcing your way through it. And like most influences, decreased oxygen at higher elevations affects everyone differently — one individual's response can even vary with time. Although being fit at sea level doesn't make you immune to the effects of high elevation, you can take precautions to minimize your risk of being delayed by altitude sickness. You will benefit from responding sensitively to your condition.

At elevations above 6,000 feet, many people experience shortness of breath and may find themselves breathing faster and deeper. Above 10,000 feet, everyone gives more attention to breathing. You may also experience headaches, nausea, fatigue, and poor-quality sleep. In extreme cases where people experience hallucinations, disorientation, or cough up blood, it is necessary to go to a lower elevation immediately. In many mountainous areas you will change elevation dramatically and often. It is wise to plan to ride at a lower energy level and cover fewer miles so you can adapt your pace to your body needs.

It requires seven to fourteen days for most people to adapt to high altitude. You can minimize your risks by taking the following precautions:

- Drink about 25 percent more water. The dry air at high altitude increases water loss both through the skin and by breathing harder. Dehydration contributes to headaches at any elevation.

- Avoid alcohol and caffeine. Their effects are intensified at high elevations.

- Get plenty of sleep.

- Maintain light exercise and pace yourself. Just sitting around will slow the acclimatization process.

- Eat frequent, smaller meals because digestion may be impaired. Eat a carbohydrate-rich diet to keep your blood sugar levels up. Your basal metabolic rate increases as much as 40 percent during the first few days at the same time that your appetite drops off. Select high quality foods and make the necessary effort to eat more. (Ryan, p. 266)

- Use conscious, diaphragmatic breathing.

- Rest when your heart rate is abnormally high. Take this opportunity to stop and enjoy the spectacular views and allow your body to catch up on oxygen. Be sure to make the best use of your gears to adjust your exertion level.

- Diminish energy loss by carrying extra clothes and putting them on when you are cool.

- At high altitude, the risk of sun and wind burn and hypothermia are ever-present so go prepared with more clothing than seems necessary. The rewards of riding in spectacular and remote high mountain areas are well worth the extra precautions to ensure your good health.

Fluids: the Medium of All Body Processes

Drink water often on all rides! The human body is a water medium — water makes up 60 percent of our body weight. Water functions as a transport medium, a structural part of body tissue, a lubricant, and a component of chemical reactions. (Manore et al., p. 239) This means that all body processes take place in water and depend on electrolyte balance to regulate the distribution of water inside and outside the cells. **When you are inadequately hydrated, all body functions are compromised**. The symptoms of dehydration are fatigue, headaches, light-headedness, heat intolerance, decreased appetite, and muscle cramps. In contrast, proper hydration will extend the distance you can ride before fatiguing, reduce stress on your body, and facilitate recovery. If you are in the habit of riding without carrying water, resolve to change that now. Install bottle holders on your bike where they are easily accessible. Or you might prefer one of the many convenient hydration systems. Many riders find that sipping frequently from a drinking tube makes it easier to stay hydrated.

Body fluids do several critical jobs:

1. Transport energy to your muscles in the form of glucose
2. Carry away lactic acid, a byproduct of high-intensity (anaerobic) exertion
3. Eliminate other waste products
4. Dissipate heat through your skin
5. Enable optimum cardiovascular function

Dehydration causes your performance and pleasure to suffer. The most serious effect of exercise-induced dehydration is the abnormal rise in core body temperature due to the inability to dissipate heat. Other negative effects of dehydration due to decreased blood volume and electrolyte imbalance are abnormal elevation in heart rate and inefficient utilization of muscle glycogen. (Manore et al., p. 232)

Fluid intake must match fluid loss. Body fluids are lost through exhalation, sweat, and urination. You need to replenish those losses with water, electrolytes, and carbohydrates. Water follows gradients, that is, it flows from areas of low concentration to areas of higher concentrations. Avoid drinking concentrated beverages that cause fluids to move from your body into the intestines resulting in a net loss.

How much should you drink? Perspiration rates vary as do base hydration levels before exertion. When you are not exercising you should drink 8 to 10 cups of fluid each day. While exercising drink 4 to 8 ounces (one-half to one cup) every 15 minutes. The basic rule is to consume one-and-a-half-times your sweat loss.

Fluids are absorbed from the stomach and the first half of the small intestines. (Ross, p. 41) The process of fluid leaving the stomach to the small intestines is known as gastric emptying. The rate of gastric emptying is important and is affected by the type of beverage used and volume drunk. Lower concentration beverages speed emptying. Increased volume also speeds emptying so drinking a half a cup of fluid every 15 minutes will empty faster than sipping every few minutes. In hot weather, cool fluids are more palatable, increase gastric emptying, and help cool your body. High exertion levels slow absorption of fluids and solid foods.

What quantity of fluids should you carry? This will vary with temperature and exertion level. In warm weather, carry 70 to 100 ounces for an all-day ride. Accurate assessment of adequate hydration is difficult. One way to determine if you are getting enough fluids is to monitor the frequency and quality of urination. Be sure you urinate every two to four hours throughout the day. Monitoring frequency is especially important during extreme heat. It is hard on your body to lose fluid waste only through perspiration. When you monitor urine color, it should be the same pale yellow color it is when you are not exercising. Color evaluation will not be useful if you are taking supplements or eating foods that strongly color your urine. If you suspect that you are not drinking enough, you could weigh yourself before and after rides if you have not stopped for a meal. Each pound lost reflects two cups of water lost.

It is always better to **carry excess water** than to run out and suffer. On unfamiliar routes, plan to carry all the water you will need for the entire ride. You may not find water where you expect to and in many remote areas there are no water sources. On the western plains where there are no streams or lakes, even the cattle tanks may be empty. Surface water that you do find may be brackish or too saline to purify. Whenever you are on tour, carry extra water reservoirs in your packs. Then when you are in the wide-open spaces, you can ride into the unknown with confidence. Plan on one gallon of water per person per day. I know water is a burden at 8 pounds per gallon but if you run out of water, your entire body is going to feel agonizingly heavy, and basic body functions will be compromised.

Your **sense of thirst** is not a valid indicator that you need fluids. Thirst indicates that you are already low on fluids so always drink before you feel thirsty. Ironically, at high altitudes, in arid climates, and during cold weather rides, when you actually require increased fluid intake, your sense of thirst is diminished. Remember to drink frequently under these special circumstances. Water loss through perspiration is common in winter too. It is disguised under several layers of clothes and can be excessive if you are not regulating your heat dissipation carefully by venting your multiple layers of clothing. You will need to take special precautions to prevent the fluids in your containers from freezing at temperatures below freezing. Try using insulated containers and filling them with warm water. Select beverages that are appealing to you so you will want to drink often.

With so many sport drinks available, how should you choose **what to drink**? That will depend on the duration and intensity of your ride. If you ride for an hour or less, drinking only water may be fine. You should begin refueling during the first 30 minutes, so riding longer than that while drinking only water will reduce your thirst and your stamina. Consider that your thirst mechanism is triggered by decreased blood volume and increased concentration of electrolytes. If you ride for several hours drinking only water, your blood volume is increased, and your electrolyte concentration is decreased. You will not feel thirsty. These conditions can result in headache, nausea, muscle cramping, and lethargy. (Burke, p. 54) Adding small amount of electrolytes and carbohydrates (salt and sugar) to your water helps maintain your sensation of thirst and facilitates absorption.

What does this mean **in practical terms**? It is easier to meet your fluid and caloric needs if you carry two beverage containers. Fill the second container with an energy beverage that will satisfy your palate and help maintain your energy reserves. If you have only one reservoir in your hydration system, try reducing the concentration of an energy beverage to facilitate absorption. Experiment to determine what concentration works best for you. Most energy beverages are four- to eight-percent concentration and empty efficiently from the stomach. For recreational riders, the concentration recommended by beverage manufacturers is generally too high. You may not like the flavor and may get a pain in your gut. I recommend using one-half the concentration suggested on the container. The concentration of soft drinks ranges from 10 to 12 percent. The higher concentration causes them to empty from the stomach more slowly. (Ryan, p.188)

Energy beverages will benefit you on any ride. You consume fluids for hydration but when you consume energy beverages, you get the bonus of additional fuel. Because energy beverages are absorbed as readily as water, they are easier and faster to digest than most solid foods. Read the labels on the many energy beverages available and disregard the advertising. The most powerful advertising campaigns are generally based on distorted information. Some sport beverages are effective electrolyte replacements, an important factor for endurance events, but they are low on sustaining energy. You will do better with a palatable energy beverage that has been formulated and tested to release an even flow of energy with less emphasis on electrolytes. If you get tired of the beverages you are carrying, remember that most fruits, yogurt, and milk will also help you hydrate.

When selecting your fluids, remember that most **popular beverages** are diuretics. That means they flush water out of your body, thus reducing their contribution to your general hydration level. These include coffee, tea, alcohol, and caffeinated soda. Consider that the hydration value of coffee is about half its volume. Hot or cold herbal infusions ("teas") and dilute juices are more healthful and easier to absorb. Dilute fruit juices to optimize absorption and their cleansing benefits. Read the ingredient labels and search for juices with no added sugar in any form. Also avoid fruit drinks since they are high in refined sugar without the benefits of micronutrients.

Drink frequently before and after rides. Drink 14 to 20 ounces (seven-eighths to one-and-a quarter cups) of fluid about two hours before exercising, especially in hot weather. (Manore et al., p. 231) This will ensure that you are well hydrated to start and give you time to excrete the excess fluid before exercising. Drinking excess fluids can cause a side ache during exercise. During the first hour after exertion, drink at least 28 ounces of your favorite energy beverage to facilitate recovery. This helps replenish the glycogen supplies in your muscles and will help you feel more energetic after your ride as well as the following day. This practice can make a noticeable difference in your stamina and fun during multiple-day events and tours. Refer to "Muscle Recovery," beginning on p. 312.

Take precautions to ensure that the water you drink is not contaminated. Essentially *all* surface and tap **water needs to be purified** before drinking. I recommend you install a purification system in your home for all water you consume. When you are away from home, use the excellent portable water-purification bottles and pumps available for backcountry and international use. The portable pumps are also useful on long rides where

continued on page 293

Things to Take Along

"Be Prepared." When you know you are able to take care of yourself and your bike, you can relax and enjoy your experience.

Store on your bike:

Helmet - wear this

Lock - put this in today's pack

Equipment to be permanently attached to your bike:

If you commute by bike or leave your bike parked in high-theft areas, you will want to incorporate these items into your pack. It will increase your fun and simplify your preparation time if you keep all your riding essentials in one pack you always carry on your back or on your cargo rack.

Bottle holders (or hydration system on your back)

Frame pump

Seat bag with emergency supplies:

Spare inner tube, tire levers, patch kit (Check the fluidity of the glue every six months.), tire boot, multi-tool, personal ID, insurance facts, emergency contact information, latex gloves, adhesive bandages, compress, rubbing alcohol, coins for pay phone (or bring a cell phone), $20 bill or credit card, and energy bar

Mirror

Bell

Sealant in the inner tubes in your tires but not in your spare tube

Pepper spray secured to your handlebars (use a fastener like Velcro®)
for personal protection

Extras that vary with the season, duration of your ride, and your destination:

Extra jacket and/or pants for rain or wind

Wind mitts, shoe covers

Maps

Sunscreen, lip balm, elastic bandage, antihistamines

Essential clothes and accessories in order of importance:

Helmet

Comfortable saddle

Cycling-specific shoes

Bar ends on flat bars

Gloves

Fortunately you can spread the expense of these things over a period of time. Encourage friends and family to give you gift certificates or these specific products for your birthdays and holidays.

you know surface water is available. It may be easier to carry a purification system rather than large quantities of water.

Food: Fuel, Function, and Fun

When you begin a regular exercise routine, you will need to nourish your body with the wholesome nutrients that it requires for energy and maintenance. You cannot enjoy an energetic life style fueled by Krispy Kreme® doughnuts and Big Macs®. When riders want to move to a higher level of athletic performance, they commonly upgrade their bikes. The truth is, they would make a more dramatic increase in stamina if they would critically and knowledgeably improve their eating habits. Consider some basic facts about food and athletic performance.

What is the significance of the calorie content of foods? A **calorie** is a unit of heat used in nutrition to indirectly measure the energy value of a food. One calorie from any source requires the same energy expenditure to burn it off. Foods that can be energy sources are divided into carbohydrates, fats, and proteins. The concentration of calories differs in these categories. Carbohydrates and proteins have four calories per gram, and fats have nine calories per gram. **If you are gaining weight, you are consuming more calories than you are expending. There is no magic involved with altering your body weight. Everyone can maintain or lose weight if they accept this basic truth and honestly track their caloric intake and output.**

Avoid letting current fads distract you from eating beneficial **fats**. The moderate consumption of fat is essential to health, especially for the distribution and storage of fat-soluble vitamins. Dietary fats also influence how much high-density lipoprotein (HDL), the so-called protective cholesterol, is in your bloodstream, how your blood clots, how susceptible your heart is to erratic rhythms, and how the inner lining of blood vessels responds to stress. (Willett, p. 58) The high-energy benefits of fats in athletic performance are especially important in endurance events and cold weather activities. Discussion of dietary fat has become critical to healthy living because most U.S. citizens consume too much fat. Weight control is only one part of the issue. Do not eliminate all fats from your diet in hopes of maintaining a healthful weight. Instead, learn to distinguish the healthful fats and avoid the regular consumption of harmful ones. Notice that plant oils form the base of the Healthy Eating Pyramid, p. 296.

Based on chemical structure, fats are **monounsaturated, polyunsaturated**, and **saturated**. The most healthful fats are the monounsaturated fats with olive and canola oils among the best and most readily available. Polyunsaturated fats are noteworthy because some of them contain omega-3 fatty acids, also known as n-3 fatty acids. The human body does not manufacture these fats so it is essential that you include them in your diet. Sources rich in omega-3s are salmon, sardines, flaxseeds, walnuts, and canola oil. Omega-3s are important components in cell membranes throughout the body but especially in the eyes, brain, and sperm cells. They also reduce blood clot formation and play a critical role in keeping the heart beating regularly. Since heart arrhythmias are a major cause of fatal heart attacks, make the effort to include omega-3-rich foods in your menus.

Avoid **saturated fats**. These are all the fats in dairy products, red meats, and coconuts. This means minimizing or eliminating these from your diet. An equally pervasive, harmful fat is **partially hydrogenated vegetable oils** that are high in **trans fats**. It is the hydrogenation process to make oils solid and extend their shelf life that produces these harmful elements. For this reason, it is worth minimizing your consumption of all *commercial baked goods that are high in partially hydrogenated vegetable oils: pastries, cookies, crackers, and chips.* A new food labeling law that goes into effect in 2006 requires that the amount of trans fat be listed with other dietary information. Some snack food manufacturers are responding by reducing the trans fats in their products. In the meantime, I encourage you to do your own baking. Quick breads and muffins are made with oils so satisfy your sweet tooth with them and avoid the cookies – even if they're homemade. Cookies require the use of partially hydrogenated vegetable oils (margarine) or butter to achieve their texture. Refer to the appendix for several recipes that are wholesome, easy to make, and are especially practical for cyclists. They taste better than energy bars and provide sustained energy.

Utilizing your own stored fatty tissue as an energy source is another story. It must be broken down into fatty acids in order to be transported in the blood to your muscles. This occurs during moderate-intensity aerobic activity that is more than 4 hours in duration. If you want to burn fatty tissue, adopt a program of consistent moderate-intensity, sustained rides that stimulate the production of the enzymes responsible for converting stored fat to energy. (Burke, p.17) Carrying 30 pounds on your bike will also burn fatty tissue.

Protein is for growth, maintenance, and repair of your body. It also assists in the production of enzymes, hormones, and key components of the immune system. It is only useful as an energy source when carbohydrates and fats run low after 90 minutes to 2 hours of high-energy aerobic activity. If the protein used for energy is taken from what the body stores, it breaks down structural and functional tissues — muscles you would probably like to keep.

Proteins are abundant from both plant and animal sources. Animals eat plants and convert and concentrate plant protein in various tissues. In addition to concentrating plant protein, animals also concentrate pesticides and other plant contaminants. The result is that the higher up the food chain you eat, the higher the concentration of pollutants you consume! This hazard can be diminished if you eat organic, range-fed animal products, especially milk. If you are concerned about the quality of protein you consume, notice that both kidney beans and beef contain 26 percent protein. Benefits of choosing the vegetable source over the meat source are that the beans are cleaner, cheaper, and easier for the body to digest and process. The amino acids (the building blocks of protein) in meat contain more sulfur, which cause more calcium loss than an equal amount of protein from plants. We now know that it is not necessary to combine certain plant proteins to build muscle. Your body can assemble a complete profile of amino acids over the course of a day when you eat a variety of foods as part of a well-balanced diet. It is difficult to become protein deficient when you are eating a balanced diet of *unrefined foods*. (McDougall, p. 43-45) Research has exposed several reasons why eating excess protein is detrimental — the excess is stored as fat if energy requirements don't burn it first. Additionally, protein does not burn as cleanly as carbohydrates.

Minerals and vitamins are vital to building and regulating your body and your energy production. As you are increasing your consumption of fruits and vegetables, place more emphasis on nutrient-rich vegetables. They are higher in vitamins and minerals and lower in sugars.

There are many **sources of information on healthful eating**. I recommend Andrew Weil's *Eating Well for Optimum Health* for honest, up-to-date, and fascinating discussions. Dr. Weil skillfully relates complex nutrition to your daily eating habits. He carefully distinguishes between scientifically documented research and conjecture. As you are looking for nutritional guidance, be wary of "new scientific" findings. Only pay attention to conclusions that are derived from rigorously controlled clinical trials that follow the rules of blind testing. This method involves designated control groups and designated experimental groups. The individuals involved are unaware of which group they are part of. The sample size must be reasonably large and must clearly define the demographic cross-section of participants. To provide reliable conclusions, studies must be conducted over a period of years to determine the permanence of outcome and to establish accurate cause and effect.

Another valuable source of information on nutrition is Walter C. Willett's *Eat, Drink, and Be Healthy*. Dr. Willett draws on years of research and his background in nutrition and epidemiology to critically evaluate the abundance of misinformation on eating habits constantly bombarding U.S. citizens. Most significant among them is the United States Department of Agriculture's (USDA) food pyramid. Many of us accepted it as the government's effort to provide a simplified guide to healthful eating when the food pyramid was established in 1992. What we received instead was a promotional piece by the USDA to market crops U.S. farmers produce in abundance. Over the years, research has eroded the foundation of the USDA pyramid. Dr. Willett explains concisely why it is harmful and offers understandable scientific documentation for the Healthy Eating Pyramid he designed specifically to improve public health. Refer to www.hsph.harvard.edu/nutritionsource.

What are **your nutritional requirements during exercise**? The first and foremost

The Healthy Eating Pyramid

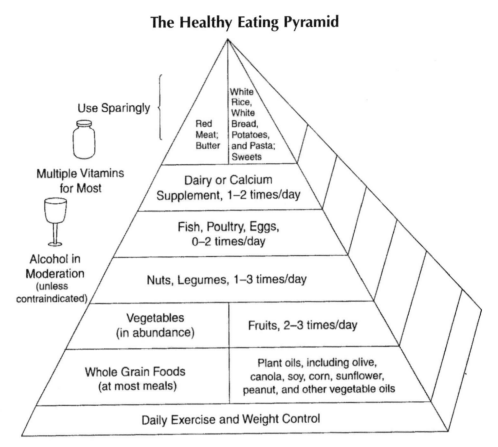

Study this carefully and notice how dramatically this rearranges popular eating patterns. It is the distillation of the best scientific evidence about links between diet and health. Most significantly, the entire healthful eating guide is based on daily exercise and weight control! There is no need to measure serving size. Just base your eating on the relative importance of these food groups and the guidance on the number of times each day to eat foods from each group. (Reproduced with the permission of Simon and Schuster Adult Publishing Group from *Eat, Drink, and Be Healthy: The Harvard Medical School Guide to Healthy Eating* by Walter C. Willett, M.D. Copyright © 2001 by President and Fellows of Harvard College.)

reason for eating well is to maintain a steady flow of energy. Your energy is supplied by muscle glycogen and blood glucose when you are exerting yourself. For about the first 90 minutes of high exertion, energy comes from the glycogen stored in the muscles and eventually from stores in the liver. These supplies are derived from the carbohydrates eaten before you exercise. When those stores are depleted, energy is drawn primarily from blood glucose. You can replenish your blood glucose during exercise but muscle glycogen supplies are replenished after exercise. Refer to the section on muscle recovery to learn how to maintain your blood glucose level and facilitate recovery.

Every ride will be more enjoyable if you **establish a personal energy base line** for eating frequency during exercise. Remember that everyone is different even though the norm established for how long you can ride at high exertion on stored energy supplies is 90 minutes. Avoid misusing this information by pushing yourself to 90 minutes and then bonking — becoming listless and unmotivated after coming to the end of your body's energy supplies. Select a time when you are well-rested, well-fueled, and well-hydrated and then ride a route in a style that is typical for you. Keep drinking your energy beverage in your characteristic manner. When you get to the point when riding becomes laborious, your shoulders and neck are tired, and your butt is sore, note how many minutes you have been riding. Repeat this test several times so you can stop just short of that time to eat, stretch, and relax a bit before resuming your ride.

Carbohydrates are made by plants and are stored in their leaves, stems, roots, and fruits. Plant sources include small-molecule carbohydrates and large ones. The small-molecule carbohydrates are known by several names: simple carbohydrates, sugars, and mono- and disaccharides. Fruits are high in these carbohydrates, primarily the sugars fructose and glucose. That is why we love their sweet taste. Large-molecule carbohydrates also have various names: complex carbohydrates, starches, and polysaccharides. The percentage of carbohydrates in foods varies. Green and yellow vegetables are low in complex carbohydrates. Wheat, rye, rice, and corn are 70 to 90 percent complex carbohydrates as are legumes (beans and lentils), tubers (yams and potatoes), and winter squashes (acorn and pumpkin). These plant sources also contain abundant proteins, fats, fibers, vitamins, and minerals. The only food from animal sources that contains significant amounts of carbohydrates is milk, which contains the simple sugar, lactose. (McDougall, p. 36)

Since carbohydrates play a key role in fueling your body during exercise, it is important to understand differences in quality of carbohydrates. Until the late 1970s, testing of carbohydrate absorption was based on laboratory testing of the foods and not on the actual response of human bodies to specific foods. In the late 70s, testing began on blood glucose levels in humans after they ingested specific carbohydrates. These tests resulted in the development of the **glycemic index** (GI). The GI is now generally accepted as a valid and important measure of the effect of an ingested food on blood glucose levels.

If you compare charts of GI values, you will see different numbers for the same food. The complexity of the human body results in different blood sugar levels from tests among individuals and from tests of one individual at different times. For this reason it is wise to consider the general range of the GI values rather than the absolute values. The index is based on glucose as 100. Low GI foods are below 55, intermediate GI foods between 55 and 70, and high GI foods are more than 70. This information is important in athletic performance, in reducing heart disease risk, in managing diabetes, and in weight control. (Brand-Miller et al., p. xii) It has replaced the earlier system that grouped simple sugars (monosaccharides: glucose, fructose, and galactose) in one category and polysaccharides (starches) in another. The discovery that two simple sugars glucose (GI 100) and fructose (GI 20) enter the blood stream at very different rates demonstrates the importance of these tests.

Fructose has a low GI and is extremely common in processed foods today. What a lot of people don't realize is that fructose is a poor energy source because it goes to the liver to be converted to glucose before it is transported to the muscles and brain for energy. When you read packaging labels on processed foods to determine their contents, notice that fructose is used abundantly as a sweetener, especially in beverages. It is popular among food processors because it is relatively cheap and easy to use. That is not so for your body. It is difficult to metabolize, interferes with calcium absorption, and may elevate fat levels in your blood, increasing risk to your heart and arteries. It is remarkable that although a person can be maintained on intravenous glucose, intravenous fructose solution causes severe damage to the liver. (Weil, 2000, p. 63) Beware of consuming large amounts of fructose.

How can **knowledge of the GI help you maintain optimum energy** while riding? If you want to prepare for a long ride, you can eat low GI foods in advance. They will provide glucose to working muscles later in your ride when muscle glycogen runs low. If you need quick energy mid-ride or to restore your glycogen and blood glucose supplies after exertion, you can choose high GI foods. The rate at which glucose enters the blood stream also influences insulin response and the availability of that blood glucose to the muscles. *The New Glucose Revolution* provides lists of GI for common foods and discusses the details of using this important tool. You will notice that the GI tends to be high in refined and processed foods like white bread, white rice, and commercial cookies. High fiber fruits, non-starchy vegetables, and whole grains have lower GI. Other factors that tend to lower the GI are high fiber content, low gelatinous starch content, digestion resistant physical forms of the foods (Grape-nuts are more slowly digested than Grape-nut flakes), high acidity (like adding lemon juice to a salad), and the fat content, all of which retard the emptying of the stomach.

You will do well to **limit your consumption of high GI carbohydrate snack foods** while you are inactive. Their sudden increase in blood sugar triggers a high insulin response that works to remove sugar from the blood and deposit it as fat. This insulin spike increases the risk of heart disease and of developing diabetes. The sugar high is followed by a sugar low causing a drop in energy level, resulting in a false sense of hunger and a yen for more food. (*Tufts University Health & Nutrition Letter*, Nov. 2000) In contrast, low GI foods do not create a false sense of hunger, which leads to eating unneeded food. (Harvard Women's Health Watch, Dec. 2000)

Before you go to the cupboard and start pitching out all your favorite snacks, let's look at food categories that will benefit you. From the following table, you will see that selecting low GI fruits is not intuitive. Notice that three dried fruits — apricots, raisins, and dates — are each in different categories. It will be worthwhile to purchase a reference book with a GI listing. I recommend *The New Glycemic Revolution*, because it includes the carbohydrate density for each food. Generally speaking, if you want to improve your nutrition you will need to eat more fruits and vegetables as well as more whole grains.

The term "whole grain" is misleading. Only 5 percent of grain foods in the U.S. diet are made from whole grains! Food coloring is commonly added to baked goods to give the appearance of whole grain. You will need to read ingredient labels. Wheat is the only grain that requires the label "whole." Oats, brown rice, barley, quinoa, and millet are whole grain without that designation. Select foods where whole wheat or another grain is the first ingredient listed. (*Tufts University Health and Nutrition Letter*, July 2002) Even so, not all bread with whole grain wheat as the first ingredient will have a low GI. Remember the physical form of a food strongly influences the GI. Whole wheat bread with a low GI must be dense and made of coarsely ground flour (stone-ground). This makes it even more essential that you bake for yourself or shop knowledgeably at health food stores.

Sample Glycemic Indexes of Common Foods
(Using glucose as the standard of 100)

Low G.I. Foods		Intermediate G.I. Foods		High G.I. Foods	
Fructose	20	Orange juice	53	Bagel	72
Grapefruit	25	Oatmeal cookie	55	Corn chips	72
Kidney beans	27	Basmati rice	58	Cheerios	74
Lentils	29	Sucrose	59	Jelly beans	80
Dried apricots	31	Pizza	61	Rice cakes	82
Whole milk	32	Granola bar	61	Pretzels	83
Yogurt with fruit	33	Banana	62	Baked potato	85
Ice cream	36	Raisins	64	French baguette	95
Apple	39	Stone wheat thins	67	Glucose	100
Pasta	41	Shredded wheat	67	Dates	103

Variations occur among brands and methods of preparation.

Use the GI values in full context and avoid "condemning" a food because it is high on the GI.

This means you will need to consider the **glycemic load** of each food. Foods not only vary in the speed of conversion from starch to sugar during digestion but also in the amount of carbohydrates in an average serving. Comparing white potatoes and carrots will serve as an instructive example. During GI testing, volunteers are given 50 grams (one-quarter cup of sugar weighs 50 g.) of carbohydrate from the test food. Carrots are a low-density carbohydrate so it would take more than a pound of carrots to extract 50 g. of carbohydrate. When would a person eat a pound of carrots in one sitting?

Further invalidating the simple comparison of GI values is the inconsistency in those values. If you compare two charts notice that some charts use glucose as the standard at 100 and others use white bread as 100. These two sets of GI values differ by at least 20 points. Furthermore, two reliable testers give different values of the GI of carrots and the carbohydrate density of carrots. That is because carrots are not synthesized to some universal standard in a laboratory but are grown in different soils with varied weather conditions, harvested at different levels of maturity, and cooked in different manners. The end products vary widely. The total rise in blood sugar from eating a serving of carrots is substantially lower than from eating a serving of baked potatoes even when carrots are given the higher GI value. When compared ounce for ounce, potatoes raise blood sugar levels faster and to a higher level.

Food description and serving size	Glycemic Index	Grams of Carbohydrate Per Serving	Glycemic Load
Carrots peeled, boiled, canned, 1/2 cup, 2.4 oz	49	3	147 (1)
Carrots (second source)	94	8	752 (2)
White Potato with skin, baked in oven, 1 medium, 4 oz	85	30	2550

(1) *The New Glycemic Revolution*
(2) "Harvard Women's Health Watch," June 2001, p. 1, 2.

In selecting carbohydrates, you also need to consider the values of micro-nutrients. Let's continue this comparison of carrots and potatoes. Carrots are lower in calories, higher in calcium and an outstanding source of vitamin A. They are also an important source of protective phytochemicals, especially carotenoid pigments, antioxidants that are strong cancer fighters. (Weil, 2000, p. 58) So you can see it is important to evaluate carbohydrate density and nutrient values of foods as well as GI.

When you combine foods in a snack or meal, the **GI of the meal** is calculated from the percentage of carbohydrate in each food and the amount of each food in the meal.

Combining foods of high GI and low GI results in an intermediate GI response. During physical activity, you can enhance your pleasure and performance by blending a variety of foods to create a reliable source of energy over a longer time period. This will help you avoid the frustration of bonking. It will also help you choose a source of quick energy before you run down. This discussion has focused on carbohydrates since they are the first source of energy. But remember that fats, proteins, vitamins, and minerals also play important roles in nutrition. Fats and proteins are generally slower to digest than carbohydrates and drawn on as energy sources only as carbohydrate sources diminish.

Balanced meals and energy beverages will fuel you well for one or two hours of riding. But for competition or multiple-day rides, invest in **commercial energy products**. They are designed to provide a steady, easily accessible source of energy in contrast to most snack foods that give a short burst of high sugar, low nutrient energy. Sport energy foods can also aid in recovery after exertion. During high-energy riding and for the hour or so afterwards, the burning sensation you might experience in your muscles is due to the production of lactic acid. You can find relief from this discomfort with energy products that replenish the blood glucose and muscle glycogen and flush the lactic acid through your system. What you eat and drink in the first hour after exertion strongly influences the rate and extent of your recovery. The producers of Cytomax® were some of the first to demonstrate that you recover faster if you drink 22 to 28 ounces of Cytomax® during the first hour after high exertion. Refer to "Muscle Recovery" (pp. 312-315) for more information on the mechanisms and tools of recovery.

Avoid limiting your food intake while riding in an effort to lose weight. Inadequate food will make riding arduous, make you vulnerable to poor judgment, and maybe even make you nauseous. In addition to being no fun, it will discourage you from riding frequently. If you are riding to lose weight, limit your food intake the following day when you may still have an energy debt.

Inform yourself about general nutrition and **change your eating habits** accordingly. Most U.S. citizens eat harmful diets. It is tragic in a land of plenty that so many citizens are malnourished. Refer to the books on the recommended reading list. They provide an excellent perspective in plain terms. Here are a few ideas to help you improve your eating habits:

- Remember it is the decisions you make each meal that determine the quality of your health now and 10 years from now.

- Read food labels carefully. Ingredients are listed in descending order by weight.

- Remember that food fads are always based on half-truths. The current obsession with coffee and bagel shops loads patrons with caffeine, high-GI white flour, and all the unhealthy, high unsaturated-fat embellishments.

- Avoid eating candy, white flour products, and fried foods. These foods are high in calories and low in vital nutrients.

- Sweet cravings are often a sign of dietary imbalance. Try eating plenty of tossed salads with lots of dark greens and vegetables high in vitamins and minerals. Avoid fat-ladened dressings and try sprinkling your salads with seeds, nuts, or lemon juice.

- Eat more whole grain foods, dried beans, lentils, vegetables, and fruits.

- Eat out less. It is difficult to find wholesome foods and balanced meals in restaurants. Restaurant food is characteristically high in salt and fat to delight the palate.

- Since you know you must eat every day, carry fresh vegetables, fruit, yogurt, and whole grain foods with you so you can avoid fast foods and unwholesome snacks. For snacking suggestions refer to Chapter 1, p. 19.

- Avoid processed foods. Cook complete meals from scratch at home. It just takes planning and it helps if you can avoid cooking while you are hungry.

- Avoid overeating; stop eating before you feel full. Try selecting your portion size visually by volume.

- When you sit down to eat, give thoughtful attention to assimilation and appreciation. You will enjoy it more and be better satisfied. You will also be more aware of the food you need and more able to adjust your intake to fit your activity levels.

More evidence is coming to light that **how you eat** is important to nutrition. Are you inclined to eat meals while driving, while working at your desk, or while dashing out the door? It is difficult to benefit from food eaten on the run. Your digestive system just doesn't work as well when you don't give it time and energy. That means you will limit the benefits from the nutrients in the food and may experience discomfort and bloating. You may increase food cravings by cramming food on the run or eating in loud, distracting settings. Plan to eat at least one meal a day seated in a quiet place and focused on absorbing and appreciating the food. As Thich Nhat Hanh says, when you eat, put your bread in your mouth, put your black beans and Swiss chard in your mouth but don't put your projects or your career concerns in your mouth. Just eat, mindful of the flavors, textures, and nourishment of your food while appreciating your body's ability to utilize it.

Whenever you eat, ask yourself **what your activity level will be** for the next three hours. Then match your caloric intake to your expected expenditure. Does skipping breakfast mean you are sedentary during the morning? Does eating your largest meal in the evening mean you are physically active at the end of your workday? I experienced a pattern on day tours of feeling low energy until early afternoon. One Sunday morning I was tired and hungry and decided to compensate by eating a breakfast that was larger than usual. I made myself a big omelet with lots of fresh vegetables, homemade whole wheat toast, and fruit. An hour later, I felt strong right from the start of my ride. Since that dramatic success, I have delighted in following the old adage: breakfast like a king, lunch like a prince, and supper like a pauper. I have just reversed my breakfast and dinner menus. I find that this caloric distribution better matches my energy expenditure. I am better energized throughout the day and sleep better at night due to lower stomach acid and reduced digestive function at bedtime. I enjoy a productive evening with a light meal of cereal, pancakes, or eggs embellished with fruit and nuts. Shaking up the traditional menus makes it easier to respond to my caloric needs throughout each day. You might experiment with your caloric intake distribution throughout the day and try to improve your stamina level at work and play.

Sleep: the Most Neglected Resource

The better you sleep, the better you ride.
The better you ride, the better you sleep.

General fatigue significantly reduces your stamina and your focus. It impairs the function of your central nervous system and reduces your capacity to perform. Try to be sensitive to how well-rested you are and select easier rides when you are tired. Not only will you have more fun but you will also reduce the chances of mishaps. A gentle, relaxing ride can turn your pattern of fatigue around. Kriyananda, a wise Yoga teacher, says, "Save enough energy each day so that at the end of the day you have the energy to think, to study, and to help others." Such self-nurture can increase the balance in your life and the lives of those around you.

The key to adequate sleep is the discipline to go to bed. How often do you wake up in the morning and yearn for more sleep but the day's work demands your attention? Longing for more sleep, you review the next few mornings searching for a morning when you can sleep in. Since this practice is usually marginally successful at best, it is fortunate that there is another option. Create a schedule that allows you to get the needed sleep. It is simple arithmetic. Work back from the time you need to get up. How many hours sleep do you need? Think over your bedtime rituals to determine how long they take. Now back up your bedtime to include the preparation time. Wow, it will certainly take discipline to hit the target! Maybe a timer would help. Avoid getting hooked on TV, the newspaper, or other "relaxing" activities. They are probably cluttering your mind and making it more difficult to quiet down and sleep soundly. No matter how enjoyable these distractions may be, they are not as renewing as the sleep you are missing by engaging in them.

How much sleep do you need? There are surely individual variations. And we all know that our need for sleep varies depending on the season as well as emotional and intellectual demands. It is only tradition to believe eight hours of sleep is the norm. The National Sleep Foundation (www.sleepfoundation.org) recommends seven to nine hours each night for adults. Sleep needs are determined genetically and do not change basically throughout adult life. You can determine how much sleep you require to stay free of infection, well-focused, and balanced in disposition. Make these observations during different seasons and circumstances. Sleep until you wake up voluntarily, without an alarm. If you feel rested, that is how much sleep you need. Keeping a sleep diary will help you identify patterns in your personal sleep needs. Often people with a lot of responsibilities or who are especially conscientious tell me that they wake up early and can't go back to sleep. I understand this problem because I experienced this when my sons were young, and my business was struggling. Now I know that I can change this pattern by using the following techniques and reminding myself that I will be more effective and productive if I roll over and get more sleep.

Perhaps it would help your conviction to get more sleep if you valued sleep more appropriately. Do you really appreciate the benefits of sleep? Are you dragging and yearning for more energy? Sleep is an energizer. Are you injured or have you over-trained and are impatient to heal the micro-tears in your sore muscles? This healing occurs during sleep. Do you feel an infection coming on or are you battling a lingering infection? Sleep is wonderfully curative. Even if you are just feeling puny or bummed, sleep will help you regain your perspective. Other benefits are brighter mood, improved mental and physical performance, improved immune function, improved glucose metabolism, and reduced accident risk. Surely sleep is worth building into your schedule.

It is reported that half of all U.S. citizens suffer from **insomnia** on any given night. No wonder we tend to careen in the extreme. Surely tension and anxiety are the main deterrents to sleep. So cultivation of all relaxation techniques will be a big help. Moderate, daily exercise is another reliable tool to improve your sleep quality. Take care to avoid eating a heavy meal within three hours before bedtime. Select foods that do not cause you digestive problems. It is best if you can abstain from all stimulants but if you do drink coffee, do it in the morning and early afternoon. Avoid all stimulants after three o'clock or four o'clock if you have any sleep problems in the evening. Experiment with this list of techniques to improve your rest and your perspective.

1. Prepare thoughtfully for bed by developing a pre-sleep routine. This routine should wind down your mind and body so you are ready to let go of all the demands that have tugged at you today and others that you face tomorrow.

2. Select your evening activities carefully. Pursuing a high adventure novel, watching sensational news on TV, or working out vigorously will make it difficult to settle into slumber.

- Spend the last hour before bedtime centering your mind and body.
- Take a walk and enjoy the sky.
- Practice your Yoga, Qigong, or stretching.
- Take a warm bath or shower.
- Read a book to your children.
- Spend some time grooming your pets.
- Practice meditation.

3. Journaling will help you get your thoughts and concerns on paper and out of your head. Refer to Chapter 4, pp. 131-133.

4. Establish conditions for the night that optimize your sleep. This is especially critical when you travel.

- Select the right blankets to keep you comfortable. You might appreciate extra warmth on your legs when you have been working out or when the weather is cold. This can reduce the risk of cramps in your lower legs and feet.

- Experiment using different pillows or not using any at all until you are completely comfortable.

- Regulate airflow so your air quality contributes to sound sleep.

- Shut out disturbing sounds. Earplugs are one of the simple ways of controlling a noisy environment. They are cheap enough for you to always have extras.

- Replace that old mattress if it does not provided adequate support. Your entire perspective and attitude depend on adequate, quality sleep, so investing in a quality bed is surely justified. You could even take to the floor. Many people have found relief from back problems by sleeping on a firm pad or futon on the floor.

5. Once you are in bed, choose a sleeping position that relaxes and aligns your body.

- The total relaxation pose of Yoga can help you drop off to sleep. Lie flat on your back and elongate yourself from the top of your head to the bottoms of your heels. Mentally broaden your shoulders, rib cage, and hips. Place your arms along your sides with palms up. This will open your chest. Check over your complete alignment and scan your body for tension. Practice controlled, diaphragmatic breathing. Close your eyes and let your body feel heavy and fully relaxed. If this position causes discomfort in the lower back, it is an indication that your back needs stretching out. You will most likely benefit from exercises for the back and abdominal strengthening exercises, pp. 225-228.

- You spend many hours in bed, and the positions you sleep in will affect your daytime posture. Notice how you sleep. Do you tense your neck or clench your jaw? Or perhaps you sleep on your side with your shoulder rolled forward and compress your lungs. Do your arms or hands go numb?

- The side-lying position is healthful for the back and chest. To lie on your right side, place your pillow diagonally across your chest from your right shoulder to your left lower rib cage and place your head, left shoulder, and upper arm on it. Raise your left forearm alongside the pillow and bend your left knee up to hip height. This position supports the natural curvature of your back, opens your chest, allows good circulation to your arms and legs, and supports your neck and head without strain.

Side-lying position

These techniques prepare you for sleep but how will you **drop off to sleep** once your head is on the pillow? Richard Shane, Ph.D., a psychotherapist in Boulder, Colo., has developed *Sleep Easily*, a technique and understanding of sleep that can help you ease into sleep, fall back to sleep, and sleep more deeply without medication! Common relaxation techniques and methods to bring on sleep require too much effort to allow the mind to move into sleep. *Sleep Easily* is a simple, neurophysiological method that uses breath, heart, and body sensations to bring on sleep. Think how distinctive the sound of sleep breathing is. It is the primordial sound of comfort inside the mother's womb. It helps you feel safe, comfortable, and fosters a sense of well-being. These three conditions are necessary to allow you to fall asleep.

Try this brief practice to experience the techniques used in *Sleep Easily*. Close your eyes.

1. Begin with your tongue. It is a bridge between the autonomic and voluntary nervous systems. Press it gently against the roof of your mouth and then let it relax heavily on the floor of your mouth. Open your throat, relax it, and create space at the back of your mouth.

2. Listen to your breathing and appreciate that it exists. Plug your ears and you can hear your breath through your bone and tissue instead of through the air. You will recognize the sounds deep within your sinuses, airways, and upper chest as characteristic of sleep.

3. As you gently and softly feel and hear this breathing in your air passages, your body will rest in comfort, and you will move in the direction of sleep. Observe and invite the sensations you individually associate with sleep. If you have tinnitus (ringing in the ears), use feeling rather than sound.

With these techniques, you will be able to quiet your mind, calm your heart, and find comfort in your breathing. If you were to look at this technique as a simple progression, it might look like this:

Deeply listen to your breath.
Your breath becomes calmer and quieter.
You feel that calmness.
Calmness "soaks" into your heart, which becomes quieter and calmer.
Calmness spreads from your breath and heart throughout your body.
Your mind rests in the comfort of your softening body sensations,
and your mind/brain becomes quieter and calmer.
This eases you into sleep.

This list will help you understand the individual elements but do not expect them to occur in sequence, one after another. Instead, the experience will spread pervasively throughout your body and mind. It is essential to remember that you do not need to make any effort for these changes to occur. They will happen effortlessly by themselves simply by your being aware of deeply listening to your breath. It is an awareness of *being*, rather than doing.

If you are experiencing difficulty breathing, physical or mental pain, inner conflict, anxiety or fear, don't struggle, just listen to your breath with a sense of acceptance and appreciation. At its own gradual and deliberate rate, your breath will become more comfortable, and this comfort will spread to other areas of your body. A model for this might be if you had an infant sleeping peacefully in your arms and you just listen to its breathing with a sense of wonder and love. Another benefit of listening to the quiet, pure, non-verbal sound of your breath is that it satisfies the mind's craving to be listening to something. When your mind is giving attention to listening, it has less need to create thoughts.

Gratefully accept incremental change. Appreciate any small progress. It is better than the other alternative of reverting to your old, sleepless habits. As you notice each bit of improvement, acknowledge it and give yourself time to change. Affirm that you are changing and will eventually succeed.

Studying Dr. Shane's *Sleep Easily* method caused me to completely remake my attitude and understanding of sleep — what it does and how I can enjoy sleep. Sleep is a time of self-nurture, healing, and re-forming my disposition and perspective for waking hours. The process of going to sleep is about creating a safe, comfortable realm of peace. There are no activities that can be accomplished from this place. Let go of tomorrow's challenges and joys and appreciate the calm and renewal of this time and place. Rehash your past activities and emotions while journaling before bedtime. When you are in bed, just rest in the present moment.

Sorting through my old, negative attitudes and experiences with sleep and nighttime helped me let go of my unpleasant and frightening associations. I'll give you my list of strongest influences hoping it will help you recall some old baggage you might release.

- From childhood, the terror of nightmares

- The displeasure of sleeping for 16 years with a partner who was thoughtless of my needs at night and demanding of sexual gratification

- Getting up repeatedly in the night to comfort wakeful or sick children and the resulting displeasure of sleep deprivation

- As a single mother of young children, fear for our nighttime safety

- The unsettling acknowledgment that I lost my perspective at night — that everything was distorted, and I seemed to lose my coping skills. This caused me to magnify any problems. I had attributed this vulnerability to darkness.

Once I sorted out these influences I was surprised to observe that none of them were valid for me anymore. Before I could acknowledge that, however, it was necessary for me to identify these factors in order to release them once and for all. I have replaced my attitudes formed out of these experiences with a new understanding that sleep and nighttime are a miraculous and mysterious time of self-nurture, abiding peace, healing, and growth. Several learning experiences have contributed to my current enjoyment of nighttime and sleep.

Years ago we employed a blind mechanic at Self-Propulsion. A professional auto mechanic, Gerry had been blind from birth and had skillfully transferred his mechanical deftness from cars to bicycles. Gerry was our constant teacher. He loved tandem riding and the outdoors so he joined us on a weekend camping trip. In the woods, I was amazed to observe him duck under low-hanging branches that he was able to sense. Inspired by Gerry, I decided to decrease my dependency on sight. I would try tuning in to my other senses so I could learn to walk in the woods at night without illumination. During an evening walk, we became preoccupied trying to locate and identify a distant sound and did not make it back to camp before darkness engulfed us. We had no lights but I gained some benefit from the light from the night sky. I reassured myself that Gerry would find our way back to camp. Indeed he did, and during that time I learned to let go of my preoccupation with sight and use my senses of hearing and sensation of my feet to remain on the road surface. Branches brushing on my sides told me I was off the track. I have continued to practice these skills by walking after dark without illumination. (It is rarely pitch black at night in Colorado.) Now I no longer feel anxious in the dark. Anytime I need to find my way or to find an object in camp, I look forward to the opportunity to use all my sensory skills. Since I devote my full attention to what is around me, I have lots more fun and learn more about myself and nature.

This love of the night combined with several other factors has led me to abandon my bed in my house and routinely sleep in my backyard on a mat with my sleeping bag. There, the soothing energy of nature always makes me feel at peace. The canopy of the night sky, the sounds of the wind, birds, and coyotes, refresh and comfort me when I wake up at night. (I have also developed patience for my neighbors' occasional loud parties. Earplugs are also my constant companions when parties or strong winds interrupt my sleep.)

Now I understand that sleep restores balance to my nervous system, is grounding, and helps me establish a fresh perspective. Through Yoga, I have learned that I am not an unconscious victim of darkness or the wanderings of my sleeping mind. In a changed-consciousness, I savor the quiet and am content. My sleeping-consciousness can result in growth, healing, and revitalization. In the moments while I lie in bed aligning my body, I purposely direct my thoughts toward positive qualities I want to develop, I review positive qualities possessed by someone I admire, or I reach out to the source of my being. The fact that I often solve problems and design projects in my sleep is a wondrous bonus of thoughtfully setting the stage for my hours of sleep rather than the product of an agitated mind. You may find Tenzin Wangyal's *The Tibetan Yogas of Dream and Sleep* a fascinating exploration of the usefulness of sleep. Since we spend one-third of our lives sleeping, cultivating our sleeping skills is a worthwhile activity.

I assure you that sleep is not a waste of time compared to activities that seem more fun or more important. Rather, it is an essential part of a healthy life that enables me to perform physically with strength and agility, to think clearly, to maintain inner calm, and to develop a deeper self-love. It gives me courage to expand my comfort level and my creativity. Being well-rested enables me to be more compassionate toward others. It surely is worth going to sleep for all these benefits!

So what can you do when you are wakeful at night? You may be inclined to intensify your anxiety by worrying about the influence of inadequate sleep the following day. Relax. Studies have shown that five-and-a-half hours of sleep lets you perform necessary tasks adequately. Additional hours of sleep contribute to your mood or attitude. They are what enable you to be cheerful, compassionate, and understanding. They make life more fun for you and your associates. Likewise, if you are troubled by "near sleep," Dr. Shane recommends you redefine your sleep goal to be content with it. While you are resting in "near sleep," you will either ease into sleep or you will experience a state of deep, quiet, nurturing connection with yourself that is healing and restful.

If you are suffering from physical pain, avoid external distractions or disassociation techniques that may help when you're awake. Instead, try to stay integrated by using internal distraction and keeping your awareness inside your body in a "safe zone." Make your breath comfortable, soak it into your heart, and let that spread throughout your body. When movement that causes pain wakens you, treat it like driving over a bump and continue driving. Continue breathing and you'll reenter sleep.

I encourage you to learn more from Dr. Shane and his recently published four CDs and guidebook *Sleep Easily*. Contact him through the Center for Personal Development, 3985 Wonderland Hill Ave., Boulder, CO 80304, 1-866-431-REST (7378), www.sleepeasily.com or www.drshane.com.

Frequently, insomnia is your body intelligence telling you to change your life style. Being scattered, unable to sleep, and forgetful are all signs that you are trying to handle more complexity than is healthy. Could it be that you have adapted to circumstances you ought not to tolerate? Unfortunately, our society rewards you for juggling many responsibilities, activities, and thoughts. However, your mind and body will reward you for simplifying. Take time to enjoy the moment. Bring your focus to the activity at hand. There is no guarantee that satisfaction will come to you at some future time. It is within your capabilities to adjust your life style and your attitude to increase your contentment *now*.

When you are feeling overwhelmed and/or overworked, it may help you find some balance if you try to put your situation in a larger perspective than today. How many people in our world would be grateful if their only worries were about too much work? How grateful they would be for adequate food, clothing, shelter, and a relatively safe environment. Re-evaluate all your activities to determine which ones are optional and eliminate one or two of them. When you are asked to do another activity, ask yourself if it will make a positive difference in your life or for your community. If not, just say no! Pursuing endless activities just for the experience is a good formula for insanity.

Being selective in activities also applies to seemingly innocuous activities like listening to background music or TV. If your mind races, you're probably not making space for yourself. Help your mind slow down and center yourself by deciding when you need quiet. Turn off the music and TV. Avoid reading every time you sit down. Try reading only when you need information or want entertainment. The next step is to try quieting your mind through meditation. This can be a spiritual, solitary practice or simply a release of all your concerns while concentrating on your breathing. In all of your day's activities, try bringing your full attention to whatever you are doing. Check the quality of your breathing. When your mind wanders off, pull it back to the job you are doing. When additional tasks crowd in on you, put them on a list and deal with them at an appropriate time. Frequently interrupting yourself diminishes the quality of your work and scatters your mind. This practice will increase your satisfaction in each task and help you stay centered.

The quality of your day is affected by **how you waken**. You may find it necessary to use an alarm clock but after you are reliably awake, enjoy lying in bed for a few minutes and transition gradually to wakefulness. Take this opportunity to activate acupoints on your neck, shoulders, arms, and hands. Take a moment to greet the day and your expected activities. Recite your affirmations. If you are really weary and finding it difficult to bring your energy up, try the stretching routine on pp. 103-105.

Freedom from Infection

A low-grade infection or the initial stages of the flu or a cold are other reasons your legs may sometimes feel like lead. You may not know you are fighting a bug but your performance is off. Several days later you can confirm that an infection was present. Riding can be healing if you adjust your energy output to respond to your current stamina level. Try not to push yourself if you are feeling drained. You can build stamina another day. If your body is telling you to slow down, heed that warning. Rest and nutritious food enhance your immune system whereas strenuous exertion stresses it.

It takes years to build dependable, consistent fitness and stamina. Avoid sacrificing today's wellness in hopes of speeding up the conditioning process. Frequently, riders drive themselves too hard when preparing for an event or a personal goal. This can result in sickness, burnout, or injury, and can set up the need for staying off their bike for weeks. Cycling can be a dependable companion through all life's phases. So let your style evolve to meet your daily and yearly needs. One effective method to establish an energy level appropriate to today's ride is to ask yourself if you could maintain this pace all day. If you sense you will run out of energy after several hours, back off your pace. Check your heart rate, breathing, muscle sensations, and mental focus. Are you enjoying what you are doing or only yearning to be finished? Just keep backing off your pace until you reach a sustainable level for physical and psychological pleasure.

Conservation of Your Resources

Conserving the resources you have will increase your stamina and pleasure. Avoid squandering your riding resources through hectic preparation and poor body temperature regulation.

Probably all of us have experienced the frenzy of last-minute preparation for a cycling event or a bicycling vacation. We rush to get our clothing organized, food collected, home in order, bicycle maintained, and everything packed. We stay up late, eat hastily, and squander energy in panic mode. When the ride begins, we are exhausted. The first day is slow, hard work. Time management will help you avoid this last-minute rush, and conscious breathing will help you avoid going into overdrive. During preparation, try shifting into the energizing, calming breathing techniques that are so useful when riding.

When you waste your energy on unnecessary heating and cooling of your body, you are taking available energy away from propelling your bike. Adjust your clothing and riding time-of-day to maximize your comfort when riding at temperatures below 60 degrees, above 85 degrees, and in precipitation. Refer to Chapter 8 for help in adapting to challenging weather conditions.

Accept weather conditions and other riding circumstances you can't change or avoid.

Let go of your grievances. Then imagine how conditions could be even worse and you may be grateful that you have been spared further discomfort or risks. Try to heighten your awareness and to search out the beauty or humor in the situation. How many times have you looked back and laughed at a miserable situation in your life? If you practice, you can gain that perspective and amusement while the mess is actually in progress. Physical and psychological comfort will allow you to put all your energies into propelling your bike and exercising good judgment.

Muscle Recovery

Do you know the feeling of riding hard one day and feeling like a noodle the next day? Understanding how your body refuels and recovers will increase your stamina, especially during all-day and multiple-day tours and cycling events. Your progress in improving your health and fitness will be more noticeable if you avoid wearing yourself down and ignoring the recovery process. Optimum recovery includes elongating, balancing, and relaxing your muscles as well as replenishing energy to your muscles, blood, liver, and nervous system.

Muscles work by contracting. They cannot apply force by expanding. One muscle pulls on a bone in one direction while an opposing muscle pulls it back to its original position. (Refer to the illustration of prime mover and antagonist muscles, p. 12.) When the first muscle contracts, the opposing muscle extends. As a muscle is repeatedly contracted during the repetitive exercise of pedaling a bike, it becomes shorter and tighter.

Carefully selected stretches will help specific muscles return to their healthy, elongated, and relaxed condition. Chapter 5 contains stretches for each part of your body to enable you to achieve and maintain a flexible, balanced musculature. It is unfortunate that few cyclists recognize that stretching is necessary to maintain a healthy body. If you ride more than 25 miles per week and do not stretch daily, your neck, shoulders, back, and hamstrings will become excessively tight. These tight muscles not only reduce comfort and flexibility, they also cause compression and impairment to organs, glands, and both the nervous and circulatory systems. Usually these impairments are ignored until injury or dysfunction result in pain or illness. Don't wait for trouble, select a few stretches and do them daily. Rotate your choice of stretches each week to meet your immediate needs and to maintain your motivation. Refer to the Alexander Technique to better understand the damaging effects of habitual misuse of your body, pp. 93-96.

During the recovery process, stretching relieves muscle tension, postpones fatigue, and stimulates the transport of nutrients and removal of waste products throughout your body. Stretching before exercise has the additional benefit of warming your muscles and preparing them for more vigorous exercise. Failure to stretch out before and after exercise reduces muscle elasticity, joint flexibility, and increases risk of injury. Refer to "Understanding Yoga Postures and Stretching," pp. 96-100 to optimize your stretching technique.

You might also enjoy massage, hot baths, or saunas to help relax and soothe tired muscles. Massage increases circulation, which promotes healing through the exchange of nutrients and waste products in the system, relaxes and loosens muscles, and is psychologically calming. In the recovery process, massage is more effective than rest alone. It provides some stretching but cannot replace an active stretching program. If you have sustained an injury, postpone massage until the swelling and pain have subsided. You can begin acupressure on distant trigger points immediately. The heat of sauna and baths reduces muscle tension and increases your overall sense of well-being. Make them leisurely to optimize the benefits, take care not to get overheated, and watch for signs of light-headedness. Be sure to drink plenty of fluids during any activity that increases circulation so you will facilitate the transport of nutrients and waste products.

Let's review a few elements of how your body is fueled during exercise and the causes of muscle fatigue and soreness. Carbohydrates are converted to glucose that is transported by the blood to your liver and to your muscles. There it is converted to glycogen for storage. For about the first 90 minutes of high-energy exercise, your muscles are fueled by stored glycogen. The blood glycogen can be refueled during exercise by consuming easily assimilated carbohydrates. This is vital to maintaining stamina and optimum body function. Glucose fuels your brain and nervous system as well as your muscles. When you experience fatigue or exhaustion, your weary brain and nervous system also contribute to your condition. This accounts for poor judgment and slow response time when you are tired. Stored fat contributes to available energy during low- to moderate-intensity exercise after four or more hours.

Muscle soreness is caused by lactic acid buildup and delayed onset muscle soreness (DOMS). During high exertion workouts, when inadequate oxygen is available, lactic acid builds up in your muscles. If you maintain a low- to moderate-intensity exercise level you will avoid this discomfort except during brief periods of climbing out of the saddle. This is experienced as a burning sensation and is short term. All lactic acid is flushed out of your system within 60 minutes after exercise. (Burke, p. 37) In contrast, DOMS occurs the day following exercise. It is due to micro tears in your muscle fibers. The soreness and stiffness you experience are caused by swelling within your muscles. Of course the best cure for both types of sore muscles is prevention by gradually building up your exercise intensity. Precede each exercise session with warm-up stretching or just begin your ride at a low-intensity level and increase your exertion as your body warms up. Complete each ride with the cool-down description that follows. If you have been off your bike for a few weeks, let your riding season build gradually by increasing your riding distance and intensity as your stamina develops. Responding to your overall level of fatigue and fitness condition during all rides will enable you to avoid soreness.

It is important to optimize recovery because it returns your body to a normal, balanced state by restoring body fluids, replenishing energy stores, and repairing muscle tissue. The late Edmund R. Burke studied the recovery process in scientific detail. He identified three phases of recovery following exercise. Although Burke's study involved high energy riders, his steps can be adapted for all riders. Along with stretching, his suggestions should become a thoughtful part of your riding routine.

The first 30 minutes after exercise is the **rapid recovery phase.** During this phase all your body processes begin to return to their pre-exercise level. These include your metabolic rate, heart rate, breathing rate, and body temperature. You will want to cool down gradually during the first 5 to 10 minutes. By keeping your circulation above normal, all restorative processes are facilitated. You might do this by completing your ride at a leisure pace or by stretching out.

For optimum recovery, you need to replenish your depleted energy stores. Consuming high GI drinks and foods will accelerate this process. Remember that high GI foods quickly raise blood sugar concentrations and stimulate the release of insulin. Insulin plays a vital role in transporting glucose through the blood to muscle cells and there converting it to glycogen for storage in your muscles. Because fluids are absorbed more quickly than solid food, energy beverages are ideal for meeting your carbohydrate needs during the first hour. Strive to consume 22 to 28 ounces of energy beverage during this period. During the first 90 minutes, the speed of glycogen synthesis is two to three times faster than normal. This gives you a window of opportunity to quickly replenish your muscle glycogen and rehydrate. If you miss this window of time, your glycogen recovery will be significantly slower, and you will notice your fatigue more acutely for the next 24 hours. (Burke, pp. 44-45)

How soon you eat solid food will depend on the energy level of each ride. Burke identified the first 90 minutes to two hours as the **intermediate phase**. For a moderate energy ride, you can select some high GI carbohydrates to eat after you have finished your sport drink and during the next two hours. Energy bars are convenient during this period if you are away from home or far from food stores. Some protein during this time period increases insulin response and increases replenishment of glycogen by as much as 30 percent. To ensure a moderate rate of absorption of foods, avoid fat intake and limit protein consumption to a 1:4 ratio with carbohydrates, that is, one gram of protein for every four grams of carbohydrates. (Burke, p. 67, 72) Refer to Monique Ryan's *Sports Nutrition* for help in selecting foods for this process.

The remaining 24 hours Burke called the **longer phase**. After endurance workouts, muscles repair and adapt to exercise. During this time period, you can rebuild your body energy stores to their normal level. Select carbohydrates with low GI because absorption will accomplish this better. Obviously if you are riding for several days or weeks, you will compress this period into the evening hours and the following morning before riding again. These meals should be composed of 60 to 65 percent of the calories from carbohydrate

(4 calories/gram), 20 to 25 percent from fat (9 calories/gram), and about 15 percent from protein (4 calories/gram). (Burke, p. 72) On multiple-day tours you will always benefit from maintaining your energy supplies while riding. One of the great delights of recreational riding is the ability to respond to your needs as they become evident. This underlines the importance of always carrying energy bars with you on any ride. Don't risk running your blood sugar low and suffering from low energy, poor judgment, and prolonged recovery.

Some riders experience the unpleasant phenomenon of muscle cramping during the recovery period. The causes of cramping are not understood but there are precautions you can take to reduce the likelihood of cramping. These involuntary muscle contractions are associated with dehydration, lowered blood volume, and inadequate oxygenation of your muscles. You might try these techniques and see if they help you prevent cramping:

- Warm up and cool down methodically when you exercise.
- Include stretching in your rituals.
- Stay hydrated using adequate electrolytes especially when overheating or if you usually sweat profusely. Do not restrict your salt consumption during hot weather.
- If you are susceptible to cramping at night, stretch out before going to bed and take special measures to keep warm. For example, if you are troubled by cramps in your calves, wear warm knee-high socks to bed to to keep your calves warm. Be sure the socks do not impair your circulation.
- When you do cramp, stretch out the cramping muscle and apply pressure to it. For calves and shins, just walk the cramps out.
- Use the "Shiatsu for the calves and Achilles tendons," pp. 174-175 whenever your calves feel tight or after you have released the muscle spasm.
- Until more is understood about muscle cramping, prevention is the best approach.

Focus: the Key to Pleasure and Performance

Mental focus is influenced by all of the above energy sources. When you are well-rested, relaxed, and well-fueled, your focus can come together for a blissful ride. However, if you are scattered with your mind going this way and that, you can choose to focus your attention and improve your riding technique on every ride. When you discover you are rattled before a ride, center yourself during your warm-up stretching. Use your abdominal muscles and diaphragm to engage the soothing parasympathetic nervous system. Then concentrate on your Slow, Even, Long, and Full inhalations and exhalations. Bring your attention to each part of your body as you stretch. Use the "Focus your mental energy" head massage to remove scattered energy anytime. Refer to p. 252.

Avoid letting your racing thoughts engage you. As they come up, just let go of them. If you start riding and discover your bike handling is poor, you could stop and stretch. If that is not practical, let go, relax, and consciously change your breathing pattern. Rather than resigning yourself to poor performance, consciously affirm that you can turn your performance around to create a positive outcome. You might say, "I'm in control, I'm doing what I love, and I am bringing my full attention to my riding." Taking time for this adjustment will brighten your attitude, increase your bike handling skills, and reduce the likelihood of mishaps.

Surely one of the pleasures of technical trail riding is the singular focus you experience that may elude you at other times. But if you rarely handle your bike on road or trail as well as you would like to, here are some suggestions. Tune in to the present moment. Be alert to your surroundings. Look up and around you at the larger scene. What do you see, hear, and feel? What feedback are you getting from your body - your knees, back, neck, and lungs? Are your hips rigid or can you flex your spine and rock your hips freely from side to side? Has your mind wandered off to other concerns? If so, bring it back to the pleasures of the place and the process of riding. Try to let your destination be secondary to your immediate enjoyment. Be ready to change your planned destination to accommodate your immediate needs.

Cycling can be meditative. It is rhythmic, it changes your breathing patterns, and it makes you more aware of nature surrounding you. Cultivating the interrelationship of cycling and meditation is at the heart of taking the peace of riding back into your daily routine. Refer to "Beginning a Meditation Practice," pp. 133-135 for practical guidelines.

On the other side of the coin, practicing meditation off the bike will bring greater focus to your riding and will increase your awareness of your entire well-being. Studies have shown that regular, conscious practice of Yoga, Qigong, or other spiritually enriching practices can improve your total wellness. It has also been demonstrated that meditation is more effective than simple relaxation techniques at reducing high blood pressure, anxiety, and the stress of high energy exercise. (Harvard Women's Health Watch, January 2001)

Balanced Development of Confidence, Muscle Strength, and Bike Handling Skills

We've examined body mechanics, equipment modifications, and energy sources. What else contributes to your riding satisfaction? At any given time, your riding skills depend on a balance of your confidence, your strength, and your technical bike-handling skills. Assessing your strengths and weaknesses in these three areas will help you understand your current performance level. We all know athletes who excel in one sport and are in excellent physical condition. However, when they begin cycling, they are not immediately able to translate their athleticism into skillful riding. Cycling performance is only as strong as the weakest link in this triad. That inadequacy can result in hesitation to achieve top performance, premature fatigue, or frequent crashes.

Perhaps you have reached a plateau in your riding ability. Consider which of these elements is weakest for you: confidence, strength, or riding technique. As you strive to improve the weakest one, you can enjoy rapid, overall improvement. By thoughtfully evaluating your current abilities, you can determine how to develop these elements at parallel rates.

Stream crossings were my personal training ground for learning the interdependence of these three elements. In the Rockies, most streams are 10 to 20 feet across, and the water is crystal clear. I would pause on the bank, choose a line trying to avoid rocks too large to ride over, and then plunge in. I would usually get as far as my momentum would carry me. Then I would become tense with apprehension, and the bike would resist my efforts at control. At this point, I would give up, put my feet down, dismount, and push my bike the rest of the way across the stream. I was frustrated with my hesitancy to ride the entire crossing because my sons would confidently cross streams with much glee. I wanted to share in the fun.

We always rode single track on multiple-day bike camping trips. About 45 pounds of camping gear and food increased my challenge. My sons have always been my technique coaches, especially in those early days. They would encourage me, "Mom, instead of giving up mid-stream, just pour on the power." "Oh, sure," I thought, "What power?" In reality, my lack of confidence obscured my awareness of my own power. After all, I was usually successful in powering the load up rock-strewn and rooted trails. I just couldn't pour on all my power when I lacked confidence and control.

Gradually I sorted out a successful stream-crossing technique. On streams wider than 10 feet, I pause to pick a line. Then I take a moment to banish apprehension. I relax my body by taking a few conscious, diaphragmatic breaths. I visualize myself riding all the way across and then I ride in. If I do tense up or lose confidence mid-stream, I begin a controlled, prolonged exhalation and pour on the power. Hooray! I motor on through. The exhalation automatically relaxes my body. Body tension causes the bike to fight back when what's needed is for it to obligingly shift with the shifting rocks at the bottom. The burst of power lets me forge through the resistance of the bigger rocks at the bottom and boosts my confidence.

The role of confidence was again demonstrated when I started using clip-in pedals. At first my confidence took a dive. I still remember my first stream crossing with clip-ins. The banks were steep, and the trail paralleled the stream. I turned into the stream and mid-way, launched myself off the bike like a novice. It was worth a hearty laugh but the reality was it took me some time to regain the same confidence I had enjoyed with toe-clips and straps.

Gay Hendricks offers a technique for regaining confidence and composure when your technique has taken a turn for the worse. If you are having an off-day, this technique will turn your performance around. Pause a moment. Take three conscious, diaphragmatic breaths, and make an irrefutable statement: "The sky is blue" or "I'm riding with Nicole today." Then continue on your way with confidence that your usual performance level is restored. Professional athletes use this technique. (Hendricks, p. 161 to 162)

Tips for Improving Your Bike-handling Skills and Building Your Riding Confidence

1. Be singular in purpose while planning your ride. Can you remember a ride with a group of friends who really frustrated you because they were a lot slower than you or rode too fast for you to keep up? Increase the chances of fun by selecting only one or two riding goals. Some of the goals you might choose from are: getting a fitness workout, limbering-up/stretching-out/winding-down, exploring new territory, practicing bike handling skills, having a social outing, enjoying nature, experimenting with new techniques or equipment, and getting renewed.

2. Ride alone or with companions who are willing to accommodate your needs today. Improving your skills is difficult when you are distracted by group dynamics.

3. Practice. Ride often enough that you are totally at ease on your bike. Practice until your shifting and braking are second nature. Take time out when you are riding to consider what you are doing technically. Practice thinking about your form and how you are using your body.

4. Relax. Breathe from the diaphragm. Refer to "Effective Breathing Integrates the Mindbody and Optimizes Performance," pp. 72-86. Begin each ride in touch with your resources and goals for today. Let your body and mind warm up gradually to the task. I have discovered it is better to save highly technical or physically demanding sections of the ride for the later part of my outing.

5. Clear your mind. Leave your present concerns behind and focus on the moment. Is the ride you planned appropriate for today? If not, change the route, the pace, or the distance and adjust to the time allocated. Set yourself up for satisfaction so you can be free of self-imposed pressure.

6. Look ahead. Run your visual focus far enough ahead to let your ride flow and to give you adequate reaction time for traffic or trail obstacles. Adjust your speed so you can be confident of your reaction time. Avoid becoming preoccupied with details immediately in front of your wheel or the next obstacle may catch you unprepared.

7. Keep your head upright and point your chin in the direction you want to go. Your chin will act as a rudder. Try this out on a switch back or any sharp turn where you need to double back more than 100 degrees. As you initiate the turn, look back to where you will be when the turn is complete. Your body and bike will follow the lead of your chin.

8. Choose the line you want to ride and focus on it. Don't get stuck looking at the obstacles. That will cause you to ride directly into them. If the situation is critical (a situation where a miscalculation might result in injury), consciously relax through a prolonged exhalation. A tense body prevents your bike from shifting to the most stable position. A relaxed body lets you subtly guide your bike with hips and weight shifts. The bike will freely follow your command. You see it is a delicate balance between letting your bike go to a secure riding surface and taking control when it needs correction.

9. Cultivate a constant exertion level. Do you pedal and coast, pedal and coast? If this is your pattern, practice shifting gears so that you can pedal continuously at a consistent exertion and cadence. This will give a better aerobic workout and will build stamina throughout the ride.

10. Apply power at the strategic moment you are beginning to lose control. This will help you regain control instead of falling. If you are about to crash, try a burst of power and right your bike instead of giving up and putting your foot (or hip) down. Success in this maneuver will give your confidence a big boost.

11. Anticipate gear changes. When your path climbs or drops steeply or you must stop abruptly, change gears before you stall out. Change gears often so your cadence is constant and you are completely comfortable and in control. Refer to "How to Use Your Gears for Optimum Health and Performance for 21 or More Speeds," pp. 283-284.

12. During rides, change your tire pressure as your riding surface changes. This will optimize your comfort and control. Carry a frame pump so you can increase the tire pressure according to what the riding surface and your stamina indicate. A soft tire increases traction and keeps the tire in contact with the riding surface, thereby increasing control and comfort. A hard tire reduces the contact patch on the riding surface, reduces traction, increases rebound, and generally reduces control. A hard tire transmits impacts to the rider but protects the rim from damage. It also affects rolling resistance. Either extreme in tire pressure increases rolling resistance. Experiment to determine for your weight, tread pattern, and riding style what pressure works best for you under various riding conditions. Many cyclists ride with too high tire pressure for optimum control or comfort. Refer to "Should I experiment with different tires to increase my riding enjoyment?" on pp. 277-279.

13. Avoid locking up a wheel with the brakes. It is difficult to control a skidding tire. Strive to ride at a controlled speed so you can skillfully handle the unexpected. If you need to slow down for a technically challenging section, apply your brakes to reduce your speed but continue to pedal. This technique will give both power and control to your rear wheel and is especially useful in snow.

14. Increase your control of your bike and your comfort by getting off the saddle often. Place the pedals so that the crankarms are horizontal and lift slightly off the saddle to avoid impacts. Rise higher off the saddle with knees bent to respond quickly to obstacles on the road or trail. Standing in a relaxed crouch allows you to maneuver your bike quickly with minimum effort. Observe which foot you use on the forward pedal. You will have a favorite foot but learning to lead with either foot forward will improve your performance and balance your musculature. Contacting or holding the nose of your saddle between your thighs will increase your control in demanding situations.

15. Shift your weight for control.
    - Shift your hips side-to-side to help steer your bike.
    - Move your entire torso forward or back to weight and unweight a wheel.
    - Project your buttocks off the back of the saddle over the rear wheel to hold the rear wheel down and avoid going over the handlebars in a sudden stop or steep descent. Refer to the photo on p. 265.
    - Shift your weight over the front wheel to prevent the front wheel from coming off the ground in a steep climb or in an abrupt rise coming out of a gully.
    - Flatten your torso low over the bike frame and spread your weight over both wheels to hold the front wheel down and maintain traction on the rear wheel during steep ascents.
    - Shift your weight onto the pedals and off the endangered wheel to avoid rim damage or pinch flats when hitting an unavoidable obstacle.

    Riding a relatively small bike facilitates all these maneuvers.

16. Regulating your speed on descents is critical to maintaining control. The optimum speed gives enough momentum to keep the front wheel rolling over obstacles. If you are going too slowly, the front wheel may jam behind obstacles and send you over the handlebars. If you are going too fast, you may be challenged to respond fast enough to negotiate the road or trail. Practice achieving just the right balance between going too slowly so you feel confident and going too quickly while striving to maintain control.

Although these techniques are frequently described in terms of single track riding, they are useful survival skills for urban riding. Just replace your visualization of obstacles with drainage grates, potholes, motor vehicles, pedestrians, and small animals. Your urban riding will be safer and more fun using these skills.

Selecting Compatible Riding Companions

Make riding more fun by selecting riding companions who are compatible with your abilities and riding priorities. People tend to ride with friends and family they enjoy socially. It is quite likely that these people are not appropriate riding companions, however. Customers coming into Self-Propulsion frequently complain about keeping up with the group they have chosen to ride with. Before they look for the reason in their equipment, I ask them to think about the experience level of their riding companions. This is especially true when joining a cycling club. Club members are usually dedicated riders who have been building their fitness base for years. Ask the riders you are considering riding with how many years they have ridden and how many miles they ride each week. Is it reasonable for you to expect to keep up with them? If you wanted to learn a new language, would you start in a third-year course? Be fair to yourself and if you want to ride with more fit cyclists to learn from their experience, carefully select less demanding routes to share with them and then ride a part of the planned ride before you turn back by yourself.

The following questions will help you evaluate how compatible you will be with other riders or groups:

1. Are you willing to ride at the same speed, technical level, and distance?
2. Are you of similar abilities?
3. Are your sense of adventure and risk taking levels similar?
4. How many of these desires do you share?
   a. Pushing for a high-energy fitness workout
   b. Enjoying nature and the surroundings
   c. Stopping to eat and relax
   d. Socializing and chatting while riding
   e. Challenging to improve technical skills
5. Is it easy to discuss and negotiate a mutually satisfactory plan to meet your immediate needs?
6. Are they supportive and encouraging to you and your improvements?

If you are not finding many aspects of compatibility, seek out riding companions who share your priorities or simply ride alone. You might find new riding friends through local cycling clubs or events. Or, you could inquire about organized rides at your local bike shop. Undertaking a thoughtful search for new riding companions is worth the time because it can reduce disharmony with friends and family that arises when trying to persuade them to ride in your style or criticizing them for choices you don't understand.

Be flexible in your expectations of how you might ride with a friend. I have learned to let my friends ride at their pace and I come along at mine. I have two friends I occasionally bike pack with. They are both high-energy riders and rarely carry heavy loads when they ride by themselves. Consequently, they have developed different muscle types than I have with carrying my camping gear and commuting supplies. When I go self-contained touring with them, they ride faster and get well ahead of me but need to stop to rest under their unfamiliar burdens. I come plodding along at my sustainable pace, greet them as I pass, and continue riding. Pretty soon they pass me again, and we play leapfrog all day. Since I have paced myself all day and am used to carrying so much gear, I have energy in the evening to go exploring while they rest in camp. We are good friends and are comfortable with our different styles.

Introducing Someone Special in Your Life to Cycling

Maybe you are hoping that riding will be a great way to spend time with your partner, child, or parent who does not ride. Here are some suggestions that might help you successfully introduce this special person to something you cherish. First acknowledge that this is a delicate undertaking. It seems to be difficult to learn from or instruct someone we love. Too often it becomes a battle of wills with unrealistic high hopes or incompatible expectations. Sharing a skill with a family member takes tact and talent. Try these tips:

1. Set the stage for teamwork. Be honest about each other's expectations. Discover your mutual reservations and fears and explore how to address them. Decide *together* when to ride, the distance, the speed, and the goal of the outing.

2. Take care of all the mechanical details. Be sure all bikes are in fine mechanical running order. Carry tools to adjust seat height and handlebar position and be sure to put sealant in the inner tubes. Nothing spoils an outing like a mechanical breakdown.

3. Select your bikes to favor the less experienced rider. If you are the stronger rider, ride a bike that is heavy or inefficient so you will have to work harder. Avoid the common error of putting the slowest rider on a clunky bike.

4. Help select clothing to ensure comfort. Offer choices to the less-experienced rider. Visit a bike store and check out helmets, shoes, gloves, and shorts. Don't worry about the investment. If the novice rider is hurting, the next ride will be difficult to launch.

5. Choose delightful weather. If it is extremely hot, threatening to rain, extremely windy, or cold, have an alternative plan and postpone the bike ride until circumstances are more enjoyable.

6. Make food and drink a fun part of the trip. Plan to stop and snack. Low energy levels reduce stamina and spoil dispositions. Always carry your favorite snacks and drinks even if you plan to stop at a restaurant.

7. Start novices at their confidence level and not at yours. Let them begin on a wide saddle, with no toe clips, and wearing loose shorts. Ride a five-mile out-and-back trip to the ice cream store or a swimming pool, setting a playful attitude. Relax! This slower, easier pace won't lock you in for a lifetime. Your mutual riding styles will evolve together gradually. In fact, your children may eventually ride farther and faster than you do!

8. Design your outing for success. Select the type of place your special someone enjoys rather than choosing your favorite cycling place. Riders with years of experience lose their ability to evaluate rides from a novice's perspective. Be ultra conservative in selecting the ride route. One time I selected a route to share with a friend and her two young children. It seemed easy and non-threatening to me but at the lunch break my friend asked her daughter how she was handling the drop-offs at the edge of the trail. Oops, I hadn't noticed any drop-offs.

9. Plan it shorter and easier than you think is necessary. Coming home with extra energy is always better than returning exhausted and irritated.

10. Discuss your mutual goals. Is your purpose to get a great fitness workout? Is it to explore a favorite route from the slower speed of a bicycle? Is it to reach a specific destination? Is it simply to share time with friends or family?

11. Provide encouragement. Praise small successes. Use creativity and humor on difficult portions of the ride, especially if your plans go awry.

12. Give just enough instructions to ensure safety and fun. Children are especially resilient so let them discover their own way. You don't need to lecture kids or adults to impart all your cycling knowledge on their first outing. Young kids could ride part of the way on their own bikes and part of the way on a child seat or in a trailer. You might even plan an all-downhill trip and have someone else retrieve the car. You could also ride to a trailhead and then take a hike.

13. Recognize differences in male and female riding styles. Men are more likely to set goals of distance, speed, and elevation gain. They tend to be attracted to the thrill of competing with a companion and often enjoy riding until they are exhausted. In contrast, most women focus more on the whole process of riding. They usually enjoy physical comfort during the ride as well as the social aspects of the outing. They usually value the views, the flowers, and the chance to take photographs. They prefer to come home refreshed and ready for the next day, not wiped out entirely. Sharing these different styles can lead us to try new things and not get stuck in our ways.

Conclusions

Optimizing your resources for blissful riding does require some life style changes. As you learn to nourish and nurture yourself for more enjoyable athletic performance, you will feel more energetic and centered for other activities in your life. Yes, those are some of the benefits your new riding priorities and skills will bring to your life. Developing skills to improve your riding technique will help you deal with life's challenges. You can justify the time and energy needed to change your cycling performance because it will benefit your health, your family, and your career.

Where will you find the time to make appropriate changes? Observe your life and determine what you do with your time. Identifying where your time goes and what preoccupies you is an excellent practice in mindfulness. Without reflecting on the choices you are making, you risk letting life pass you by. Success is in the details of the choices you make every day.

Robert K. Cooper introduces the concept of "time competency" — using time wisely — as a prerequisite to success in health and fitness programs. (p. 32) Most of us have times when we feel victimized by the inexorable march of time. We feel frustrated because time flies so fast we go into overdrive trying to accomplish what we have planned. Time is as important a resource as food and sleep yet we rarely learn to manage and utilize it wisely. By recognizing that our lives are made of minutes and learning to spend them wisely, we can change our perception of time from an uncontrollable, fleeting element to a highly valued tool. We can learn to distinguish between being busy and being productive. We can avoid being preoccupied with the immediate schedule and work our long-term goals into the day-to-day schedule. Time competency eliminates the anxiety that results from working in a constant state of urgency and makes contentment a daily reality. Thoughtful scheduling brings our dreams to life.

Motivation always follows behavior. Waiting for just the right moment to go for a ride or to change your eating habits is fruitless. There are always complicating circumstances. But when you *act as if* you had time to ride or *act as if* you desire to eat an orange rather than drinking a soda pop, soon it will be true. Change your behavior first and you will want to continue later. How often we attach burdensome consequences to today's decisions. Just try an experiment and see what results. I even find that experimenting on myself is cheap entertainment. I was laboring over whether eliminating dairy products from my diet would improve my wellness. I tried to gather a lot of answers and tried to speculate whether such a change would be worth the effort. Finally I had a revelation, just stop eating dairy products and don't labor over the decision! I love cheese and yogurt but decided that for six weeks I could try it. *Acting as if* enabled me to discover that eliminating dairy products reduced my nasal drainage by half and ended the discomfort in my teeth that came from referred pain from my sinuses! At last I could chew on the left side of my mouth. No more dairy products for me. I use tapioca pudding made with soymilk substitute to satisfy my desire for dairy products. I'd still be suffering from sore teeth if I hadn't *acted as if* I wanted to eliminate dairy products from my diet!

Life style changes must be rooted in genuine self-respect and the desire to care for ourselves. Using the affirmations "I love myself and I am worthy" will eventually serve as rudders to steer you back on a healthful course even when you are weary.

Changing your habits will change your condition. Believe it, affirm it, visualize it, and practice it. You'll find that the healing powers of your mindbody will be activated. Gradually in small increments or dramatic steps, you will be transformed over the months and years.

chapter 8

Proper Clothing Extends Riding Seasons

- Understanding Clothing Technology
- Regulating Your Energy While Heating and Cooling
- Riding in the Heat
- Dealing with Precipitation
- Wind Alert!
- Riding in Temperatures Between 40 and 60 Degrees
- Riding in Below-freezing Temperatures
- Stoking Your Inner Fire

At Self-Propulsion I have observed that most cyclists enjoy their bikes from April through August. In Colorado, September through mid-November is predictably cool and sunny. Why do many riders just hang up their bikes in September, missing the opportunity to maintain their fitness and enjoy the fresh air of the changing seasons? I guess it's habit. After a busy and active summer, many are glad to withdraw and relax in seclusion. Another factor is familiarity. Most people are active outdoors at temperatures between 60 and 80 degrees. Although riding when the temperature is between 30 and 45 degrees can be more comfortable than riding in high temperatures, it does require more clothing and preparation. Surely darkness is a deterrent during the shorter days of winter. By gradually increasing your tolerance for riding at cooler temperatures and by acquiring adequate lighting, you can extend the pleasures of your riding season.

Just as I encourage you to exercise moderately every day of the week, I recommend that you exercise moderately every month of the year. You will build a strong fitness base if you progress every season rather than falling back during fall and winter. At one time in the Rockies, many people maintained their winter fitness by skiing. Recently it seems that traffic congestion, increased expenses, and complexity of planning are keeping more would-be snow sport enthusiasts at home. Could it be that you too experience the joy of improved fitness throughout the summer and then lose conditioning during the winter?

To quote a wise Scandinavian saying: "There is no such thing as bad weather, only inadequate clothing." Its truth may be lost in an era of big houses, big offices, and big motor vehicles. But it is true nonetheless. Once adequately dressed and outdoors, we can discover nature's beauty in all but the most destructive weather patterns. Strong winds are unsafe for cyclists and can be difficult to ride in but most other weather can be enjoyed when cyclists know how to dress. Gradually begin to acquire technical cool-weather clothing for cycling.

Your reward will be sustained fitness and a more intimate view of each season. How long has it been since you watched low clouds wrapping around the hills, birds forming flocks getting ready to migrate, and fallen leaves sweeping across the street in the breeze? Have you discovered that riding in rain or snow is not as intense as driving in those conditions? Do you still enjoy the spring thrill of seeing the first buds on the trees ready to burst or the crocuses peeking through the leaves? Have you compared the aroma of the roses in someone's garden as you interrupt a ride through the neighborhood? I suggest that you dress for the weather and try exploring all seasons.

Just as with bicycle hard goods, technical clothing choices are complicated by misinformation. Some of this is due to vast differences in personal comfort expectations and personal experiences. When you are seeking advice on clothing for specific temperature ranges, ask your advisor to define "comfort." I define it as warm and relaxed. On the other end of the spectrum are riders who are "comfortable" as long as they are not getting frostbitten. You will need to experiment to determine what keeps *you* comfortable when selecting clothing.

Understanding Clothing Technology

Any garment's performance is influenced by its design, the construction and fiber content of its fabric, and any chemical treatments.

You are probably most aware of the garment design aspect of this statement. You might describe a jacket as red with long sleeves, zip front, vent across the back and front, and slash pockets with zippers. These style characteristics are important for looks and specific functions. Fabric construction will determine whether the jacket is a raincoat of tightly woven and coated pack cloth; whether it provides wind protection and is lightweight, tightly woven, with a light coated rip stop; or whether it insulates and is made of fleece pile. Fiber content is especially critical in high-tech clothing. If it is nylon, for example, the fabric will be very durable but not insulative. If it is cotton, it will dry slowly and have limited durability. If it is polyester, it will transport moisture well, be durable, and dry quickly.

Additional performance characteristics are influenced by the *quality* of the fiber, the fabric, and the garment construction. The use of chemical finishes, lamination, and the blending of several fibers also contributes. Some garments are constructed of a combination of fabrics with different construction and fiber content. Here are some textile terms to help a wise shopper.

- Dimensional stability — The fabric or garment retains its shape with use and laundering.

- Hand — This refers to how the fabric feels to your touch.

- Knit — This type of fabric is constructed with yarns looping through rows of yarns that cross the fabric. Lycra® shorts are an example of a knit.

- Lycra® — refers to the elastic core of a yarn that may be wrapped with nylon, polyester, cotton, or any other fiber. Lycra® usually makes up 15 percent or less of the fabric content.

- Monofilament yarn — The yarn is extruded like a fishing line. It is most commonly found in Lycra® shorts and tights. Fabrics made of monofilament yarns are durable but less comfortable. A common example is rip stop nylon.

- Pilling — This is the formation of small balls of fiber on the fabric surface. It is characteristic of fabrics made of strong fibers that prevent the balls from breaking off the surface of the fabric.

- Spun yarn — Short fibers are twisted together to make a yarn. It is used for all cotton and wool and any synthetic where the extruded fiber is chopped in short pieces and twisted. These are slightly less resistant to abrasion but more breathable and absorbent. Spun yarn is used in Supplex® nylon.

- Wicking — This refers to the transporting of moisture through a fabric — a valuable method of moving perspiration away from the body.

- Woven — This fabric is constructed of interlacing lengthwise and crosswise yarns. Supplex® is woven.

- Yarn — This thread is made of fiber and is used in weaving or knitting fabrics.

Give special attention to the fiber content when selecting a garment. The Textile Labeling Act requires that every garment have a fiber-content label sewn in. If you don't find the content on the hangtag, search for the content label, which is often stitched into a side seam. The fiber information chart, on the next two pages, can help you understand the properties that fiber content contributes to a garment.

Regulating Your Energy While Heating and Cooling

Wise energy use is at the heart of maintaining your stamina and wellness when cycling. The mental and physical energy you use to tolerate hot and cold weather cannot be used to propel your bike. Learning to regulate your body temperature by careful selection and use of technical clothing will increase your pleasure and your performance. Avoid being one of those riders who invests without restraint in a fine bike but wears humble, low-tech clothing.

Here are some of the specific challenges you face in regulating your body temperature.

1. Dissipating the heat constantly generated during highly aerobic activity

continued on page 332

Textile Fiber Information Useful for Bicycling Clothing

Fiber	Benefits	Drawbacks	Durability
Cotton	Economical, natural low-allergic response, comfortable in hot weather.	Cold when wet, retains moisture, poor durability, becomes smaller and harsher with age	Progressively shrinks, doesn't hold shape, poor color retention, low strength, vulnerable to rot/mildew
Wool	Beautiful, stays warm when wet, low pilling	Dries slowly, heavy when wet, wide range of qualities	Progressively shrinks, less durable than synthetics, damaged by moths
Nylon	High durability, dyes in bright colors, dries quickly, wide variety of fabrics — monofilament or spun	Doesn't breathe well, builds static, poor moisture transport in monofilament, no muted colors, narrow range of comfort	Doesn't rot, high tensile strength, long wearing, good shape retention
Acrylic	High loft, economical	Pills easily, high flammability	Moderate to poor resilience, loses shape easily
Polyester	Fleece warm when wet, dyes well, good loft, moderate to expensive, good wicking properties	Some shrinkage after years of wear, fuses in high heat	Can't get rid of it
Polypropylene	Highest wicking, wide range of temperature comfort, warm when wet, nonabsorbent, high warmth to weight ratio	Requires washing each wearing for some people, some retain body odors, vulnerable to heat	Industrial fiber, strong, chemically resistant, high abrasion resistance

Care	Best Use	Avoid Use	Common Use
Easy, avoid hot washer and drier — rumples easily	Hot days, day trips, as sleep shirt when bathing isn't possible	*Don't use in winter* or temperatures below 70 degrees F. Poor for socks	T-shirts
Requires gentle, cool water wash, special soaps and hand wash for most	Fashion and warmth	When need clean, dry clothing in extreme sports	Sweaters, socks, traditional winter pants
Easy, quick dry, tolerates abuse, tolerates heat better than other synthetics	Water sports, durability in sock blends	In monofilament: when you need moisture transport and comfort over wide range of temperatures	Wind suits, sock blends, Lycra® shorts and tights, running and hiking shorts
Easy	Economical warmth	Socks cause perspiration. Don't use around flames	Socks, economical winter wear, beautiful Berber fleece
Easy, dries quickly, looks great	Fleece, base layer	Business suits	Fleece, knit base layer, cotton blends in shirts
Requires low temperature wash and dry	Base layer	In outerwear that can't be washed frequently	Moisture transport layer

2. Mitigating the intense effect of overheating and chilling during hill climbing and descending

3. Dealing with the ever-present wind, either self-generated or imposed on you by the elements

4. Reducing your sense of exposure to rain, snow, sleet, and hail

5. Limiting your exposure to the sun's harmful rays

The consequences of inadequate temperature regulation include nausea and dizziness from overheating, dehydration, painful sun and wind burns, and the misery of getting chilled or frightfully cold. This sounds like a great sport. Shall we take up chess? Fortunately, our bodies are remarkably adaptive to most of these conditions. When it is hot, perspiration provides cooling and is aided by increased circulation near the skin. When it is cold, our surface blood vessels constrict to conserve our energy and to help stabilize our core temperature. What can we do to augment our body's adaptive systems?

Riding in the Heat: Temperatures Above 80 Degrees Fahrenheit

Adequate hydration is the most important consideration when you are riding in hot weather. Your body's evaporative cooling system cannot work well if you are not drinking lots of water and energy beverages. Refer to the section on fluids in Chapter 7, pp. 288-291.

Your body requires one or two weeks to adapt to riding in temperatures over 80 degrees. Begin your conditioning with frequent rides that are shorter than you are conditioned for. If you live where there are dramatic changes in temperature, and gradual conditioning is not always possible, be conservative on those unexpected hot days. Decrease your distance and exertion level. If you are surprised by high temperatures during a cycling event, adjust your riding plan to avoid suffering from heat exhaustion or needing to be hooked up to an IV. Learn to recognize when extreme heat and humidity make it unwise to ride at all. It does take some courage to abandon an event ride that you have been anticipating for months. I vividly remember how disturbing it was to see one of our friends collapse on the pavement from heat stress while we were providing mechanical support for a summer benefit ride. To avoid these extremes, refer to the following chart to determine if you should cancel your ride and exercise indoors instead.

How to use the Heat Index Chart:

1. Locate the relative humidity (%) across the top.

2. Select the air temperature (F.) down the left side of the chart.

3. Follow across and down to find the *apparent temperature*. Apparent temperature is the combined index of heat and humidity. It is an index of the body's sensation of heat caused by the temperature and humidity. In other words, it is what the temperature "feels like" to the body.

4. Note: Exposure to full sunshine can increase heat index values by up to 15 degrees F.

Heat Index (Apparent Temperature)

Relative Humidity (%)

F	40	45	50	55	60	65	70	75	80	85	90	95	100
110	136												
108	130	137											
106	124	130	137										
104	119	124	131	137									
102	114	119	124	130	137								
100	109	114	118	124	129	136							
98	105	109	113	117	123	128	134						
96	101	104	108	112	116	121	126	132					
94	97	100	103	106	110	114	119	124	129	135			
92	94	96	99	101	105	108	112	116	121	126	131		
90	91	93	95	97	100	103	106	109	113	117	122	127	132
88	88	89	91	93	95	98	100	103	106	110	113	117	121
86	85	87	88	89	91	95	95	97	100	102	105	108	112
84	83	84	85	86	88	89	90	92	94	96	98	100	103
82	81	82	83	84	84	85	86	88	89	90	91	93	95
80	80	80	81	81	82	82	83	84	84	85	86	86	87

Air Temperature

With prolonged exposure and or physical activity

1.	Extreme Danger	2.	Danger	3.	Extreme Caution	4.	Caution
	Heatstroke or sunstroke likely		Sunstroke, muscle cramps, and/or heat exhaustion likely		Sunstroke, muscle cramps, and/or heat exhaustion possible		Fatigue possible

This Heat Index Chart provides general guidelines for accessing the potential severity of heat stress. Individual reactions to heat will vary. It should be remembered that heat illness can occur at lower temperatures than indicated on the chart. In addition, studies indicate that susceptibility to heat illness tends to increase with age.

Reprinted from National Weather Service 1998.

First of all, select light-colored clothing that will reflect the sun's rays. Next, change your riding time to the cooler part of the day or at night. It is hard to believe just how draining riding in temperatures about 90 degrees can be. On one ride at 6,000 feet and 95 degree temperatures, my family and I were so sapped by the heat that we rode as far one evening from five o'clock to seven o'clock as we had ridden the whole rest of the day. There are times when it is important to get up at five a.m., such as when you need to avoid searing temperatures and conserve energy to avoid stressing your body. You can catch a catnap during the heat of the day. We discovered that riding in the evening after the sun's intensity fades diminished the effects of extreme heat. Adequate lighting systems enable you to enjoy night rides. The wind may subside, and the moon and stars accompany you. For information on choosing lights refer to Chapter 9, pp. 368-370.

In arid climates, you can augment your perspiration by wetting your clothing. Your body regulates its temperature in hot weather by dilating blood vessels close to the skin to help cool your body's core. Wetting your clothes increases the temperature differential cooling your blood, which then cools your entire body more effectively. I hope you will experience such great relief from wet clothing that you will overcome the embarrassment of your semi-wet appearance. When I was a student living in southern Arizona, I commuted by bike in temperatures over 100 degrees. At these temperatures, it is simply impossible to drink enough fluids to protect yourself from heat exhaustion. I developed the technique of riding in wet or damp clothing. Because clothing dries so quickly at these temperatures, they must be rewetted often. Before setting out on my ride, I would soak my cotton T-shirt in a sink of warm water and then put it on. During the ride, I would stop and soak myself by standing in lawn sprinklers. If you are riding along rivers or streams, just jump in the stream and soak yourself. This technique works best where there are frequent water sources. If there is no water available, put two or three wet shirts in a plastic bag and put on a fresh wet one as each one dries. In this way, you can stave off dehydration and heat exhaustion. In fact, this technique can make riding in extreme heat highly amusing.

One summer afternoon I was returning from a three-day self-contained tour. The late afternoon temperatures were in the 80s, and I was pulling up a gradual hill with a strong head wind sweeping down off the foothills of the Rockies. I motivated myself to keep pushing by thinking of the cool dip I would take in Bear Creek at the foot of the next hill. I dropped down onto the bike path along the creek, lay my loaded bike over on the bank, and eased myself down into the cool mountain stream. I could instantly feel the vitality returning to my body. When I was completely cooled down and with my long pants and Sun Precautions® shirt clinging unflatteringly to my body, I climbed up the bank to my bike. Just as I emerged, a man came riding along the bike path. Imagining that I had crashed into the stream, he asked with alarm, "Are you all right?" "Oh yes, I'm quite refreshed," I replied with satisfaction. I'm sure I missed seeing him rolling his eyes in

Not dead, just cooling off. I enjoy my favorite cooling technique for hot weather riding.

disbelief as he rode on.

Another rapid cooling technique that is especially useful for commuting in warm or hot weather is to run cold water over your wrists. As soon as you get to your destination and before the flush of body heat makes you perspire profusely, go directly to a restroom and put your wrists under cold running water for several minutes. A gentleman businessman who commuted everywhere by bike in his fine business suits used this technique to maintain his professional dignity. Jerry called it the three-minute shower.

In temperatures above 70 degrees, cotton can be a good choice. It absorbs more water than synthetics and dries more slowly, absorbing more heat. However, these very characteristics are also the reasons why cotton should *not* be worn below 70 degrees. A cotton T-shirt saturated with sweat can put you at risk of chill if the temperature drops suddenly.

Last and of great importance is the need to protect yourself from sun and wind burn. This is always a hard sell due to the social dictum that tan is beautiful. With an ever-increasing number of people having to deal with skin cancer, the idea of sun protection is gaining in popularity. **Complete clothing cover**, including head and neck, provides better protection for your skin from ultraviolet (UV) rays and wind damage than any sunscreen lotion developed to date. Even when you're in temperatures higher than 80 degrees, you can have more comfort, be better protected, and stay cleaner by covering your body with clothes rather than using the popular bare skin and sunscreen approach. Why is that? Specially designed, lightweight fabrics cut out more damaging UV rays than lotions. Lotions impair the function of your sweat glands interfering with your cooling system. Lotions also attract dust and grime, producing the gooey mess on your skin familiar to most cyclists. You will not need these messy lotions when you wear long-sleeved shirts with high collars and long pants. Full cover also minimizes your exposure to dust and grime and blots off perspiration. Air flows through your garments and keeps your cooling system working.

Full-cover clothing protects against UV, dust, and insects. It blends in with other outdoor enthusiasts and is quite suitable for restaurant and errands along the ride route. The unique sun protective gloves (SPF 30) are designed by Glacier® for fishing but are also ideal for cycling.

The air flowing over your body when you ride lifts the loose-fitting clothes off your back and provides you with the sensation of riding nude in the shade! If you are dousing yourself with cooling water, your full cover will also retain more water and contribute further to your cooling.

I know this outfit is not sexy but neither is skin cancer. Surely the long robes of desert people around the world give us evidence that clothing is good protection against the sun *and* the heat. Several manufacturers are making sun protective sports clothing that is sensible, attractive, and durable. Select light-colored clothes that reflect the sun and are highly visible. Since these clothes are made of synthetic fibers, they are great for touring because they wash clean even when quite soiled and dry quickly. One of the companies that makes these synthetic fiber clothes, Sun Precautions®, was established by Shawn Hughes, who survived malignant melanoma at age 26. Most cycling jerseys and athletic clothing offer less than 10 SPF when dry and less than 5 SPF when damp or wet. The fabric developed by Sun Precautions®, Solumbra®, is so effective in sun protection that it is regulated by the Federal Drug Administration as a medical device. It provides 30+ SPF all day from both UVA and UVB even when it is wet. It is lightweight, breathable, and comfortable even at high exertion. (Edmund R. Burke, "The Burning Question," *Adventure Cyclist*, June 2002, p.12, 13) If you sew, you can also make your own fine riding clothes. An unexpected advantage of these unobtrusive clothes over traditional Lycra® is that you blend in with the locals. This is especially important during international bicycle tours. Wearing functional, ordinary clothes helps you experience a closer connection to other cultures by making you more approachable.

Protecting your face and lips from sun and wind is another challenge. Mouth breathing in dry, hot weather can cause severe lip burn and cracking. For multiple-day tours, begin applying lip balm on the first day. Painful damage can appear suddenly and not heal well as long as exposure continues. Cheeks and nose need protection from direct sun as well as from the reflection off your glasses. One creative tourist fashioned a guard for nose and cheeks out of leather and secured it under the bridge of her glasses. Again, not flattering, but remarkably functional.

In arid climates where sun exposure is excessive, you will be wise to avoid riding between ten a.m. and three p.m. when the sun's rays are most damaging. High altitude further intensifies sun damage because there is less atmosphere to protect you from those rays. If your skin is especially vulnerable to burning or to skin cancer, you can get many scientifically documented methods of sun protection from Buck Tilton and Roger G. Cox's *Ozone, UV and Your Health, 50 Ways to Save your Skin*.

Quality glasses will protect your precious eyes from damaging UV rays as well as from insects, dust, and flying debris. Because you may lose control of your bike when you are reacting to the discomfort of something caught in your eye, glasses can help you avoid crashing. Invest in glasses with wrap-around clear lenses that reduce air flow across your pupils. Clear lenses will make the glasses useful in limited light conditions. Interchangeable lenses convert one pair of glasses to varied light conditions and night riding. This means you will have to shop carefully to find glasses that conform to the contours of your face. It is worth the investment of time and money to prevent impaired vision and reduce the chances of crashing. Wearing goggles and using anti-fog compounds can help keep your glasses clear in rain and snow but slowing down when visibility is poor will help you avoid mishaps.

Dealing with Precipitation

Preparedness

Most riders are reluctant to invest in quality rainwear until they are caught out in a cold rain with no protection and become chilled to the bone. In climates where rain is usually cold, routinely carrying rainwear will give you peace of mind: you know you are prepared and can thoroughly enjoy riding even when it looks like it could rain. Riders frequently postpone a ride when the weather is uncertain. However, with your rainwear, you can ride in spite of threatening weather. Not only is this more fun than shifting to Plan B but it can enable you to ride many more miles every year.

Realistic Expectations for Comfort in Rainwear

Let's take a realistic look at comfort in rainwear. If you would like to stay dry and comfortable on a rainy day, you should probably stay in your living room. It really is possible to ride in the rain and stay warm. Because it is difficult to stay dry during long periods of riding in the rain, I see the function of rainwear as keeping the water on your body *warm*. This is particularly true for your legs because pants just can't vent well enough to prevent perspiration from accumulating on your legs. Even in cool temperatures, you may feel clammy under rainwear. Wearing a wicking layer next to your skin will increase your comfort especially on your arms and legs. You will do well to select a rain jacket with a wicking mesh lining in the sleeves. Even so, while touring on rainy days you will have to stoically disregard your clammy condition. Take solace in the scenery and in your fine fitness level.

Experiment in your climate to determine what is comfortable. Although in warm, humid climates you may not need any rainwear in summer, a sudden rainstorm in mountainous areas can cause hypothermia. Be prepared and always carry what you need to be safe and to have fun.

Tips on Optimizing Rainwear Performance

As with any tool, rainwear requires some skill to enjoy it. Adjust your riding speed to reduce perspiration and wind-driven water penetration. Usually the difficulty of seeing through your wet eyewear will cause you to slow down. Open garment vents as soon as you start warming up. Test any garment before buying it to determine whether you can open and close the vents with one hand while riding. Rainwear designed for hiking often hides zippers under Velcro®-secured flaps, making it necessary to stop to adjust the vents and the front opening. Be sure that the front opening allows you to open from both the top and the bottom while riding to optimize venting for various wind and rain conditions.

Guidelines for Selecting Rainwear

The most important step in rain protection is selecting a jacket appropriate for your wet weather riding style. In spite of manufacturers' claims for micropore-breathable fabrics, they do not protect you fully from wind and rain nor breathe adequately for the highly aerobic demands of cycling. Microfiber jackets provide excellent wind and moderate water protection but they will not keep you dry in a steady rain. Microfiber garments do a good job of protecting you from the risks of chill during showers. Jackets made of coated pack cloth with venting designed into the structure of the jacket are the most economical, reliable, and compact protection from heavy rain. If you like to tour and continue to ride even when it pours, look for these design features: vents across the back, zip-pits under the arms and down the sleeves, Velcro® tabs at the wrists so you can regulate air flow, and a stand-up collar lined with polyester fleece to protect your neck and prevent water entry. Avoid jackets with elastic at the wrists that prevent air flow up the sleeves. Make sure the collar design actually prevents water from running off your helmet and down your back inside the jacket. Use the venting at the neck opening as your final venting tool if you begin to overheat. Burley Design Cooperative® jackets are designed, tested, and manufactured in rainy western Oregon. An outstanding value, they are thoughtfully

The Noj® head cover allows freedom of movement and gives the best protection from water running down your neck in rainy or cold weather.

researched and developed over many years' experience. Rain Shield® lacks sophisticated design and fit but the jackets are made from a high tech, inexpensive material that breathes well while providing water protection. Their jackets and pants offer an excellent, affordable weather guard for fair-weather riders.

What other rain garments should you consider in addition to a good jacket? A helmet cover will make an important contribution to your comfort in cold rain. The numerous vents in helmets make them poor protection in inclement weather. Have you ever gotten home and taken off your helmet to discover little piles of snow on your head, exactly the shape of each vent? Or how about the feeling of cold water trickling down your scalp under your helmet? A great invention for keeping precipitation from running through your helmet and down your neck is the Noj® head cover. It was developed for motorcyclists and adapted for bicyclists. This "little tent" sheds water off your head and neck and will keep your head and torso dry in heavy rain or snow. If you prefer using a hooded jacket, be sure you can secure the hood so it does not impair your vision when you turn to look back at traffic.

Now your upper body is protected from precipitation, but the water runs off your jacket and soaks your hips until your wet buttocks are soggy on the saddle. This is not much fun! Each level of protection you add requires another level below it to shed the water running down. Once you add rain pants, you will need shoe covers to prevent water from running off your pants directly into your shoes. How you cover your legs depends strictly on temperature and on the duration of your ride. As already mentioned, it is difficult to vent pants adequately and they get pretty clammy inside. If it is cold, and you are at risk of serious chill, use coated, pack-cloth rain pants and put them on as soon as it starts raining. For warmer temperatures, you may find microfiber pants are a good compromise because they breathe well and provide wind protection even when they are wet. Other riders find it more satisfactory to wear middle- to heavyweight polyester or polypropylene tights and just get wet. A waterproof saddle cover will help reduce soggy-butt syndrome. Commercial saddle covers can be bought but a plastic grocery bag is cheap, readily available, and can be tied on with the handles.

Shoe covers will serve you well in rain and cold. Burley Design® has created shoe covers that are lightweight, are low in bulk, and keep your feet and ankles reasonably warm. Select a size that fits your cycling shoes snugly and then, if you ride with clip-in pedals, cut out a hole in the bottom just the size of your cleats. Obviously, water will come through the hole but because these covers are wind-proof, you can be comfortable at moderate temperatures.

Burley® rainwear with Noj® head cover and homemade rain mitts are my favorite rainwear.

Neoprene is commonly used for shoe covers. Reserve your use of neoprene clothing for water sports and avoid it for cycling. It traps all your sweat and makes you vulnerable to chilling. It is a poor insulator.

Over-mitts will keep your hands warm above 50 degrees but mitts and gloves have so many seams, the water comes through. Give special attention to hand protection because cold, wet, stiff fingers can't reliably operate your control lever. In temperatures between 40 and 60 degrees, you can wear loose-fitting rubber dishwashing gloves over polypropylene liner gloves. At warmer temperatures, wear hand covers that keep you warm and let your hands get wet.

What does all this mean in practical terms? Commuters and touring cyclists will be wise to carry a full rain suit, helmet cover (or Noj®), mitts, and shoe covers whenever they ride. When unexpected rain or snow strikes, you can protect yourself with this extra layer of clothing. Inclement weather is fun when you are prepared. If you are a day fitness rider, *always* carry a jacket. You will appreciate this extra layer on long chilling descents after having gotten sweaty on the ascent. Emma suggests that if you perspire profusely on a climb, and your jacket is wet inside, at the summit, before you descend, pull your zipped jacket off over your head and put it on inside out. It will protect you from chill on the descent and will be dry when you reach the bottom. Then you can put it on right-side out again and proceed in comfort. All riders can ensure increased comfort by making a habit of carrying a microfiber jacket (and pants in cooler weather) in their seat bags.

Wind Alert!

Why is wind so unpopular among cyclists? The direct answer is that it makes us work harder, it can make it difficult to control our bikes, and in severe cases, it can put us at risk of injury. Wind is psychologically unsettling and scatters our minds. Since we erroneously assume the normal weather condition is calm air, it is especially unnerving that we have no control of the wind's presence, intensity, or direction. Strong winds can also be frightening. Not only can high winds blow us over, they can carry dust, debris, and large objects that could injure us. I vividly remember the challenge of riding through dust devils in Arizona and trying to maintain control of my bike while riding with my eyes closed to protect them from the wind-driven sand, tumbleweeds, and debris.

Those of you who live in regions where wind is uncommon, please bear with me while we consider how to deal with the wind. Understanding the wind will make it less frustrating to ride in it. Wind does deserve healthy respect from cyclists and since wind in the foothills of the Rockies and the neighboring plains is common and often intense, I equip myself with an anemometer (wind gage) and have fun observing my response to wind and measuring its speed. My new understanding of wind has greatly improved my attitude toward riding in it.

The first step in understanding wind is to distinguish between self-generated wind and wind imposed by weather. When the air is calm, **our bodies slicing through the static air perceive our own movement as wind of the same speed we are riding**! The only time the air feels calm is when we are riding with a tail wind of the same speed as our riding speed. Before you become bored with this self-evident observation, let me assure you that acknowledging this truth will help you realize how often you perceive that you are riding into the wind when in fact the air speed is negligible. On the other hand, the cumulative effect of a rider's speed and wind speed can be dramatic. You set out in a pleasant breeze of five mph. You then turn a corner and head directly into the wind. At your 15 mph riding speed, you are now in a 20 mph head wind. Is this an unpleasantly windy day? No, you are just feeling the effects of your own speed. Confirm this by looking at the passing trees and grasses when you're riding to see if they are actively moving. This awareness can greatly reduce your impatience with the wind. You can further reduce your discontent with wind by studying its behavior where you commonly ride.

First, purchase an anemometer. If you are willing to spend $70 to $80, Kestrel® makes a fine, digital meter that is convenient and easy to use. For less than $20, you can purchase a Dwyer® wind meter like those used by the U.S. Forest Service fire fighters. Either of these will tuck into your jersey pocket so you can begin to calibrate your sense of wind speed. I discovered that before I started carrying a wind meter I had systematically over-estimated wind speed. Consider your immediate terrain when evaluating the wind speed. Are you on the leeward or windward side of a ridge? Are you mid-slope or on a valley floor?

We glance at thermometers to help us select appropriate clothing before a ride. We need to be able to quantitatively evaluate wind, too, because it plays such a prominent role in cycling. How often have you stood in the comfort of your living room, looked out the window, and concluded that this sunny day requires only lightweight clothing. Once outside and exposed to the wind, you discover you are quite inadequately dressed. Why not measure the temperature *and* the wind, accurately accessing its speed, gusts, and direction, and then decide whether to ride, where to ride, and what to wear. After that, accept responsibility for your decision, determine to make the best of the wind, and befriend it as your companion.

After you have measured the wind, what can you conclude? If you are a casual, fair-weather rider, you will probably want to exercise inside if the wind speed is greater than 15 mph. At wind speeds less than 20 mph, the challenge is mostly psychological. Remember to use your gears and maintain your cadence just as if you were riding hills. For more adventurous riders, safety becomes an issue between 25 to 30 mph. At these speeds, it can be challenging to maintain control of your bike. If you are planning a road ride, you will also have to consider the erratic behavior of motorists and your ability to ride a straight line on a narrow shoulder. Try selecting a route that is somewhat protected. Consider canyons, valleys, gullies, or forested areas.

If you are caught mid-ride by unexpected winds that make it difficult to control your bike, it is advisable to take temporary refuge, discontinue your ride, or return home as directly as possible. In many regions, the wind's direction and strength are so capricious, it is difficult to decide what to do. In any case, adjust your pace and shorten your distance. Let go of your irritation with this change of events and befriend the wind by carefully observing its effects. Pull out your trusty wind meter and measure the speed. What is the prevailing direction and how often does it change? How does it sound in the trees, power lines, and grasses? What are the birds doing? Are they playing on the currents or have they taken refuge? These observations can distract you from dwelling on your increased exertion and efforts to control your bike.

Another trick to help you enjoy your ride is to cover your ears to diminish the noise that constantly reminds you that you are working against the wind. For years, each spring and fall, I went to Pawnee National Grasslands to ride with friends. On the open prairie, the wind howls most of the time. We were delighted to discover that when we put on our ear bands, we could enjoy riding in the wind when the weather was otherwise pleasant. I often fantasize about taking a self-contained tour on the prairies with no other route plan than to keep the wind at my back. Every time the wind would change direction, I would take the next available road or trail heading out of the wind. My only deterrent is finding someone to pick me up in Kansas and take me home at the end of the tour.

When the wind is powerful, and no alternative is available but to ride home, another wind-taming technique is to focus on each pedal stroke as the unit of forward progress. My house is located on a rise in the foothills of the Rockies where high winds are common. This means that when I ride home from the east, I usually ride into a head wind for the last two miles. In the winter, when the high winds are driving snow, I have learned to bend down low, sight off the curb for direction, and focus on each pedal stroke instead of the total distance left to cover.

Be sure to refer to the wind chill index chart on page 355 to help you evaluate the effects of wind during cold weather. During windy warm weather you are more vulnerable to dehydration so be sure to drink adequately while you are distracted by the wind.

Riding in Temperatures Between 40 and 60 Degrees Fahrenheit

This is a good temperature range to start adapting to cool-weather riding. I think that many riders stop riding as weather cools because they fail to adapt their clothing and end up getting cold. Try these pointers:

1. Wear protection over your entire body. All body parts work better when they are warm. It is faulty to wear only a jacket to maintain your core temperature and leave your legs exposed. Your core temperature is strongly influenced by heat lost through your extremities. Your legs have a large surface area relative to their mass and will affect your temperature dramatically in cool weather if you don't cover them. Your legs do not sense the cold as acutely as your torso does, fooling you into thinking they are comfortable. Riding with inadequate leg cover is like riding without warming up gradually. Warm muscles work better so do your legs a favor! Compare the number of layers you have on your torso with the layers on your legs. If you will add layers to your legs and remove them from your torso, making the protection nearly equal, you will discover that you perspire less, reducing the risk of chill. Additionally, your legs will work better while you stay comfortably warm.

    I learned this lesson dramatically on my first bike tour. The only leg cover I had was my blue jeans. During the heat of the day, I enjoyed the freedom of riding in shorts. When the late afternoon temperatures dropped, and fatigue and hunger set in, I became tired and uncomfortable. I resisted putting on my stiff, confining jeans. When I finally gave in, I was amazed and delighted to discover new stamina and lifted spirits. I felt like I had new legs.

2. Lightweight pants will keep your legs performing well and will reduce the risk of injury. You can choose either loose-fitting pants or traditional tights. Select polyester or spun nylon (avoid monofilament nylon) for breathable moisture management. Always wear shorts under your tights so you can remove the tights when you warm up. Over-heating is as detrimental to pleasure and health as chilling. If you wear loose-fitting shorts, wear loose-fitting pants rather than tights to avoid the scarecrow look. Some riders wear Lycra® tights or long underwear under loose-fitting shorts but this makes it more tedious to remove your leg coverings in public. There are many types of polyester pants that provide excellent moisture management. They may be tights or loose-fitting, spun woven fabric, or fleece. Test the wind resistance of any pants before buying them by placing the fabric over your mouth and trying to blow air through it. Knits usually lack wind resistance due to their loose construction. Woven fabrics can be tightly constructed and highly wind resistant. In fleece, look for Malden®'s 100-weight. They make two types of fleece:

stretch and basic. You can differentiate these visually. The stretch fleece looks fuzzy and has *no* wind resistance. It is a poor choice for cycling because it provides no warmth without a wind-breaking layer over it. The basic 100-weight Malden® fleece looks more like felt and has excellent wind resistance. Laminated fleeces that claim to be wind resistant vary in effectiveness. If your insulative layer of fleece has good wind resistance, you can simply take off your wind layer when you begin to warm up and still have adequate warmth from your wind-resistant insulative layer.

Leg warmers with shorts and arm warmers are popular for moderately cool temperatures. They enable you to adjust your leg and arm coverings without stopping. Just shove them down around your ankles and wrists when you warm up and pull them back up if you cool down.

3. Use a single-layer wind jacket. If it is made of coated fabric, adjust the venting frequently to prevent perspiration build-up and eventual chilling. For temperatures above 25 degrees, avoid jackets with insulative linings that prevent you from incrementally adjusting your temperature.

4. Carry polypropylene or polyester liner gloves. They require little space to carry and are thin enough to fit under your fingerless cycling gloves. Cold hands make it difficult to control your bike and to relax.

5. Carry an ear band or Dog Earz®. These convenient ear covers attach to your helmet straps with Velcro® and keep the wind off your ears without affecting your hearing. They can quickly be secured or removed as temperatures change.

6. Guard against over-heating by adjusting your neck opening and removing or adding layers as frequently as is necessary to maintain a constant body temperature. Over-heating not only makes you sweat and risk chilling it can also cause nausea or loss of stamina.

Dog Earz® provides convenient warmth and wind protection for moderately cool temperatures.

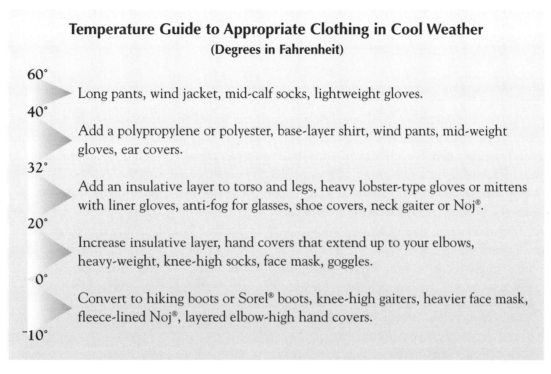

Temperature Guide to Appropriate Clothing in Cool Weather
(Degrees in Fahrenheit)

60°
Long pants, wind jacket, mid-calf socks, lightweight gloves.

40°
Add a polypropylene or polyester, base-layer shirt, wind pants, mid-weight gloves, ear covers.

32°
Add an insulative layer to torso and legs, heavy lobster-type gloves or mittens with liner gloves, anti-fog for glasses, shoe covers, neck gaiter or Noj®.

20°
Increase insulative layer, hand covers that extend up to your elbows, heavy-weight, knee-high socks, face mask, goggles.

0°
Convert to hiking boots or Sorel® boots, knee-high gaiters, heavier face mask, fleece-lined Noj®, layered elbow-high hand covers.

–10°

Climates and individual differences vary greatly. These guidelines are for arid, sunny climates. For other conditions, wear additional clothing for wind, high humidity, predominantly downhill riding, low stamina level, or if you are inclined to be cold. Install an outdoor thermometer on the north side of your dwelling so you can base your clothing on your local temperature readings each day. Use weather forecasts as a form of entertainment and not as a guide to clothing selection.

Riding in Below-freezing Temperatures

If you've never ridden in the cold, you're probably wondering why you would want to start. Here are several reasons:
1. To maintain your fitness level year round
2. To embrace the winter and its unique beauty
3. To improve your bike handling skills if snow is part of the fun
4. To feel the exhilaration of freedom while combating cabin fever
5. To maintain your routine of commuting by bike

You will need to invest in additional, high-tech, cycling-specific clothing. You may already have some appropriate clothing from other winter sports. The unique demands of cycling, which are highly aerobic and generate lots of heat and wind, will probably require some specialized garments that breathe well. Cycling appropriate gloves or mitts are especially important to provide adequate warmth but also permit some dexterity to operate your control levers.

Layer From the Inside Out

Dressing in layers means that each layer can be designed to perform a specific function. This system reduces bulk and at the same time increases your freedom of movement. If for each layer you have two choices to select from, you can create comfort with a minimum number of garments and you can adapt to changing conditions during any ride by adjusting your layers. In any climate, you will want to build your clothing protection on a three-layer system: next to skin, mid-layer, and outer layer.

Begin selecting your clothing for any ride from the base layer out. When cycling, you must protect your entire body. When riding in below freezing temperatures, you should be able to choose from as many layers of clothing for your arms, legs, and extremities as you can for your torso. Uniform clothing on your torso and legs will make your entire body uniformly comfortable without overheating your torso. In all aspects of comfort in cold

Angie models ideal layering technique: a base layer of polyester with zip-neck, 100-weight Malden® fleece insulation, and wind and water resistant outer layer. All together it is lightweight, not confining, and can be adjusted to regulate changing temperatures.

weather, remember that less is more. The goal is to stay warm while sweating as little as possible. That means three well-chosen layers on legs and torso will give you more comfort than a heavy bulky jacket and lightweight leg covering.

The **base layer** or garment that is next to your skin is most important. To conserve heat, it should be form-fitting and clinging to your skin. Its task is to conserve heat and move perspiration away from your skin because the same sweat that is so vital to cooling in warm temperatures can cause chilling during cold weather. Transporting moisture away from your skin is essential to cool-weather comfort. Polypropylene and polyester are the high performance fibers for this layer. Because they are totally non-absorbent, polypropylene yarns transport moisture better and dry faster than any other fiber. However, they are thermally sensitive and require special care during both the manufacture process and during home care. If you are fortunate enough to own polypropylene base layers, launder and dry them with gentle heat. Polyester base layers run a close second in performance, are more readily available, and easier to care for. Both fibers are very durable and worth the investment. Cotton should be completely excluded from any layer of clothing at temperatures below 70 degrees. Because it holds a lot of moisture within the fiber, it does not transport moisture. It will not dry in the cold, it's heavy, and it's non-elastic. Resist the temptation to use it simply because it is cheap. Although wool is being promoted as a base layer, it takes hours to dry and can cause chilling during prolonged exposure to low temperatures. You will do better for economy and performance to use synthetics.

As a regular bicycle commuter, Ken has chosen more classic cycle wear for cooler temperatures. The insulated jacket and tights are easy to slip on after work for the night ride home. His wrap-around clear-lensed eyewear protects his eyes from cold air and dust and therefore help him see well after dark.

Insulation is the primary task of the **mid-layer**. It also needs to be absorbent to accept moisture from the base layer. Polyester fleeces excel for this layer by trapping warm air in their loft. You can choose from many weights of fleece for different temperatures. Malden Mills® is the developer of this revolutionary fabric and continues to make superior quality. Wool was the standard for insulation for many decades and is still acceptable as an alternative to polyester. You will find that it is heavier and requires hours at warm temperatures to dry. Both polyester fleece and wool continue to insulate even when they are wet. Traditional cycle clothing is often too form-fitting to provide adequate warmth at moderate exertion levels in below-freezing temperatures. **Remember: thickness is warmth.**

The **outer layer** protects you from the elements. It must keep out precipitation and wind and allow moisture to escape, while keeping the trapped warm air inside. Again, disregard manufacturers' claims that one fabric does all these tasks equally well. The better protection from precipitation and wind a fabric gives, the less breathable (able to release moisture) it is. Designing the garment with vents is the best way to release moisture but remember that precious warm air also escapes with the moisture. The best compromise seems to be achieved by using a water-repellent fabric in garments designed with strategically located vents.

Once you have all these layers on, you may find three layers of seams under your crotch are quite uncomfortable. You will be wise to re-evaluate your saddle to eliminate the pressure from these seams.

Be Prepared for Change

Meteorologists demonstrate every day how unpredictable the weather is. It is certain folly to leave home confident that the weather will remain constant or even follow the predictions. Have more fun by being prepared for change! Dressing with three layers makes it easy to remove one layer if the temperature warms up. Where will you put it? You can tie it around your waist or use a large seat bag or rack and pack. Tying clothing to your bike or body can cause a serious crash if the clothing tangles up with the moving parts of your bike. As you increase the length of your rides and you extend your riding season, you will need a secure way of carrying extra clothes.

In addition to adapting to the weather, you will need to remove clothing as your body heats up. The following circumstances make you vulnerable to overheating:

1. Warming up at the beginning of any ride
2. Increasing your exertion level while riding from a valley filled with cold air to warmer surrounding hills
3. Subsiding winds
4. Sun shining through the clouds
5. Benefiting from the heating quality of food you have recently eaten, as it moves through your digestive tract and warms your body

You will need to add warmth to counteract cooling under these circumstances:

1. Decreasing your exertion level
2. Descending
3. Expending all your energy supplies
4. Eating too much and diverting all your energy to digestive processes
5. Increasing winds
6. Sun moving behind cloud cover

With all these variables, it is foolish to think you could ride all day with the same layers of clothing and not suffer discomfort. So don't be caught unprepared — tuck your lightweight, compact, microfiber jacket and pants into a pack

Summary of Clothing Tips for Cold Weather Riding

- Layer from the inside out.

- First, wick moisture away from your skin, then insulate to retain body heat, and finally protect yourself from wind and snow.

- Disperse perspiration away from your body.

- Choose clothing with vents and let perspiration escape.

- Avoid constricting clothing that diminishes your warming blood flow.

- Avoid cotton in any layer in temperatures below 70 degrees.

- Give special attention to your extremities, especially your head.

or pocket. Their added warmth will help you tolerate several-degree temperature changes and light precipitation.

Adjusting your layers for comfort does require frequent stops. These stops give you the opportunity to thoughtfully evaluate your condition. Are you hungry? Are you pushing yourself beyond a sustainable exertion level? I find it all too easy during cold weather rides to become preoccupied by the sand, ice, and snow on the road; erratic traffic behavior; increased air pollution; and the complexity of clothing layers and glasses fogging. With these distractions, I lose touch with my condition and need to use conscious breathing and frequent stops to ensure that I am still having fun and to respond to my comfort and stamina needs. So rather than resisting stopping to adjust clothing, use these stops to improve the quality of your riding experience.

How to Regulate Your Body Temperature

When you ride at temperatures above 20 degrees, the challenge is regulating your temperature rather than keeping warm. To avoid overheating, ride at a sustainable energy level. At temperatures below freezing, you will need to adjust your concept of "comfortable." Your body will feel different than it does when you ride in 70-degrees weather: your core temperature should be warm but your skin should feel cool and clammy.

It can take three to five miles to warm-up thoroughly if you leave home without an indoor warm-up. Warming up in the protection of your home makes it easier to go out in the cold and may eliminate the need to stop at the beginning of your ride to adjust your clothing. The sun salutation and the elephant are efficient and enjoyable warm-ups. Review these exercises on pp. 102-108.

It requires about two weeks of regular activity in the cold (or heat) for your body to adapt. You can accelerate the process by keeping your home thermostat at 55 or 60 degrees. Try wearing your fine fleece indoors and enjoy lower utility bills.

You can easily regulate your temperature by using your body's radiators: your midriff, neck, and head. Select zip necks that you can open and close while riding and install long zipper pulls that you can grasp while wearing bulky gloves or mitts. Air blown down your neck onto your midriff has a splendid cooling effect, and you can open and close each layer to achieve exactly the appropriate amount of cooling. The body loses about 40 percent of its heat through the head. Although some would consider this a disadvantage, cyclists can use this to their advantage to help regulate heat gain as well as heat loss. It is a good idea to add an ear band and liner gloves to your "always carry" list. Also carry a variety of head covers for different conditions. Choose from an ear band, an under-helmet skull cap, neck gaiter, Maxit® head gaiter, face mask, Noj®, and helmet cover. Refer to the section on "Protecting Your Extremities" on the next page.

Perspiration Management

In cooler temperatures when you must wear more clothes, perspiration management is vital to avoid getting chilled. First, pace yourself to minimize sweating. This will ensure that your base layer does not become saturated but continues to transport moisture away from your body effectively. Use your "neck vent" and add or remove layers to avoid overheating and sweating profusely. If the terrain is demanding, and you think you must ride at high energy levels to get where you are going, shift into easy gears and use conscious breathing. These measures help your body run cooler and mitigate the negative effects of higher exertion levels.

The release of moisture from among your layers is critically important because moisture trapped inside your outer layer creates your own humid microclimate. You know how much more penetrating humid cold is than dry cold. Let the vapor-saturated air out of your clothes so you can benefit from as low humidity as the climate permits. Wet clothing next to your skin puts you at risk of severe chilling if you have to stop, if the wind increases, or if the temperature drops. If you still own a "low-tech" uncoated, rip stop nylon windbreaker, it will serve well on cold days when precipitation is unlikely. Garments without coating allow complete escape of vapor and can make you considerably warmer.

Let your perspiration remind you that you are using fluids. Drink systematically while riding in cold weather. The body's thirst mechanism responds poorly in the cold, and you will need to remember to drink in relation to your exertion level. Certainly do not restrict your fluid intake to avoid having to urinate in the cold.

Protecting Your Extremities

Have you ever noticed that it is more difficult to keep your neck, head, hands, feet, and lower back warm? These areas have little body insulation but abundant blood circulating near the surface. Without careful protection, your blood cools off as it passes through these uninsulated areas, reaching your hands, feet, head, and lower back at a temperature that is too low to keep them comfortable. By clothing these areas with adequate insulation, you may be surprised to experience warm extremities for the first time.

Many riders mistakenly think they have poor circulation in their hands and feet due to a protective temperature-regulating mechanism. When your body is at risk from too much heat loss, it preserves heat by altering your blood circulation pattern. Blood vessels in your extremities contract, which reduces flow and keeps the blood closer to your vital organs to maintain your core temperature. For this reason, your torso will feel warm while your extremities are uncomfortably cold. Avoid being fooled by this important survival mechanism and focus on better insulation on your *entire* body. Add thin layers until you are comfortable. Be careful not to add so much more clothing that you perspire profusely.

The **lower back** is easily protected with long-tailed shirts and jackets. These will overlap your leg covers and give double protection to your lower back. Be sure waist bands are not so tight that they interfere with circulation in the area.

Hand and wrist protection is available at reasonable cost down to about 28 degrees. Remember that the function of fingerless cycling gloves is to protect your palms from abrasion in case of a crash and to offer some shock absorption. They provide little warmth since the fingertips and wrists are exposed. For this reason, the liner glove is essential in cycling hand wear. Made of thin polyester or polypropylene, they are useful in rain and cool temperatures. If your fingerless gloves fit loosely, you can put the liner underneath for an unexpected chill. In temperatures below 40 degrees, you can wear your liners under heavy mitts. When you need to remove a mitt for increased dexterity to adjust clothing or eat a snack, a liner glove will prevent you from exposing your bare hand to the cold.

Next in warmth is a mid-weight, full-fingered glove with reasonable bulk to provide warmth. They too should be padded on the palm for insulation. Usually this weight of glove has a ribbed cuff. Stretch out the cuffs of your gloves and jackets so that the double layer of ribbed cuffs does not constrict the flow of blood into your hands. In fact, check all your hand cover layers for constriction that can impair circulation and cause chilling. Be sure that your handlebars and bar ends are insulated with padded tape or grips. Gripping a cold handlebar draws the heat directly out of your hands.

When temperatures are below freezing, wear well-insulated mitts or lobster mitts with long, insulated cuffs. Gloves isolate your fingers, preventing them from retaining and sharing their warmth. Fit your heavy mitts loosely enough to accommodate liner gloves inside. Further warmth can be added with wind-proof, water-resistant over mitts. Waterproof hand covers sound good but they make your hands sweat profusely.

Hand protection needs to extend over your forearms up to your elbows in temperatures below 20 to 25 degrees. When your forearms are adequately insulated, your blood will stay warm into your wrists and hands and keep them comfortable. Many mountaineering mitts that are warm enough at these temperatures do not allow the dexterity you need to control your brakes and gears. You may find that the best solution is to make custom mitts yourself. I have made

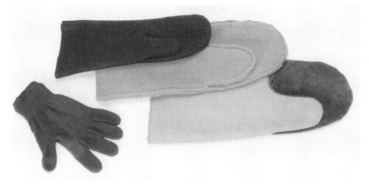

Homemade, elbow-length mitts can be specially made to layer together or separately to achieve the desired warmth.

layered mitts that are quite comfortable and practical between zero and 25 degrees. The base layer is my commercially available liner glove. Then comes a mitt of wind-stopper fleece stitched so the wind-stopper layer is toward the outside. The third layer is 300-weight Malden® fleece, topped off by Cordura® mitts with thick, suede leather palms. Each layer is progressively larger so that they fit loosely over the inner layers. Because they are not stitched together, each layer can be separated from the others to adjust for temperature.

There are lots of functional products available for **protecting your head and neck**. Be sure that these are thin enough to fit under your helmet without constricting circulation in your scalp. One great feature of the adjustable helmet fitting systems is that you can easily change the inside circumference of your helmet to accommodate various head coverings. Well-ventilated helmets are fine in summer but you will want to cover the vents in cooler temperatures. Rain covers work well for this purpose. If you cover some vents with duct tape, be advised that manufacturers warn that adhesives can cause your helmet shell material to deteriorate. The simplest head coverings are Dog Earz®, ear bands, and skull caps that cover your ears, all of which are lightweight, economical, and easy to carry. If your helmet provides adequate warmth for your head, neck gaiters can be adequate and have several benefits for cyclists. They allow you to adjust them with one hand while you are riding whereas face masks require you to stop, remove your gloves, helmet, eyewear, and face mask, and then put them all back again. Neck gaiters can also help to warm cold air before you inhale it. Use a fleece neck gaiter thick enough to retain some warmth and pull it up over your mouth. Then you can breathe through it and not choke on the cold air. The Duster® is a neck gaiter with a zipper for temperature regulation, and you can also let the flaps cover your cheeks while you breathe through its V-shaped opening.

For more complete head cover, there are several choices. You will want to consider

The Duster® is a zippered neck gaiter and is fully adjustable under your helmet and around your cheeks without having to remove your helmet.

The Maxit® gaiter is so versatile that it is another "always carry" item. Shelley models it as an ear band, head cover/neck gaiter, and a face mask. Made of polypro Lycra®, it is remarkably warm for its weight.

their protective value *and* how confining they are. Select clothing that does not interfere with your vision or freedom of movement for watching traffic. The lightest weight for convenient carrying is the Maxit® gaiter. It is a tube of polypropylene Lycra® that can be worn as a neck gaiter, ear band, cap, or face mask.

It is so compact that it fits in a pocket. It will stretch out with a little wear so it is not as confining as when new. Face masks come in many weights and cover the entire head and neck except the eyes, nose, and mouth. The Noj® comes in two weights — one is lined with Coolmax® mesh, and the other, designed for colder temperatures, is lined with fleece. They are great for keeping out rain or cold and allow complete protection and freedom of movement. They also fold down to pocket size. Refer to the rainwear photos on pp. 339-340.

Preventing frostbite to your face is critical at low chill factors and on longer rides. The challenge is to cover your face without fogging up your glasses. The only sure solution is to cover your nose and cheeks with a mask that has an opening for your nostrils. Select one made of polyester fleece for the best comfort. Avoid the more common masks made of neoprene: not only are they disgusting to wear but they make your face completely wet and vulnerable to frostbite. For temperatures below 10 degrees you will need to wear goggles. Spend whatever it costs for ones that go over your prescription glasses and are vented to prevent fogging. Fogged-up glasses are a visual impairment but more importantly, fogging can be disorienting. Cold, dry air is punishing to your eyes, making eyewear extremely important in freezing temperatures. It takes at least one mile for your eyes to adapt to the cold and stop tearing excessively *even* with good protective eyewear. Ride conservatively until you can see clearly. If tears run down your cheeks, blot them to prevent them from freezing.

Now, this sounds like lots of fun! At this point it will be helpful for you to look around. The landscape may be hushed in a blanket of snow, the sun turning snowflakes into glistening diamonds. The moon and stars may be sparkling extra bright. In any case, you can look forward to refueling with a hearty dinner. Many cold weather riders believe that some inconvenience and discomfort outside is a lot more fun than a workout inside. We have discussed proper clothing at length but psychological comfort is equally important. Breathe consciously, relax, and enjoy the weather. Gradually condition yourself to harsh conditions. In any case, avoid becoming obsessive or heroic while riding in difficult weather. These mindsets obstruct good judgment and can cause nausea or muscle strains from overexertion.

Because **keeping feet warm** is often the limiting factor at extreme temperatures, here are some suggestions. Fit your shoes loose enough to accommodate thicker, insulating socks and insoles. In 20 to 40 degrees, you may find that shoe covers and maybe old wool socks over your shoes will keep your feet warm. Purchase winter riding shoes that are all leather and have no open mesh panels. Trade out your clip-in pedals for pedals with toe clips and straps or Power Grips®. Clip-in pedals drain heat out of your feet. The cut-out in the soles and the bolts for cleats transmit the warmth of your feet into your cold, metal pedals. Only the insole and sock separate your feet from these metal conductors. Be sure that your calves are adequately insulated. Try wearing knee-high socks and gaiters. For extreme temperatures, abandon your cycling shoes completely and use hiking or Sorel®-type boots.

Clothe each part of your body in proportion to its ability to keep itself warm. The greater its mass and more abundant its blood flow, the warmer it will be. This means you should dress your torso and head in moderate to light cover; your legs and neck moderately; and provide the most protection to your forearms, wrists, and hands, calves, ankles, feet, and lower back.

Optimizing Conditions

My goodness, who went off on those extremes? Let's get back to 20 degrees. You can improve conditions on any given day with these careful choices:
1. Ride mid-day when it is warmest.
2. Try two shorter rides rather than one longer one.
3. When the roads are clear, find a riding partner with whom you can take turns drafting. The drafting position is remarkably protected in the slip-stream of the front rider.
4. Wear dark colors to absorb the warmth of the sun and wear a caution triangle for visibility.
5. Select a route with a lot of southern exposure and stay out of deep canyons and valleys. The cold settles into valleys and can make more than a 10-degree difference.
6. Carry a warm energy beverage in an insulated bottle or hydration system. Take care not to make the beverage too hot and burn yourself during the first 10 to 20 minutes.
7. Ride more slowly than usual to reduce the chill factor of self-created wind.
8. Increase your energy output — ride a mountain bike, reduce the tire pressure, or carry a load.
9. Ride on roads with little traffic. The challenges of a runny nose, diminished vision and hearing, and dust from sanded roads require greater focus and make it difficult to be alert to traffic.

Assessing Wind Chill Factor

The Wind Chill Temperature Index Chart from the National Weather Service will help you assess perceived cold under various windy conditions. This was recalculated in 2001 using new advances in science, technology, and computer modeling to provide a more

Wind Chill Temperature Index

Temperature (°F)

Calm	40	35	30	25	20	15	10	5	0	-5	-10	-15	-20	-25	-30	-35	-40	-45
5	36	31	25	19	13	7	1	-5	-11	-16	-22	-28	-34	-40	-46	-52	-57	-63
10	34	27	21	15	9	3	-4	-10	-16	-22	-28	-35	-41	-47	-53	-59	-66	-72
15	32	25	19	13	6	0	-7	-13	-19	-26	-32	-39	-45	-51	-58	-64	-71	-77
20	30	24	17	11	4	-2	-9	-15	-22	-29	-35	-42	-48	-55	-61	-68	-74	-81
25	29	23	16	9	3	-4	-11	-17	-24	-31	-37	-44	-51	-58	-64	-71	-78	-84
30	28	22	15	8	1	-5	-12	-19	-26	-33	-39	-46	-53	-60	-67	-73	-80	-87
35	28	21	14	7	0	-7	-14	-21	-27	-34	-41	-48	-55	-62	-69	-76	-82	-89
40	27	20	13	6	-1	-8	-15	-22	-29	-36	-43	-50	-57	-64	-71	-78	-84	-91
45	26	19	12	5	-2	-9	-16	-23	-30	-37	-44	-51	-58	-65	-72	-79	-86	-93
50	26	19	12	4	-3	-10	-17	-24	-31	-38	-45	-52	-60	-67	-74	-81	-88	-95
55	25	18	11	4	-3	-11	-18	-25	-32	-39	-46	-54	-61	-68	-75	-82	-89	-97
60	25	17	10	3	-4	-11	-19	-26	-33	-40	-48	-55	-62	-69	-76	-84	-91	-98

Wind (mph)

Frostbite Times ☐ **30 minutes** ☐ **10 minutes** ■ **5 minutes**

Wind Chill (°F) = $35.74 + 0.6215T - 35.75(V^{0.16}) + 0.4275T(V^{0.16})$
Where, T = Air Temperature (°F)   V = Wind Speed (mph)   effective 11/01/01

The wind chill temperatures are based on:
• Wind Speed at an average height of five feet (typical height of an adult face) based on readings from the national height standard of 33 feet (typical height of an anemometer).
• The lower threshold of calm at 3 mph.
• The clear night sky It assumes no impact from the sun.
• Constant humidity.   Reprinted from the U.S. National Weather Service

accurate, understandable, and useful formula for calculating the dangers from winter winds and freezing temperatures. Clinical trials were conducted at the Defence and Civil Institute of Environmental Medicine in Toronto in conjunction with the Meteorological Services of Canada. The new values are not as extreme as the prior values calculated in 1945. It is interesting to me that the factors used in calculating the wind chill are temperature and wind speed but not humidity. This chart shows you that at 30 degrees with a wind of 20 mph, the wind chill temperature is 17 degrees. Be sure to dress accordingly. Now you can see the importance of measuring wind speed with an anemometer rather than guessing.

I would say at mild temperatures the pleasure of riding is lost at about 30 mph, and risk is too high as the wind speed approaches 40 mph. In cold weather, riding becomes unpleasant at wind speed closer to 15 mph. When you add that to your self-created wind, you can see why I encourage you to be conservative in evaluating cold, windy days for riding suitability.

Stoking Your Inner Fire

Riding in the cold requires more calories because you burn them both for propulsion *and* to keep warm. No amount of care in dressing will keep you warm if you don't have the fuel to burn. Eat adequately, well in advance of starting your ride. Carry easy-to-eat snacks that don't freeze and store them next to your body where body heat will keep them palatable. Drink a warm energy beverage and carry it in an insulated container so it will stay warm throughout your ride. Some caution is needed here. If you use a highly insulated thermos and hot beverage, you are at risk of burning your mouth at the beginning of the ride. On the other hand, it is frustrating to have your fluids freeze during your ride. Prepare a warm bottle and a second hot bottle for longer rides so you can maintain your hydration without burning your mouth. You may like to plan your route so you can go inside to warm up. Visiting an eatery is a convenient way of doing that.

Eat lightly but often on longer rides. More substantial meals will draw the warming blood out of your extremities to your stomach and cause cold hands and feet. Swen Wiik taught me this lesson during his legendary Nordic Ski Dealers Clinics. The food at the Nordic Lodge was exceptionally nutritious, tasty, and abundant. We tanked up on huge breakfasts and finished each day with delicious, well-balanced dinners. Each day, as we headed out onto the trails, we would pick up our sack lunches. Anticipating how hungry we would get during a full day of cross-country skiing, we looked forward to savoring our lunches. How surprised I was the first year I participated to open my lunch and find one piece of substantial, homemade bread with a slice of meat or cheese sticking to it and a piece of lettuce. The lunch was completed by one piece of fruit and a cookie. How would this heat me and propel me throughout the afternoon? I discovered that not only was I well-fueled, but to my amazement, my hands and feet remained warm after lunch even in the severe cold. You too can benefit from carrying substantial snacks and light lunches on all-day, cold weather rides.

Conclusion

Riding in challenging weather conditions keeps you fit in body and mind. You will need to know your priorities and adhere to them. I first began riding through winter storms to avoid feeling confined to my house. I needed to get to work and my '59 Plymouth wouldn't start at temperatures below 10 degrees. The colder the weather, the more likely I was to be riding my bike. For my short ride of two miles, I used the dash technique: dress warmly and ride hard before my hands and feet got uncomfortably cold. Now, 20 years later, I know better. I have adequate clothing and ride "my snow rig," a 38-pound mountain bike equipped with knobby Continental® tires, fenders, and front and rear cargo racks. I top it off with 10 to 20 pounds of cargo. I stay present at each phase of the journey. My focus is on my condition, my pleasure in getting to know nature in yet another mood, and on adjusting my clothing, food, and comfort whenever I need to. How delighted I was to discover that the big fir tree in the park actually warmed me when I snuggled up to it to get out of the wind and eat a winter lunch on a snowstorm ride.

Shift your priorities during winter riding to discovery and adventure. You can learn a lot about yourself and nature by letting go of your fair-weather riding priorities and consciously choosing different reasons for riding. As safety takes on wider meaning, you will need to change routes to establish shorter rides with little traffic and less exposure. It is vital to maintain awareness of your body under all those layers. Breathe consciously and stop frequently to assess your condition. Study nature's unique displays of light, air currents, and snow drift patterns. A helmet light gives a new perspective during winter night rides.

By maintaining your fitness level through summer heat and winter storms, you will continue to feel strong, maintain the higher metabolic rate of an active life style, and be less susceptible to seasonal mood changes. Take on these challenges gradually, stay within your confidence level, and recapture the childhood joy of discovery.

chapter 9

Riding with Contentment in Urban Areas Requires Special Attention

- The Three Rs of Riding in Traffic
- Project an Agreeable Attitude
- What to Do If You Are Hit
- Routine Maintenance Guidelines
- Avoiding Collisions
- Selecting Headlights
- Games to Play

As our urban areas become increasingly congested, riding with satisfaction becomes more challenging. In addition, drivers are giving less attention to driving because they are distracted by cell phones, computers, eating, and their ever-present mind chatter. This is also true on multi-use trails where walkers, runners, skaters, and other cyclists listen to earphones, talk, or are simply lost in their own thoughts. Toss in a few geese, and dogs on retractable leashes, and you have a mix that demands alertness. How can we urbanites enjoy our bikes for transportation and recreation close to our homes?

Begin by accepting the status quo: acknowledge that conditions have changed and will continue to evolve. Riding while you are irritated and ready to lash out at the next inconvenience or threat will surely backfire on you. Instead, direct your energy more effectively toward advocacy for non-polluting means of transportation and recreation. Seek out your local human-centered, sustainable transportation groups and lend your support. Understanding that change takes time and that many improvements for non-motorized transportation have already been made will help you be more patient while riding.

Second, take time to research and seek out the best times and routes to ride. Stubbornly continuing to ride on heavily-trafficked routes during peak hours adds to your risk of injury, exposes you to increased pollution, and certainly has a negative impact on your disposition. How can you pay attention all at once to the movement of each vehicle, each traffic signal, other road users, the riding surface, bike control, and weather conditions? Under these conditions, the statistical chance of mishap is greatly increased. When you have time and curiosity, explore the recreational trails and transportational routes you will need to shop, to ride to work, to visit friends, and to relax and renew.

Third, practice your conscious breathing and maintain moderate exertion levels when you ride in the city. These techniques will heighten your awareness, acceptance, and openness as you mix with traffic. Avoid putting your head down and hammering out a fitness ride while denying the heightened risks of traffic congestion.

The Three Rs of Riding in Traffic with Contentment and Reduced Risk

Responsibility

Accept responsibility for all your actions: know the law and follow it to the letter. The vehicle code for motor vehicles also applies to bicycles. Because these are evolving codes that need further enlightenment, there are few privileges for cyclists at this time. Work toward improving these codes through your state legislatures, city councils, and state bicycle advocacy organizations. *Do not take liberties with them while riding.* Each time motorists see cyclists breaking the law (or even demonstrating poor judgment), their intolerance for cyclists ratchets up another notch. The result could be aggression directed at you or the next cyclist who comes along. For this and other reasons, it's important for cyclists to go the extra mile, so to speak, and pay attention to more than what the basic rules require. Accept the responsibility of being part of a cycling community and encourage your cycling friends to demonstrate their best riding behavior. Some packs of cyclists are notorious for their irresponsibly and arrogance. Use any influence available to you to encourage responsible riding behavior among club members and training groups.

When you are in traffic and make a poor choice that results in an unnerving situation, accept *your* contribution to the near miss and concentrate on avoiding another poor choice. Carrying irritation into traffic will only increase the likelihood of mishaps.

Respect

Respect everyone's right to share the roads and trails with you. This is especially important when other people's choice of vehicle and style of driving does not match your priorities. Comparing their choices with what you think they should have done is an exercise in futility and will only spoil your disposition. While we cannot change other people's ways, we can change our own attitudes toward them. Is it worth getting irate, spoiling your ride, and diminishing your safety for the sake of righteous indignation? Try to accept the fact that these people are doing the best they understand at this time. That is all any of us can do.

Renewal

Every ride can be renewing and bring you to your destination refreshed and content. Maintain a broad perspective and practice your breathing and pedaling techniques. Look at the sky and your surroundings. Many bike commuters believe that a difficult bike commute is better than any kind of motor vehicle commute. If the circumstances you left behind were unpleasant, consciously shift your focus to the pleasures of riding and shed your frustration. The showman Peter Glenn says that even with the many trials and tribulations in our modern world, it is always possible to find joy and perspective as you ride your bike. Try making that happen every day.

Project an Agreeable Attitude Toward Traffic, and It Will Be Returned to You

We all have had the experience of starting the day feeling grumpy, and then finding that everything and everyone we encounter reflects our poor attitude. When we make poor choices and expect the worst, by golly, that is just what we get! Most often we notice this in the negative but it also works in the positive. When we set out expecting the best, projecting an open, gracious attitude to fellow road and trail users, we have a pleasant ride with fewer frustrations. This does not mean that each interaction will be cheerful but that we will experience the best that is available in each situation. I notice that many citizens seem pretty unhappy. They probably need our smiles and good cheer in our voices.

How can you manifest a positive attitude? Be alert to all activity around you. Signal your intentions so that motorists and trail users can accommodate you. Always ride defensively and do not take risks. Interact with motorists. Try waving and nodding thanks to every motorist who gives you the right of way. I find it helps to pretend I am in another country. I'm trying to understand how this different culture works. My judgmental attitude evaporates as I think, "Oh, that's the way they do it here."

It is wise to be gracious even with motorists who put you at risk. As cyclists, we are extremely vulnerable and have no recourse except to call a law enforcement officer. Trying to "educate" other road and trail users will only escalate a risky situation. When people lash out with aggression, either ignore them or simply wave back and smile. This is a harmless way to express yourself and may help offenders put their behavior in perspective. Try this friendly response on motorists who startle you by shouting or blowing their horns. See if when they try to startle you, you can be so relaxed that you don't even jump, much less become irritated.

This is not to suggest that you be submissive because there are times when it is important to be assertive. In some parts of the United States, I have found that it is necessary to put my hand up in the "stop" gesture to encourage motorists to give right of way in heavy traffic. Still, by maintaining an attitude of goodwill and acceptance, I maintain the positive energy that's necessary to attend to my safety and to ride defensively.

On multi-use trails, actively give the right of way to all users. Mount a cheerful sounding bell on your handlebars and signal your approach well in advance. We cannot know how well people perceive our approach. Sounding a bell usually elicits a more cheerful response than calling out. As you approach trail users, sound your bell and then slow down enough so you can actually stop. Tell them, "I'd like to pass," then wait for them to acknowledge you and give permission. This means that you will constantly have to slow down and interact. Is that what you want to do today? If not, choose another route. Instead, try this trail early some weekday morning. Riding on public trails is a privilege, and this inconvenience is the price we pay to use them. Be accommodating. Who knows what burdens the other trail users are carrying today?

What to Do If You Are Hit by a Motor Vehicle

Unfortunately, no matter how careful you are, you may be hit by a motor vehicle. Be prepared by thinking through what to do before you're in that situation. You might carry a copy of these instructions in your seat pack along with your emergency equipment.

When a motor vehicle hits you, the driver may stop and ask if you are all right. The appropriate answer is: **"No! I am not all right!"** Why? Because you have just been hit by an object weighing more than one ton. You are no match for this contest with a combined weight of maybe 200 pounds.

When most riders are hit, their first thoughts are about severe injury or death. When they discover they are still breathing and mobile, they are inclined to brush off the incident too casually. Later, alas, they discover that they do need costly medical care as well as expensive bike repair or replacement.

Being hit is bad enough: don't add insult to injury. You do have a right to the road and you also have responsibilities. Avoid taking an apologetic attitude for your involvement in a crash. In our society, where people's personal identities are entwined with their motor vehicles, your identity as a cyclist can be regarded as less important. Therefore, projecting an apologetic attitude in a crash situation can reduce your chances of getting fair, respectful treatment.

Be as business-like as possible and gather as much information as you can if you're part of a collision.

1. Take a good look at the driver. No legal procedures are possible if you cannot identify the driver. Memorize the license plate number. Though this can be difficult when you are shaken up, do your best. Carry pencil and paper at all times.

2. Record the driver's name, address, phone numbers, driver's license number, and the name of his or her insurance company. If possible, also take the names, addresses, and phone numbers of any witnesses.

3. Call 911 and ask for the police. If you are hurt, also ask for an ambulance.

4. Ask the motorist to stay at the scene until the police arrive. If the motorist leaves, he or she is guilty of hit and run, which is a serious crime.

5. When the police arrive, ask the officer to take an accident report. If the crash involves serious bodily injury, death, or more than $1,000 total property damage, a report is required by law.

6. Record the reporting officer's name, badge number, and department or agency.

Check with local and state law enforcement agencies to confirm your rights and responsibilities and local laws.

Routine Maintenance Guidelines Based on Weekly Mileage

Regular care of your bicycles will extend the useful lifetime of their components and reduce the chances of crashes or mechanical failures. An odometer will help you know what maintenance you should undertake based on mileage since the last service. I have provided a chart with further instructions in Appendix C. Make copies and record maintenance dates for each bike you are responsible for.

Bike Care for Low-Mileage Riders (less than 20 miles per week)

Keep your bike clean and dry and resist the temptation to lubricate the chain more than three to five times a year. Lubricate the chain sparely with non-aerosol, "dry" lubricant. I recommend T-9® by Boeshield®. Avoid lubricating a dirty chain. Whenever your drive train makes enough noise to irritate you or you can see a thin film of rust on it, wash the bike thoroughly according to the following description, let it dry completely, and then lubricate the chain with one sparing drop on each roller. If you frequently get your bike wet, you may want to lubricate the plates of each link to retard rusting.

Bike Care for Middle-Mileage Riders (between 20 to 80 miles per week)

Weekly -

Keep your bike clean, dry, and lubed as just described. In addition, evaluate your chain for elongation every 500 miles. Use an accurate ruler. Replace the chain before it has elongated a sixteenth-of-an-inch over a 12-inch segment. If it has elongated more than a sixteenth-of-an-inch, you will also need to replace your cassette.

Measuring 12 inches of your chain every 500 miles will save you the expense of replacing the cassette every time you replace the chain.

Monthly -

Put your bike in a repair stand that lifts the

rear wheel off the ground and run through the gears to evaluate their precision. Inspect your tires for cuts, bruises, aging cracks, and general wear. If you ride in mud or water, check the brake pads for wear.

Every six months -

Learn how to evaluate the bearings and check all the bearing assemblies for proper adjustment as an indication of excessive wear or damage. If you ride often in mud or water, check the braking surface of your rims for heavy wear indicated by a concave surface.

Bike Care for High-Mileage Riders (more than 80 miles per week)

Weekly -

Keep your bike clean, dry, and lubed as described. Inspect your tires for cuts, bruises, and general wear.

Monthly -

Evaluate the chain, brake pads, derailleur performance, and bearing assemblies, as described. Spin the wheels slowly and sight-off the brake pads to evaluate the wheel trueness.

Every 10 weeks or 1,000 miles -

Take a maintenance class or find a competent mechanic and have your bike evaluated. High-mileage riders can significantly reduce wear on their components by keeping their bikes clean, riding at a minimum cadence of 80 rpm, and skillfully shifting gears.

Basic Bike Washing Instructions

Whatever your average weekly mileage, keeping your bike free of mud and grime is the most important maintenance job you can do. Your bike will perform better and last longer if you prevent grime from building up in the pivots and cable guides. If you only ride in fair-weather, you will not have to wash your bike often but if you get the equipment to make washing easy and get used to washing, it will no longer be a laborious task.

Equipment: You'll need a recycled five-gallon bucket: a traditional, loop-shaped, long-handled toilet brush or smaller brush to reach tight places; and a non-corrosive cleaner. I recommend Shaklee®'s Basic I®.

Technique: If you get your bike muddy, it will be easier to clean if you wash it immediately before the mud dries and sets up. Make your job easier by remembering that in arid climates where it is easy to damage wet trails, it is best to ride on dirt roads until the earth dries out. Protecting public trails from excess wear will also help cyclists maintain access to them.

1. Put a dime-sized drop of Basic I® in the five-gallon bucket and fill it with about four gallons of warm water. Lean up your bike in a suitable washing place.

2. Slosh water generously over the bike. If the day is hot, slosh water on a small area so you can clean it before it dries.

3. Scrub around each rim, one side at a time, rotating the wheels as you progress.

4. Scrub both brake assemblies, brushing until they are clean, and then slosh them with clean water.

5. Now scrub the chain drive. Brush both sides of the chain, rotating the crank until you have cleaned the entire length. That is about three crank rotations. Brush the cogs by brushing down on the side toward the back of the bike and then drawing the brush back up. Brushing down will rotate the cassette. Continue to do this until the cogs are clean. Thoroughly brush the pivots in the bodies of both derailleurs.

6. Throw the remaining water over the entire bike. If the tires are muddy, and a hose is convenient, lay the bike down on its side so the wheels will turn freely. Let the wheels spin while you spray at one point on the tires. Avoid aiming high-pressure water at the bearing assemblies where it could penetrate and cause corrosion. Protect the saddle with a plastic bag.

7. Dry your bike completely either in the warm sun or in a warm room.

Note: Resist the temptation to clean your bike at a car wash. The high-pressure spray will force corrosive soapy water into the bearing assemblies and cause damage.

Precautions to Reduce Your Chances of Collision or Injury

One part of taking full responsibility for your safety is equipping yourself appropriately for urban riding. This means making yourself highly visible and using all your senses to identity activity near you. Check this list to see how well-prepared you are.

1. Keep your bicycle in good mechanical working order at all times with routine, preventive maintenance. Take classes or train yourself and purchase a good reference book. I recommend Lennard Zinn's *Zinn and the Art of [Mountain or Road] Bike Maintenance*. Find a reliable bicycle mechanic and take your bike in every 500 miles for a mechanical evaluation. Riding in messy weather requires more frequent cleanings.

2. **Always wear a well-maintained helmet**. Properly position it with the front over the forehead one inch above your eyebrows. This is the only facial protection you have. It is best to optimize it. The straps and fitting mechanism should be washed and

readjusted periodically. Replace your helmet after about five years because the Styrofoam® deteriorates gradually and becomes less protective.

3. Always wear high visibility clothing. Consciously seek out bright yellow, white, or neon yellow jackets, riding shirts, and helmets. Save your concern for fashion for other occasions. It is better to be gaudy and alive than beautiful and dead.

4. Always wear protective eyewear and don't be cheap. Can you place a price on the value of your sight? Eyewear will reduce the chance of getting an insect or dust particle in your eye and crashing while reacting to the discomfort.

5. Use a rearview mirror. Why trust your life to the motorist behind you? Would you drive your car without rearview mirrors? You are so much more vulnerable on your bike. When you must ride *in* the lane with traffic, make a habit of checking that each passing vehicle pulls out around you. This is easiest when you watch the relationship between the vehicle and the lane stripes on the pavement. Handlebar-mounted mirrors allow you to check behind you without losing peripheral vision in front. The Mirrycle® is the most stable and durable mirror on the market.

6. Never ride with earphones. It is illegal as well as a demonstration of poor judgment. Hearing is essential to staying informed about conditions around you. You need to be able to hear approaching danger.

7. When you ride into the rising or setting sun, be especially defensive and alert. Motorists driving into the sun will not be able to see you.

8. Use adequate illumination at night and whenever the visibility is poor due to the weather, dawn, or dusk. Though the law requires reflectors, they are not adequate by themselves. The majority of car/bike collisions that occur at night are head-ons where the cyclist had only a front reflector. Front reflectors have too narrow an angle of reflectivity to warn oncoming traffic of your presence.

    a. First secure an LED (light-emitting diode) taillight to your bike. These run up to 500 hours on a pair of AA batteries. This means that they will function in emergencies when you have miscalculated your ride duration and need illumination at dusk or dark.

    b. If you ride regularly at night, LED leg lights worn on the outsides of both calves define you as a cyclist. They surely are the most effective lights for alerting motorists to your presence. They are lightweight, economical, and allow cyclists to be seen from 360 degrees.

    c. Battery operated lights that fit into the spokes of your wheels really get people's attention. They are particularly effective for traffic approaching from the side.

I ride through several roundabouts on my commute. After I mounted lights in my front wheel, I observed that motorists were more likely to yield to me. The lights also delight bystanders. I have had many people, who are otherwise too cool to talk to me, shout out, "Cool lights!"

Be sure your illumination helps people see you from all directions.

d. The law requires the use of headlights between dusk and dawn. Common sense also dictates that helping motorists see you will reduce your risks. Proper illumination can make night riding delightful, quiet, and solitary. Refer to the section on the next pages on selecting headlights.

9. Lock your bike if your hand is not on it. This includes when it's at your own dwelling. It takes only a few seconds to steal a bike. If the thief rides your bike away, you have little chance of recovering it on foot. It's true that professional thieves with appropriate tools can break even the most secure locks but most bikes are stolen by amateurs who want a cheap ride. Always carry a quality lock made of U.S. steel and use it wisely. You will also be wise to remove all accessories when you leave your bike parked. In many urban areas, it is not even safe to leave your bike locked up. Either insist on bringing it inside and locking it up or drive to these locations. Many transportational riders find that riding an old, cheap bike is the only solution in high-risk theft areas.

10. Do not defend your bike if you discover a thief stealing it. It is a sad commentary that cyclists have been hospitalized with serious injury incurred after trying to defend their bikes from thieves in their own neighborhoods. Instead, yell at thieves from a safe distance to try and scare them off. If they are determined, however, let them take your bike and avoid personal injury.

11. Secure all cargo in containers where they will not become entangled in the wheels or other moving parts of your bicycle and cause a crash. You can select a backpack or bike packs. Remember that backpacks increase the weight on your seat bones and increase saddle discomfort. If they are heavily loaded, backpacks can compromise your bike handling skills and cut off circulation in your shoulders. If you frequently carry cargo on your bike, give up the notion that a cargo rack clutters your bike. Many riders have crashed when a loaded grocery sack hanging on the handlebars or a dangling jacket sleeve caught in a wheel! Increase your bike's functionality and

your safety by installing a practical rack and packs. Many of us consider a bike without a cargo rack only a shadow of a bike.

All these precautions are common sense and economical insurance offered to reduce your risk of collision and injury.

Factors to Consider When Selecting Bicycle Headlights

You can choose from a wide variety of practical bicycle headlights. What factors should you consider in making a wise decision? Each manufacturer and owner tells you that his or her choice is outstanding. Which will best serve your needs and priorities? I recommend that you personally test a variety of lights because it will help you make a decision based on your own perceptions and expectations.

Front lights, both handlebar and helmet-mounted, fall into two categories. The first category is inexpensive (under $40) and primarily useful in helping motorists see you. These lights provide moderate to dim illumination. The second category allows you to see where you are going, requires a greater investment, and includes rechargeable battery packs to provide much greater illumination and running duration. These lights range from five to forty-five watts. Details change with ever-improving technology. They are generally available from less than $100 to more than $300.

Handlebar-mounted lights under $40 usually use ni-cad AA or AAA batteries and provide short running times. This means the batteries may be discharged right when you need them but having to buy lots of batteries can be costly. Additionally, most of these batteries are difficult to recycle and end up contaminating our landfills. Using rechargeable batteries lessens environmental impact.

More powerful lights with rechargeable battery packs have made night riding fun and much safer. With proper care, they will last for many years and are versatile. Most battery packs weigh one to two pounds. Of course, the lightest most compact ones are the most expensive. It may help you justify the cost of any bicycle headlight by using them for household and camping applications.

Answering the following questions will help you select appropriate lights.

1. Where should you attach your lights and battery packs? You can choose among handlebar-mounted, helmet-mounted, or a combination. Helmet-mounted lights, especially useful for urban riding, allow you to scan where you are riding, alert motorists to your presence, and continue to illuminate your way when you get off your bike. Consider a scenario where you are making a left turn across heavy traffic. A handlebar-mounted light will shine across the street but the cars that need warning are approaching on your *right*. With a helmet-mounted light, you can make the turn while directing your beam towards the oncoming traffic. A helmet-

mounted light can also help you see whether the noise beside the trail is a busy squirrel or a dog about to take a bite out of your leg.

There are two disadvantages to using a helmet-mounted light alone. They limit your ability to see while riding in dense fog. Also, the beam does not project shadows, and that limits your depth perception. Handlebar and helmet-mounted lights used together afford the best overall coverage, especially for riding technical, single track. The combination of a spot beam for the helmet light and flood beam for the handlebars is especially useful. A cautionary note: before you ride on single track in your area check with the authorities to find out if public trails are open to riders at night. Many public trails are closed between dusk and dawn.

TurboCat®'s Trail Guide 10® is an outstanding example of an affordable, helmet-mounted headlight. The purchase price includes the lead-acid, rechargeable battery pack and battery charger.

Many manufacturers and experienced riders recommend carrying the battery pack for your helmet-mounted light in a backpack or pocket rather than attaching it to your bike while in use. This practice could prevent damage to you or your light in a crash and makes the light useful for non-biking application.

2. How bright a light do you need? Unfortunately, wattage is only a measure of power and not of actual brightness of useable light. Wattage alone does not tell the whole story. The actual illumination is determined by wattage, reflector design (which determines the beam pattern), and the efficiency of the bulb, battery, and wiring. Higher wattage systems may not be better for your chosen application. Handlebar-mounted lights with more than 15 to 20 watts will make it difficult or impossible to see outside the beam your light projects. If you are looking for that animal along side the path, 30-watt lights on the handlebars will prevent you from seeing it while your eyes are adapting to the bright light of the beam. The addition of a helmet light solves this problem.

3. How long do you need your battery to last? For commuters, this is easy to calculate. If you have a long commute, you may want to keep one battery charger at home and one at work to charge your batteries at both ends of your commute during winter's short days. Generally, it is wise to choose a system with longer running time than you think you will need. Carrying a back-up LED headlight or an extra battery pack will give you additional illumination if your primary battery pack runs out before

you reach your destination.

4. What characteristics do you want in a battery pack? Many riders who are concerned about weight like the more expensive nickel-metal-hydride batteries. Not only are they lighter weight but they charge somewhat faster than lead-acid or ni-cad batteries. They do have fewer recharging cycles than other batteries. Others prefer lead acid batteries because they are the least costly, kinder to the environment, and can be charged without as much concern for charging duration. Ni-cads are in wide use and generally work well. However, cadmium is toxic to the environment.

5. What are you willing to spend? The most expensive lights may not be the best lights for your use. But do plan to spend a minimum of $100 for a good, dependable light. Give special attention to conditions and duration of product warranties. You will get the best value by buying a light from a respected manufacturer who specializes in lighting, is knowledgeable about the technology involved in lighting design, actually uses the product, and provides cheerful maintenance and warranty service. TurboCat® ranks high in all these areas.

Bicycle lights make up another product category where the purchase price is an investment in your safety and quality of life.

Exercises to Help You Develop a Peaceful Attitude in Traffic

Exercise I: That's not a jerk but a driver exercising poor judgment in choice of speed.

Avoid labeling careless and reckless drivers with unkind names. Using judgmental expressions, even in thought, increases your irritation. Instead, describe them in objective, accurate terms. Most drivers are not actually stupid but are simply demonstrating poor judgment. Isn't "that stupid speed maniac" actually just "a speeding guy using poor judgment?" Can you remember the last time *you* used poor judgment driving, and another motorist avoided a collision with you by reacting fast? By golly, that *has* happened.

Exercise II: Ha Ha! You didn't make me jump!

You are riding along peacefully enjoying the noon-day sun and are rudely startled out of your peace by a loud, prolonged honk from a motorist right on your rear wheel but out of your peripheral vision. Do you give the motorist the satisfaction of seeing you jump several inches off your saddle in alarm? Another trick some motorists enjoy is shouting at you from close range but out of sight. Try using these surprise situations to test your level of relaxation. Can you be so content and relaxed that you don't startle at all?

Exercise III: I'm taking the emergency exit!

Many cyclists believe that motorists want to hit them when they drive too closely in passing. Holding this belief surely diminishes your contentment as you ride in traffic. When inattentive drivers look at you, their energy follows their glance and they unconsciously steer toward you. It is the same phenomenon some novice riders experience when they see a pothole, focus on it, and then ride directly into it. The result is that an inattentive motorist may see the cyclist and drift toward him or her rather than driving consciously around them. Here is a situation where a rearview mirror is essential. Under these circumstances, you must be ready to ride into the ditch or jump the curb to avoid being hit. Can you execute these self-preservation measures as a test of your skill *and* avoid angry thoughts about the motorist?

Conclusions to *Bicycling Bliss*

Bicycling bliss is the result of conscious cycling. I do hope that practicing conscious breathing and projecting a positive attitude will result in greater peace and contentment in a world that tends toward the unsettling extreme. One of my intentions with this book is to share my experiences from cycling for more than 50 years. I've learned that bicycle riding provides benefits that extend far beyond physical fitness and lessons that contribute to my entire well-being: physical, mental, psychological, and spiritual.

As children, we love to ride bikes, sensing the freedom and independence they provide. We love being capable with our new riding skills. Now, in adulthood, it is possible to expand those pleasures by developing new adult riding skills and by cultivating new attitudes toward our world. I hope you will return to **Bicycling Bliss** often in the years ahead since repetition supports learning. The first time I hear a new idea it sounds strange. The next time it becomes familiar. Yet another time, and it begins to take on meaning. Finally, I discover its nuances as I make it my own.

I welcome your comments and feedback. Please send them to:
   Portia H. Masterson
   P.O. Box 16334
   Golden, CO 80402-6006
or e-mail: portia@bicyclingbliss.com
Visit our website at www.bicyclingbliss.com

Recommended Readings

Alexander Technique

Conable, Barbara and William Conable, *How to Learn the Alexander Technique: A Manual for Students*, Andover Press, OH, 1991. ISBN 0-9622595-4-3

Gelb, Michael J., *Body Learning: An Introduction to the Alexander Technique*, Henry Holt and Co., NY, 1981. ISBN 0-8050-4206-7   615.82

Rickover, Robert, *Fitness Without Stress: A Guide to the Alexander Technique*, Metamorphous Press, OR, 1988. ISBN 0943920329

Human Anatomy

Calais-Germain, Blandine, *Anatomy of Movement*, Eastland Press, WA, 1985 (French), 1993 (English). ISBN 0-939616-17-3   612.76

————, and Andrée Lamotte, *Anatomy of Movement Exercises*, Eastland Press, WA, 1990 (French), 1996 (English). ISBN 0-939616-22-X   612.76

Dox, Ida G. Ph.D. et al., *The HarperCollins Illustrated Medical Dictionary: The Complete Home Medical Dictionary*, Harper Perennial, New York, 1993. ISBN 0-06-273142-4   610.3

Jenkins, David B., *Hollinshead's Functional Anatomy of the Limbs and Back*, W.B. Saunders Co., PA, 1951, 1991. ISBN 0-7216-5128-3   611.98

Yokochi, Chihiro, M.D. et al., *Photographic Anatomy of the Human Body*, Igaku-Choin, Tokyo-NY, 1989, 2001. ISBN 0-89640-160-X   611

Bicycle Maintenance

Van der Plas, Rob, *Bicycle Technology: Understanding, Selecting and Maintaining the Modern Bicycle and its Components*, Bicycle Books, San Francisco, CA. 1991. ISBN 0-93321-30-3   629.28772

Zinn, Lennard, *Zinn and the Art of Mountain Bike Maintenance*, VeloPress, Boulder, CO, 2001. ISBN 1-884737-47-1   629.28

————, *Zinn and the Art of Road Bike Maintenance*, VeloPress, Boulder, CO, 2000. ISBN 1-884737-70-6   629.28

Breathing

Douillard, John, *Body, Mind and Sport: the Mind-Body Guide to Lifelong Fitness and Your Personal Best*, Crown Trade Paperbacks, NY, 1994. ISBN 0-517-8838-X   613.7

Hendricks, Gay, Ph.D., *Conscious Breathing: Breathwork for Health, Stress Release, and Personal Mastery*, Bantam Books, NY, 1995. ISBN 0-553-37443-5   613.192

Iyengar, B.K.S., *Light on Pranayama: The Yogic Art of Breathing*, CrossRoad Publ. NY, 1992. ISBN 0-8245-0686-3   613.192

Zi, Nancy, *The Art of Breathing: Six Simple Lessons to Improve Performance, Health and Well-being*, Vivi Co. Glendale, CA, 1997. ISBN 1-884872-72-7

Foods and Nutrition

Brand-Miller, Jennie et al., *The New Glucose Revolution: The Authoritative Guide to The Glycemic Index*, Marlow & Company, NY, 2003. ISBN 1-56924-5064   612.396

Burke, Edmund R., *Optimal Muscle Recovery*, Avery Publishing Group, NY, 1999. ISBN 0-89529-884-8   613.711

Colgan, Michael, *Optimum Sports Nutrition: Your Competitive Edge*, Advance Research Press, NY, 1993. ISBN 0-9624840-5-9   613.2

Gregory, Patricia R., *Bean Banquets From Boston to Bombay: 200 International, High-Fiber, Vegetarian Recipes*, Woodbridge Press, Santa Barbara, CA, 1994. ISBN 0-88007-139-7   641.6

Manore, Melinda, Ph.D. R.D., Janice Thompson, Ph.D., *Sport Nutrition for Health and Performance*, Human Kinetics, Champaign, IL, 2000. ISBN 0-87322-939-8 (55)   613.2

McDougall, John A., M.D., and recipes by Mary McDougall, *The McDougall Program for a Healthy Heart: A Life Saving Approach to Preventing and Treating Heart Disease*, Dutton, NY, 1996. ISBN 0-525-93868-0   613.2

Ryan, Monique, R.D., *Complete Guide To Sports Nutrition*, VeloPress, Boulder, CO, 1999. ISBN 1-884737-57-9   613.2

Weil, Andrew, M.D., *Eating Well for Optimum Health: The Essential Guide to Food, Diet, and Nutrition*, Knopf, NY 2000. ISBN 0-060959584   613.2

Willett, Walter C, M.D., *Eat, Drink, and Be Healthy: The Harvard Medical School Guide to Healthy Eating*, Simon & Schuster, New York, 2001. ISBN 0-7432-2322-5   613.2

Integrated Health and Healing

Cohen, Kenneth S., *The Way of Qigong: The Art and Science of Chinese Energy Healing*, Ballantine Books, NY, 1997. ISBN 0-345-39529-8   613.71

Sarno, John, M.D., *Mind Over Back Pain*, The Berkley Books, NY, 1982. ISBN 0-425-17523-5   617.56

————, *The Mindbody Prescription: Healing the Body, Healing the Pain*, Warner Books, NY, 1998. ISBN 0-446-67515-6   616.0472

Weil, Andrew, M.D., *Health and Healing*, Houghton Mifflin Co., Boston, 1988.
    ISBN 0-395-36200-8   615.53   Part II, Chapters 4,5, and 6

———, *Natural Health, Natural Medicine: A Comprehensive Manual for Wellness and Self-Care*, Houghton Mifflin, NY, 1995. ISBN 0-395-73099-6   613

General Health and Fitness

Cooper, Robert K., *Health and Fitness Excellence: The Scientific Action Plan*, Houghton
    Mifflin Co., MA, 1989. ISBN 0-395-47589-9   613

Crossen, Sue, *Back Pain Breakthrough: A Revolutionary Approach to Cure Back Pain!*,
    www.healingresults.com, 2001. ISBN 0-9711436-0-9

Goldberg, Kenneth A., *How Men Can Live as Long as Women*, The Summit Group, TX,
    1993. ISBN 1-565300254   613.04234

Ross, Michael J., M.D., *Maximum Performance: Sports Medicine for Endurance Athletes*,
    VeloPress, CO. 2003. ISBN 1-931382-22-0   612.044

Schroeder, Charles Ray, *Taking the Work Out of Workout: A Revolutionary Approach for
    Making Exercise More Exciting and Easier to Stick to*, CHRONOMED Publishing, MN,
    1994. ISBN 1-56561-049-0   613.71

Tilton, Buck and Roger G. Cox, *Ozone, UV and Your Health, 50 ways to save your skin*, ICS
    Books, Merrillville, IN, 1994. ISBN 0-93802-95-5   616.5

Meditation and Spirituality

Ferrini, Paul, *Love Without Conditions: Reflections of the Christ Mind*, Heartways Press, 1994.
    ISBN 1-879159-15-5   248.4

Kriyananda, Goswami, *The Spiritual Science of Kriya Yoga*, The Temple of KriyaYoga, IL,
    1976. ISBN 0-9613099-1-1

Nhat Hanh, Thich, *Being Peace*, Parallax Press, CA, 1987. ISBN 0-938077-00-7   294.3444

———, *The Long Road Turns to Joy: A Guide to Walking Meditation*, Parallax Press, 1994.
    ISBN 0-938077-83-X   294.3443

Pressure Point Therapy

Coseo, Marc, *The Acupressure Warm-Up for Athletic Preparation and Injury Prevention*,
    Paradigm Publ., Brookline, MA, 1992 ISBN 0-912111-34-8   615.822

Ellis, Andrew et al., *Fundamentals of Chinese Acupuncture*, Paradigm Publications,
    Brookline, MA, 1991. ISBN 0-912111-33-x   615.892

Forem, Jack and Steve Shimer, LAC, *Healing with Pressure Point Therapy: Simple, Effective Techniques for Massaging Away More than 100 Common Ailments*, Prentice Hall, NJ, 1999. ISBN 0-7352-0006-8   615.822

Gach, Michael Reed, *Acupressure's Potent Points: A Guide to Self-Care for Common Ailments*, Bantam Books, NY, 1990. ISBN 0-553-34970-8   615.822

Namikoshi, Toru, *The Shiatsu Way to Health: Relief and Vitality at a Touch*, Kodansha International, Tokyo, 2002. ISBN 4-7700-2894-6   615.822

Strength Training

Cook, Brian B. and Gordon W. Stewart, *Strength Basics: Your Guide to Resistance Training for Health and Optimal Performance*, Human Kinetics, IL, 1996. ISBN 0-87322-843-X 613.71

Delavier, Frederic, *Strength Training Anatomy*, Human Kinetics, Paris, 2001. ISBN 0-7360-4185   611.73

Schmitz, Eric and Ken Doyle, *Weight Training for Cyclists*, VeloPress, Boulder, CO 1998. ISBN 1-884737-43-9

Stretching and Massage

Anderson, Bob, *Stretching*, Shelter Publications, Inc., CA, 1980. ISBN 0-936070-01-3 613.7

Johnson, Joan, *The Healing Art of Sports Massage*, Rodale Press, Emmaus, PA, 1995. ISBN 0-87596-186-x   615.8

Wharton, Jim and Phil Wharton, *The Wharton's Stretch Book: Featuring the Breakthrough Method of Active Isolated Stretching*, Time Books, NY, 1996. ISBN 0-812926234 613.714

Yoga

Couch, Jean, *The Runner's Yoga Book: A Balanced Approach to Fitness*, Rodmell Press, Berkley, CA, 1990. ISBN 0-9627138-0-5

Coulter, H. David, *Anatomy of Hatha Yoga: A Manual for Students, Teachers ,and Practitioners, Body and Breath*, Honesdale, PA, 2001. ISBN 0-9707006-0-1   613.7046

Kraftsow, Gary, *Yoga for Wellness: Healing with the Timeless Teachings of Viniyoga*, Penguin Group, 1999. ISBN 0-14-019569-6   613.7046

————, *Yoga for Transformation*, Penguin Group, 2002, ISBN 0-14-019629-3   613.7046

Glossary

Abdominals - Commonly refers to all abdominal muscles, including the rectus abdominis, transversalis, pyramidalis, and internal and external obliques. Illustration p. 115.

Abduction - Movement of the arms or legs away from the midline of the body; the opposite of adduction.

Acupressure - An ancient Chinese art that uses pressure applied to specific points on the skin to stimulate the body's healing abilities.

Adduction - Movement of the arms or legs toward or across the midline of the body; the opposite of abduction.

Aerobic exercise - An exertion level at which the heart and lungs are capable of supplying the muscles with enough oxygen to fuel them adequately. Contrast to anaerobic.

Agility - The capacity to change position and direction quickly with precision and without loss of balance.

Anaerobic exercise - Literally means in the absence of oxygen; exercise that demands more oxygen than the heart and lungs can supply to the muscles. Such explosive exertion can only be maintained for a few minutes and produces undesirable metabolic byproducts such as lactic acid. The oxygen debt created is paid when the exertion is reduced to sustainable levels. Contrast to aerobic.

Anterior - As a directional term it refers to the front of the body. Contrast with posterior.

Autonomic nervous system - The system that controls vital functions and is also referred to as the involuntary nervous system. It is composed of the sympathetic and parasympathetic divisions. Contrast with the somatic nervous system.

Ayurveda - (pronounced aa-your-vay-da) Means "science of life." It is an ancient Indian healing system with a history going back more than 5,000 years. It emphasizes the spiritual nature of humans, body types, food, right timing, and life style. It focuses on healing the root causes of illness. Only natural therapies are used. It seeks to balance all life's elements.

Ball of the foot - The prominent joint at the base of the big toe; the important flex point in the foot in walking and shoe fitting.

Bar ends - Add-ons to flat handlebars to provide alternative hand positions; also known as climbing bars. Illustration p. 242.

Bliss - An enduring form of contentment derived from being fully present and practicing simplicity, moderation, self-nurture, reflection, and conscious breathing.

Bonking - The state of complete exhaustion when a rider depletes all energy supplies; when motivation ceases, legs become leaden, and the fun is over. Eating foods with a glycemic index of 60 or more will help get through this unpleasant state.

Brake lever reach - The distance between the brake lever and the handlebar grip; an important factor in reducing hand strain on long rides and controlling the brakes.

Bursa - A fluid-filled sac between tendon and bone that allows the tendon to glide over the surface of the bone. Bursitis is the inflammation of the bursa due to direct trauma or friction from the overlying tendon(s).

Cadence - The revolutions per minute of the pedals. Maintaining an rpm of 80 is efficient: it reduces strain on your legs, fatigue of the bicycle frame, and wear on bicycle components.

Clamp-on stem - The stem used with a threadless fork steerer so the horizontal portion of the stem clamps onto the steerer instead of the traditional stem type where the vertical portion of the stem inserts into the steerer. Raising the handlebar position can be more complex with clamp-on stems and requires a stem riser and perhaps riser handlebars. Illustration p. 269.

Clavicle - Also known as the collarbone; the horizontal bone at the top of the chest cavity on the front of the shoulder.

Clip-in pedals - Pedals that accept the cleat on the bottom of the cycling shoe that attaches the foot/shoe to the pedal; commonly known as clipless pedals. Illustration p. 160.

Condyle - A rounded knoblike prominence at the end of a bone that enables it to articulate with another bone.

Dan tian - An energy center in the middle of the body, half-way between the navel and the pubic bone.

Diaphragm - In general terms it is a separating sheet of muscle. For our purposes it refers to the respiratory diaphragm that horizontally separates the chest and abdomen cavities. Illustration p. 77.

Drafting - Riding in the slip-stream of the rider ahead. This requires that the front wheel of the person who is drafting be within 12 to 18 inches of the front rider. The slip-stream advantage reduces effort needed to keep up. Obviously, the drafting rider must pay close attention to every move of the front rider.

Dual control levers - Also known as STI® or Ergo® levers; they are used on drop handlebars, and both the brake and gear control levers are incorporated into one mechanism.

Endo - Slang for a rider launching over the handlebars usually followed by the somersaulting bicycle.

Extensors - A general term for the muscles that extend or straighten a limb when contracted.

Fascia - A sheet of connective tissue that supports and gives form to organs and muscles.

Flexors - A general term for muscles that fold or bend a limb. One muscle can be an extensor or a flexor depending on the relationship to the reference joint. For example, the quadriceps femoris is a flexor of the hip and an extensor of the knee.

Float - The side-to-side movement of the foot on clip-in pedals. It minimizes ankle and knee strain throughout the pedal stroke.

Gluteals - Commonly used to refer to the gluteus maximus, medius, and miminus; also known as the buttocks.

Hamstrings - Commonly used to refer to the muscles of the back of the thighs; technically the tendons on either side of the back of the knee that appear like strings. The inner one is the tendon of the semimembranosus, semitendinosus, gracilis, and sartorius. The outer one is the tendon of the biceps femoris.

Hyperextend - The extreme extension of any part of the body beyond the normal limit.

Iliotibial band or tract - Often referred to as the ITB; a thick, fibrous band that runs along the outside of the leg from the ilium of the pelvis to the tibia in the lower leg. The tensor fascia lata muscle is embedded in the ITB and abducts, flexes, and rotates the thigh inward. Illustration p. 189.

Ischial tuberosities - The seat bones that are meant to bear the rider's weight on the saddle.

Kinesthetic sense or kinesthesia - The sense perception of muscular movement by which one estimates the position of body parts.

Lateral - A directional term refering to the side of the body in contrast to medial. In motion it refers to side-to-side movement as opposed to fore and aft movement.

Ligament - A fibrous connective tissue that binds bones together or a membranous sheet or cord-like structure that holds organs in place.

Line - as in "cutting a line" or "riding a line" - The path ridden through obstacles on the trail or road. First the line is traced visually and then followed through with your bike when your focus is clear and your body supple.

Lumbar vertebrae - The portion of the spine at the waist and midriff. Illustration p. 148.

Medial - A directional term referring to the midline. Contrast with lateral.

Meridian - In traditional Chinese medicine, an invisible channel of energy flow that runs the length of the body and into the extremities. Chart p. 139.

Mindbody - The integrated whole of tangible and intangible aspects of the human being.

Mindfulness - Probably of Buddhist origins; to be fully alert and engaged in your present activity, surroundings, and circumstances and responding to them with grace and humor.

Paraspinals - Commonly used in weight training to refer to the spinal erectors along both sides of the spine. They stabilize, flex, and extend the back.

Parasympathetic nervous system - The system concerned with maintaining the everyday functions of the body, especially the orderly activity of the digestive and eliminative tracts and the activity of slowing the heart. Contrast with the sympathetic nervous system.

Perineum - The area of the body bound by the pubic bone, the tailbone and the thighs, which is vulnerable to damage from constant pressure on a bicycle saddle.

Phytochemical - Non-essential micronutrients that help protect us from dangerous organisms and toxins like pollutants and pesticides.

Pinch flat - Usually two small cuts in the inner tube caused by compression of the tire and inner tube against the rim during impact on the edge of a pothole or obstacle in the trail.

Power Grips® - A foot-to-pedal attachment system that uses a strap diagonally across the pedal. When the foot is aligned forward for riding, the strap holds the foot firmly on the pedal. Illustration p. 161.

Pushers - Riders whose downward pedal stroke dominates the rotation. Contrast with spinners.

Qi - The Chinese word meaning "life energy."

Qigong - The art and science of developing qi and controlling its flow and distribution throughout the body. The open flow and even distribution of qi improves the health and harmony of the mindbody.

Quadriceps - Commonly known as quads; the extensors of the knee at the front of the thigh composed of three superficial muscles: rectus femoris, vastus medialis and vastus lateralis, and the deeper vastus intermedius beneath the other three component muscles.

Rolfing - An organized method of deep tissue work that heightens ones internal awareness through reeducation of internal muscular structure. Rolfing is concerned with the integration of human structures. It asserts that the human body is so plastic that it can be brought into alignment with gravity through reeducation and deep structural work.

Sacrum - A slightly curved, triangular bone formed from five fused vertebrae between the coccyx and lumbar spine and between the two hipbones, forming the posterior section of the pelvis.

Saggital plane - An anatomic directional term that describes the plane that bisects the body just as the bicycle frame bisects the rider. It is a useful term for cyclists since the legs move through saggital planes while pedaling.

Shiatsu - Developed in Japan as a "hands-on" method of preventative health care and therapy that increases vitality, relieves fatigue, and stimulates the body's natural healing power by pressure applied to key points on the body.

Single track - A term used in mountain biking to describe an off-road riding trail. Contrast with double track, a dirt road.

Somatic nervous system - This system voluntarily controls skeletal muscle contraction and receives information from the sensory organs and pain and touch. Contrast to the autonomic nervous system.

Spinners - Riders who power effectively on the full rotation of the crank. See pushers.

Straddle height - The distance measured between the floor and the rider's crotch. This is used in determining proper bicycle frame size. It is contrasted to stand-over height, which is measured on the bicycle from the floor to the top of the frame top tube half-way between the head tube and the seat tube (see illustration of the bicycle on p. 258).

Sympathetic nervous system - The system concerned with preparing the body for emergency actions and functions especially anger, fear, and flight. It slows digestive function and increases cardiac output. Contrast with parasympathetic nervous system.

Taiji quan - An ancient, slow, and graceful choreographed Chinese exercise form designed to open the body meridians for a free flow and even distribution of qi. It is one form of Qigong practiced for health, self-defense, and meditation. It emphasizes relaxation and grounding. Also known as T'ai Chi Ch'uan.

Tendon - A fibrous band that attaches a muscle to a bone.

Threadless headset - The bearing assembly that provides smooth turning of the handlebars. It fits on the steerer of the fork without threads. Adjustment is made with the stem cap nut bolt and retained by a clamp-on stem. Illustration p. 269.

Thoracic - Any part of the anatomy having to do with the thorax or chest.

Tinnitus - Noise in the ears such as ringing or buzzing rather than the sensation of external stimuli.

Track stand - Balancing on a bicycle without forward movement maintained by small adjustments in weight shift and small movements of the pedals. It is used in track racing where track bikes have a fixed-gear (no free-wheeling mechanism).

Trigger point - In Eastern medicine, an acupoint that stimulates healing and release at a distance location or organ in the body. In Western medicine, a group of muscle fibers that are constantly contracted inside a tight band of muscle. They feel like a knot to the touch. Pressure on these points may be painful locally or cause referred pain at a distant part of the body. The terms are interrelated but differ subtly.

Trocanter - The bony prominences where muscles are attached. Common reference is to the upper end of the femur that you can feel at the hip joint.

Triceps of the arm - The muscle that extends the forearm; located at the back of the upper arm. Tri indicates it has three heads (or distinguishable parallel parts).

Vascular bundle - The ridge of blood vessels and nerves along the male perineum; the base of the penis.

Index of Exercises

Index of Acupressure Point Instructions

Index of Illustrations and Charts for Reference

A Personal and Professional History

My Early Years of Cycling

My life perspective has been strongly influenced by my view from a bicycle seat. Nature has been my intimate companion, whether in a city park, in a remote forest, or on a spacious prairie.

My cycling adventures began in Upper Montclair, New Jersey. When I was eight years old, I learned to ride my neighbor's 26-inch-wheeled road bike. I remember repeatedly shoving off the curb trying to propel the bike further with each try. I can still feel the joy of playing bicycle kickball and bicycle follow the leader. Curbs at least one-foot high flanked one side of our street, and the space between that curb and the big, old trees was very narrow. To pass through, we had to tilt our handlebars to one side to avoid hitting the trees or falling off the curb. Mastering this maneuver on that big bike taught me the balance between momentum and steadiness.

Eventually I asked my father for a bike of my own. My eagerness to have one was intensified by his immediate refusal to buy me one, insisting they were too dangerous. His denial became my challenge, and I began to scheme. Since kindergarten, I had participated in our school's banking program by depositing a quarter in my savings account every Wednesday. I figured that by combining all these savings with my future allowance, I could put together the $55 needed for the beautiful three-speed bike in the Sears catalog by early summer. To my surprise, my father agreed to this proposal and even offered to buy me a horn.

The arrival of my new bike made that summer blissful. We spent our summers in a cabin we built in the woods of the Pocono Mountains in eastern Pennsylvania. During the week my father worked in New Jersey, and my mother, sister, brother, and I lived in the woods. We walked two miles to the swimming hole every afternoon and to church on Sundays. What a joy it was to have a bike so my sister and I could extend our range of travel whenever we wanted to.

My sister earned money by selling her oil paintings of the summer homes near our cabin. Many days we packed a lunch, a blanket, and a book into a paper grocery sack and set out for the painting site. She tied her metal box of painting supplies onto the touring bars of my bike, and we took turns walking and carrying the bag or riding my prized bike. At our destination, Priscilla painted while I read to her. I especially remember reading Thomas Costain's *The Silver Chalice*.

In other situations, my bicycle became an escape to safety and freedom. I rode my trusted companion to a friend's house or just cruised the neighborhood when my home life became tense with conflict. Now I find it intriguing to hear other adult cyclists describe their emotional attachment to cycling and even their riding styles as being rooted in childhood riding experiences. The connection is certainly there for me.

While working on a cycling merit badge in Girl Scouts, I organized and led a 15-mile round trip bicycle ride with 10 girls. This outing was a great adventure and a test of my stamina and independence. I look back on experiences like this with a special appreciation of my mother's support. She didn't warn me of potential dangers or caution me to "be careful." She let my sister and me explore and wander and never scolded us when we came home scraped, muddy, or disheveled. Her support gave us the freedom to meander through open country and find joy and peace in nature.

When I was 13, my mother, sister, and I moved to Oregon and spent our summers on my uncle's ranch near Salem. There I tested my bike's all-terrain worthiness even more than in the woods of Pennsylvania. During the winters near Astoria, riding was much more limited. More than 100 inches of annual rainfall made riding less desirable, especially when I was wearing a heavy wool coat and scarf. The loaded log trucks speeding down the narrow street past my house intimidated me, and that deterred me from frequently venturing out to find enjoyable roads.

During my last two years of high school and my years at Oregon State University, I rode through the rolling farmland of the Willamette Valley. None of my friends enjoyed bicycling the way I did so during the fifties and sixties I rode alone. I had no cycling models and did not know about bicycle touring but I wanted to ride from my home west of Salem to my uncle's ranch east of town, about 25 miles. Having no tour packs, I put my lunch and jacket into satchels and hung them on my handlebars. As I rode through Salem, I happened to pass a bike store and stopped in hoping someone would strike up a conversation so I could talk about my adventure. To my disappointment, no one even greeted me. Riding through the farmland, I mulled over that experience and decided from that point on I would enjoy the momentary pleasures of any activity and not expect recognition from others.

In the late sixties at the University of Arizona, I was happily part of an active cycling community. In Tucson, I developed techniques for riding the short distance to campus at temperatures above 100 degrees. At that time, I was married and although we owned two old cars, my husband and I rode our bikes to campus and on errands. I spent many happy hours touring Tucson with our first son, Bernhard, taking in the world from his child seat. For a time I cared for another baby while his mother worked. We made quite a spectacle with Bernhard in the child seat, her son in the Gerry Carrier on my back, and me obviously pregnant. I was lucky that our neighborhood was reasonably flat.

Becoming a Bicycle Retailer

In 1977, we moved to Golden, Colorado, nestled in the Foothills of the Rockies. I quickly discovered that my trusted three-speed was quite inadequate for getting around with two-year-old Kirk now in the child seat. I therefore retired my old bike after 27 years of service and moved up to a new Raleigh ten-speed. The wider range of gears and the drop handlebars delighted me.

In 1980, my cycling evolution took a quantum leap. With both Bernhard and Kirk in school, my husband and I joined five other partners to open a bicycle store, Self-Propulsion, Inc. The events leading to this partnership began during my first week in Golden. While I was buying new bikes for us at the only Golden bike store, I became

Bernhard and I set out on errands. I definitely made a fashion statement in this cycling attire. Notice my corduroy shirt and purse on the handlebars, sandals, and rubber pedals, and alas, no helmets in 1975.

acquainted with the young mechanic, Karl Hummel. The bike store he managed closed in 1980, and Karl was much in need of work. An unholy alliance of seven riders combined their skills and capital to build Self-Propulsion to support Karl. I'll spare you the details, but during 1982, Karl left, I divested all six partners, divorced my husband, and did my best to nurture Bernhard and Kirk, who were then six and ten years old. Now that was a character-building experience: more growth through cycling!

Up to this point my experience with bike stores was extremely limited. Back in New Jersey, I had hung out with an old European man who refurbished used bikes in his garage. Besides my brief visit in Salem, I had not been in another bike store until we moved to Tucson. For 16 years, I had ridden on the original tires and tubes that in those days were heavy and made of natural rubber.

Having no preconceived notion of what a bicycle store should be, I set out to discover what bike stores were like. First, I visited bicycle retailers in Denver. I was happy to discover that my closest neighbors were Doug and Jo Stiverson of Westside Cyclery, and Eugene and Nora Kiefel of Wheat Ridge Cyclery, who have remained close friends and generous supporters of Self-Propulsion throughout the years. Their examples taught me that there is no substitute for professional expertise and genuine caring. Doug taught me to build wheels while Eugene taught me that being a devoted parent should take priority over running the bike store. When fatigue and loneliness threatened my equilibrium, I went to them for solace and advice.

I was highly motivated to succeed in business because of my love for bicycles and people and my need to put food on the table. My first impulse was to try to mimic successful bike stores in the Denver-Boulder area. Fortunately, I was diverted from this course by Interbike®, a bicycle trade show that was introduced in 1981. Its founder, Steve Ready, is passionate in his pursuit of cycling and truth and he created a new genre of trade shows with a strong learning environment. The show offered many critical seminars where I learned about creating a unique bicycle retail experience and providing top quality bicycle service and knowledgeable attention to customers. This complemented my desires to provide the highest quality in mechanical work and bicycle fitting and to share my love of cycling with others.

Self-Propulsion's Business Principles

One benefit of being a small business owner is the integrity of working and living by one set of principles. Self-Propulsion was founded on **honesty**, fairness, and good stewardship. Our business practices evolved out of my personal commitment to these principles. We were honest in all matters even when the truth was not what customers wanted to hear. We didn't make promises we couldn't realistically fulfill. When we didn't know the answers to customers' questions, we frankly told them we needed to research answers and would get back to them. Without honesty, there can be no trust. Without trust, life is long and tedious.

Fairness means that every customer received our best effort on each visit. We discovered it was more fun for us and for our customers when we avoided stereotyping them based on their appearances or initial comments. Instead, we encouraged them to tell us about their riding style and needs so we could specifically address them. In 1986, John Mita reinforced the wisdom of this style for us. He was in his late seventies and came in to buy one of our first mountain bikes. He was a bit stooped, stocky, and shuffled a bit when he walked. He pointed to our demo mountain bike and casually told me he wanted a bike like that with cargo rack, fenders — the whole works. We were not accustomed to that style of buying, and I tried discretely to explain that this bike was designed for off-road riding and was one of our more expensive bikes. John was not deterred. He told me he was an avid cyclist and had read all about the new mountain bikes in the cycling magazines. He was making an informed choice. We dutifully prepared it for him and in the years to come enjoyed his frequent visits to the store and seeing him on his daily rides far into the countryside.

I have a soft spot for underdogs and found myself giving special attention to people society neglects. We went the extra mile for the differently-abled, people of color, international students, women, citizens 50 and better, and the gay and lesbian community.

We gave special support to riders whose styles are overlooked by the industry: bicycle commuters, self-contained tourists, leisure riders, family recreational riders, riders motivated by environmental concerns, and people who only ride a few time a year.

We provided encouragement and support to riders at all stages of their cycling experience. Regardless of customers' dedication to cycling, we sought to discover how we could support them in their desire to ride. When customers discovered the joy of cycling and lamented that they hadn't started riding earlier in life, we commended them and pointed out that everyone starts riding as a beginner. If they would ride often, they would quickly progress to a new level.

Good stewardship means managing our resources well. We have been rewarded economically and environmentally for this commitment. I try to live as a world citizen and make my material choices while keeping an eye on the living conditions of people in other places in the world. Whenever I contemplate bringing something new into my life, I ask, "How will this object leave my life?" In business, we encouraged customers to avoid frivolous consumption and to instead purchase products and services based on safety, improved performance, or preservation of their equipment. We recycled all materials discarded at the store and offered to recycle customers' used bicycle stuff. This took training, time, space, and energy but I was motivated by my desire to have as little impact on our earth as possible.

Our commitment to these principles required that we continually reevaluate the ideas that made us comfortable. Whenever I have discovered that an idea is outmoded or wrong, I have appreciated the knowledgeable people who have helped enlighten me and been patient with me while I was learning. Being aware that what I believe to be true is only my current understanding, I am open to the ideas of other people. I strive to learn something from each person and their experiences.

The Evolution of a Distinctive Business Style

Serving on the board of the National Bicycle Dealers Association (NBDA) helped me create a vision for Self-Propulsion. When I was elected to the board in 1985, I was the first woman to serve. I was also the only current board member who was new to retail and who owned a small store (2,200 sq. ft and less than $250,000 gross annual receipts). In fact, at least a third of the board members had inherited their stores from their fathers, and their fathers had served on the NBDA board before them. These were kind, community-oriented men with years of experience and confidence in their ways of doing business. One-by-one, each retailer gave me his formula for success: One said I needed to publish a product catalog for my customers. Others said I needed to reach a particular size, I needed multiple stores, or I needed to compete on price. Gradually I learned to accept their advice as caring support for my fledgling business. I finally realized that their priorities were quite different from my own, and that was why their suggestions didn't fit Self-Propulsion. Our first priority has always been to help people find joy in cycling rather than to build a large, impressive business establishment. In fact, Self-Propulsion was small by design because it helped us provide personal attention to all customers and it gave us the luxury of making sound environmental choices.

About the same time I discovered I was on a different path from these retailers, I realized I was specially qualified to meet the needs of women and older riders. I also realized that business patterns established by men generally wouldn't fit my style. So we set out to establish a team of employees who shared my vision. We nurtured the vision through weekly sharing and training meetings. Sales staff took each customer's concerns seriously and gave him or her respectful attention. We also changed our product mix. We offered a large selection of comfortable saddles as well as loose-fitting alternatives to Spandex® clothing. We discontinued stocking bicycles with only two chainrings because women and older riders appreciate a wide range of user-friendly gears to enable them to climb with less effort. We became sensitive to their desire to balance fitness with pleasure through nature, family, social interaction, and good food. These observations helped us create an environment where non-traditional riders felt better served.

Most older riders have a heightened appreciation for their physical capabilities. At some point after turning 50, their bodies surprise them with a few unanticipated changes. Shapes change, a few aches and pains develop, and they figure out it is wise to preserve the capabilities they have. With increasing years, many people become comfortable with their idiosyncrasies and place a higher value on having their personal needs met than on following trends set by other people. Many older riders have the resources to create the exact bike and style they desire. We learned to listen carefully and modify bicycles to fulfill their wishes. Our reward was serving people who knew their priorities and who enjoyed a hearty laugh at themselves.

Riding as a Family

The first seven years at Self-Propulsion demanded all my energy and creativity to achieve profitability. Even though we were advantageously located next to the popular Foss General Store and had the privilege of doing business in a town where the citizens value honesty and integrity, Golden was a drab little byway. Thirty percent of the downtown buildings were vacant, and I wondered if we were doomed by our location. I worked six days a week from dawn to dark. Since my sons' summer break was during peak season, and they worked in the store from an early age, we could not share school vacations together. We addressed this dilemma by closing the store for three days on all Memorial and Labor Day weekends to make it possible to get away together.

We began a tradition of taking all our vacations on bikes. On two experimental self-contained bike tours, I gained some experience bike touring. At eight years old, Kirk demonstrated that he could ride 18 miles a day. We toured with a motley array of equipment and rode on heavy, affordable road bikes in blue jeans and tennis shoes with no attachment to the pedals. Kirk was in

Here we are fresh and clean at the start of another adventure. This trip we rode along the Foothills north of Boulder when it was still open farmland.

charge of carrying the tissue and lemon drops. Bernhard carried the sleeping bags, sleeping pads, one tent, and a sack of clothing. Everything else went on my bike: a second tent, more clothes, and the food. We rode to places we had never been to provide the excitement of discovery.

Our first tours were out-and-back rides. In this way we could stop and camp when we found a suitable place and could always turn back when fatigue diminished our fun. Bernhard was always a strong and eager rider. Kirk, however, was not sure that riding all day was his idea of a good time. To sweeten his perspective, we carried treats to coax him up the steep hills. "See that corner up there? You can have five yogurt-covered raisins when you get there." When parents lament that their cycling is curtailed by small children, I chuckle to think of all those miles I coasted half the time and braked the other half. However, I believe allowing my sons to propel themselves in their own style not only helped them feel capable but also demonstrated that I valued them enough to ride as slowly as they needed me to go.

When mountain bikes became available, we headed into the woods — first on to dirt roads and then mountain trails. We were beside ourselves with joy when we were able to take a week off one August. By this time we had better bikes and more equipment, which increased our options and our comfort. Many wonderful years of touring followed, culminating in a two-month-long cycling trip in Mongolia. We chose this destination in order to visit our dear Mongolian friends who had come to Golden in 1991 to study at the Colorado School of Mines. The endless miles of dirt tracks, spacious vistas, occasional

Bernhard rewards Kirk with jellybeans. No wonder! On this trip we rode uphill for two days before enjoying the rewards of the descent.

motor vehicles, and friendly people made Mongolia a mountain biker's dream.

In retrospect, how did my sons' childhood cycling experiences influence their adult riding styles? Today, Bernhard rides to work, on urban errands, and on self-contained bike tours with his partner. He only uses his compact pickup for hauling things and for distant vacations. Kirk rides regularly for fitness and recreation and always joins our family tours. To this day, we get together at least once a year to tour by bike or by sea kayak.

My early pattern of riding for transportation and adventure has remained the same, even while I have increased my stamina and improved my equipment. I drive my car about 3,000 miles a year, and the rest of my transportation is by bike. I have stayed true to my cycling beginnings, riding for fun and for environmental reasons rather than riding as an equipment junky.

Reaching Beyond the Essentials of Retailing

I love to teach. As a graduate student, I taught German and after Bernhard's birth I taught childbirth education for six years. During Self-Propulsion's first year, I began teaching bike maintenance classes. This first class ran for six-weeks, and the students overhauled their bearing assemblies and cleaned the drive train. From simple beginnings in 1981, it evolved into a sophisticated program. Gradually other classes were added: family cross-country ski classes, basic bike maintenance, and a three-week sequence on adjusting bearings, brakes, and derailleurs. I have enjoyed frequently giving presentations on bicycle maintenance and defensive riding techniques in the schools and for civic organizations.

Through student questions and suggestions, I have expanded my own understanding of the subjects.

Self-Propulsion News has also contributed to my teaching tradition. It began as a single page schedule of events and friendly visit with customers. Soon it was published in March, June, and November each year covering events, product information, mechanical instructions, featured customers, and philosophical discourse. When customers' questions made the need obvious, I published free information sheets to help riders have more fun sooner. In fact, the original idea for **Bicycling Bliss** was to create another free handout on riding technique.

When I joined the National Bicycle Dealers Association board, I was invited to present seminars at Interbike®. This was the best learning experience of all. After receiving my assigned topic each year, I researched the subject and often interviewed other retailers. Some of the topics focused on managing the service department, serving neglected markets, writing a mission statement, and bike fitting. During seminar discussions and in conversations with retailers on the show floor, I gained direct insight into the workings of the industry and retail-related issues. Each Interbike® stimulated creative problem solving and re-evaluation of Self-Propulsion's direction.

During this period of active involvement in the cycling industry, I also organized a special project to heighten awareness of women riders' needs, wrote monthly articles for the NBDA newsletter, and tried to promote cycling from within the industry. Part of the NBDA Women's Project included soliciting letters from women riders across the U.S. The many personal letters I received revealed the strength, perseverance, and courage of many capable riders. These women demonstrated a profound love of cycling as they coped with challenges that confronted them.

During my work in bicycle advocacy, I was a founding member of the Colorado Bicycling Advisory Board. Here I gained first-hand experience in promoting cycling interests in the community and working with government agencies. I had the opportunity to make presentations and listen to other advocates at bike/pedestrian conferences in Toronto, Minneapolis, and Indianapolis.

Each one of these opportunities expanded my understanding of cycling and grounded my belief that the bicycle is a vehicle that meets diverse individual, community, and global needs.

Developing the Basic Concepts of *Bicycling Bliss*

I continued to search for ways to bring broader cycling satisfaction to more riders and to discover ways to attract more novice riders to this healthful activity. With the naiveté and enthusiasm of a beginner, I hoped service on the NBDA board might facilitate change. During those eight years I met many caring and creative retailers and learned many lessons essential to my growth. I also discovered that the industry is conservative and limited by the confines of tradition and low profitability. So I withdrew from my responsibilities in the industry and shifted my focus to finding solutions to riders' problems. I put my energy into serving Self-Propulsion's customers, training our staff, and refining my understandings, concepts, and services.

To better serve customers I needed to understand why people weren't clamoring to ride bikes. What negative influences in the contemporary cycling environment deter people from getting started riding and progressing to full commitment?

Certainly the media's and general cycling industry's preoccupation with equipment, competition, speed, and extreme riding styles obscures the pleasures of cycling from many people. Glance into any bicycle publication and you will see images of riders flying through the air, of sprays of mud, and of blood and injury. These abuses put off people who want to ride for health and fitness or for their love of nature.

If instead, the bicycle media and industry would give the highest priority to health and fitness, more riders would be comfortable riding. It is essential to creatively and critically match riders' needs to equipment options. Let me share this story about Rick as an example of how critically weighing equipment options can help riders find appropriate solutions to their cycling problems.

Rick was in his late thirties and had several neck vertebrae fused making it uncomfortable for him to ride leaning over. His doctor suggested that a recumbent might enable him to ride comfortably. Recumbents are lots of fun, and in the early nineties, Self-Propulsion offered three models at various price points. Over the years, we have gained experience servicing and riding them. Many people like the comfort of the supportive seat and they enjoy the attention these unusual conveyances attract from passersby. *However*, one does need to weigh the pros and cons of choosing a recumbent. First, they are a significant investment. Prices begin at $1,000 for a safe and serviceable vehicle. Many styles are available but prices climb steeply from the classic rigid models. Surely, Rick's neck is worth more than $1,000, and his neck would be comfortable riding a recumbent. He would also enjoy the benefits of the aerodynamic position.

Would a recumbent meet Rick's other cycling requirements? He and his wife wanted to resume riding off-road. Well, recumbents really don't lend themselves to off-road riding. I suggested he could ride a conventional bike leaning forward only ten degrees. That would eliminate strain on his neck, enable him to ride off-road, and let him choose from a wide selection of bicycles. Using a suspension fork and seat post would reduce transmission of impact to his neck. He was delighted to know he had options and could enjoy cycling again.

How We Learned to Match Rider Needs with Bicycle and Component Designs

As musculoskeletal problems became more common among riders, I focused on learning more about biomechanics and the causes of stress and repetitive motion injuries. I was delighted to discover that my concentrated study of body use while cycling enabled me to help riders solve their problems. I began writing **Bicycling Bliss** in the fall of 1996. As I wrote, I uncovered many questions. Using Self-Propulsion as my "laboratory," I developed the following methods to identify possible solutions and verify their validity:

- Listening to the needs of customers
- Identifying recurring concerns and needs
- Observing my own riding experiences and testing theories on myself
- Carrying out measurements to clarify or substantiate my theories
- Identifying the causes of rider discomfort originating from bike design
- Modifying customers' bikes to enhance their riding experiences
- Asking customers for feedback on the extent of our success at meeting their needs
- Modifying new bike models during the assembly process to better meet the needs of most of our customers

We were always motivated by the desire to match recreational riders' priorities with available bikes and components.

We Developed a Practical Fitting System to Ensure Optimum Fit for All Customers

By 1997, I realized that poor bicycle fit and inappropriate design were limiting the growth of cycling and the bicycle industry. Numerous bicycle fitting systems were available but were based on the experience and priorities of racers and not appropriate or affordable for many recreational riders. That fall, bike designer and fitting expert, Lennard Zinn, and I presented a seminar at Interbike® to help specialty bicycle retailers learn how to knowledgeably fit bikes to shoppers. Lennard and I designed a simple system to make optimum fitting economically feasible for all retailers. You will find that system presented in Chapter 6, pp. 257-263.

After the show, Self-Propulsion staff began measuring shoppers who were looking for new bikes and regular customers who were wanting to eliminate riding discomfort. We took a few minutes to measure the rider and to create a Customer Reference Card. While we made the measurements, we interviewed customers to get to know their needs, develop trust, and identify riders' experience, physical requirements, and riding priorities. This proved to be a revolution in improved service *and* in our ability to fit each customer to a bicycle appropriate in size, price, and style!

To enable us to match the measurements to bike frames, we measured all bikes during the assembly process. We then recorded the standardized measurements for effective top-tube length and stand-over height on each price tag along with the manufacturers' frame size. Now, with the customer's calculated guideline measurements in hand, we were quickly able to select appropriate bikes for them to test ride and set the seat height appropriately. This procedure increased our confidence in fitting riders, which in turn increased customers' confidence. We all were having more fun!

Modifying Bicycles During the Assembly Process

By quantifying fitting procedures, we began to observe trends in bicycle designs that satisfied the needs of our customers. By modifying our new bikes during assembly, we were able to increase our efficiency and provide customers with immediate pleasure during test rides.

Rider position was our foremost concern. That meant our first modifications replaced stock stems with taller ones that had shorter horizontal reach to bring the handlebars closer to a rider's shoulders. When adjustable stems became available, we were able to fine-tune the handlebar position before each test ride. By adjusting these stems in their most vertical position we were able to raise the handlebars dramatically and to enable riders to sit with their torsos nearly vertical.

Riser bars limited our ability to shorten them for more responsive handling. We found that the curve in the bars prevented us from moving the controls far enough toward the stem to achieve a more comfortable width of 21 inches. On smaller frames, we replaced the riser bars with flat bars. We added bar ends to most of our bikes. Of course, we increased the retail price to make these modifications profitable.

The choice of gear shifters should be a matter of personal preference. It can be disappointing when bike shoppers find bikes that fit, respond well, and are in their budget but don't have the shifters they like to use. To ensure that bike shoppers found immediate delight in bikes they test rode, we converted common sizes of our best selling models so they were ready to test ride with either Shimano Rapid Fire® (lever-actuated shifters) or SRAM's Grip Shift® (twist shifters).

Changes in component design and increases in chronic tension in riders' necks and shoulders resulted in a gradual progression to offering only flat-handlebar bikes. First, we realized that the handlebar style does not dictate the forward lean of the rider's torso. Then in 1993, the ever-innovative and rider-oriented Shimano® introduced STI® (Shimano Total Integration®) levers for drop handlebars. This incorporated both gear and brake controls into the brake levers, making brake and gear control easily accessible and wonderfully accurate. Campagnolo® was quick to follow with Ergo® levers. Dual levers often cause hand strain since the hand movements required to actuate these levers are not used in other manual activities, and the levers are designed for large hands. This is especially true for riders with average to small hands who ride bikes with three chainrings. To access the controls, the riders' hands must be on the brake hood or the drops and that increases neck and shoulder tension.

Traditionalists loved the dual levers but riders who wanted the comfort of an upright position and freedom from neck, shoulder, and hand strain asked for something else. So we began modifying customers' road bikes installing taller stems, flat handlebars, bar ends, and mountain bike controls. We created some unusual looking bikes but after the initial adjustment to the esthetics of the new configuration, customers were delighted by the benefits and renewed their commitment to cycling.

In the late nineties, the demand for road bikes increased dramatically. Many riders returned to cycling in the eighties when mountain bikes were introduced. Mountain bikes were fun, stable, and made climbing easier. Now these riders wanted the greater efficiency of road bikes. They were delighted to discover that they could ride with greater ease on a performance road bike without giving up their comfort, control, and carefree riding style. Responding to riders' requests, we have progressively converted higher priced road bikes to flat bars with bar ends. I believe that by 2010 most road bikes will be equipped with flat bars with bar ends!

These bike modifications have all been driven by our evolving understanding of the biomechanics of cycling and the positive responses of riders to our comfortable bike setups. One of the great attractions of cycling is the potential for each rider to have a bike customized to his or her personal style. Although this evolution parallels my own experience, the popularity of these changes among a wide variety of cyclists confirms the theories we have developed.

Our discovery process has been facilitated by our willingness to experiment and create any bike configuration that our customers asked for as long as it was safe. It is my belief that *everyone* should ride a bike. To make this happen, I focused on one rider at a time and welcomed the challenge of creating vehicles that encouraged everyone to ride, even when they had limitations due to injury or illness.

Conclusion

I have enjoyed sharing my evolving love of cycling and cyclists with you. I hope this story will provide some insights into my perspective and that the ideas I offer will increase your own bliss. In hindsight, I understand that my empathy with a broad spectrum of cyclists stems from my own gradual and independent cycling development. I rode around blithely for 30 years quite unaware that my equipment was outmoded, and my riding style was unusual. I was isolated from other cyclists in the countryside of Oregon and didn't visit bike stores or read cycling magazines. Then I became a bicycle retailer and realized I had some catching up to do. I had to search for explanation of the mystifying customs and problems of the riders who came into the store. Through this process, I have developed an appreciation for the potential and diversity of cycling styles. I not only accept all riders for where they are in their evolving understanding of cycling but delight in encouraging them to keep riding in whatever way they enjoy. I am often able to guide them in the first tentative steps toward increasing their body awareness and improving their riding skills. I delight in whatever part I can play in helping riders find their rhythm and increase their joy on the seat of a bicycle.

Bicycle Frame and Component Terminology

Appendix C

Chart for Recording Bicycle Maintenance

The appropriate frequency of routine bicycle maintenance varies widely. On one extreme are the fair-weather, moderate-mileage road riders and on the other are the all-weather, high-mileage mountain bikers. The road riders can go many more miles between maintenance checks than the mountain bikers. You will need to service all aspects of your bike more frequency if you:
- ride more than 50 miles per week.
- let your bike get dirty and wet and stay that way.
- ride at a high-energy level.
- usually pedal at a cadence of less than 80 rpm.

1. Preserve your chain drive by lubricating it sparingly, riding at a cadence of 80 rpm or more, and washing your bike and chain drive every time they get muddy or covered with road grime. This can happen on the rack on the back of your car. Frequent washing and complete air drying will make the job quick and easy. Use a five gallon bucket and long-handled loop-style toilet brush. Avoid corrosive cleaners and high pressure water such as at car washes.

2. Since resistance in the gear cables and housings reduces precision in shifting, cables and housings should be replaced with each chain drive cleaning. Use new housing end-caps too. Any time the housings are bent or the protective plastic cover is damaged, they need to be replaced. If the bike has cable guides under the bottom bracket, clean and lubricate them frequently. Turn your bike over and visually inspect them and brush them clean and put a drop of chain lubricant on them.

3. Brake cables and housing should also be replaced when there is any sign of damage or resistance.

4. Check your brake pads on your mountain bike for wear and position on the rim each time you ride. Water, mud and grit can wear them out quickly. Don't let worn pads damage your rims or tires, or diminish optimum braking function. Know the thickness of your pads when new and replace them when the pad compound wears low. Road bikers and fair weather mountain bikers should check their pads every 500 miles. Be sure your wheels are precisely centered in the bike frame and the quick release properly secured *every time* you remove a wheel!

5. Tire quality varies widely. Poor quality tires age and crack whether you ride your bike or not. Continental® road tires last 1,000-3,000 miles, mountain bike tires 2,000-8,000 miles. Front tires always wear longer than back. The back tires bear more weight, and more significantly, apply friction to the ground as they power the bike forward, depositing rubber in the process. An accidental cut can occur on your first ride, or never. Inspect your tires regularly for cuts, damage, or wear.

6. Learn to inspect your rims. Slowly rotate the wheel while checking the distance between the rim and the brake pad. You should find less than a sixteenth-of-an inch variation. Repeat this process and check the roundness of the wheel by sighting off the top of the brake pad to check for hop or flat spots in the rim. Then evaluate the uniformity of spoke tension around the entire wheel by grasping pairs of spokes and squeezing them together. The integrity of the wheel depends on uniform spoke tension.

7. The quality and type of seals influence durability and performance, but proper adjustment during new bike assembly and each bike service is more critical to durability. The best quality hub can be damaged in less than 500 miles if it is not properly adjusted during assembly. Take your bike to an experienced mechanic and have all the bearing assemblies evaluated on any new or used bike when you buy it.

8. The standard bottom brackets with square spindles that come in new bikes are always of minimal quality. When you replace them, upgrade to the top quality to get the best seals, bearing quality, performance, and durability. Cartridge bottom brackets can creak in the frame and need to be removed. Grease the threads of the fixing cups and tightly re-secured them in the frame. To check the condition of the bottom bracket assembly move the crankarms side-to-side to test for lateral movement. Then drop the chain off the small chain ring onto the frame and spin the crank. Replace the bottom bracket assembly if there is lateral spindle movement, high resistance, or grinding.

Record of the Mechanical Service of Your Bicycle

I suggest you copy and prepare a record-keeping chart for each bike in your family. If you use a bike computer, you can also record the mileage between checks and get an idea of service frequency for your riding style.

Procedure/ Assembly	Date & Mileage	Date & Mileage	Date & Mileage	Suggested Frequency
Measure Chain				Every 500 miles
Replace chain				Elongation>1/16″ over 12″ length
Lubricate chain				When too noisy or rusty film forms
Clean Chain Drive (1)				400-1,000 miles
Replace gear cables and housing (2)				With each chain drive cleaning
Replace brake cables and housing (3)				As wear and damage indicate
Replace brake pads (4) Front Rear				As wear indicates
Replace tires (5) Front Rear				As wear and damage indicate
True Wheels (6) Front Rear				Whenever out of true
Overhaul bearing assemblies (7) Headset Front hub Rear hub Replace cartridge bottom bracket (8)				Every 1,000-3,000 miles Every 1,000-3,000 miles Every 1,000-2,000 miles Every 2,000-3,000 miles
Suspension tune-up				See manufacturer's specification

Human Anatomy Illustrations

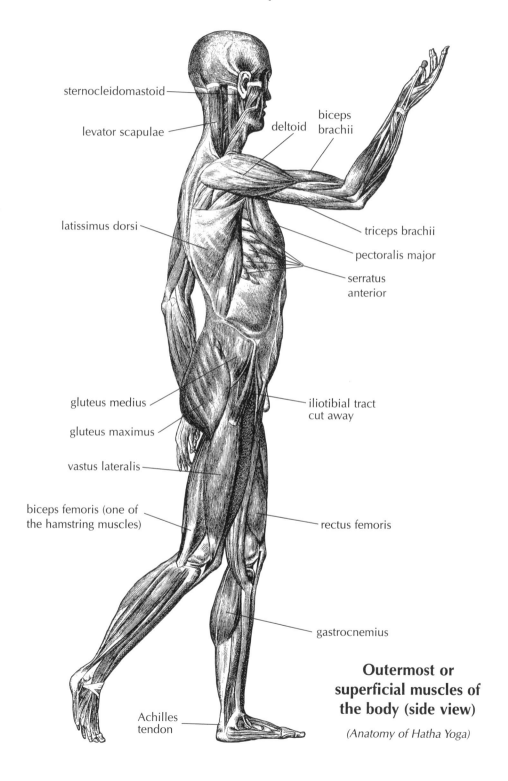

sternocleidomastoid

levator scapulae

deltoid

biceps brachii

triceps brachii

pectoralis major

serratus anterior

latissimus dorsi

gluteus medius

gluteus maximus

vastus lateralis

iliotibial tract cut away

biceps femoris (one of the hamstring muscles)

rectus femoris

gastrocnemius

Achilles tendon

Outermost or superficial muscles of the body (side view)

(Anatomy of Hatha Yoga)

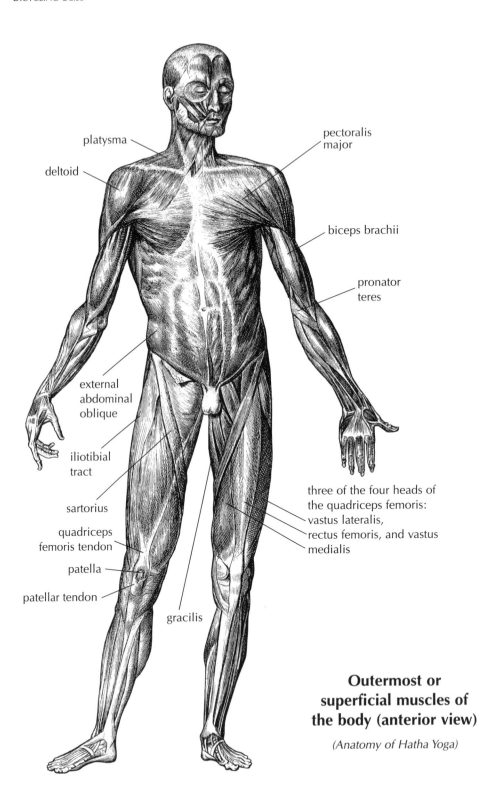

platysma

deltoid

pectoralis
major

biceps brachii

pronator
teres

external
abdominal
oblique

iliotibial
tract

sartorius

quadriceps
femoris tendon

patella

patellar tendon

gracilis

three of the four heads of
the quadriceps femoris:
vastus lateralis,
rectus femoris, and vastus
medialis

**Outermost or
superficial muscles of
the body (anterior view)**

(Anatomy of Hatha Yoga)

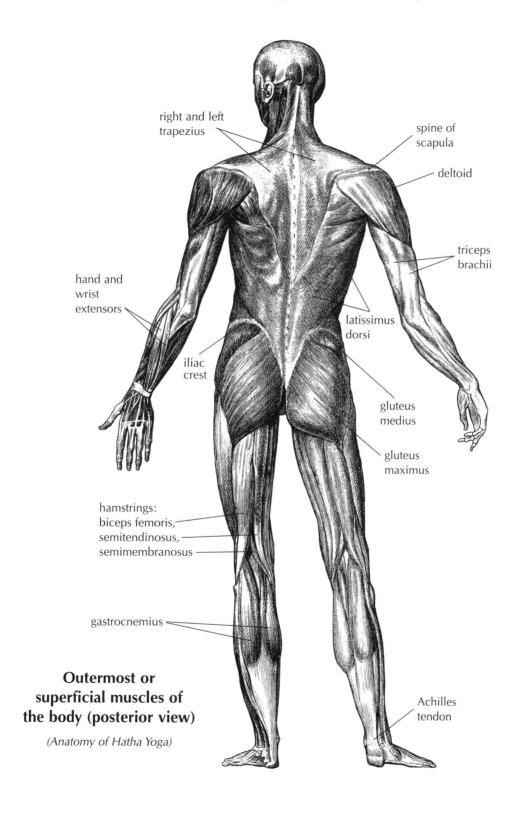

right and left
trapezius

spine of
scapula

deltoid

triceps
brachii

hand and
wrist
extensors

latissimus
dorsi

iliac
crest

gluteus
medius

gluteus
maximus

hamstrings:
biceps femoris,
semitendinosus,
semimembranosus

gastrocnemius

**Outermost or
superficial muscles of
the body (posterior view)**

(Anatomy of Hatha Yoga)

Achilles
tendon

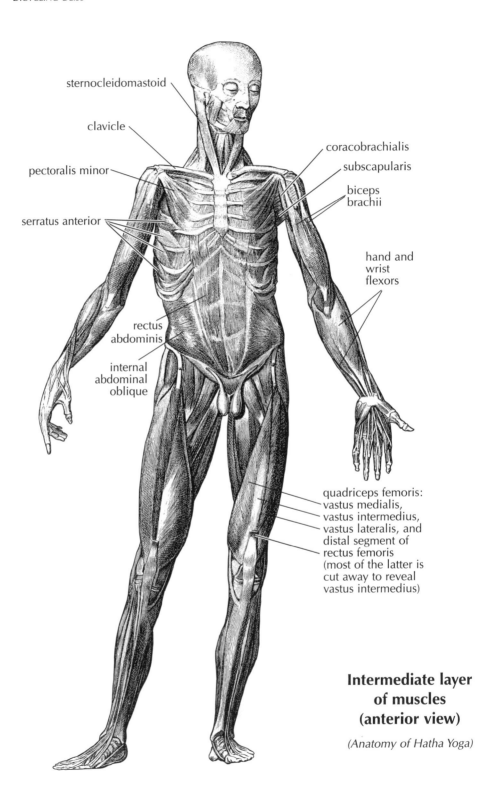

sternocleidomastoid

clavicle

pectoralis minor

serratus anterior

rectus
abdominis

internal
abdominal
oblique

coracobrachialis

subscapularis

biceps
brachii

hand and
wrist
flexors

quadriceps femoris:
vastus medialis,
vastus intermedius,
vastus lateralis, and
distal segment of
rectus femoris
(most of the latter is
cut away to reveal
vastus intermedius)

**Intermediate layer
of muscles
(anterior view)**

(Anatomy of Hatha Yoga)

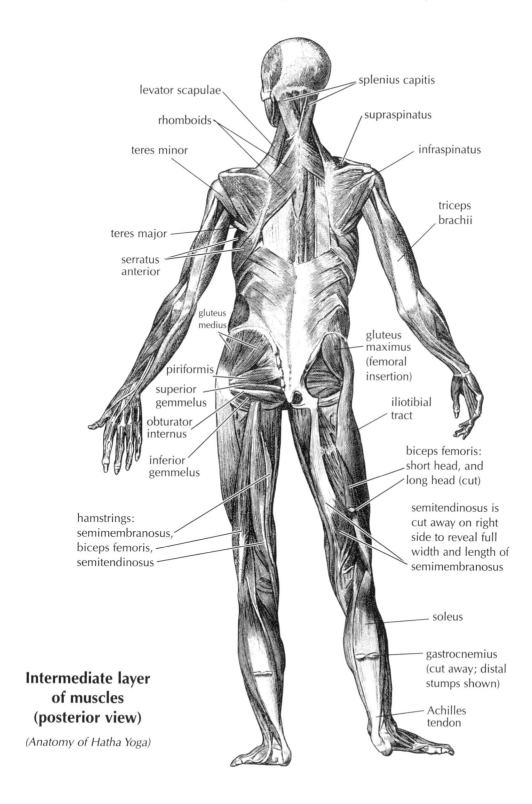

levator scapulae

splenius capitis

rhomboids

supraspinatus

teres minor

infraspinatus

triceps
brachii

teres major

serratus
anterior

gluteus
medius

gluteus
maximus
(femoral
insertion)

piriformis

superior
gemmelus

iliotibial
tract

obturator
internus

inferior
gemmelus

biceps femoris:
short head, and
long head (cut)

hamstrings:
semimembranosus,
biceps femoris,
semitendinosus

semitendinosus is
cut away on right
side to reveal full
width and length of
semimembranosus

soleus

gastrocnemius
(cut away; distal
stumps shown)

Achilles
tendon

**Intermediate layer
of muscles
(posterior view)**

(Anatomy of Hatha Yoga)

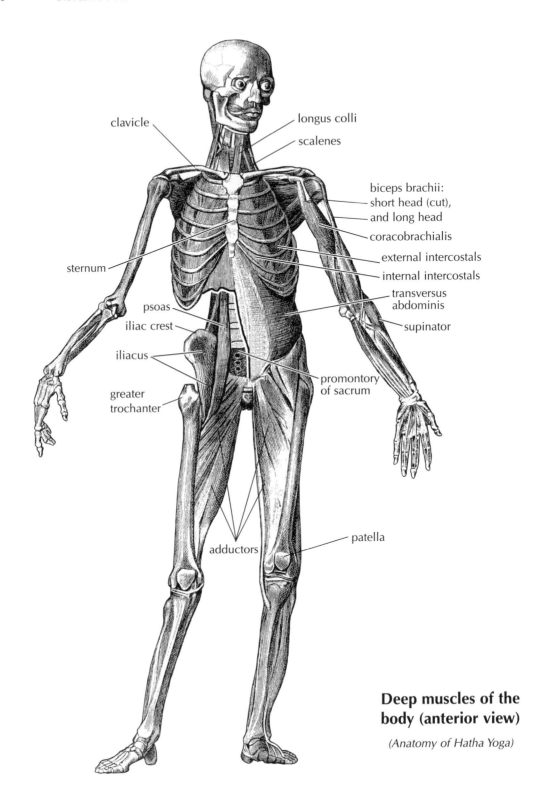

clavicle

longus colli

scalenes

biceps brachii:
short head (cut),
and long head

coracobrachialis

external intercostals

internal intercostals

transversus
abdominis

supinator

sternum

psoas

iliac crest

iliacus

greater
trochanter

promontory
of sacrum

adductors

patella

**Deep muscles of the
body (anterior view)**

(Anatomy of Hatha Yoga)

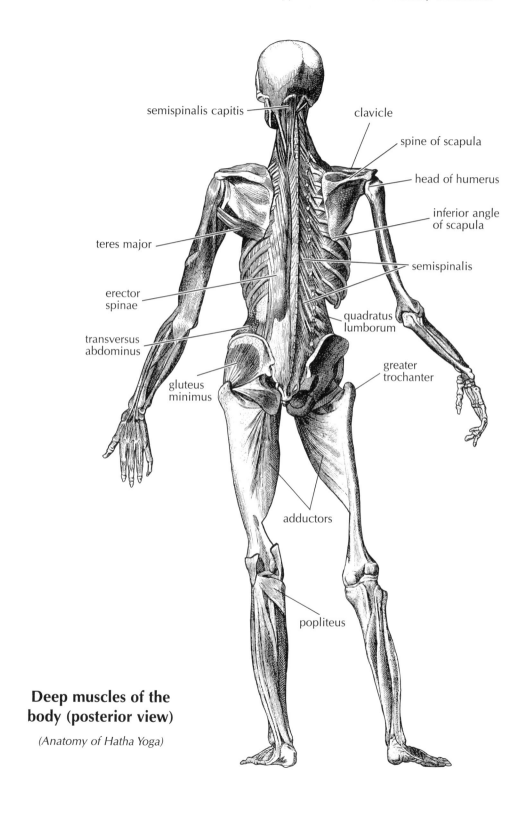

semispinalis capitis

clavicle

spine of scapula

head of humerus

inferior angle
of scapula

teres major

semispinalis

erector
spinae

quadratus
lumborum

transversus
abdominus

greater
trochanter

gluteus
minimus

adductors

popliteus

**Deep muscles of the
body (posterior view)**

(Anatomy of Hatha Yoga)

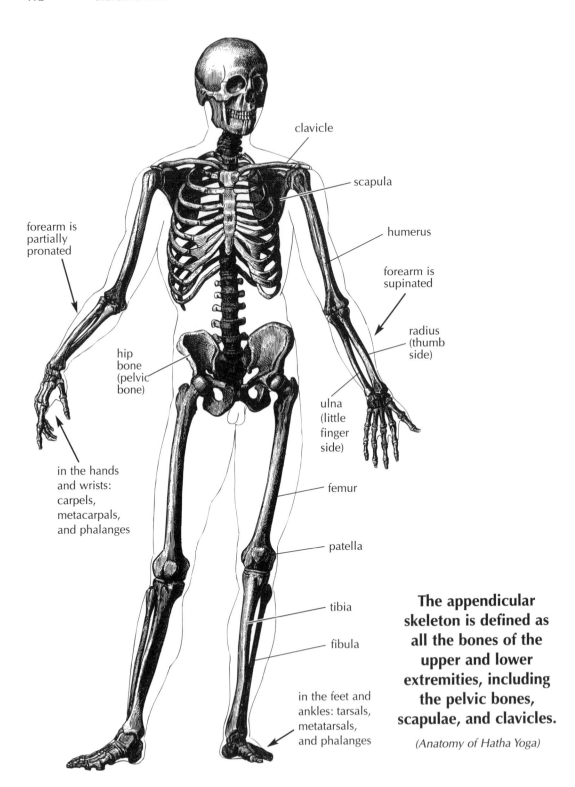

clavicle

scapula

humerus

forearm is
partially
pronated

forearm is
supinated

radius
(thumb
side)

hip
bone
(pelvic
bone)

ulna
(little
finger
side)

in the hands
and wrists:
carpels,
metacarpals,
and phalanges

femur

patella

tibia

fibula

in the feet and
ankles: tarsals,
metatarsals,
and phalanges

**The appendicular
skeleton is defined as
all the bones of the
upper and lower
extremities, including
the pelvic bones,
scapulae, and clavicles.**

(Anatomy of Hatha Yoga)

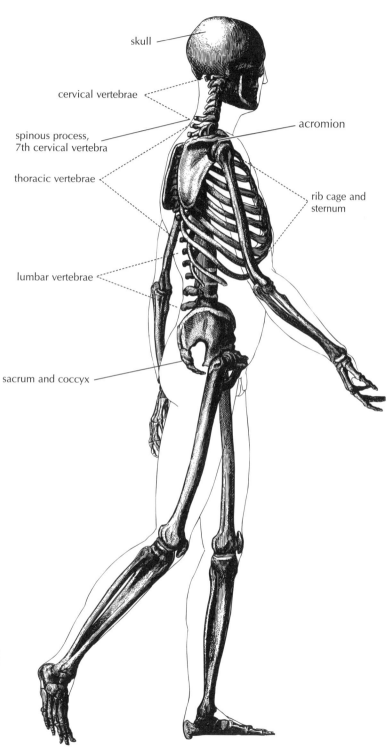

skull

cervical vertebrae

spinous process,
7th cervical vertebra

thoracic vertebrae

lumbar vertebrae

sacrum and coccyx

acromion

rib cage and
sternum

**The axial skeleton
includes the vertebral
column, skull, rib
cage, and sternum.**

(Anatomy of Hatha Yoga)

Appendix E

Preparing Food for Fun and Nutrition

Recipe Index

Healthful Eating is the Foundation of Wellness and High Performance

I love to prepare and eat my favorite foods. I prepare them when I want them in the style I like them and then I enjoy eating them outdoors in the quiet nurture of nature. After a tiring day at work followed by a nutritious bowl of hot cereal and fruit, I peacefully settle into baking whole grain treats, simmering a big pot of bean soup, or cleaning and storing fresh greens I bought the night before at my local organic grocer. I may listen to quiet music, read a bit of news, and generally wind down to my before bedtime exercise. Since these indulgences are renewing to me, I wonder why many people avoid cooking for themselves and instead choose to suffer the consequences of eating harmful foods in the distracting environment found in most commercial eateries.

Kirk tells me that people don't cook from scratch for themselves because it requires planning and moving good nutrition to a top priority. My commitment stems from my strong desire to feel full of energy and to stay centered and grounded. I know that for me to be comfortable and vital in my later years, I need to maintain good nutrition habits and eat high quality foods every day.

Each of us is capable of maintaining good health and of healing imbalance, injury, and illness. We all choose whether or not to inform ourselves, to cultivate our natural healing powers, and to practice skills to support healing. **Healthful eating is the foundation of high performance, health maintenance, and healing capabilities**. The scientific literature is clear that illness and premature death can be avoided by eating wholesome, nutritious meals and by maintaining a routine of daily exercise.

It's easy to convince ourselves that changing our eating habits is not worth the effort. I encourage you to listen objectively to your mental and verbal defenses. I hear them daily from friends and customers. We remembered Dave as an energetic, confident cyclist who worked long hours at his successful career. We didn't see him for three years and when he returned, he told us he had suffered a heart attack while still in his forties. His perspective was quite changed, and he was afraid to go anywhere without his cell phone with GPS. He had lost his joy in cycling for fear of another heart attack. As I encouraged him to return to his riding and inquired about his eating habits, I was astonished when he told me he couldn't reduce his meat consumption "...because I am such a carnivore." Wait a minute here! He chose to limit his full recovery by confining himself to eating habits that destine him to remain at high risk for heart disease? I'm sure he is not aware of the irrationality of this thought sequence. He would shoot himself in the foot by refusing to change his eating habits and choose illness and fear over health and confidence.

We all benefit from freeing ourselves from our traditional eating patterns. Initiate change by making a realistic survey of your eating habits over the last three months. List the types of food you eat frequently and your eating schedule throughout the day. What is a typical breakfast, lunch, supper, and snack for you? Do you have long periods of fasting or do you nibble much of the time? I have found that by eating my main meal in the morning between my morning Yoga and Qigong practice and work, I have been able to free myself of less healthful eating patterns and to maintain enjoyable energy levels by adjusting my food consumption more accurately to my energy needs.

Our habits tend to evolve by circumstance. I encourage you to evaluate your habits and question if you are eating in a way that will sustain your vitality throughout your life. After surveying your current habits, gather information about healthy eating habits. Use the sources in the recommended reading list. Then allow time to process the information and let it settle into your consciousness. Gradually your habits will begin to change as you get a clear idea of what changes will benefit you. Use the tools for integrated wellness in Chapter 4, pp. 67-151 to support your commitment to health and fitness excellence.

Learn to eat the minimum amount of food that supports your energy needs. It will help you maintain your body weight, avoid gastric distress, and regulate elimination while maximizing your energy output and your focus. Measure all the servings of your favorite foods that you eat at home to determine what quantities enable you to maintain your weight. Then increase or decrease these basic amounts depending on what your physical activity level will be in the three hours following that meal. For example, when I am setting out on a 20-mile bike ride, I increase my intake by 10 to 20 percent depending on the stamina level required. When I am going to sit at the word processor for the next three hours, I decrease my basic serving size. At each meal ask yourself "What are my energy requirements for the next three hours?"

When social commitments tempt you to eat a larger meal than usual, simplify and reduce the size of your next meal. When you eat at a restaurant, take an airtight container with you and plan to take the excess portions home with you. In other words, make your meal decisions consciously and avoid over-eating or consuming harmful foods out of habit.

Let your taste shift gradually from over-processed wheat flour products to whole-grain baked products, from foods containing partially-hydrogenated vegetable oils to those with unsaturated oils, and from high-salt- and sugar-containing foods to high quality fruits and vegetables that you can savor for their natural goodness.

When you need to eliminate dairy products or other categories of food due to intolerance or their harmful effect on your health, make your commitment, design your affirmations to support that choice, and make the change in one dramatic step without looking back. Teasing yourself with an occasional indulgence just makes the task more difficult.

Food Planning and Time Management

I hope the following suggestions will make your food preparation easier:

- Avoid cooking when you are hungry. Prepare your main course a day in advance. The flavors will blend and taste their best when you are ready to eat the next day.

- Prepare large enough quantities of soup or bean dishes to last three to four days. Prepare your fruits and vegetables before sitting down to enjoy an easy meal.

- Record the number of hours each week you spend on TV and computer entertainment. Replace time spent on sedentary recreation with grocery shopping and food preparation.

- I make grocery shopping fun by riding my bike to the store with trailer or tour packs and remembering that I am truly privileged to have the means and access to this wealth of food.

- Make your basic grocery list throughout the week by jotting down foods as they run low and as you plan the next week's menus. Avoid unscheduled trips to the store. I have created some tasty dishes by making do with the foods available at home.

- Soaking whole grains (intact kernels) in advance will shorten the cooking time.

- Soak and cook dried beans the day before you plan to prepare the bean dish.

- Wash dishes while you visit on the phone or with family and friends. Pans used for steaming vegetables can be rinsed and turned up to dry and don't need to be washed with each use.

- Make it easy to brush oil into baking and cooking pans by keeping handy a shallow, covered container of oil.

Basic Utensils to Get You Started

Vegetable peeler	Potholders
Paring knife	1-quart saucepan
Chopping knife	2 to 3-quart heavy
Bread knife	saucepan
Cutting board	Cast-iron skillet
Large wooden spoon	6 to 8-quart soup pot
for bread dough	4-quart mixing bowl
Utility spoon	8-quart mixing bowl
Wire whisk	Electric skillet
Potato masher	Loaf pans
Spatula for sautéing	Muffin tins
Spreading spatula	Baking sheet
Measuring spoon set	Cooling racks
Dry ingredient measuring	Plastic storage
cup set	containers
2-cup liquid measuring cup	Blender

Use a natural-bristled, one-inch-wide paint brush to lightly brush your pans with oil before placing food in them.

Kitchen Organization

- Store ingredients and utensils so you can stand in one place and reach commonly used products.

- Transfer grains and bulk ingredients to airtight containers that provide easy access.

Storing and Cleaning Food

- Store prepared foods in airtight containers in the refrigerator.

- Buy quality nuts from reliable sources where they are refrigerated and store them in your refrigerator so the fat content does not become rancid.

- Clean leafy, green vegetables, especially spinach and lettuce, and store them in airtight containers in the refrigerator. This will maintain their freshness, retard spoilage, and encourage you to eat more of them.

Simplicity

- Plan simple meals and eat the same main dish for several days in sequence. This will reduce preparation time as well as reduce the quantity you consume. The greater the variety, the more you will eat. Think of how you load up your plate at a buffet. Just sampling each dish results in over-eating.

- Avoid making a mess and you won't have to clean it up. Save time and resources. Use one drinking vessel between dish washings. If you live alone, use one bowl, one plate, one fork, and one spoon. Rinse and air dry them between uses. This works especially well for low-fat meals.

- Clean up fish odor immediately by placing the oils, skin, and bones in a plastic bag and taking it directly to the trash. Wash up the food preparation containers and air out the kitchen.

- Simplify your life style to reduce stress and minimize gastric distress.

Choice of Foods

- Quality ingredients are the secret to savory, clean flavors.

- Quality vegetables require less preparation since you just combine them, steam them lightly, and enjoy their natural good flavor.

- Eat fresh organic produce whenever possible for the best nutrients and flavors. Produce grown by conventional methods may be satisfactory if they can be washed with detergent and rinsed or peeled. The following products are more healthful when grown organically since the conventional forms are highly contaminated:

  - Strawberries - Conventional growers use the fungicide, methyl bromide, a known carcinogen. Strawberries cannot be cleaned adequately to remove it so only eat strawberries when they are certified organic.

  - Leafy, green vegetables - Their large, textured surfaces make it impossible to remove all chemicals.

  - Vegetables that are waxed - This includes apples and cucumbers unless you will wash *and* peel them.

  - Other highly contaminated foods are peaches, apricots, cherries, and grapes from Chile; and cantaloupes, green beans, celery, and spinach from Mexico. (Weil 2000, p. 142)

  - Milk - Environmental toxins and hormones and antibiotics given to dairy cows may accumulate in milk.

- Equip yourself with basic reference books so you can look up the nutritional values of foods and not be led astray by hearsay. I recommend the USDA's *Nutritive Value of Foods* Home Bulletin No. 72, Revised October 2002. You can purchase this from the U.S. Printing Office or print it out in PDF format from www.nal.usda.gov. The best reference for glycemic index is Jennie Brand-Miller's *The New Glucose Revolution. Food: A Handbook of Terminology, Purchasing and Preparation* will answer all your food preparation questions and can be purchased at www.aafcs.org from the American Association of Family and Consumer Science.

Recipes

Abbreviations with metric and English equivalents used in these recipes are as follows:

t. = teaspoon =	T. = tablespoon =	c. = cup =
0.16 fluid ounce	0.5 fluid ounce	8 fluid ounces
1/3 tablespoon	3 teaspoons	16 tablespoons
5 milliliters	15 milliliters	238 milliliters
4.2 grams of sugar	12.5 grams of sugar	200 g. of sugar
0.15 ounces of sugar	0.44 ounces of sugar	7 oz. of sugar

Dips and Spreads

Use these as sandwich spreads or dips for fresh vegetables to carry with you on bike rides or for sack lunches at work. They are economical and wholesome. You'll find them to be good alternatives to chef's salads and cheese sandwiches.

Hummus with Herbs   Yield: 2 cups

Combine in a heavy saucepan:

  3/4 c. dried chickpeas
  3 c. water

Bring to a boil, remove from the heat, and let stand 1-8 hours. Cook over low heat until thoroughly tender. The amount of time depends on the freshness and quality of the chickpeas but allow two or more hours.

When tender, combine the chickpeas and remaining cooking fluids with the following ingredients and puree in a blender or food processor until creamy smooth:

  1/4 c. Tahini (sesame butter)
  3/4 c. pine nuts
  Juice of 1/2 lemon or lime
  1 clove garlic
  1 1/2 T. olive oil
  1 t. paprika
  2 T. each of the following fresh herbs: basil, cilantro, parsley
  Dash of salt

Add enough water to facilitate processing but still maintain a thick, creamy, spreadable mixture.

I like to puree the ingredients in two batches so my blender will perform well. Experiment with what works best for your equipment. Hummus will thicken in the first few hours after preparation, and the flavors will blend in the next 24 hours. It keeps well for a week when refrigerated in a sealed container or for two days when unrefrigerated while bike touring or camping at temperatures below 70° F.

Serve with fresh tomatoes, dark greens, whole wheat bread, cheese, or chips and fresh vegetables.

Layered Bean Dip

Build this popular dip in a plastic 9-inch by 9-inch square container with airtight lid. The preparation time is about one hour but it's worth it. It keeps 3-4 days in the refrigerator.

The combined layers should be about 1 1/2 inches deep when completed. Layer from the bottom:

- 1 - 15 oz. can of refried beans, thinned to the right consistency for dipping with picante sauce
- 2 large Roma tomatoes diced finely.
  Do not use all the juices or the dip will be too soupy.
- 2 - 3 chopped green onions including part of the green portion
- 3 1/2 oz. chopped ripe olives
- 5 oz. cheddar cheese, grated
- 2 ripe avocados, mashed with a potato masher leaving them a bit lumpy.
  Mix in lemon juice (to retard browning) and garlic salt.
- 2/3 c. sour cream or 1/3 c. sour cream and 1/3 c. yogurt

Serve with corn chips or fresh vegetables.

White Bean Spread

Yield: 1 1/2 cups

Fully cook the dried beans until all the fluid is absorbed. Use:

- 3/4 c. dried white beans, great northern and limas.
- 2 1/2 c. water

If you prefer, use 1 1/2 cups low-sodium, water-packed canned beans, drained:
Sauté until dark brown:

- 2 T. canola oil
- 1 small yellow onion, finely chopped
- 1 clove garlic, crushed
- 2 T. chopped green chilies

Blend in thoroughly:

- 1/8 t. cayenne
- 1/2 t. salt

Cook the beans until they are easy to mash. Use a potato masher to create a smooth paste.
Then thoroughly blend the beans with the sautéed vegetables.
Add:

- 1 T. low-sodium soy sauce
- 2 t. apple juice frozen concentrate

Use as a sandwich spread or dip. This spread will keep for at least a week when stored in an airtight container in the refrigerator. I also like to spread it thinly on a whole wheat tortilla and then warm and brown them in a lightly-oiled skillet on medium heat. Then I top this combination with chopped tomatoes and greens.

Beans and Soups

Beans are nutritious, economical, and have many ecological benefits. They are the staple food in many countries but are not valued appropriately in the U.S. Let me encourage you to overcome any resistance you may have to eating dried beans regularly.

Dried beans and peas are so economical that you can buy organic beans and still prepare meals cheaply. Beans, peas, and peanuts are legumes. These plants take the nitrogen from the air and fix it in the soil, enriching the soil for other plants. They contain high quality protein that metabolizes cleaner than meat during digestion. Growing legumes does not pollute our soil and streams with excess nitrogen as does the run-off from manure created by livestock production. Legumes are high in fiber, have a low glycemic index, require little processing, and are low on the food chain so they contain few contaminants.

Cultural attitudes about foods often lead us to make unwholesome choices. Let me contrast our attitudes toward dairy products with those toward legumes. Dairy is surely a sacred cow in the U.S. The American Dairy Council spends millions of dollars convincing us that dairy products are essential to our health. The facts are: most people have some level of intolerance to cow's milk and products made from it. It may be a lactose intolerance that causes gastric distress or an allergy to the proteins that increase sinus problems or other symptoms. As already mentioned, milk is likely to contain a concentration of contaminants, and organic milk is expensive. However, expense and health problems stemming from dairy products are largely ignored because we feel it is un-American not to enjoy ice cream, cheese, and cow's milk.

In contrast, legumes are nutritious, low in contaminants and processing, economical, and beneficial for the earth. Without understanding the cause or seeking remedies, many people complain that beans give them gastric distress and simply refuse to eat them. Some people see the preparation time as a deterrent. Let's look at the facts in hopes that you will experiment and adapt to eating these delicious morsels regularly.

Legumes are composed of protein, fiber, and complex sugars called oligosaccharides. We can only digest simple sugars so the complex sugars pass to the large intestines where they are broken down by fermentation. The fermentation process produces hydrogen, methane, and carbon dioxide, and the resulting flatulence is unpleasant. Another factor is that legumes contain a mixture of protein and carbohydrates. The carbohydrates require more basic pH in the digestive track, and proteins require a more acid pH – a combination that also contributes to gastric distress. Most U.S. residents eat low-fiber diets so their digestive tracks are not accustomed to processing it. This needs to be corrected since soluble fiber lowers blood cholesterol and stabilizes blood sugar while insoluble fiber maintains bulk in the bowels and promotes regular elimination. What can we do to reduce gastric distress caused by these digestive challenges?

Select recipes low in sugars and meat to facilitate digestion. Typically, we eat chili with meat and baked beans high in added sugar. Meat slows the digestion of the complex sugars by increasing acidity and contributing acid indigestion to the already complex digestive process. Select bean dishes that do not use sugar. Avoid fruits and sweet desserts in the same meal that will not digest until after the protein in the beans is processed.

Introduce dried bean dishes into your diet by selecting the beans that are lower in complex sugars and easier to digest. Pinto beans that are so popular in the U.S. are some of the most difficult to digest. Some of the best beans are Anazasi beans that have 75 percent less oligosaccharides than many other popular beans. Also try adzuki beans, black beans, chickpeas, lentils, mung beans, split peas (without ham), and black-eyed peas. Use seasonings that reduce flatulence like ginger, cumin, chilies, and cayenne. Mix your bean dishes with easy to digest carbohydrates to dilute their effects. Serve them with equal volumes of brown rice, polenta, whole wheat bread, cornmeal muffins, and vegetables that calm digestion like yams and winter squash. (Lesa Heebner, *Calypso Bean Soup*, HarperCollins, San Francisco, CA 1996, pp. xvii-xviii.)

You may find that a few drops of Bean-O® on the first spoonfuls of beans will reduce flatulence. Others people find that it reduces gastric distress to add a few strips of kombu seaweed (at health food stores) during the cooking process. The best route to quiet digestion of legumes is to eat them often, and you will develop the bacteria needed to ferment the complex sugars.

If you eat a low-fiber diet, help your body adapt to this important food by adding more fiber found in whole grains, fruits, and vegetables.

You can quiet gastric distress by simplifying your life style, reducing stress, and surrounding your mealtime with conscious breathing and a peaceful attitude since the parasympathetic nervous system controls digestion. I find that most foods cause gastric distress when I am anxiously pursuing a high-demand schedule. Rather than finding fault with the meal I just ate, I take the gastric distress as warning that I'd better calm down and give attention to my health needs.

Recipes offer a variety of ways to prepare beans that are supposed to increase their digestibility. Experiment with these to determine if any of them are helpful for you. I think my general level of stress is more important than cooking tricks. I do know, though, that I must limit my bean consumption to one meal per day.

Cooking Tips for Dried Beans

Soaking beans shortens the cooking time and increases tenderness and texture. Some legumes do not need to be soaked and are tender after 30 to 45 minutes of cooking. These include lentils, mung beans, split peas, and black-eyed peas. Depending on your source of beans, sort and rinse them to eliminate debris. Choose your soaking method based on your time schedule. You can place the dried beans in a large pot and cover them with three to four times the volume of water. You soak them for eight hours or bring them to a boil, turn off the heat, put a lid on the pan, and let them soak for one hour. Then you can begin to simmer them slowly for one-and-one-half to three hours. You may find that draining off the soaking water will decrease gastric distress. I have not found that to be true and choose instead to retain the water-soluble vitamins that may be lost by draining off the soaking water and use the same water for cooking. You will need to watch water absorption and occasionally add more water to keep the beans covered during cooking.

Cooking time depends on the length of time the beans have been stored so the best test of doneness is tenderness. Test them every fifteen minutes after the first hour to know when they are done. After a year in storage, dried beans tend to be tough so store a limited quantity in a closed container in a dry place. Cooking time can be shortened to about half by using a pressure cooker.

Several factors influence **tenderness**. Cook the beans slowly and avoid letting them boil. Do not add salt and acid ingredients like tomatoes until the beans are tender. If your tap water is highly saline, you will be wise to cook beans in filtered or bottled water.

Cooked beans **store well** for four to six days in the refrigerator. Since beans ferment easily, do not leave them out after cooking but promptly put them in the refrigerator. Cooked beans freeze better if they are stored without salt or other ingredients.

Serving size can be estimated by remembering that one cup of dried beans produces three to four servings as a side dish or about two servings as a main dish.

The **seasonings** in these recipes are mild so if you like spicy food increase the chilies and spices. After burning my mouth a few times too often, I learned not to serve soup "piping hot" but to serve it before it boils.

Anasazi Bean and Roasted Chili Soup   Yield: 10 servings of 1 1/4 cups

Anasazi beans are also known as Aztec beans, Appaloosa beans, or cattle beans. Their low complex-sugar content makes them a wise choice to substitute in other recipes.

Rinse, sort, and place in an 8-quart soup pot:
>   2 c. dried Anasazi beans
>   6 c. water

Bring to a boil, remove from the heat, and let soak for one hour. Then simmer until tender.

While the beans are cooking, roast the chilies. Always wear rubber gloves while handling chilies to prevent the oils from getting in your eyes and making them sting.

Wash, remove the stems, veins, and seed. Cut the peppers in lengthwise strips that will lie flat on a baking sheet for roasting:
>   3 ancho chilies

    3 jalapenos

Chilies vary widely in spiciness so select your favorite chilies and be prepared to add some hot sauce when the soup is finished to achieve the flavor sensation you would like.

Place the chili slices on a lightly-oiled baking sheet with the skin-side up. Roast them until the skins turn brown and blister. Transfer them to a covered airtight container to steam. This will make the skins easier to remove.

While the chilies are steaming, clean, core, dice, and spread evenly on a baking sheet:

    1 large red sweet pepper

Roast under the broiler until somewhat dried.

During the last 30 minutes the beans are simmering, prepare and add to the pot:

    1 bay leaf
    1 c. broccoli trunks, peeled and diced
    1 large carrot, sliced
    1 large yellow onion, diced
    6 cloves of garlic, pressed or finely minced

Put your gloves on again and remove the skins from the chilies, dice them, and add to the bean pot along with:

    1 - 15 oz can of stewed, diced tomatoes with all the fluid
    1 t. ground cumin
    1/2 t. dried thyme
    1/4 t. ground coriander
    1/2 t. ground black pepper
    1 T. low-sodium soy sauce

Place one-third of the soup in the blender and puree it. Return it to the soup pot for a creamy, flavorful soup. Adjust the seasonings and fluidity. This may seem like a lot of work but the results are delicious.

Serve hot, garnished with chopped, fresh cilantro, hot cornmeal muffins or other home-made bread of your choice.

Armenian Lentil Soup   Yield: 6 servings of 1 1/4 cups

Rinse, sort, and simmer for about 20 minutes:

    1 1/2 c. green lentils
    4 c. water

Sauté until translucent:

    1-2 T. olive or canola oil
    1 1/2 - 2 c. onion, diced
    1 red sweet pepper, diced

Add to the lentils along with:

>   2-3 c. butternut squash, peeled, seeds removed, and cubed (or eggplant if you like but squash is more nutritious)
>   1/2 c. fresh tomato, chopped
>   1/2 c. dried apricots, diced
>   1 1/2 t. salt
>   1/4 t. each - cinnamon, allspice, and cayenne
>   2 t. paprika

Add fluids as needed to create the consistency you like. I recommend the following:

>   1 c. water
>   1 c. soymilk

Simmer another 30 minutes. Prevent boiling or the soymilk will curdle.

Before serving stir in:

>   3 T. fresh parsley, chopped.
>   1 T. fresh mint, chopped (or 1 t. dried)

Serve with whole wheat bread or muffins and dark green vegetable.

The unusual blend of spices makes this soup a guest pleaser. The flavors blend and this keeps refrigerated for a week.

Black Beans with Polenta   Yield: 2 quarts or 6 servings

Combine in a large pot, bring to a boil, remove from heat, cover, and soak 1-8 hours:

>   1/2 lb. black turtle beans
>   5 c. water

Then simmer 1-2 hours or until tender.

When nearly tender, sauté for about 3 minutes watching constantly so it won't burn:

>   3 T. olive oil
>   3 large cloves garlic, minced
>   1/4 t. cayenne pepper

Remove from the heat and cool the oil slightly, then add:

>   6 oz. tomato paste
>   1 c. tomato sauce

Add to the beans along with:

>   4 c. water
>   3 t. salt
>   2 T. fresh parsley, chopped
>   1 T. fresh sweet basil, chopped

When this mixture is simmering, gradually sprinkle over the top of the bean mixture while stirring constantly to prevent lumps from forming:

    1 c. polenta or coarsely-ground corn meal

Continue to cook and stir for the first 5 minutes so the polenta does not sink to the bottom and burn. Simmer over low heat for 20 minutes until the polenta is cooked. Control the fluids to produce the desired consistency.

Serve with chopped fresh cilantro, tomatoes, and warmed whole wheat tortillas or fresh bread and salad.

Black Turtle Beans Asian Indian Style
Yield: 8 servings of one cup

I have simplified this recipe to make it easy to prepare and versatile.

Bring to a boil, remove from the burner, cover, and let stand 1-8 hours:

    1 pound dried black turtle beans (about 3 cups)

    6 c. water

Simmer for 1 1/2 -3 hours . Add more liquid as needed to keep the beans covered. When they are tender, add:

    3/4 c. tomatoes, diced with juice, either fresh or canned

    2-4 t. fresh ginger root, grated finely

    1/2 t. ground cardamon

    1 T. ground coriander

    1/2 t. cayenne pepper

    2 t. salt

Sauté until golden:

    4 T. ghee (*see below) or canola oil

    2 c. onions, finely chopped

Stir into the onions:

    1/4 c. fresh coriander leaves (same as cilantro), chopped

In the last 10 *seconds* or until brown, stir in:

    1 1/2 t. cumin seeds

Pour some fluid from the beans into the skillet to transfer all the flavors to the beans. Cook for 15 minutes to blend the flavors. Remove one third of the mixture and mash with a potato masher or puree in a blender. Return to the beans pot for a creamy texture.

When the cooking is completed and the beans are cooled a bit so the cream does not curdle, add:

    1/2 c. heavy cream

    1 c. plain, low-fat yogurt (If you prefer, substitute with 1 - 1 1/2 c. soymilk.)

Serve with short-grained brown rice. Steamed greens make a complementary side dish as well as yellow winter squash.

* You can buy ghee at an Indian grocery or make your own. It keeps for months in a jar in the refrigerator. Heat butter over low heat and let it simmer until the water in the butter evaporates. Place in the refrigerator for 4 hours to let the clarified butter float to the top. Spoon it out into another pan and boil for 2 minutes. Strain through a muslin cloth. Cool and store in an airtight jar.

Chicken, Red Bean, and Rice Chili   Yield: 6-8 servings of 1 1/2 cups

Prepare this soup a day in advance. It tastes much better when the flavors blend.
Bring to a boil, remove from the burner, cover, and let stand 1-8 hours
   1 c. dried red beans, any red bean will do, Anasazi, kidney (or 15 oz canned red beans):
   3 c. water
Cook over low heat until tender. Depending on the quality and type of beans, cooking could require 1 1/2 - 3 hours.

Cook separately until tender:
   1/2 c. short-grain brown rice
   1 c. water
As the beans and rice near completion, sauté in a large, heavy skillet:
   3 T. olive or canola oil
   2 lb. chicken breast or thigh, skinned, boned, and cut into bite-sized pieces
   1 1/2 medium onions, chopped coarsely
   2 cloves garlic, crushed
Combine these with the following ingredients in a 10-quart soup pot:
   28-32 oz. canned, stewed and diced tomatoes
   1 3/4 c. chicken or vegetable broth
   1 1/2 t. salt
   1/8 t. ground, black pepper
   Enough water to make the consistency you like
Now you choose your favorite chili flavoring making it as spicy and flavorful as you like.
I use:
   2 ancho chilies, roasted, skinned, and diced (Refer to instructions under Anasazi Chili.)
If you are in a hurry you could use any of the following: 1-2 T. ground chili powder, hot sauce, or canned roasted chilies or dried chilies. Experiment with what you like and record your favorite.

Serve with whole wheat toast or corn bread, grated cheese, a tossed salad of dark greens, and mixed fruit dessert.

Greek Stove-top "Baked" Beans   Yield: 4 servings

Place in a heavy 2-quart pot:
>   1 1/2 c. dried great northern beans or other white beans
>   4 1/2 c. water

Bring to a boil, turn off the heat, cover, and let them stand 1-8 hours. Simmer until tender, about 1 1/2 - 2 hours.

Sauté until transparent and golden, then add to the fully-cooked beans:
>   2 c. onions, diced
>   1 clove garlic, minced
>   3 T. canola oil

Continue cooking over low heat and add the following:
>   1 c. tomato sauce
>   2 T. vinegar
>   3 T. honey
>   1 bay leave
>   2 whole cloves

If there is more fluid than you like, remove the cover and simmer, stirring often until the mixture reaches the thickness you like. The flavor improves the next day. Before serving remove the cloves and bay leaf.

Of course you can bake these but I think slow stove-top cooking in a heavy pot makes it easier to control the consistency.

Asian Indian Chickpeas   Yield: 3-4 servings of one cup

Combine in a 2-quart saucepan:
>   1 c. dried chickpeas
>   3 1/2 c. water

Bring to a boil, remove from the heat, cover, and soak 1-8 hours.

After soaking, cover, and simmer for 2 or more hours until tender.

When the chickpeas are nearly tender, sauté until translucent and golden brown:
>   3 T. canola oil
>   1 c. onions, chopped

For the last minute stir into the onions:
>   1 t. ground cumin
>   1/4 t. ground cayenne pepper

Transfer fluid from the chickpeas to the skillet to ensure that all the flavor in the oil gets in the pot.

Add to the chickpeas along with:

1 t. salt
1 lb. canned, diced tomatoes and enough liquid to make a thick mixture.
2 T. flaked, sweetened coconut
1 T. fresh lemon juice

The flavors improve and blend the second and third day. I like to carry one cup of Indian Chickpeas in my lunch and eat them cold with 3/4 c. yogurt and peanut butter on whole wheat bread.

Lima Beans and Greens   Yield: 4 main-dish servings

Prepare Greek Stove-top "Baked" Beans using 2 cups of dried, large lima beans and 5 cups of water. I like to make these with plenty of fluid when serving them over the greens.

When the limas are hot and ready to serve, steam the following just long enough to wilt them:
>   2 c. of greens per serving, cut in 1-inch x 2-inch pieces Choose any of your favorite
>   fresh greens or a mixture including kale, chard, collards, and spinach.

Place each serving in individual soup bowls and top with about a cup of hot beans.
Serve with rye or whole wheat bread, toast, or muffins, sliced jack cheese, sliced cucumbers and tomatoes.

Lima Bean and Winter Vegetable Soup   Yield: 4-6 servings

Combine in a heavy soup pot:
>   1 c. dried lima beans
>   6 c. water

Bring to a boil, turn off the heat, and let stand 1-8 hours depending on your planning. The longer they stand the shorter the cooking time. Then simmer for 1-2 hours until soft but not mushy.

In a heavy skillet, sauté until a rich, *dark* brown:
>   1 large onion, cut in 1/2" chunks
>   2 cloves garlic, mashed
>   2 T. olive oil

While sautéing, stir often to prevent burning.
Add the following seasonings to the beans:
>   1 t. salt
>   1/8 t. black pepper
>   1 bay leaf
>   1/2 t. dried thyme
>   1/2 t. dried marjoram
>   1/4 t. crushed fennel seeds

1/2 c. dry white wine (optional, I don't use it)

2 c. vegetable stock, canned

Peel, cut into cubes, and add to the beans:

1 large yam

4 oz. turnips

4 oz. mushrooms without stems and roughly chopped, use shiitake or portobello

These vegetables require 30-45 minutes to become tender but not mushy.

Add shortly before serving:

1 c. shredded kale and stalks

Adjust fluid and seasonings to taste. Serve with bread, green salad, and cheese if you like.

Mosh Awa - An Afghan soup of mung beans and chickpeas   Yield: 4 servings

Place in a saucepan, bring to a boil, remove from heat, cover, and soak 1-8 hours:

1/2 c. dried chickpeas

1 1/2 c. water

Simmer 2 hours or until tender.

In a separate saucepan combine and simmer until tender, 30-45 minutes:

1/2 c. whole, dried mung beans

1 1/2 c. water

While the beans finish cooking, sauté until transparent:

3 T. olive oil

1 medium onion, chopped

1 clove garlic, mashed or minced

When the onions and garlic are finished, stir in:

1/4 t. ground cayenne pepper

Combine the chickpeas, mung beans, and onions in a 2-quart pan and add:

1/2 c. tomato sauce

1/2 t. dried mint or 2 t. fresh or frozen mint chopped

1/2 t. dried dill weed

1/2 t. salt

Simmer until it is quite thick so when you dilute it with the thinned yogurt it will be a desirable consistency. Just before serving when the soup is slightly warmer than the right temperature for eating, add the thinned yogurt. Don't add the yogurt to boiling soup or it will curdle.

1/2 c. yogurt thinned with

1/4 c. water

(Use 3/4 c. soymilk in place of dairy and water.)

Serve with whole wheat bread, salad, and fruit.

Persian Bean and Barley Soup   Yield: 8 cups

Clean, bring to a boil, cover, and soak 1-8 hours:
    1/4 c. dried kidney beans
    1/4 c. dried chickpeas
    2/3 c. hulled barley (or pearl barley if that is what you have on hand)
    4 c. water - add more if needed to keep the beans covered
Simmer over low heat for 1 1/2 - 2 hours or until tender:
Combine in another pot and simmer for 30-45 minutes:
    1/4 c. mung beans (or substitute lentils and cook 1 hour)
    2 T. rice, I like short-grain brown rice
    2 c. water
As the beans approach tenderness, sauté:
    2 T. canola or olive oil
    2 stalks celery, diced (or broccoli stumps, peeled and dice)
    1 red sweet pepper, diced
    1 carrot, peeled and diced
    1 medium onion, diced
Combine all these pots into one large soup pot and add:
    1 c. vegetable broth
Adjust to your taste and stir in:
    1/4 c. fresh parsley, minced
    1/4 c. fresh cilantro, chopped
    1/4 c. fresh dill weed, chopped (or 1 1/2 t. dried)
Stir in:
    3/4 c. sour cream, yogurt, or milk substitute
    2 t. sugar
    1 t. salt
    Black pepper to taste
Remove one quarter of the soup and puree it. Return it to the soup pot. Do not boil, but keep at serving temperature to avoid curdling.
Just before serving add:
    Lacinato kale cut in bit-sized pieces.
Delicious served with fresh whole-grain bread, sliced cucumbers and tomatoes and tapioca mixed fruit for dessert.

Swiss Chard and Black-eyed Peas   Yield: 6-8 servings

Clean, bring to a boil, remove from burner, cover, and soak 1-8 hours:

1 pound dried black-eyed peas (about 2 c.)

5-6 c. water

Simmer, covered for about 1 1/2 hours over low heat:

As beans approach tenderness, sauté:

2 medium onions, chopped

2 cloves garlic, mashed

When onions are lightly brown, stir in:

1/4 t. cayenne pepper

1/4 t. allspice

Transfer some fluid from the peas to ensure all the flavors in the oil are included in the peas.

Combine with the beans and add:

1/2 c. Thompson raisins

1 c. black olives, pitted and halved

Heat and let the flavors blend.

Before serving, add:

2 pounds Swiss chard or other favorite greens, cut in bit-sized pieces.

Serve with whole-grain bread and carrot or beet salad.

Dried Bean and Pea Soup

Yield: 8 servings of 1 1/2 cups

Measure out, sort for junk, and rinse:

3/4 c. dried pinto beans

1/2 c. dried baby lima beans

Combine with:

4 c. water

Bring to a boil, remove from heat, cover, and soak 1-8 hours.

Then simmer until tender, 1-2 hours.

As these are cooking, simmer until tender in another covered pot:

3/4 c. dried lentils

3/4 c. dried split peas

5 c. water

These will require 45-60 minutes.

Sauté until translucent and golden:

3 T. canola oil

1 medium onion, diced

2 cloves garlic, mashed or minced

1 c. broccoli trunks, peeled and diced

Combine the beans, peas, and onions with:

2 carrots, peeled and diced

1/2 t. oregano
2 t. salt
1/8 t. grounded black pepper
1 T. fresh parsley, chopped
28 oz. canned, diced tomatoes

Add as much of the tomato juice as you like to achieve the consistency and flavor balance you like.

Breads - Quick

Quick breads use baking powder and/or soda as leaven. The best texture results from mixing the dry ingredients in one bowl, the moist ingredients in a second bowl, and then pouring the moist ingredients into the dry ones. Stir them just enough to moisten all the dry ingredients. If you will carry the baked goods on your mountain bike or backpacking, you may want to make them more durable by stirring them a bit more and including eggs.

Choose your sweeteners wisely. These recipes are mildly sweet. If they taste bland to you, use a little more sweetening and reduce it gradually as you learn to appreciate the other subtle flavors. Any type of sugar has the same number of calories per tablespoon. Honey is used for flavor but is high in fructose so you may want to use white sugar instead. Honey is about one-and-one-half times sweeter than cane sugar so you can use a little less if you like. Molasses provides zippy flavor and a few minerals. Brown sugar is generally cane or beet sugar with molasses added. Dried fruits provide sweetening but again it is fructose that sweetens.

Muffins and quick breads are not sensitive to high elevation baking until over 9,000 feet.

Learn to adjust the amount of fluid in each recipe to produce a texture you like. I like dense bread. It is more satisfying and results in a lower glycemic index. Use a bit more fluid if you like light baked goods.

I have not included conventional cookies for several reasons. It is difficult to create the traditional texture without using partially hydrogenated oils, saturated fat, or non-traditional ingredients. Cookies are time-consuming to bake. They also tempt you to over-indulge because they are usually excessively sweetened and so convenient to eat. I find that the more wholesome a baked product, the easier it is to eat moderate amounts.

Recipes for bread and muffins tolerate many modifications without sacrificing flavor or quality. If you don't eat dairy products, substitute soymilk and/or applesauce. Just omit the eggs if you don't eat eggs. Without eggs the product will be more fragile since eggs function as a binder while adding flavor. If you don't tolerate wheat but can eat spelt, substitute spelt flour. Once you are able to identify the consistency of batter that produces the texture of baked goods you like, you can make substitutions liberally.

Oat Bran Muffins   Yield: 18 muffins

In Bowl I, combine and stir briskly:
> 3/8 c. oat bran
> 1/2 c. quick-cooking rolled oats
> 1 c. boiling water
> 3/8 c. chopped yellow raisins

Allow to cool until lukewarm.

Blend in Bowl II and pour into Bowl I:
> 1 egg, beaten
> 1/2 c. yogurt mixed half and half with water (or soymilk)
> 1/4 c. canola oil
> 3 T. molasses
> 3/4 c. dark brown sugar

In Bowl III, combine the remaining dry ingredients:
> 1 c. quick cooking rolled oats
> 1 c. whole wheat, stone-ground flour or spelt
> 3/4 t. salt
> 1/4 t. soda
> 3/4 t. baking powder

Pour the moist ingredients into the dry ingredients and stir just enough to moisten the dry ingredients. If the batter is too stiff, add 1/4 c. applesauce or water to achieve the consistency you desire. More fluid batter results in lighter muffins.

Lightly brush the muffin tins with oil. Fill the tins two-thirds full. Bake at 375° F. for about 25 minutes or until lightly browned. Serve hot or cold, with dinner or with jam.

Cornmeal Bread or Muffins   Yield: one 9-inch x 9-inch pan or 12 muffins

This quick bread is wonderfully moist and dairy-free.

Combine the dry ingredients in a medium-sized mixing bowl:
> 1 c. yellow cornmeal
> 3/4 c. whole wheat flour
> 3/4 t. baking powder
> 3/4 t. soda
> 3/4 t. salt
> 2 T. sugar

Blend the wet ingredients in a second bowl:
> 2 eggs, beaten
> 1 c. apple sauce, unsweetened

3/4 t. vinegar, unflavored
2 T. canola oil
1/2 -3/4 c. water or soymilk

Pour the wet ingredients into the dry ingredients and stir just enough to moisten the dry ingredients. Again, adjust the consistency of the batter to create the texture of muffin you like. Lightly brush the baking pans with oil and pour the batter into the pan or spoon it into the muffin tins.

Bake at 375° F. for 20-25 minutes or until they just begin to become golden brown on the top. Remove muffins from the pan to a cooling rack if you will store them.

Corn bread is great with sweet toppings or plain with soups, salads, and bean mixtures.

Master Mixes for Pancakes

Pancakes are quick and nourishing when you use a master mix. Store the drymix in an airtight container and it will keep for months. You can use these basic mixes for waffles by adding more oil and water for a more fluid batter.

Wheat Bran Pancakes

Blend thoroughly in a large canister:
    3 1/2 c. whole wheat flour
    2 c. unbleached white flour (wheat or spelt)
    2 c. wheat bran (buy in bulk at health food stores)
    1 T. sugar
    2 t. salt
    2 t. soda
    3 t. baking powder

Cornmeal Pancakes

Blend thoroughly in a large canister:
    4 1/2 c. yellow cornmeal
    2 1/2 c. whole wheat or spelt flour
    1 T. sugar
    2 t. salt
    2 t. soda
    3 t. baking powder

To mix for eight 4-inch pancakes, place in a mixing bowl:
    1 egg, beaten
    1/2 c. plain yogurt

1/2 c. water (or substitute 1 c. soymilk for yogurt and water)

2 t. canola oil

Blend these ingredients and stir in with a few strokes:

1 c. master mix

A few lumps are okay since they will disappear during cooking.

Set the skillet at 350° F. The batter will thicken while the skillet heats. Brush the skillet with oil and pour the batter. Turn the pancakes when the top side has lost its gloss and begins to look a little wrinkled. Cook briefly on the second side. You can peak under them to see if they are lightly brown. Overcooking will make them tough.

For wholesome topping try peanut butter instead of margarine or butter, unsweetened apple sauce, rhubarb sauce, or other ripe fruit mixture.

Pineapple Nut Muffins   Yield: 18 medium-sized muffins

This is a basic fruit nut muffin recipe. You can substitute any fruit sauce or pureed fruit for the pineapple. Just give attention to the fluid-dry ingredient balance to produce the muffin texture you prefer.

In one medium-sized bowl, combine:

1/4 c. canola oil

1/2 t. butter flavoring

3/8 c. honey

1 c. crushed pineapple (or other fruit choice not drained)

1/2 c. chopped and plumbed yellow raisins

In another larger bowl, combine:

2 c. whole wheat flour

1 t. baking powder

1/2 t. baking soda

1/2 t. salt

1/2 t. cardamon (try additional spices appropriate to your fruit blend choice.)

Pour the wet ingredients into the dry ingredients adding:

3/4 c. chopped raw almonds or other nuts

Stir only enough to moisten the dry ingredients. Add:

1/4 - 1/2 c. unsweetened applesauce to achieve the desired consistency. If you like firm muffins, this may be adequate moisture. If you like them light, you may need to add some water or yogurt.

Brush the muffin tins with oil and fill three-quarters full with batter. The batter does not rise much during baking. Bake at 350° F. for 25-30 minutes or until lightly golden on top.

Pumpkin Bread
Yield: 2 loaves

Combine in a large mixing bowl, beating with each addition:

3/4 c. dark brown sugar

3/4 c. white sugar

1/4 - 1/2 c. canola oil

3 eggs

2 c. pureed pumpkin (If you use canned pumpkin, add 3/8 c. water.)

Then add gradually:

2 1/2 c. flour - I use all whole wheat. You can use any combination of unbleached white flour and stone-ground whole wheat flour

1/4 t. baking powder

1 t. soda

1 t. ground cinnamon

1 t. ground allspice

1 t. ground cloves

Finally stir in:

1/2 c. raisins, chopped and soaked in hot water to plump and then drain off the water

3/4 c. walnuts, chopped coarsely

Prepare the loaf pans by cutting pieces of wax paper to fit the bottom of the pans and then brush the sides with oil. Pour the batter into two loaf pans and bake at 350° F. for 50 minutes. (At 6,000 ft. elevation use 375° F.) Take care to bake them enough since pumpkin bread can be soggy. This batter also makes fine muffins. Brush the muffin tins with oil, fill three-quarters full with batter, and bake about 40 minutes.

Remove the loaves from the pans by running a spreading spatula around the edges and turning the loaves out onto a pot holder in your hand. Peel the wax paper off the bottom and place the loaves on a cooling rack to cool thoroughly. Store in plastic bags. Pumpkin bread keeps well for a week in the refrigerator.

Wheat Bran Muffins
Yield: 36 muffins

Combine in Bowl I:

3 c. wheat bran

1 c. boiling water

1 1/4 t. soda

When it is blended add:

1/2 c. canola oil

2 eggs, beaten

1 1/2 T. molasses

5/8 c. yogurt

3/8 c. water (or substitute soymilk for the yogurt and applesauce for the water.)

1 c. dark brown sugar

1 c. pitted, cut-up dates

Combine in Bowl II:

2 1/2 c. whole wheat flour

3/4 t. salt

1 1/2 t. baking powder

1/2 c. chopped walnuts

Pour Bowl I into Bowl II and stir just enough to blend all the ingredients. If the dough is too dry add more applesauce.

This is an unusual dough since it will keep well in an airtight container in the refrigerator for a week. You can mix them up when you have time and then bake them fresh for breakfast. They are sweet and taste great just plain.

For baking, spoon into lightly-oiled muffin tins and bake at 350° F. for 25-30 minutes.

Whole Wheat - Dried Cranberry Super Cookies   Yield: 15 large cookies

These make tasty, wholesome energy bars.

This recipe is versatile and can be made by substituting applesauce for any or all of the yogurt, canola oil, or egg. If you are going to carry them on the trail, the egg increases their durability.

Combine in Bowl I, being sure the honey is fully dissolved:

1 egg, beaten

1/2 c. plain yogurt or soymilk

3/8 c. water

3/8 c. honey

1/4 c. canola oil

1/4 c. currants

3/4 c. dried cranberries, chopped

In Bowl II combine:

2 c. stone-grounded whole wheat flour or spelt

1/2 c. quick rolled oats

1 t. salt

3/4 t. baking powder

1/2 t. soda

1/2 t. cinnamon

1/4 c. sunflower seeds, roasted and unsalted
1/2 c. chopped walnuts

Pour the wet ingredients into the dry ingredients and stir just enough to moisten the dry ingredients. If the dough is too dry, add some applesauce. You will discover the consistency of batter needed for the desired end product. Let it stand for 5 minutes to absorb moisture and form thicker cookies on the baking sheets.

Drop in large spoonfuls on an oiled cookie sheet. Bake at 350° for 20-25 minutes. They should be lightly browned. Remove to a cooling rack. Eat hot or cold, at home or on the trail. They keep well for several days.

Breads - Yeast

Few aromas are more tantalizing than the smell of freshly baked bread. You can enjoy it regularly, eat lots of wholesome bread, and build strength in your triceps, wrists, and hands when kneading it. I find great joy and satisfaction in kneading bread and am amused by the popularity of bread machines.

To get you hooked on bread baking, I have included two casserole breads. These require no kneading. Just stir the ingredients together into a moist dough, let it rise, and turn it into loaf pans. These casserole breads make delicious complements to salads and bowls of soup or beans.

Cinnamon Raisin Casserole Bread   Yield: 2 small loaves

Combine in a 2-cup glass measure and stir until partially dissolved:
1 pkg. dry yeast
1/2 c. hot tap water
2 t. sugar
Let stand until it froths up to the 1 1/2-cup line.
While the yeast is activating, combine in an eight-quart mixing bowl:
3 c. water
1/2 t. salt
1/4 c. honey
1/2 c. flax seed meal (or 3 T. vegetable oil)
1 c. rolled oats
2 1/2 c. whole wheat, organic, stone-ground flour
1 t. cinnamon
Stir vigorously to develop the gluten strands, then add:
Yeast mixture
Finally add:

2 1/2 c. unbleached white flour or whole wheat flour if your palate
    has adapted to whole-grain breads.

1 c. raisins

1/3 c. walnut pieces

Stir again to create a uniform texture with well defined strands of gluten. Cover the bowl with a plate and let rise in a warm place until almost double in bulk. Stir the dough down and divide in half. Prepare the pans by brushing the bottom and sides with oil and dusting with flour. Turn the dough into the pans and let rise 30 to 45 minutes until almost double in bulk.

Heat the oven to 350° F. and bake loaves for about 30 minutes. They should be golden brown and sound hollow when turned out of the pans and tapped on the bottom. Cool on a rack. When thoroughly cooled, place in plastic bags and close with a twisty. The loaves keep well in the refrigerator for a couple weeks. This bread makes great toast.

Dilly Casserole Bread   Yield: 2 small loaves

Combine in a 2-cup glass measure and stir until partially dissolved:

1 pkg. active dry yeast

1/2 c. hot tap water

2 t. sugar

Let stand until it froths up to the 1 1/2 cup line.

While the yeast is reactivating, combine in a heavy saucepan and heat to lukewarm:

2 c. small curd, creamed cottage cheese*

2 T. minced onion

2 T. canola oil

4 t. dill seed

In an eight-quart mixing bowl, combine:

2 eggs, beaten

1/4 c. sugar

2 t. salt

1/2 t. soda

Blend in the cottage cheese mixture and finally add:

2 c. whole wheat flour

Stir vigorously until the gluten strands are visible.

Add and stir to form a stiff dough:

2 c. whole wheat flour

Cover the bowl with a plate and let rise in a warm place until double in bulk. Stir the dough down and divide in half. Prepare the pans by brushing the bottom and sides with oil and dusting with flour. Turn the dough into the pans and let rise 30-45 minutes until double in bulk.

Heat the oven to 350° F. and bake the loaves for about 30 minutes. They should be golden brown and sound hollow when turned out of the pans and tapped on the bottom. Cool on a rack. When completely cool, place in a plastic bag and close with a twisty. Store in the refrigerator. This makes great sandwiches and is durable enough to carry bike touring.

*If you do not eat dairy products you can substitute 1 1/2 c. soymilk and 1/2 c. applesauce for the cottage cheese. If you do eat dairy, a pleasant variation is to add 1 c. grated cheddar cheese, and 1 t. each of oregano, thyme, and parsley.

All **kneaded yeast breads** can be handled the same way. Use these basic instructions for each of the following bread recipes.

Handle the yeast wisely and you can use one, quarter-ounce package of active dry yeast for any size batch of bread. Since yeast is the most expensive ingredient by weight, this treatment is a real savings.

Use a two-cup glass measuring cup and combine:

1/2 c. hot tap water

2 to 3 t. sugar

1/4 ounce active dry yeast

Stir these ingredients until most of the yeast granules are dissolved. Let the mixture stand for at least 10 minutes until the foam froths up to the one-and-one-half-cup mark. Stir it down so you can pour all the yeast into the bowl of ingredients you have been preparing while the yeast was multiplying.

Add the yeast to the mixture of flavor-giving ingredients before you begin adding the flour. Add the flour in two additions. There is no need to be ceremonial about this. You will develop the gluten during the kneading. This preliminary mixing is just to blend the ingredients and make the dough stiff enough to turn out onto the counter to knead. Gluten is the protein in the flour that forms elastic strands during kneading and gives the baked bread its strength and elasticity. The amounts of flour given in each recipe are approximate. Differences in humidity cause the dough to respond differently. Use the consistency of the dough as your guide to flour amounts rather than using the exact amounts in the recipes.

When the dough is too stiff to stir with a big wooden spoon, clean the counter and cover a 12- to 14-inch diameter circle with about a quarter-inch deep layer of flour. Turn the dough out onto the counter. Set the bowl aside and return the dough to the same big bowl for rising.

Now knead the bread for 15 minutes. This is the secret to good bread. Time yourself and don't cheat. Wash and flour your hands before beginning. Add flour to the counter to prevent the dough from sticking to it or your hands. Be sure you are using your body well. Most kitchen counters are too high. Place your thickest phone book on the floor in front of your dough to lift yourself to a height that enables you to knead without scrunching your shoulders. Breathe rhythmically into your kneading with SELF breathing and put your love and joy into your kneading. Your bread will be more nourishing from the effort.

Since the purpose of kneading is to develop the gluten strands, use your hands so they fold the dough over repeatedly, stretching it on each rotation. Let me see if I can give helpful verbal instructions on kneading. I'll give these for right-dominant people so lefties just reverse the hands. Lift the back of the dough pile with the out-stretched fingers of your left hand. Fold it toward your right hand, intercept the fold of dough with the heel of your right hand, and press it firmly back into the ball. Repeat this over and over, each time folding the dough from a position slightly left of the previous fold so the dough slowly rotates clockwise. The dough should quickly form a cohesive ball and become progressively more elastic and firm. If the dough is so stiff it makes it difficult to push the right hand back into the dough ball, you have added too much flour. Make a note on the recipe and add less flour the next time you make the recipe. Kneading is great exercise and will warm you up quickly. At the end of 15 minutes, the dough should be elastic, firm, and less sticky. The potato bread is great to learn on because the dough is easy to handle. The rye bread dough is sticky and less elastic.

Now it is time for the yeast to work. The temperature at which the dough rises influences the flavor of your bread. For optimum results the temperature should be 75-80 degrees Fahrenheit. If your house is cool, warm your oven with its light by turning it on when you begin making bread. Cover the bowl with a plate or damp cloth to prevent the top surface of the dough from drying during this rest period. Let it rest until almost double in bulk. You can test the readiness to form loaves by stabbing two fingers into the dough. It is ready if the dough retains the shape of the holes your fingers made. If they close up quickly, the dough needs to rise more. The time required will vary with warmth, altitude, and the vitality of the yeast. Generally it will take two to three hours.

Forming the loaves is simple using a rolling pin. Punch the dough down into the bowl with your fist and draw it away from the edges of the bowl with your hand or a rubber spatula. This will knock the air out of it and make it easier to handle. Turn it out on a lightly floured cutting board. Use a large knife to cut the dough ball into the same number of wedges that you will make loaves. One at a time, place each wedge on the clean, lightly floured counter. Place the broad end of the wedge toward you on the counter in front of you. Sprinkle the top surface of the wedge lightly with flour and lightly flour the rolling pin (or a sturdy quart jar if you don't have a rolling pin). The challenge is to use just enough flour to prevent the dough from sticking to the counter or rolling pin but not so much that it won't adhere to itself as you roll it up. Roll the dough out about two feet long so it is about a quarter inch thick. This will eliminate coarse air bubbles formed during the rising process. It should be about the width of your loaf pan.

Now roll up the dough. Beginning at the far end, start rolling the dough toward you, pausing every two inches to press the rolled dough against the dough on the counter with the heels of your hands. This creates a solid loaf without gaps of air. Seal the end of the dough in the same manner. Lightly dust the dough roll with flour and place it in a loaf pan that is lightly brushed with oil.

Cover the loaves with a damp cloth and place them in a warm place to rise to *almost* double in volume. This will require 30-45 minutes. This timing will determine how light your bread will be. If you let it rise more than double, the bread will be fragile and crumble easily.

When the loaves are ready to bake, place them the oven without pre-heating it, spacing them so the hot air will flow around them. Set the temperature at 400 degrees F. and bake them at this high temperature for only 10 minutes. Then reduce the heat to 350 degrees F. and bake another 25-35 minutes. The initially hot oven causes the yeast to go wild before it is killed by the heat and results in lighter bread.

Test for doneness by turning the loaves out onto a potholder in your hand, lifting the pan off, and thumping the bottom of the loaf. The bottom should be lightly browned and sound hollow when thumped. When a loaf does not pass the test return it to the pan and the oven. Check each loaf separately since oven heat is not uniform. The tops and bottoms will brown uniformly if you rotate the loaves between the top and bottom shelves of the oven during the last 5-10 minutes of baking while you are checking them for doneness.

When the loaves are done, remove them from the pans and place them on cooling racks until they are thoroughly cooled. This will take several hours. To avoid mold growth during storage, be sure they are completely cool and place each loaf in a clean, stout plastic bag (or double bag them). They can be stored in the refrigerator for as much as four weeks. I prefer to store them in the refrigerator rather than the freezer to avoid any change in texture or moisture.

Anadama Bread

Yield: 4 small loaves

This is an early colonial bread and the mix of grains makes it lighter in flavor than all whole wheat or rye.

Follow the detailed instructions beginning on page 442.

Combine in a 2-cup measuring cup and let grow until the foam froths up to the 1 1/2-cup line:
  1 pkg. dried yeast (1/4 oz.)
  1/2 c. hot tap water (115° F.)

     2 t. sugar

Select a 2-quart bowl with a lid and pour into it:

     3 1/2 c. boiling water

Using a potato masher, slowly add while stirring vigorously to prevent lumps from forming:

     1 1/2 c. yellow cornmeal

Let this stand for 10 minutes with the lid on.

While the cornmeal is absorbing water, combine in an 8-quart or larger bowl:

     3 T. salt

     3/8 c. molasses

     3/8 c. honey

     2 c. tepid water

     1/2 c. canola oil

     1 c. powdered milk (optional)

When 10 minutes have elapsed, stir in the cornmeal and water mixture.

When the flavor-giving ingredients have cooled so it won't kill the yeast, stir in the yeast mixture.

Now stir in and mix thoroughly:

     1 1/2 c. rye flour

     3 c. stone-ground, whole wheat flour

While you are getting used to whole wheat bread you can use some unbleached white flour to lighten the flavor. You'll add another 6-8 cups of flour.

Now refer to the detailed instructions above on kneading, rising, forming loaves, and baking.

Hearty Rye Bread
Yield: 3 small loaves

Follow the detailed instructions beginning on page 442.

Activate the dry yeast in a 2-cup measure. Combine:

     1/2 c. hot tap water (115° F.)

     2 t. sugar

     1 pkg. (1/4 oz.) active dry yeast

Let stand until the froth grows to 1 1/2 cup in volume.

Meanwhile sauté until dark brown but not burned:

     1 medium onion, finely diced

     3 T. canola oil

Combine in a large mixing bowl:

     1/2 c. molasses

     3 1/2 c. tepid water

     2/3 c. sugar or honey

2 T. salt

1/4 t. ground black pepper

1/4 t. nutmeg

When the yeast and onions are ready, stir them into the water and seasonings.

Now add the flour and choose the flavor you like among dark rye, regular rye, and whole wheat flour. To start with I recommend:

3 c. whole wheat flour

4 c. regular rye flour

Stir vigorously before adding another 2-3 cups of rye flour.

Knead for 15 minutes in unbleached white flour

Return the dough to the mixing bowl, cover, and let rise until double in bulk. The dough will take hours to rise so mix it up in the morning and let it rise during the day.

Form the loaves, place in loaf pans and let rise to almost double in bulk.

Place them in the oven without preheating and set the oven at 400° F. Reduce the heat after 10 minutes to 375° F. and bake another 35 minutes. Test for doneness by tapping the bottoms of the loaves. Place on a cooling rack and cool completely before storing in plastic bags. The bread makes great sandwiches with white cheese, turkey, or egg salad.

Rocky Mountain Whole Wheat Bread   Yield: 4 loaves

Follow the detailed instructions beginning on page 442.

Activate the dry yeast by mixing the following ingredients:

1/2 c. hot water

2 t. sugar

1 pkg. active dry yeast

Combine in a large mixing bowl:

6 c. tepid water

2 T. salt

1/4 c. sugar

1/2 c. molasses

3/8 c. canola oil

1 c. wheat bran

Add yeast when it is ready and stir in:

7 c. whole wheat flour

You'll use about 11 cups of flour total so add enough to turn out on the counter and knead. Knead for 15 minutes, let rise, form loaves, let rise in baking pans, and bake as detailed above. Bake at 400° F. for 10 minutes and at 375° F. for 25-35 minutes more. Remove from pans and cool thoroughly before storing in plastic bags in the refrigerator.

Swedish Limpa Rye Bread   Yield: 3 loaves

Follow the detailed instructions beginning on page 442.
This bread is aromatic and tastes like cake. It makes good sandwiches with white, mildly-flavored cheeses and egg salad. For a treat it is especially tasty toasted and adorned with honey.

Activate the yeast:
    1/2 c. hot tap water (115° F.)
    2 t. sugar
    1 pkg. active dry yeast (1/4 oz.)
While it is frothing up, combine in a large mixing bowl:
    1/2 c. molasses
    1/2 c. sugar
    2 T. salt
    1/4 c. freshly ground orange peel
    2 T. fennel seed
    1 T. anise seed
    1/4 c. canola oil
    3 1/2 c. warm water
Add the yeast when it is ready.
Begin adding flour, first:
    5 c. rye flour
Then add:
    unbleached white wheat flour until the dough is difficult to stir.
Turn it out, knead for 15 minutes, return to the mixing bowl to rise in a warm place. Punch it down, divide in thirds and form the loaves. Let's make round loaves. Take the ball of dough for one loaf and begin turning the dough into itself with the tips of your fingers. Stabilize the ball with your thumbs and repeatedly fold some of the dough from the sides up and into the bottom. When the top is smooth and no more big air bubbles appear, place it on a baking sheet that is lightly oiled and sprinkled with cornmeal.

Let it rise again and just before it becomes double in bulk (again this is rye and will take longer to rise) make three parallel cuts about 1/8 inch deep on the top of each loaf. Bake 10 minutes at 400° F. and 25 minutes longer at 375° F. Test for doneness by thumping on the bottom. Cool thoroughly and store in plastic bags in the refrigerator.

Whole Wheat Potato Bread   Yield: 4 loaves

Follow the detailed instructions beginning on page 442.
Activate the yeast by mixing:

1/2 c. hot water

2 t. sugar

1 pkg. active dry yeast (1/4 oz)

Meanwhile, cook until mushy:

1 medium-sized white potato, peeled and cubed

This will take about 20 minutes. While the potato is cooking, combine the following ingredients in an 8-quart mixing bowl:

2 eggs, beaten

3 T. salt

2/3 c. honey

2 c. warm water

1/3 c. canola oil

Mix in the yeast when it is ready. When the potatoes are tender, drain the potato water into a measuring cup so you can include it in the liquids in the bread. Mash the potatoes so there are no lumps.

Add to the potatoes before combining with the other ingredients so the heat of the potatoes doesn't kill the yeast:

3 c. cool water (this includes the water from cooking the potatoes)

Begin adding the flour and stir until ingredients are well mixed:

4 c. whole wheat flour

Make two further additions of flour totaling another:

8 c. whole wheat flour

When it is difficult to stir, turn it out on the counter to knead for 15 minutes. Return to the bowl to rise. Punch it down, divide in fourths for the loaves. Roll out and form the loaves, rise again and bake first at 400° F. for 10 minutes and then at 375° F. for another 25-35 minutes until it tests done when thumped on the bottom. Cool thoroughly and store in plastic bags in the refrigerator.

This dough makes fine raisin bread. Just spread raisins and cinnamon sugar on the flattened dough before rolling up the loaf

Fruit Delights

Fresh fruits make convenient, wholesome snacks. Just wash and/or peel and eat them out of hand. Here are some starter recipes to help you develop your own fruit treats for snacks and desserts. When shopping, select fruit with the most color. Avoid citrus fruits that are too firm. They are likely to lack juice. If you like firm bananas, remember that the sugars are not fully developed until all green is gone from the skins and they are beginning to brown. These ripe bananas are best for these snacks and baking. Pears ripen from the inside out so don't let them deceive you. They should be a bit soft and have just lost the hint of green on the skins. If you wait until they look ideal on the outside, they will probably be mushy or rotten at the core.

Sunny Tapioca and Fruit Dessert   Yield: 6 servings

Total preparation time is about 30 minutes plus 2 hours chilling time.

Mixed fruit compotes provide a satisfying blend of flavors, and the binding sauce retains the natural color of the fruits so they will keep for several days in the refrigerator. If you eat dairy products, you can enjoy plain, fat-free yogurt mixed with frozen juice concentrate to blend the fruits. If you do not eat dairy products, tapioca made with fruit juice is a tasty bright alternative.

Combine in a heavy saucepan and let stand 10 minutes.

> 3 T. minute tapioca
> 1 c. pineapple juice (drain this off a 1-pound can of pineapple)
> 1 c. orange juice
> 2 T. granular sugar

Cook and stir over medium heat until the mixture comes to a boil. Remove from the heat and add:

> 1 T. fresh lemon juice

Cool, stirring occasionally. You can speed up the cooling process by transferring the tapioca from the hot pan to a plastic storage container, covering it, and setting it in another container of cold water. When it is cool, stir in your favorite mixture of fresh and canned fruits.

I like the following combination:

> 1 c. drained pineapple, crushed or tidbits
> 3 apples, washed, cored, and diced with the skins on
> 3 oranges, peeled, sectioned, and sliced
> 2 bananas, peeled, and sliced
> 1 pear, washed, cored, and diced

Blend well.

I like to make the tapioca a day in advance. The following day I add the pineapple, apples and oranges. Just before serving I add the bananas and pear so their texture and color are optimum.

Pink Drink   Yield: 2 cups

Smoothies can be created from any combination of your favorite fruits. Try these suggestions for the most tasty results:

Select fruit that is fully ripe so your mixture will be adequately sweet without refined sugars.

Use bananas to thicken smoothies to a desirable consistency.

Add eye-appealing color with berries. Selecting organic berries will reduce the contaminants in this wholesome treat.

If you eat diary products, use yogurt or milk. Otherwise use enriched soymilk. Compare the labels of milk substitutes because the nutritional contents vary widely.

Place in a blender and puree until smooth:

   2 c. fresh, organic strawberries, stemmed and rinsed

   1 large, ripe banana, peeled and cut in 1-inch chunks

   1 c. soymilk

   1/2 t. vanilla extract

Pour into a glass and enjoy a refreshing "pick-me-up."

Apple - cranberry Treat   Yield: 6 to 8 Servings

It is peculiar how foods are categorized. This delightful fruit treat is usually called a salad but could just as well be a dessert. Eat it whenever you would like a light, fresh mixture of fruits and nuts.

Two to three days in advance, prepare the Fresh Orange-cranberry Relish from the following recipe. I make a big batch of this just before Thanksgiving using two 12 oz. packages of fresh cranberries and then freeze part of it in 1 1/4-cup portions. I take it from the freezer any time during the year to make this cooling, gelled dessert.

Combine in a 2-quart bowl:

   1 1/4 c. Fresh Orange-cranberry Relish

   3/4 c. orange juice

   1 c. apples, washed, cored, and diced with skins on

   1/2 c. pecans or walnuts, coarsely chopped

   1 c. canned crushed pineapple

   Combine in a saucepan:

   3/4 c. cranberry or other fruit juice

   1 T. (1/4 oz) packet of unflavored gelatin

Stir constantly over medium heat until the gelatin is completely dissolved. Cool until warm and blend into the fruit mixture. Let it gel partially before pouring into a mold and stir it to ensure an even distribution of the fruit. Refrigerate overnight or until firm.

Fresh Orange - cranberry Relish   Yield: 6 cups

Prepare at least two days in advance of serving.

Wash and sort out spoiled berries:

6 c. (24 oz.) fresh cranberries

Select:

3 oranges. Choose ones that are sweet, thin-skinned, and deeper orange in color.

Prepare the oranges as follows:

Wash the skins with soap and water. Rinse thoroughly.

If they are thin-skinned, quarter, pick out the seeds and set aside for grinding. If they are thick-skinned, cut off the orange outer skin with a knife. Then peel off the white bitter pulp and throw it out. Now quarter the oranges and remove the seeds, the core pulp, and the bulky navel end if they have them.

Grind the cranberries and oranges together with an old-fashioned food grinder or modern food processor. Collect all the juice and add it to the pulp.

Stir into the pulp and juice:

1 c. honey

1 1/2 c. white sugar

Transfer to a closed container and let the mixture blend in the refrigerator for at least 24 hours. Test for sweetness. Oranges vary in sweetness and cranberries are really sour so you may want to add more sweetening. Let stand another 24 hours and test again.

Serve cool and fresh with Thanksgiving dinner. It is delicious in turkey sandwiches.

Grains

Whole grains are versatile and digest slowly giving sustaining fuel. Served either as a hot cereal, side or main dish, or dessert they are great fuel for long rides because they stave off hunger or bonk better than anything I know, yes, even better than pasta!

Remember that soaking grains in boiling water reduces cooking time. Try cooking a large amount and freezing small batches so you can enjoy them whenever you like. Refer to Dr. Willett's *Eat, Drink and Be Healthy*, for preparation instructions and descriptions of a wide variety of whole grains.

Steel-cut Oats and Amaranth   Yield: 4 one-cup servings

The high protein content of amaranth and the low glycemic index of steel-cut oats gives this hot cereal more "staying power" than most cereals.

Measure and place in a heavy 2-quart sauce pan:

3/4 c. steel-cut oats

Cover with two-inches of water, swish around and drain the water off in a sieve. Steel-cut oats always make the water milky and the cereal will have a cleaner flavor if the oats are rinsed.

Dump the oats from the sieve back into the pan and add:

3/4 c. amaranth

4 c. water

1/2 t. salt

Bring the mixture to a boil, turn down to simmer, and cover. The total cooking time is about an hour and some stirring is necessary to keep the grains from sticking on the bottom of the pan as they soak up water and the mixture thickens.

You can cook them for 20-30 minutes in the evening, turn off the heat and let them sit and soak up water until morning. Before breakfast you can cook them another 15-20 minutes and have hot cereal ready quickly.

This cereal refrigerates and freezes well. I just fill recycled one-cup containers with the three extra servings and store them ready to warm and eat on following days.

Create your own sugar-free treat by adding any combination of the following ingredients that you would enjoy:

Add while cooking:

Raisins

Chopped tart apples

Sprinkle over the cereal in your bowl:

Broken walnut pieces

Granola

Three-Rice Main Dish with Dried Fruits and Nuts   Yield: 4 main-course servings

Combine in a heavy pot and cook slowly for about 1 hour:

1/2 c. wild rice

1/2 c. short-grain brown rice

3 c. water

1/4 t. salt

With about 15 minutes remaining before the rice is tender, add:

1/2 c. long-grain white rice

While the rice is still warm, stir in:

1 c. (4 oz) dried cranberries, chopped

1/3 c. dried currants

1/2 c. dried apricots, cut in sixths or eights

When cooled combine:

1/4 c. fresh lemon juice (the juice from one lemon)

2 T. olive oil

1 small clove garlic, minced

1 T. onion, minced

2 green onions, thinly sliced

1/2 c. fresh parsley, chopped
2 T. fresh mint, chopped (or 2 t. dried)
1 T. fresh basil, chopped (or 1/2 t. dried)
1/2 t. salt
Black pepper to taste
2/3 c. broken pecans (or favorite nuts)

Serve with spinach and mandarin orange salad with a hint of red wine vinegar, water and sugar dressing, and bran muffins.

This is refreshing in the summer but another fine main dish to carry on cold bike and ski trips. It is easy to eat with a spoon wearing heavy mitts and provides sustained energy.

Wheat Berry and Dried Fruit Treat

Yield: 4-6 servings depending on whether it is main- or side-dish.
The wheat berries will cook faster if you bring them to a boil and let them stand one hour or overnight before cooking. Cooking time varies with hardness of wheat. It could take 1-2 hours.

Rinse, sort and cook until tender:
2 c. dried wheat berries (whole kernel wheat, spelt or oats)
3 1/2 c. water

Try to balance the water so all of it is absorbed in cooking
If excess fluid remains, drain it off. Transfer the wheat berries to an airtight storage container. While still warm, stir in:
1 t. cinnamon
2 t. vanilla extract
1/4 c. honey (or 2 T. brown sugar and 2 T. white sugar)
1 t. lemon juice
1 t. lime juice
Dash of salt
1/2 c. chopped dried cranberries
1/4 c. chopped dried apricots

Let cool completely and stir in:
3/4 c. broken pecans or other favorite nuts

This recipe originally was made with one large pomegranate instead of dried fruit and served for Thanksgiving. If you have a source for fresh pomegranate, try it.

I serve this as the main dish with fresh vegetables and crackers. It is especially good on cold weather rides or ski trips. You can eat it with a spoon with your big mitts on and stay warm at lunch. It provides energy for several hours.

Vegetables

You probably need to incorporate more vegetables into your diet. To start, you will need to include them in all your meals to obtain the recommended five to six servings a day. Secondly, you will need to refer to the charts of nutritive contents to sort out which vegetables are brimming with nutrients and which ones are more traditional than valuable. Finally, let the rich and varied flavors of vegetables stand alone and resist the tendency to add oils and seasonings that make them less wholesome and require more time to prepare.

Notice I have left out tossed salads – you don't need a recipe to blend your favorite vegetables. Tossed salads can be inefficient because they take time to prepare and time to eat. Many salads are made of low-nutritional-value foods and people often drown them is unwholesome dressings. If you do make a tossed salad, use dark-colored greens and a selection of highly nutritious vegetables such as: spinach, red lettuce, romaine, broccoli, asparagus, carrots, cooked beets, red sweet peppers, chickpeas, tomatoes and top them with tamari nuts or seeds.

My favorite greens are Swiss chard, Lacinato kale (curly leaves), and collards. These are especially easy to grow in your garden and readily available at your organic grocer all year long. I recommend you steam **dark-green, leafy vegetables**, sprinkle with a hint of salt in your serving bowl and eat heartily. Southerners know the secret of greens and beans. Try some of the recipes under beans. When you use spinach don't steam it but pour the hot beans over the washed and chopped spinach for the best texture and flavor.

Greens also combine well with yellow vegetables. My favorites are garnet yams but try yellow winter squash or sweet potatoes if you like them better. These **yellow vegetables** require longer cooking times than greens so cook them for about 10 minutes before adding the greens and cook for three minutes more. When winter squash is in season, bake it as a side dish for every day. It complements curries especially well. Just cut the squash in half, place the cut side on a cookie sheet (the ones you don't use anymore for cookies), pour boiling water in the sheet to prevent burning if you like and bake at 350 degrees F. for 45-60 minutes. Scoop out the seeds just before serving and add a dash of salt. High quality winter squash is so sweet and rich you can learn to eat it with no fat or sugar and then eat it in abundance.

Although the use of salt is a controversial topic these days, I suggest that you use it as your primary flavor enhancer. You know your health challenges and perhaps you will need to use a low-sodium alternative like Bragg Liquid Aminos® or Kikkoman®'s Lite Soy Sauce. But most cyclists sweat enough to need some salt and if you avoid chips and crackers, you can enjoy salt on your vegetables without hesitation. Salt is also the secret to savory black beans.

Try steaming raw vegetables for three to five minutes in a quarter inch of boiling water even when you will eat them cold. This brief heat makes them more tender without causing them to loose their crisp texture while bringing out the flavors with only minimal nutrient loss. I briefly steam the broccoli I carry in my lunch, then cool it on a stoneware plate and add five or six florets to my carrots for lunch. Several spinach leaves and slices of tomato in my sandwich complete my vegetable quota for lunch.

Bean and Cheese Salad

Yield: 4 servings as a main dish

Combine and chill:

    2 c. Greek Stove-top "Baked" Beans
    1 green onion, chopped
    3/4 c. red sweet pepper, diced
    1 1/2 c. cucumber, cut in half lengthwise and sliced thinly
    1 1/2 c. zucchini, sliced the same way
    1 T. olive oil (optional)
    1 T. wine vinegar
    1/4 t. oregano, ground

Just before serving, add:

    1 c. jack or mozzarella cheese, diced, or 4 hard-boiled eggs, chilled and cut up

Serve on a bed of greens with whole wheat bread or muffins. This will keep well in the refrigerator for 3 days when you keep the cheese or eggs separate until just before serving.

Layered Vegetable Salad

Yield: Serves 10 or more people

Wash, drain, and cut into bite-sized pieces. Layer the following sequence of ingredients into a 10-inch x 10-inch airtight container:

    Red lettuce
    Fresh spinach
    1 1/2 c. celery or broccoli trunks, diced
    1/2 c. diced red sweet peppers
    1/2 c. diced green onions including some of the tops
    10 oz. frozen peas, unthawed
    Cauliflower
    Scant layer of crisp, crumbled bacon (optional)
    4 oz. water chestnuts, sliced

Sprinkle with grated parmesan cheese.

Blend and spread over the salad to completely cover it:

    1/2 c. mayonnaise
    1/2 c. sour cream or yogurt

Seal the lid leaving an airspace at the top so the sour cream does not stick to the cover. Refrigerate for 24 hours.

Whole Wheat Pasta and Vegetable Salad

Yield will depend on quantities of vegetables added. I usually make 6 main-dish servings.

Boil until tender but still retains a firm shape:

   1 1/2 c. whole wheat pasta This product varies widely so test brands and shapes until you find one you like. Currently I find the best flavor and texture with Annie's® Organic Whole Wheat Penne.

While it is cooking, prepare the following ingredients in an airtight container:

   1 1/2 c. high protein food Choose among:

        1 1/2 organic chicken breasts, sautéed with onions

        8 oz. canned tuna and 3 hard-boiled eggs

        Cooked dried beans, try chickpeas or black beans

   Cauliflower florets

   Broccoli florets and diced trunks

   Carrots, peeled and sliced thinly

   Red sweet peppers

   Cucumbers, half peeled, quartered, and sliced

   Any other fresh vegetables you like and have available

Drain the pasta when it is cooked and mix it into the vegetables while it is still hot.

Promptly stir in so the flavors blend:

   1/4 - 1/2 c. mayonnaise

   2 t. prepared mustard

   3 T. mild, sweet pickle relish

   1/2 t. salt

   Sprinkle with ground black pepper and garlic powder

Blend completely. Adjust flavor and moisture content. The pasta will absorb some fluid while it is stored. Just before chilling in the refrigerator, stir in:

   3/4 c. frozen peas.

This makes great lunches and group meals or for potlucks and picnics. Serve with fresh lettuce and crisp, flat rye bread like Wasa® or Finn Crisp®.

Wholesome Indulgences

What do I eat when I want to splurge? Of course I have my favorites. I try to choose things that are rich in vital nutrients and dairy-free. Obviously I love muffins and quick breads. Here are some other suggestions.

Raisins and Nuts

I always carry a bag of yellow raisins (dried without chemicals) and raw almonds. Sometimes I eat dark raisins and walnuts. This mix satisfies my sweet tooth and provides a balanced release of energy. The raisins give quick energy and the slower digesting nuts provide energy later.

Roasted Walnuts

Walnuts are rich in omega-3 fats, and I eat a quarter-of-a-cup as a snack most days. Be sure to buy your nuts at an organic grocery store to be sure they are fresh and stored under refrigeration. When I get a batch that is somewhat bitter, I roast them. I spread them on a cookie sheet and roast them in a 300° F. oven for 45 minutes. Cool them completely before storing in an airtight container.

Stove-top Rice Pudding   Yield: 2 servings

Blend in a heavy saucepan:
    1 egg, beaten
    1 c. cooked brown, short-grain rice
    1/8 t. cinnamon
    3/4 c. milk or milk substitute
    3 T. dark brown sugar
    Dash of salt
    2 T. dried fruit, chopped (optional)
Heat over low burner for 10-15 minutes. This will curdle if you heat it too hot or too long. Eat it warm and top with fresh fruit if you like.

Baked Rice Pudding   Yield: a 9-inch x 9-inch baking dish, 4 to 6 servings

Baking takes longer but produces a better texture.
Cook in advance:
    5/8 c. short-grain, brown rice
    1 1/2 c. water
You can bring this to a boil, simmer for 15 minutes, and then turn off the burner. Let it stand overnight or all day, and it will be ready to bake.
Combine:
    3 eggs, beaten
    1 3/4 cooked rice from above
    1/2 t. cinnamon
    1 5/8 c. milk or milk substitute

1/2 c. dark brown sugar
1/4 t. salt
1/3 c. raisins, dried cherries, or cranberries

Pour into an oiled, nine-by-nine baking dish. Preheat the oven to 350° F. Place on the top shelf of the oven on a cookie tray and then fill the tray with boiling water. Bake for 45-50 minutes or until the middle is almost firm.

Pumpkin Custard   Yield: 5 servings

I love pumpkin but don't want to waste time making crusts that are not good for me. So I am a fan of custard.

Combine:

3 eggs, beaten
2 c. canned pumpkin, If you use home-grown pumpkin puree,
    reduce the milk to 1 1/4 c.
1/4 c. dark brown sugar
1/4 c. honey
1/2 t. salt
1 t. cinnamon
1/4 t. ground ginger
1/8 t. ground clove

When thoroughly blended, add:

1 1/2 c. milk or milk substitute

Pour into a 9-inch pie pan. Preheat the oven to 350° F. Place on the top shelf of the oven on a cookie tray and then fill the tray with boiling water. Bake for 45-50 minutes or until the middle is almost firm. The traditional test for doneness is to insert a clean table knife close to the middle. If it comes out clean, the custard is done. If the custard sticks to the knife, bake it 5 minutes longer. Serve hot or cold with your favorite trimmings. Try chopped walnuts.

Apple Crisp   Yield: 6 servings

This recipe provides another escape from piecrust.

Combine in a mixing bowl and blend with a pastry blender or fork:

5/8 quick-cooking rolled oats
1/4 c. whole wheat flour
1/4 c. unbleached white flour, or use any combination of spelt and oat flours
1/2 c. brown sugar
1/2 t. cinnamon

1/8 t. nutmeg

4 T. margarine

When the margarine is blended, sprinkle with:

2 T. water

and blend to give the crumb texture.

Now pare, quarter, core, and slice:

5 Granny Smith or other tart apples

Spread them in the bottom of an oiled 9-inch by 9-inch baking dish. Spread the oat mixture evenly over the top. Bake at 350° F. for 40-50 minutes. The top should be golden brown, and the apples completely tender. Serve hot with milk or milk substitute. Oh, I know you like ice cream but you can eat more apple crisp with a clear conscience and a trim waistline if you use something more wholesome such as soymilk or warm tapioca.

Conclusion

Perhaps you are wondering if you will have time for anything else in life if you prepare these recipes. I assure you that you will and you will have increased energy for other things. I believe life is quite simple. Our tasks are to care for our bodies and find meaning in life. Caring for our bodies means nurturing it with adequate shelter, clothing, and **food**. Finding meaning means working to understand and develop all the intangible aspects of being human: intellect, psyche, spirit, and social relationships. If you are worried today about something that doesn't nurture yourself, the Earth, and other people, just get out your journal and figure out why you are sweating the small stuff.

Please accept my love and encouragement in building greater contentment in life.

General Index

Exercises and reference illustrations are listed in separate indexes, pp. 383-386.
Recipe index is on p. 414.
Italic page numbers indicate illustrations on that page.

stress to, 222
See also Brachial plexus; Lumbosacral plexus
Visibility, 336, 337, 354, 365, 366
Visualizations, 112, 126-31, 141
    broadening upper back, 221, 230
    elongation of spine, 221
    energy movement, 134, 147
    preventing hand numbness, 230
    as retraining tool, 81, 95, 156-57, 166, 325
Vital energy, 126, 138, 139, 142-150
Wangyal, Tenzin, 309
Warming up, 89, 98, 112, 142, 315, 318, 356
Water, 23, 48, 334-35, 337, 364
    purity, 291, 293
    See Fluids
Weight control, 10, 48, 111, 293, 295, 297, 301
Weight distribution
    on rider, 190, 221-22, 260, 266
    on wheels, 54-55, 210
Weight training. *See* Strength training
Weil, M.D., Andrew, 21, 70-72, 295
Wellness, 68, 146, 149-51, 316
    See also Health
Western medicine. *See* Allopathic medicine
Wharton, Jim and Phil, 42, 91
Wheel base, 259, 261
Whole grains, 298-99
Wiik, Swen, 356
Willett, M.D., Walter C., 295
Wind, 21, 27, 223, 287, 340-342
    chill index, 354-55
    protection from, 335-36, 339
Wool, 329, 330-31, 347
Wrists, 247, 260, 335

exercises for, *103*, 121, 216, 234-35
keeping warm, 351
neutral position, *231*, *241*, 271
pain relief, 235, 273
optimum use, *240*, *241-43*
Yoga, 24, 28, 44, 70, 109, 144, 303, 309
    technique, 96-101
    warm-up sequences, *102-08*
    See also Stretching
Zimmerman, Ph.D., Alan, 130-31
Zinn, Lennard, 17, 164, 365